Hume's Sceptical Enlightenment

Edinburgh Studies in Scottish Philosophy

Series Editor: Gordon Graham
Center for the Study of Scottish Philosophy, Princeton Theological Seminary

Scottish Philosophy Through the Ages

This new series will cover the full range of Scottish philosophy over five centuries – from the medieval period through the Reformation and Enlightenment periods, to the nineteenth and early twentieth centuries.

The series will publish innovative studies on major figures and themes. It also aims to stimulate new work in less intensively studied areas, by a new generation of philosophers and intellectual historians. The books will combine historical sensitivity and philosophical substance which will serve to cast new light on the rich intellectual inheritance of Scottish philosophy.

Titles

Hume's Sceptical Enlightenment by Ryu Susato
Adam Ferguson and the Idea of Civil Society: Moral Science in the Scottish Enlightenment by Craig Smith

Hume's Sceptical Enlightenment

Ryu Susato

To Harumi

Edinburgh University Press Ltd
The Tun – Holyrood Road
12(2f) Jackson's Entry
Edinburgh EH8 8PJ
www.euppublishing.com

Typeset in 11/13 Adobe Sabon by
Servis Filmsetting Ltd, Stockport, Cheshire,
printed and bound in Great Britain by
CPI Group (UK) Ltd, Croydon CR0 4YY

A CIP record for this book is available from the British Library

ISBN 978 0 7486 9980 3 (hardback)
ISBN 978 0 7486 9981 0 (webready PDF)
ISBN 978 1 4744 0486 0 (epub)

Contents

Acknowledgements

This book could never have been realised without at least three fortunate encounters. Firstly, I was blessed with a supervisor, Tatsuya Sakamoto, who recommended when I was a postgraduate student that I should write papers in English. Without his encouragement, I would have never dreamt of publishing papers – much less a book – in English. My debts to Japanese senior scholars and friends are too immense to enumerate here, but I must mention a few individuals by name. I first and foremost thank Hajime Inuzuka for reading and commenting on my entire typescript. Hiroyuki Takezawa kindly facilitated my research in the libraries of Kyoto University during 2012. I have greatly profited from the useful suggestions of Daisuke Odagawa and Yuichiro Kawana on Chapter 8, and from those of Hiroyuki Yorozuya on Chapter 2. Discussions with Taro Okuda, Akira Kume and Naohito Mori have been especially illuminating. My thanks also go to my colleagues in the Department of Economics of Kansai University, and above all to Kunihiko Uemura, Nobuhiko Nakazawa and Masanobu Sato. I extend my thanks to the late Hiroyuki Noji for introducing me to my later supervisor.

My second blessing was getting to know many gentle and wonderful scholars and friends through international conferences – mainly the Hume Conferences and the Eighteenth-Century Scottish Studies Society Annual Meetings – and receiving much encouragement from them. When I attended a Hume Conference in Canada for the first time as a postdoc, I had the nerve to ask some senior members for comments on my first, terribly badly written, English paper. Shortly after coming back to Japan, I received two emails with attached files. One was from the late Ian Simpson Ross, who generously gave sentence-by-sentence comments on my paper; the other was from Roger L. Emerson, who rewrote it from scratch. I am still deeply touched by the thoughtfulness they extended to a young Japanese neophyte. My special thanks also go to James E. Alvey, Moritz Baumstark, Francis W. Dauer, Lívia Guimarães, Willem Lemmens, James Moore, Neil McArthur, Miriam McCormick, Margaret Schabas, Mark G. Spencer, Carl Wennerlind, John P. Wright and many others for their support and thoughtfulness.

My third piece of good fortune was spending one year as a visiting senior research scholar at the History Faculty of the University of Oxford from 2008 to 2009. During that stay, I had many opportunities not only to attend stimulating seminars (including the Enlightenment Workshop run by the Voltaire Foundation), but also to discuss my on-going research with John Robertson (now at the University of Cambridge). He gave me a number of important pieces of advice regarding the initial idea of this book. I was also fortunate to see the late István Hont, who came to Oxford for the Carlyle Lectures in the Hilary term. I recall my conversation with him at Café Rose on the High Street the morning after the lecture with both fondness and sadness.

In addition, I stayed as a visiting fellow at the Adam Smith Research Foundation in the University of Glasgow during the summer of 2010, through the good offices of Christopher J. Berry. He also made many useful comments on the original version of Chapter 2. My gratitude is extended to Yushin Toda and Fumiko Nakabachi for their help during my stay in Glasgow. From October 2014 to March 2015, Laurent Jaffro not only accepted me as an invited researcher in the Philosophy Department of the Université Paris 1 Panthéon-Sorbonne, but also afforded me many facilities. This sojourn enabled me to incorporate (if not sufficiently) some excellent literature on Hume in French into this book, and to concentrate on revising and finishing the final typescript in a tranquil setting. I received financial support from the Kansai University's Overseas Research Project (2008), and the Domestic Researcher (2012) and Researcher (2014) schemes. I also received grants from the Ministry of Education, Culture, Sports, Science and Technology, and the Japan Society for the Promotion of Science (MEXT/JSPS KAKENHI grant numbers 16730107, 18730140, 20730140, 22730174 and 26380264). All of them helped me a great deal to continue my project in these hard times for humanities and historical research. As for the publication, Christopher J. Berry (again), Fredrik Albritton Jonsson and Craig Smith gave me much valuable information and advice. I would also like to thank Taraneh Wilkinson and Isabelle Chandon for their friendship.

Let me take this opportunity to express my gratitude to the two reviewers whose comments on my synopsis and Chapter 1 have been consistently encouraging and constructive, especially for a first-time author. Mark G. Spencer, one of these reviewers, also gave me many detailed and supportive comments on the full version. I equally thank my excellent editors at the Edinburgh University Press, Carol Macdonald, Michelle Houston and James Dale, and indexer Janet Zimmermann.

Some parts of this book were based on articles published in journals, although they have all been revised and expanded. Parts of Chapter 4 were published in *Hume Studies*, 32: 1 (2006), pp. 167–86; the original versions of Chapters 5 and 7 were published in the *Journal of the History of Ideas*, 73: 2 (2012), pp. 273–93, and in the *History of European Ideas*, 32: 3 (2006), pp. 263–77, respectively. I am grateful to the editors of these journals for their kind permission to reproduce the works in this book. Some parts of the remaining chapters have been read at Hume Conferences or ECSSS Annual Meetings at one time or another. I cannot name each individual involved in these events, but am indebted to all of the commentators, chairpersons and participants.

Finally, I am grateful to my parents for their deep understanding and immense patience towards a difficult, irritable and stubborn child – characteristics I still possess. During my work on this book, the birth of our daughter, Hana, drastically changed our family life; since her first breath, she has been an unfailing fountainhead of wonder, smiles and joy in our lives. I dedicate this book to my better half in the real sense of the term – Harumi, who has always been generous, thoughtful and receptive even under difficult circumstances.

R. S.

List of Abbreviations and Conventions

A. *An Abstract of a Treatise of Human Nature*, in T.

DP. 'A Dissertation on the Passions', in *A Dissertation on the Passions; The Natural History of Religion*, ed. Tom L. Beauchamp, Oxford: Clarendon Press, 2008; all references are cited as 'DP' followed by the section and paragraph number.

DNR. *Dialogues concerning Natural Religion*, in *Dialogues concerning Natural Religion and Other Writings*, ed. Dorothy Coleman, Cambridge: Cambridge University Press, 2007; All references are cited as 'DNR', followed by the section and paragraph number, followed by the page reference to *Dialogues concerning Natural Religion*, ed. Norman Kemp Smith, 2nd edn, London; New York: T. Nelson, 1947.

EHU. *An Enquiry concerning Human Understanding*, ed. Tom L. Beauchamp, Oxford: Clarendon Press, 2000; all references are cited as 'EHU' followed by the section and paragraph number, followed by the page reference to *Enquiries concerning Human Understanding and concerning the Principles of Morals*, ed. L. A. Selby-Bigge and P. H. Nidditch, Oxford: Clarendon Press, 1975.

EPM. *An Enquiry concerning the Principles of Morals*, ed. Tom L. Beauchamp, Oxford: Clarendon Press, 1998; all references are cited as 'EPM' followed by the section and paragraph number, followed by the page reference to *Enquiries concerning Human Understanding and concerning the Principles of Morals*, ed. L. A. Selby-Bigge and P. H. Nidditch, Oxford: Oxford University Press, 1975.

E. *Essays: Moral, Political and Literary*, ed. Eugene F. Miller, Indianapolis: Liberty Fund, 1985; all references are cited as 'E' followed by the page number.

H. *History of England: from the Invasion of Julius Caesar to The Revolution in 1688*, 6 vols, Indianapolis: Liberty Fund, 1983; all references are cited as 'H' followed by the volume and page number.

L. *The Letters of David Hume*, ed. J. Y. T. Greig, 2 vols, Oxford: Clarendon Press, 1932; all references are cited as 'L' followed by the volume and page number.

NHR. 'Natural History of Religion' in *A Dissertation on the Passions; The Natural History of Religion*, ed. Tom L. Beauchamp, Oxford: Clarendon Press, 2008; all references are cited as 'NHR' followed by the section and paragraph number.

NL. *The New Letters of David Hume*, ed. Raymond Klibansky and Ernest Campbell Mossner, Oxford: Clarendon Press, 1954; all references are cited as 'NL' followed by the page number.

T. *A Treatise of Human Nature*, ed. David Fate and Mary Norton, 2 vols, Oxford: Clarendon Press, 2000; all references are cited as 'T' followed by the book, part, section and paragraph numbers, followed by the page reference to *A Treatise of Human Nature*, ed. L. A. Selby-Bigge, revised by P. H. Nidditch, Oxford: Clarendon Press, 1978.

TA. *A True Account of the Behaviour and Conduct of Archibald Stewart, Esq.; late Lord Provost of Edinburgh. In a Letter to a Friend*, London: Printed for M. Cooper, 1748, transcribed by M. A. Box, David Harvey and Michael Silverthorne in 'A Diplomatic Transcription of Hume's "Volunteer Pamphlet" for Archibald Stewart: Political Whigs, Religious Whigs, and Jacobites', *Hume Studies*, 29: 2 (2003), pp. 233–66.

Italics within quotations are those of the original authors, unless otherwise noted.

I usually use the English (modern or contemporary) translations for the quotations from French texts. If the English translations are not available, I translate them from the originals, which are placed in footnotes.

Series Editor's Introduction

It is widely acknowledged that the Scottish Enlightenment of the eighteenth century was one of the most fertile periods in British intellectual history, and that philosophy was the jewel in its crown. Yet, vibrant though this period was, it occurred within a long history that began with the creation of the Scottish universities in the fifteenth century. It also stretched into the nineteenth and twentieth centuries for as long as those universities continued to be a culturally distinctive and socially connected system of education and inquiry.

While the Scottish Enlightenment remains fertile ground for philosophical and historical investigation, these other four centuries of philosophy also warrant intellectual exploration. The purpose of this series is to maintain outstanding scholarly study of great thinkers like David Hume, Adam Smith and Thomas Reid, alongside sustained exploration of the less familiar figures who preceded them, and the impressive company of Scottish philosophers, once celebrated, now neglected, who followed them.

Gordon Graham

Mr Hume is a very subtile man himself and believed to be allowed the help of lawyers. Whenever a trial is made the supporters of the overture will perhaps find more than they imagine att present how much such subtile men can puzzle & perplex. They will have a particular advantage in having Mr Hume's writings for their text for this Gentleman, having so much of the sceptick in him, rarely admitts any thing on any one side of a Question but he finds out something to plead for the other. This humour appears in his Philosophy, Divinity, History, & every thing else.

Robert Wallace (quoted in Mossner 1980: 350)

1

Introduction

1 The Purpose of this Book

David Hume (1711–76) is a many-faceted and extremely equivocal thinker. The first characterisation is evidenced by the scope of his intellectual activities; the second by the variety of assessments of his works among his contemporaries and later generations. This book aims to place him in wider intellectual contexts in which he could be depicted as an Enlightenment thinker. For some, this might sound redundant, as it could be contended that Hume has already been widely recognised amongst the foremost philosophers of the period (the term 'philosopher(s)' used for these intellectuals here and in its eighteenth-century usage encompasses historians, political economists and scientists). Nevertheless, the conventional definition of the Enlightenment failed to resonate with many alleged characteristics of Hume's social philosophy and for this reason he has often evaded definition as an Enlightenment thinker. Peter Gay, for example, still wonders 'what, after all, does Hume, who was a conservative, have in common with Condorcet, who was a democrat?' (1966–9: I, x). Despite his positive appraisal of luxury, civilisation and conversable society, Hume's criticism of social contract theory, his respect for convention and his famous thesis that '[r]eason is and ought only to be the slave of the passions' (T 2.3.3.4; 415) sat uncomfortably with the contract-based, individualistic and rationalistic image of the Enlightenment. In sum, while he has been widely recognised as a philosopher of the Enlightenment, several significant qualifications have always been necessary to accompany such a classification.

As Gay's comment attests, the ambiguity in evaluations of Hume as an Enlightenment thinker is closely related to the relationship that has been claimed to exist between Hume's philosophical scepticism and his alleged political conservatism. One classic example of this assumed relationship is found in John Stuart Mill's evaluation:

> [Hume's] absolute scepticism in speculation very naturally brought him round to Toryism in practice; for if no faith can be had in the operations of human intellect, and one side of every question is about as likely as another to be true, a man will commonly be inclined to prefer that order of things which, being no more wrong than every other, he has hitherto found compatible with his private comforts. (Mill [1838] 1963–91: 80n.q–q 38)

In fact, the allegation of political conservatism as a logical result of scepticism was not new at the time of Mill, but had a long legacy from the history of scepticism: Sextus Empiricus clearly asserts in his *Outlines of Scepticism* that '[t]hus, attending to what is apparent, we live in accordance with everyday observances, without holding opinions [*adoxastôs*] – for we are not able to be utterly inactive'. He goes on to count 'the handing down of laws and customs' as one of four aspects of these everyday observances with which the philosopher may comply. As for religion, Sextus also argues, 'following ordinary life without opinions, we say that there are gods and we are pious towards the gods and say that they are provident' (Sextus Empiricus 1994: 1.23; 3.2; see also 2.102). For Sextus, as far as we can avoid holding opinions, merely following the rules of everyday life does not hinder us from attaining tranquillity.[1]

Mill's assessment of Hume, despite its banality,[2] has resonated among present-day Hume scholars in various ways (Miller 1981; Whelan 1985; Livingston 1998).[3] In addition, Hume was often considered a prominent Tory historian in the late eighteenth and early nineteenth centuries (and much later too). It may also be said that Hume shares with Burke a certain distrust of reason, and that both criticised the social contract theory based on the abstract idea of natural rights. In this sense, Hume is one of the important philosophical figures within the Enlightenment world to have viewed the cult of reason as possibly dangerous. This position could be reinforced by his deep scepticism concerning the attainability of truth and the idea of human perfectibility. Hence, Donald Livingston claims that Humean criticism of 'false' philosophy 'is an affirmation of the liberal way of life but a rejection of the foundationalist tradition of liberal philosophizing'. In the sense that '[t]he form of liberalism we have inherited is foundationalist liberalism', he continues, 'Hume is not a liberal but one of its most devastating critics' (1995: 56–7).

There are two points to make in response to this argument. Firstly, what Livingston terms 'the humanistic, historical, rhetorical, and virtue-centered liberalism' (allegedly found in Hume, Smith and Burke alike) should not necessarily be the only option as the antipode of foundationalist liberalism. We can claim that, for example, Richard Rorty's 'postmodernist bourgeois liberalism' could be another one, because his anti-foundationalism does not impede his support of liberal democracy. Interestingly, Rorty himself frequently mentions Hume, and even declares that 'Hume is a better advisor than Kant about how we intellectuals can hasten the coming of the Enlightenment utopia for which both men yearned' (1993: 128; see also Rorty 1998; 1987: 578n.24).[4] I will not delve into this subject here; suffice to say that foundationalist and/or humanistic liberalism are not all we have inherited from the tradition of liberalism, despite the former's dominance.

And yet, it does not necessarily follow from such a reading that Hume can be neatly pigeonholed into the camp of what we now call the 'liberal'. The second point to make against Livingston's claim is that any simplified image of Hume based upon such 'either/or' types of question about his legacy has clouded our understanding of the 'historical' Hume (I borrow this expression from Forbes 1975b: 127) in some significant respects. This book will not (at least directly) deal with the 'liberal/conservative' issue of Hume's social philosophy (see, for example, Miller 1981: 193–205), but rather elucidate the complexity of the 'historical' Hume more accurately.

There is another, more recent, research trend that has emerged in relation to Hume's politics or political philosophy: some recent studies tend to separate his philosophical scepticism from his politics. Andrew Sabl asserts that '[t]he most prevalent labels are probably "skeptic" – long rejected by scholars as completely misleading when applied to Hume's social and political thought which is empirical to the core' (2012: 4). For twenty-first century readers, some of Hume's scepticism in moral and political writings could be better described as 'empiricism'. There are two points to make. Firstly, as far as the concern of this book lies in investigating the 'historical' Hume, it is still worthwhile to understand how his thoroughly sceptical/empirical thinking as regards morals and politics was received in the intellectual context of his contemporaries and later generations. Secondly, as we will see below, Hume's scepticism can be neither simplistically nor completely replaced with empiricism. Some of the 'Humean' features can be properly described as an attitude or style rather than a strictly philosophical position or a technical methodology, and what he calls 'the spirit of scepticism' permeates his philosophy, morals and politics. This feature of his thought has provoked the complex images of Hume as conservative on some points and as subversive on others, among his contemporaries and later generations.[5] This is exactly why Forbes declares that Hume continues to be 'terrible campaign country':

> The more of his writings one takes into account the less confident one feels that one can ever break through. This is the 'general impression' that one ought to get; but one will not get it by trying 'to get a general impression'. And this perhaps is the ultimate mystery of Hume's 'scepticism', which the devotees eventually attain to. (1975b: viii–ix)

While avoiding plunging into ideological dichotomies and keeping Hume's scepticism in sight, this book will delineate this 'ultimate mystery' – Hume's complex, sometimes apparently contradictory, standpoint in context. The strategy adopted for this purpose will be to redefine Enlightenment in a more historiographically valid sense and to characterise and locate the historical Hume within this newly defined Enlightenment discourse.

2 A Working Definition of Enlightenment in this Book

The intellectual genealogy of the term 'Enlightenment' is more or less a history of verbal anachronism in two ways. Firstly, many philosophers who are now counted as Enlightenment thinkers did not ask the question 'what is the Enlightenment?' Even the German thinkers who, following Kant, self-consciously committed to the debate 'Was ist Aufklärung?' in the 1780s, did not frame it in today's terms. These Germans generally confined themselves to arguing over more specific questions, such as whether the authorities should remove restrictions on the freedom of the press (Schmidt 1996: 4).[6] It is doubtful whether those thinkers who are taken together to constitute the Enlightenment ever made their own efforts at self-definition. Secondly, 'Aufklärung' was originally applied 'to a period of German literature, very roughly from 1720 to 1785, from Gottsched to Lessing' (Lough 1985: 1; see also Schmidt 1996). The term gradually expanded to include other countries such as France and Britain. By the end of the nineteenth century, Aufklärung, and its English translation 'Enlightenment' had a much wider meaning, designating the spirit of the French philosophes. In the 1960s–70s, when Peter Gay published his influential work, *The Enlightenment: An Interpretation*, the term had taken on at once a narrower scope and wider meanings. In this book, Gay confined his analysis to 'the Enlightenment of the *philosophes*', while admitting that their thought 'was embedded in a wider, more comprehensive atmosphere' (1966–69: II, ix–x). This double meaning of the Enlightenment has sometimes caused an abuse of synecdoche: the French philosophes have been on occasion inadvertently treated as if they were the 'orthodox' Enlightenment thinkers, and have become the yardstick to gauge the distances of other eighteenth-century thinkers' standpoints. Considering the fact that most eighteenth-century philosophers never used the word and that some Germans omitted the definite article in their discussions, the recent debate over whether there was *the* Enlightenment has been perhaps always inevitable. 'There is no single or unifiable phenomenon describable as "the Enlightenment",' argues J. G. A. Pocock, 'but it is the definite article rather than the noun which is to be avoided' (2008: 83). On the other hand, John Robertson's recent book, tellingly entitled *The Case for the Enlightenment*, defends the concept of a transnational phenomenon of shared values: 'What characterized the Enlightenment was the new primacy accorded to human betterment, to the possibility – not the inevitability – of progress in the present world' (2005: 30; see also Robertson 2000).

I do not wish to dwell on the details of this debate here, but just point out that both parties tend to share (at least) two presuppositions. Firstly, they have no fundamental disagreement in the commensurability between various Enlightenment groups. When Pocock argues that 'we find ourselves using the word "Enlightenment" in a family of ways and talking about a family of phenomena, resembling and related to one another in a variety of ways that permit of various generalizations about them' (2008: 83), he assumes that the family metaphor can still provide the greatest common understanding of this intellectual movement.[7] In his claim that various issues in the Enlightenment are 'connected but not continuous', Pocock is distinct from those who argue that we should completely avoid using the phrase 'Enlightenment' to designate any eighteenth-century intellectual activities because there was no fundamental agreement among them (see, for example, Lough 1985: 14). If so, it would be possible or rather necessary to discover such a common ground among various Enlightenment groups, while leaving room for the diversity of specific goals and objects in each. Secondly, however, both parties seem to assume that the Enlightenment as a whole, if it exists at all, *must* have been a project or agenda containing practical and concrete ideologies. This supposition has been closely related to the double meaning of the word 'Enlightenment'. As I outlined above, the presence of the French philosophes, prominent among them the contributors to the *Encyclopédie* of Diderot and d'Alembert, seems still fundamental to Enlightenment studies in general. The 'Discours préliminaire' to the *Encyclopédie* (1751) is still considered an important exposition of 'the Enlightenment' ideals. It has been natural to assume that Enlightenment thinkers committed themselves to a clear agenda, no matter what the content is considered to be. But it is not quite evident that we must primarily define the Enlightenment as a project or agenda. (One might argue that the term 'project' or 'agenda' need not necessarily refer to any clear or concrete reform manifesto, but might apply to a weaker or more speculative one. Be this as it may, these words still appear misleading, both generically and historiographically.) We should shift the centre of the debate from whether there was *the* Enlightenment project to whether it is appropriate to define the Enlightenment as a project at all. Curiously enough, as John Robertson (2005: 1) points out, the phrase 'the Enlightenment project' was originally coined by Alasdair MacIntyre in *After Virtue* published in 1981 (MacIntyre 1981: esp. chaps. 5–6),[8] although some sporadic and passing usages of the term can be found before that year. Considering the surprising recentness of this widely used phrase, it seems appropriate to suspect its implicit premise. I will not deny the capacity of each philosopher to possess a clear and consistent individual agenda; it is quite a different matter to attempt to define a set of overall agendas for the Enlightenment and one I will not undertake here.

The tentative working definition for my present research is that the Enlightenment might be regarded as a shared sensitivity among philosophers to the on-going process of civilisation in early modern/modern Europe and the New World, and a series of questions and issues posed by those intellectuals based on this historical awareness. Among these questions are: the identity of the engine and driving forces of civilisation; whether the process was considered a blessing or curse; and whether and how it is possible to break the historical cycle of the rise and decline of civilisations. The betterment of human society through philosophical investigations into the structures of human nature and society is one of the most considerable and fundamental issues; but even this should be deemed not an indispensable element of its definition but a derivation from their historical consciousness. The point of this definition is that the Enlightenment was nothing but these thinkers' perceptions of their own times, a process in which they consciously participated as its agents. This approach is very close to one suggested by Dan Edelstein, who emphasises the Enlightenment itself as a living experience of the French philosophes and their 'self-reflective understanding of the historical importance and specificity of eighteenth-century France' (2010: 2; see also Brewer 2008: 3, 15–16).[9] Importantly, his definition has much resonance with Pocock's idea of 'the narrative of Enlightenment' in a rather unexpected way. Despite many differences between the two scholars, Pocock's emphasis on the narrativity of Enlightenment also aptly draws our attention to the way in which these philosophers grasped and described what was happening before their eyes, correlating it with their understanding of the past. The term 'Enlightenment' is understood in this book, therefore, not as a specific agenda or abstract concept, but rather as a historical and narrative one. This definition seems more flexible and open to the possibility of a more historiographically accurate and informed understanding of one of the most important intellectual phenomena in the modern European world.

It seems no coincidence that the age of Enlightenment is also considered 'the Age of History': a label that is employed in a different sense from the way in which it is used for the nineteenth century. For most Enlightenment thinkers, the Renaissance and Reformation should be considered particularly, although not exclusively, significant for their historical understanding of the changes they observed in their own times. Many of the issues that sparked debate among Enlightenment thinkers can be considered to have been triggered by the religious conflicts that engendered devastating wars in early modern Europe. This is not to say that Enlightenment thinkers were necessarily committed to secularism, although in what follows I will emphasise Hume's anti-religious aspect (Chapter 5). It is rather to recognise that the Enlightenment as a historical phenomenon is not conceivable without consideration of the fundamental bewilderment that these events caused for those who held Christianity as a belief system. Some thinkers of the age made efforts to comprehend the historic developments that unfolded before them within, or in a way that chimed with, their religious framework (Pocock 1985a; 1989; Goldie 1991; Haakonssen 1996b; Burson and Lehner (eds) 2014). The powerful political, economic and scientific innovations, including the growth of global trade and colonisation in an environment marked by the establishment of modern sovereign states, and the development of Newtonian science affected intellectual developments in a different sense. I do not wish to imply here that these latter (or any other) factors were insignificant in forming the historical awareness of the on-going civilising process; merely to suggest that the impact of these historical factors did work not as common historical premises but rather as current issues that were to be grasped and tackled precisely because they were contemporary phenomena and concerns for most Enlightenment thinkers.

With such a sensitive and self-reflective view of the drastic historical changes within the modern world as the starting point of their discussions, some philosophers embarked on the study of the science of man; others investigated the role of religion in the process of civilisation, whether critically or favourably. Accepting this wider definition will enable us to discuss the relationship of some members or groups of Enlightenment thinkers with those who pose problems for conventional definition of the Enlightenment, including such an 'anti-modern' modern as Vico, or Rousseau, *enfant terrible* of the Enlightenment. The latter, in fact, seems more sensible of the historical consciousness he shared with his contemporaries, even when he opposed their views, than any other thinker of the period.

Adopting the above definition of Enlightenment, it is my intention to cast the net as far and wide as possible, and provide the most inclusion possible. I am referring to what Gay called 'a wider, more comprehensive atmosphere, the atmosphere of the eighteenth century, which may be called, without distortion, the Age of the Enlightenment' (1966–9: I, x; see also Muthu 2003:

chap. 7). However, I attempt here not to offer a general analysis of Enlightenment discourses in any wider sense, but rather to re-locate Hume within the Enlightenment thus defined. For this purpose, it is necessary to choose a concept that enables us to best comprehend the essential features of Hume as an Enlightenment thinker. My proposal is 'Sceptical Enlightenment'.

3 'Sceptical Enlightenment' as a Heuristic Device

The phrase 'Sceptical Enlightenment' is, of course, not of my own coinage. The phrase appears perhaps for the first time in Henry May's *The Enlightenment in America*, where it is used to distinguish a chronological phase of Enlightenment in the eighteenth-century American intellectual milieu. He used it for the period ranging roughly from 1750 to 1789, along with three other Enlightenment epochs: the Moderate Enlightenment (1688–1787); the Revolutionary Enlightenment (1776–1800); and the Didactic Enlightenment (1800–15). He emphasised the centrality of French philosophes such as Voltaire in his understanding of this specific type of Enlightenment, and he also clearly admitted that Hume was 'the greatest figure of the Sceptical Enlightenment, the chief sceptic of Europe' (May 1976: 111). Although I doubt whether May's chronology of four distinctive Enlightenments can still hold its ground in the light of recent studies (Pocock 1989; Israel 2001; Robertson 2005), I have repurposed this specific phrase to represent the distinctive features of Hume as an Enlightenment thinker.

On choosing the term 'Sceptical Enlightenment' as the most appropriate for Hume, the debt to what Duncan Forbes calls 'Sceptical Whiggism' is frankly acknowledged. His phrasing has the advantage that Hume actually used it in one of his letters (L I, 111). However, there are two reasons why I propose the phrase 'Sceptical Enlightenment' instead of 'Sceptical Whiggism'. Firstly, Forbes himself does not cling to Hume's wording, but prefers to adopt the term 'Scientific Whiggism' to designate the characteristics of his political philosophy. This is because he originally coined the phrase 'Scientific Whiggism' in order to account for Adam Smith and John Millar who, from his point of view, were ahead of their times (1954; see also Forbes 1975a). Later he discovered the counterpart to his own idea in Hume's 'Sceptical Whiggism'. Forbes's original concern, therefore, lay with these two philosophers rather than with Hume.

Secondly, considering recent developments in Hume scholarship, the distinction between Sceptical Whiggism and what Forbes terms 'vulgar Whiggism' in Hume's writings does not seem as stable as before. For Forbes, vulgar Whiggism is 'something which cuts right across the whole spectrum of politics from commonwealth-men to Tories and Jacobites' (1975b: 140), and this contrast 'is seen in Hume himself'. According to this definition, it seems clear that Forbes underestimates some of Hume's allegedly 'Tory' attitudes as examples of vulgar Whiggism, or aspects of his thought that have nothing to do with 'the historical Hume'. However, recent studies have shown that some, if not most, of these examples – 'Hume's approval of the established Church of England, his opinion of the National Debt, his disapproval of the stock-holders and stock-jobbing [...], his dislike of continental wars, etc' (127) – are significant for our understanding of the historical Hume in various ways (Pocock 1985b; Robertson 1993; Hont 2005). Taking into account these developments in recent Hume scholarship, what the noun Whig or Whiggism now denotes seems to restrict the range of its applicability because of its apparent 'Britishness'. Of course, using the controversial term 'Enlightenment' runs the opposite risk of overly broad interpretation, but I think that the noun 'Enlightenment' is a more appropriate modificand in order to encompass Hume's extensive intellectual activities.[10]

The theoretical potentiality of the term 'Sceptical Enlightenment' as a heuristic device is yet to be investigated, especially compared with what Jonathan Israel terms the 'Radical' and 'Moderate' Enlightenments: the former is characterised as 'the radical democratic and, in metaphysics, materialist-determinist, or alternatively Christian-Unitarian', while the latter 'the "moderate" and positively providential (Deist or religious), championing the monarchical-aristocratic order of society' (Israel 2010: 12). If his sharp dichotomy is followed, Hume apparently falls into the latter camp (excluding its religious aspect). Along with other contemporary philosophers, Hume recommended a spirit of 'moderation' among the public. Moreover, his endorsement of mitigated scepticism might naturally lead us to expect a consequent moderation in his thought. Nevertheless, Jonathan Israel's presentation of the Radical Enlightenment not only seems too rigid in its categorisation (Spencer 2010) – despite the author's own denial of such a criticism (Israel 2006: postscript) – but also atavistic in its exclusive emphasis on the historical impact of the period on the formation of the modern world (LaVopa 2009). This appeal reminds us not only of more conventional readings of the period, but also of Friedrich Engels's depiction of the combative French Enlightenment thinkers: 'The great men, who in France prepared men's mind for the coming revolution,' wrote Engels in 1880, 'were themselves extreme revolutionists. [...] Reason became the sole measure of everything' ([1880] 1920: 1–2). Furthermore, as will be shown in the following, Hume's sceptical philosophy sometimes had radical implications, both among his contemporaries and for the generations who followed him (Marshall 1954: 250; McMahon 2007: 614; see also Baumstark 2012: 256). My position is, again, to avoid the 'either/or' types of categorisation on this point, as well as on the issue of the 'conservative/liberal' Hume. The notion of the Sceptical Enlightenment, therefore, does not so much replace Israel's daring dichotomy as grasps what I believe to be the central core of Hume's thought, in order to seek an alternative interpretation of one form of Enlightenment at the micro level.

Richard H. Popkin also addresses the issue of 'Enlightenment scepticism', asserting that 'what scepticism there was in the Enlightenment seems to have been located mainly within the person of one man – David Hume' ([1963] 1996: 1). My primary concern is neither to delineate the 'tradition' or 'extent' of scpeticism as a philosophical school in the Enlightenment (Popkin [1963] 1997; [1976] 1997; [1992] 1997; Charles 2013),[11] nor to follow May (1976: 105–11, 126–32) in grouping certain philosophers – among whom he includes Voltaire and Franklin – in the same category.[12] The focus of this book is rather to delineate a much wider import of Hume's scepticism mainly in his non-epistemological writings.

4 What is Hume's Sceptical Enlightenment?

The above-mentioned aim and strategy of this book lead us to the central question: what does Hume's Sceptical Enlightenment mean? Fuller discussions will be given in the following chapters, but a pitfall to avoid here is to make this concept a 'catch-all' term. In order to avoid this error, an overview of its essence will be useful at the outset. This will also serve as an introduction and guide for readers. The first step is to explain the relationship between Hume's philosophical scepticism and his social, political and historical writings. As we saw above, some recent studies of Hume's political thought tend to undervalue the connection between his philosophical scepticism and his politics. For example, Neil McArthur points out that 'there is not a single passage [in Hume's writings] where he explicitly extends his scepticism to the realm of politics' (2007: 117; see also 5, where McArthur regards a passage in T 1.4.7.12; 270–1 as a single exception). Yet Hume actually acknowledges the significance of scepticism in politics as well as in philosophy, though inconspicuously. Commenting on Hobbes's political philosophy in the *History of England* he critically states that '[t]hough an enemy to religion, [Hobbes] partakes nothing of the spirit of scepticism; but is as positive and dogmatical as if human reason, and his reason in particular, could attain a thorough conviction in these subjects [politics]' (H VI, 153; see also Long 2013: 210). It is unlikely that his mention of the 'spirit of scepticism' here would have nothing to do with his own scepticism. Hobbes's materialism in his understanding of human nature and his rationalism in his political theory seem far removed from Hume's 'spirit of scepticism' (Chapter 2). As another example, Hume suggests in a letter that he maintains his sceptical position even in political writings, mentioning the debate on the ancient population with Robert Wallace:

> I should be much afraid that I am entirely refuted, had I not, all along, in my essay, kept on the sceptical and doubtful side, which, in most subjects, gives a man so much the advantage of the ground, that it is very difficult to force him. (L I, 177)

This avowal of taking the 'sceptical side' sounds strange, considering his adamant claim that the modern world is more populous than the ancient. In the essay 'Of the Populousness of Ancient Nations', however, he professes his belief in remaining sceptical about the metaphysical issue of whether or not our world has attained an advanced age, and he limits his analysis to his experimental observations concerning the moral causes that affect the population in ancient and modern worlds. To these we can add his self-definition as a 'sceptical' Whig: 'The conclusion [of the essay 'Of the Protestant Succession'] shows me a Whig, but a very sceptical one' (L I, 111), on which Duncan Forbes characterises Hume's politics. Certainly Hume sometimes seems to deny putting scepticism into his historical narrative: 'I composed [the *History of Great Britain*] *ad populum*, as well as *ad clerum*, and thought, that scepticism was not in its place in an historical production' (L I, 189). He also says that 'what would become of *history* had we not a dependence on the veracity of the historian according to the experience which we have had of mankind?' (EHU 8.18; 90). However, these simply indicate that Hume does not build his narratives around philosophical scepticism on historical testimonies in the *History* to the same degree or in the same way as he does in the essay 'Of Miracles'. In the *History*, as the occasion demands, he does discuss various debatable and controversial issues critically (Mossner 1941a; Popkin 1976; Costelloe 2013: 188–91).[13] 'The philosophical Spirit, which I have so much indulg'd in all my Writings,' Hume states in a letter to the abbé Le Blanc, a French translator of Hume's *Political Discourses*, 'finds here [in the *History of Great Britain*] ample Materials to work upon' (L I, 193) – it seems unnecessary to comment on what kind of 'philosophical Spirit' he mentions here. These examples suggest that Hume does not explicitly apply specific doctrines of scepticism, but believes in maintaining the 'spirit' of scepticism even in his non-metaphysical writings.

In order to understand this point, we do not need to enter into detailed discussions about the status of Hume's scepticism in specific epistemological issues such as causality. Despite the significance in its own right of the 'New Hume' debate – over whether he should be best characterised as sceptic or as sceptical realist – it will suffice for our purpose to demonstrate how Hume believes his mitigated scepticism should not be limited to epistemology. In the last section of *An Enquiry concerning Human Understanding* (the first *Enquiry*) he contrasts mitigated with excessive scepticism under two forms respectively: antecedent and consequent. While criticising Cartesian (excessive) antecedent scepticism, he argues that this scepticism 'when more moderate, [...] is a necessary preparative to the study of philosophy, by preserving a proper impartiality in our judgements [...]' (EHU 12.4; 150). In consequence, he also criticises scepticism arising from the investigation of the infirmities of our cognitive faculties for its excessive Pyrrhonism: but he defends the usefulness and durability of 'a more *mitigated* scepticism'. This scepticism not only makes us more modest and reserved, through encouraging us to reflect on various defects of human understanding, but also serves to limit our enquiries 'to such subjects as are best adapted to the narrow capacity of human understanding', that is, 'to common life, and to such subjects as fall under daily practice and experience' (12.24–25; 161–2). He goes on to list these subjects. Along with abstract science (knowledge) and demonstrations concerning quantity and number, he includes moral reasoning on particular/general facts among '[t]his narrow limitation [...] of our enquiries' (12.26; 163). Significantly, 'history' falls under the former category (moral reasoning on particular facts) along with chronology, geography and astronomy, while 'politics' comes under the latter (on general facts), along with natural philosophy and chemistry. He further argues that 'morals and criticism' could also be proper objects of reasoning and enquiry. As is clear, this is a further elaboration of Hume's manifestation of the 'science of MAN' in the introduction of the *Treatise* (intro. 4–5; xv–xvi), though he does not mention 'history' there. He ends the first *Enquiry* with the following famous declaration:

> If we take in our hand any volume; of divinity or school metaphysics, for instance; let us ask, *Does it contain any abstract reasoning concerning quantity or number?* No. *Does it contain any experimental reasoning concerning matter of fact and existence?* No. Commit it then to the flames: for it can contain nothing but sophistry and illusion. (EHU 12.34; 165)

Although his example is a book on divinity or metaphysics, the subject is of little consequence. The fault line lies in whether the content of these arguments is limited according to the proper range of human capacity. According to Hume, this proper limitation can be realised only by a mitigated scepticism. Then, could he have completely forgotten the role of mitigated scepticism in his non-metaphysical writings? Or does he mean a totally different type of scepticism when he characterises his own political position as sceptical? In either case, he should commit his own non-metaphysical books to the flames, but this seems unlikely. On the contrary, even amid his bold claim that politics can be a science, he is always conscious of the limitations of human capacities (Chapter 5).

In order to explain the content of Hume's Sceptical Enlightenment, however, it is necessary to further particularise the nature of his 'spirit of scepticism'. Clearly Hume's scepticism is often directed against religious dogmatism. In the first *Enquiry* he describes 'the sceptic' as 'another enemy of religion' along with the atheist (EHU 12.1–2; 149). In the passage of the *History* quoted above, Hume uses almost the same phrase 'enemy to religion' for Hobbes. It is in this sense that Henry May classifies the thought of Hume and Voltaire (and some others) under the term Sceptical Enlightenment. Yet scepticism itself does not always entail antipathy to religion. Catholic Pyrrhonism in sixteenth- and seventeenth-century France, notably that of Pierre Charron, was used as an apologetic of fideism – a doctrine that consolidated the claims of faith against the appeal to reason in Christianity (Popkin 2003: 100–2; see also Penelhum 2008: 330–1; Broadie 2012: chap. 3). As is typified by the case of Bayle, it has often been difficult to evaluate the intentions of those who were suspected of scepticism on religious issues in this period, because they were (intentionally or inadvertently) deemed to be either extreme devotees or disguised atheists, or both.[14] Hume called them 'those dangerous friends or disguised enemies to the Christian religion' (EHU 10.40; 129–30), but he himself sometimes used a similar strategy in his religious writings or in his defence (Hume [1745] 1967: 19–21; Wright 2006: 11), although in his case such a gesture functions neither as an excuse nor as a disguise. Apart from the inconclusive debate over his personal belief in God, his mitigated scepticism never hindered him from looking at religions, including Christianity, critically. Moreover, Hume seems quite different from the sceptics of antiquity in general who allowed themselves to conform to the religious practices of their own community *only* when they did so undogmatically (Penelhum 2008: 328; cf. Whelan 1985: 313–14).

Despite that, scepticism as anti-religious dogmatism itself is not peculiar to Hume, especially in eighteenth-century Europe: another more specific characteristic should be counted. Among many possible intellectual strands of Hume's anti-religious thought and securalisitic orientation, Humean adaptation of modern Epicureanism seems vital to the essence of his Sceptical Enlightenment. 'Modern Epicureanism' here refers to a loose intellectual tradition, rather than any systematic school, influenced by the Greek philosopher Epicurus and his Roman follower, Lucretius, after its revival in the Renaissance. It consists of several distinctive doctrines – including atomistic, corpuscularian and materialistic views of the natural world; utilitarian and hedonistic (but not necessarily self-indulgent) ethics; and an emphasis on the stadial progress of the human world and the artificiality of justice

(Jones 1989: chap. 2; Wilson 2009). In religion, Epicurus was not an atheist, but nor yet a providentialist: gods were supposed to neither be interested in, nor to intervene in human affairs. Hence religious superstition and priestly privileges became the subject of criticism by the Epicureans (Wilson 2008: intro). Along with these claims, the Lucretian account of the unpredictable 'swerve' (*clinamen*) of atoms and the contingency of the universe could give its critics the impressions of relativism and scepticism (Nisbett 2009: 138–9). As is always the case with intellectual 'traditions', however, Epicureanism is protean and subject to various modifications: its physics (and even its ethics) could be subsumed under the Christian framework, and this is exactly what some seventeenth-century natural philosophers, such as Pierre Gassendi and Robert Boyle, attempted to do amidst the rise of experimental science (Joy 1992; Wilson 2008: chap. 9; Thomson 2008: esp. chaps. 2 and 3). As this book does not aim to give a strict definition of Epicureanism, the following chapters will rather delineate at what points and in what ways Hume critically adopts or rejects aspects of the doctrine in each specific context. In particular, the significance of Hume's Epicureanism is manifested chiefly in his theory of imagination (Chapter 2), his defence of luxury (Chapter 4) and his criticism of priesthood (Chapter 5). The Epicureanism in Hume's moral philosophy has recently attracted much more attention than before and the approach to these topics adopted here owes much to previous studies, including those of E. J. Hundert, James Moore, John Robertson and Paul Russell (for a brief but good discussion on this point, see Sagar 2013: 811–13). In the following discussions, much wider implications of this strand in Hume's social philosophy will be elucidated and placed in a different perspective. Here is another key point. While he shared many critical characteristics of Epicureanism, and scepticism has been closely linked to Epicureanism in the eighteenth century (Buckle 2007), Hume directed his scepticism even towards the Epicurean's supposedly 'true' principle: its materialistic explanation of the world. James A. Harris is right in pointing out that 'Hume maintains the sceptic's agnosticism about what is responsible for the ordered complexity discovered by scientific investigation' (2009: 168). Obviously Hume is not a materialist in the Hobbesian or Hartlean sense. He always keeps his distance from physiology or the theory of vibrations (Chapter 2). In this sense Hume's version can be better characterised as 'modern Epicureanism without its materialistic foundation', which lies at the core of his Sceptical Enlightenment. But the emphasis here is placed on the way he adopted it rather than Epicureanism itself.

As exemplified in his adaptation of Epicureanism, Hume's scepticism as anti-dogmatism often manifests itself as anti-reductionism (De Dijn 2003). He usually stops short of any metaphysical claims, simply because presupposing the existence of eternal relations of things or materialistic metaphysics goes beyond 'the narrow capacity of human understanding' (EHU 12.25; 161). Curiously enough, he is reserved even in justification for his own agendas. According to its context he often appeals to general opinion (Chapter 3), the public utility or the concept of the 'natural course of things' (E 260), all of which are important for our understanding of his social and political philosophy. However, the question of which is the most fundamental and primary for him seems to be ill posed, at least for the present purpose. Hume does not blindly accept any one of them as absolutely valid, and he remains sceptical of the possibility of providing any single, clear-cut and versatile rationale to settle specific issues. This might sound anti-fundamentalist for post-modernists (Parusnikova 1993),[15] but he does not deny these justifications in themselves. Rather his point is the way in which, and the extent to which, we can assume any of them to represent an undogmatic rationale. Moderate justification for any principle could at a certain point become otherwise if it is taken too far. Hume even considers that 'the dispute between the sceptics and dogmatists is entirely verbal, or at least regards only the degree of doubt and assurance, which we ought to indulge with regard to all reasoning' (DNR: 12.8n11; 219n; Marshall 1954: 252). If so, there is no wonder that Hume, who often appeals to established manners, was no less critical of ancient constitutionalism: a false philosophy expressed in historical form. Despite his somewhat exaggerated emphasis on the infallibility of general opinion, such opinion should, in Hume's view, be taken not as the supreme authority but as a practical guide at most (see below, pp. 84–5).

From the scepticism thus described are derived several, more particular, manifestations of Hume's 'spirit of scepticism'. The first one is his naturalistic account of human nature and society (Forbes 1975b: chap. 2). By holding to what he believes to be an empirical and psychological (not physiological) analysis of the workings of human imagination and sentiments, Hume concentrates on giving an *explanatory* and descriptive understanding of human nature and societies rather than on peremptorily asserting his normative claims in a deductive way (Hardin 2007: 41). His consistently realistic and empirical observations lead him to focus on the contingencies of the real world, and he attempts to explain how diverse our social institutions are. Admittedly, many Enlightenment thinkers invoked non-European customs and manners in order to relativise the traditional Christian and the contemporary European values. For Hume as 'anatomist' of human nature, unlike (or at least far more than) them, the observations on these diversities provide rather the basic starting point for his analysis. This does not necessarily mean that he was reticent in articulating his own agenda, but merely that he always embedded his claims in social and historical context (Dees 1992).

Related to his keen awareness of contingency and his naturalistic account of human nature and society is a second characteristic: his scepticism about the clear demarcation of various issues in the real world. This appears in various forms and contexts. In Book 3 of the *Treatise*, he argues '[h]ow far these fundamental laws extend is not determined in any government; nor is it possible it ever should', because of 'such an indefensible gradation from the most material laws to the most trivial, and from the most ancient laws to the most modern'. Thus, he concludes that 'it would be impossible to set bounds to the legislative power, and how far it may innovate in the principles of government' (T 3.2.10.14; 561). Similarly, while admitting that 'the rules of justice may be dispensed with in cases of urgent necessity', he condemns 'a preacher or casuist, who should make it his chief study to find out such [exceptional] cases' (E 'Passive Obedience' 490–1). His awareness of this difficulty in legal and constitutional issues is often, if not always, concomitant with his observations of the workings of imagination, which in turn underlies his account of 'the general rules' as one of the causes for unphilosophical probability. While he argues that 'the general rule carries us beyond the original principle' (T 3.2.12.7; 573), he does not aspire to spot the exact point where or the precise moment when it does so in each particular case. This is because in complex cases related to property rights 'the whole question hangs upon the fancy, which [...] is not possess'd of any precise or determinate standard, upon which it can give sentence' (T footnote 73.4 to 3.2.3.7; 508). At the same time we should heed that this scepticism does not entail a total relativism: his point is not in the denial of distinctions themselves, but rather in the difficulty in spotting or establishing boundaries in each context.

Hume's scepticism about demarcation is not always related to legal and constitutional issues involving distinctions between essential and trivial points, or emergency and non-emergency cases. Hume also exerts this scepticism on the distinction between something normal and abnormal, or moderate and extreme in politics and religion. On this point Hume can be characterised as non-essentialist. For example, in his essay 'Of Refinement in the Arts', Hume distinguishes innocent and vicious luxury, and leaves us the merely formal definition of innocent ways to enjoy luxury. The definition is conceptually sufficient for his discussion, but he frankly admits that the distinction is a matter of degree (E 278–9): this leaves the door (wide) open for various possible assessments in different contexts. The same is true about his distinction between moderates and hard-liners in politics. Despite his criticism of political (and religious) extremists, Hume admits that this distinction differs only in the intensity of political belief or frenzy. He also confesses the difficulty in deciding '[a]ll questions concerning the proper medium between extremes' in the essay 'Of the Independency of Parliament'. This is not only because of the difficulty in finding '*words* proper to fix this medium', but also 'because the good and ill, in such cases, run so gradually into each other, as even to render our *sentiments* doubtful and uncertain' (E 46). For Hume, many, though not all, of these issues differ not in kind, but in degree: such criteria differ in each context. With his claim of the universality of human nature, he admits that the normal or ordinary workings of human nature and the abnormal ones (such as enthusiasm) are distinct in their manifestations but continuous in nature (Guimarães 2009).

Thirdly, according to Hume, because of the flexibility of the workings of human imagination and the instability of opinion (Chapters 2 and 3), even civilised societies are always susceptible to unpredictable and potentially sudden vicissitudes. Considering this way of looking at the world, Hume naturally cannot uphold the attainability of eternal truth by reason; much less the perfectibility of human nature (Chapters 6 and 7). He pays continuous attention to the fact that even seemingly well-established conventions are easily demolished, partly because of sudden or slow changes in various circumstances and partly because of abnormal and excessive passions and workings of imagination. Despite the fact that many Enlightenment thinkers held the cyclical visions of civilisation in its broad term, Hume clearly and consciously retains a more sceptical tone than others in his foresights of future progress.

All these typical, if not exhaustive, manifestations of his 'spirit of scepticism' give his social philosophy an impression of indecisiveness, aloofness and ambiguity, which is further augmented by his avowed impartiality of political biases ('Advertisement' to the *Essays, Moral and Political* in Hume [1886] 1992: III, 41–2) and his deliberate self-concealment. The former appears in his nonchalant and dispassionate style, while the latter is best embodied in his adoption of dialogical forms (Sessions 1991; Immerwahr 1989) and in his use of irony (Price 1992) especially in his religious writings.[16] These literary styles themselves are a part of, if not central to, his 'spirit of scepticism'. Such a seemingly uncommitted attitude and style sometimes, especially in the early nineteenth century (Chapter 8), evoked an image of Hume as an overly indifferent and detached philosopher.

Hume's conviction that we can neither access eternal truth nor prove the existence of God through reason, nevertheless, did not leave him disillusioned as to the potential for human happiness, which he considered attainable in this world. What Hume considers the most effectual and steady means of curbing enthusiasm and promulgating soberness is to encourage people to stick to worldly interests and develop human sociability by fostering a culture of conversation and politeness. An early example of his strong commitment to worldliness can be found in a letter written by the young Hume to Hutcheson, in which he complains:

> I cannot agree to your Sense of *Natural*. Tis founded on final Causes; which is a Consideration, that appears to me pretty uncertain & unphilosophical. For pray, what is the End of Man? Is he created for Happiness or for Virtue? For this Life or for the next? For himself or for his Maker? (L I, 33)

This attitude later came to constitute the backbone of Hume's robust defence of luxury: our freer pursuit of worldly pleasures (Chapter 4). He clearly accepted the normative core of the distinction between barbarism and civilisation, and committed himself to defend or even encourage the latter (Berry 2006; McArthur 2007: chap. 1). This is because, Hume believes, promoting attachment to earthly concerns has a much lower likelihood of producing devastating effects in human societies than to set one religious commitment against another, which could promote nothing but hypocrisy or enthusiasm (Chapter 5). His acceptance of the inherent instability of social realities does not compel him to abandon his pursuit of regularity in the system of government; on the contrary, the theme pervades his political writings (Chapter 6). Seen in this light, Hume shares not a few normative claims for the betterment of our world with some other contemporary thinkers, despite many differences in terms of the intensity of their claims, their decisiveness and their views of the prospects for the future of humanity. (It may be added that such a positive commitment is not a necessary qualification for an Enlightenment thinker according to our definition.)

Taken individually, these characteristics might not be peculiar or exclusive to Hume; similar traits can be identified in other thinkers. Yet it seems extremely difficult to find all of these characteristics in any one thinker but Hume. It is also undeniable that the emphasis on these various components of Hume's 'spirit of scepticism' varies according to context: precisely how this variation manifests itself I will clarify as far as possible in what follows. Viewed in this light, the question that we must consider – and my primary concern in this book – is how Humean defence of such positive values as 'industry, knowledge and humanity' is supported by seemingly conservative, though actually sceptical, aspects of Hume's thought, such as his criticism of rationalism in morals, his rejection of the social contract theory in politics, and his deep doubt concerning the possibility for progress in human civilisation. In sum, Hume's Sceptical Enlightenment is the concept representing his distinctive way of supporting what he believes to be the core of modern values (refinement and politeness), while avoiding falling into any kind of dogmatism, including philosophical dogmatism. In doing so, Hume levels his criticism against what has been considered the alleged 'Enlightenment' credo of 'Reason and Progress', while simultaneously refusing to side with naive traditionalism.[17]

5 Outline of the Following Chapters

In what follows, the discussions in Chapters 2 and 3 will mainly deal with the theoretical basis of Hume's Sceptical Enlightenment, which reveals the reasons he frequently betrays his anxiety about the unstableness and fragility of human civilisation. In the *Abstract* of the *Treatise of Human Nature*, Hume is proud of his own treatment of the theory of association of ideas: a topic on which Thomas Hobbes, John Locke and other philosophers had led the way. Hume was well aware of the strong implications of the associationist theory as a part of Epicureanism, but he consistently distances his theory from the materialistic account of associationism. He also remained constantly committed to the issue of the wide latitude for the course of development of human conventions as an inevitable consequence of the variable workings of the human imagination (Chapter 2). Although Hume does not explicitly equate the works of imagination with what he terms opinion in his political and historical writings, his thesis that every government is founded on opinion has a clear resonance with his sensitivity to the changeableness of our perceptions. Chapter 3 will demonstrate that the notion of opinion plays a central role in enabling him to criticise both the social contract theory and the myth of the ancient constitution. Hume's keen awareness of the volatility of our political opinion does not plunge him into an obstinate defence of the *status quo*; rather it leads him to a deeper and critical understanding of the actual flexibility of what people believe to be 'what is established'.

Building on this foundation, Chapters 4 to 7 will examine the way in which this foundational perspective is combined with his theoretical contributions to the betterment of society in the several crucial issues of the Enlightenment – luxury, religion, democracy and civilisation. Hume's pro-luxury and anti-religion standpoint was well known – or, rather, notorious – among his contemporaries. As Chapter 4 will argue, Hume's method of advocating luxury is quite different from those of Mandeville and Smith, and by combining both elements of Epicureanism and Stoicism he attempts to demonstrate how to refine social intercourse through the enjoyment of luxury. Compared with his support of luxury, Hume's criticism of priesthood has been a more disputed point; despite the notoriety of his anti-religious attitude, Hume's alleged support for the established Church in the *History of England* has been considered one of the most significant pieces of evidence that Hume became increasingly conservative with advancing age. However, in Chapter 5 I will emphasise the consistency between his life-long criticism of priestcraft since the essay 'Of Superstition and Enthusiasm' and the ironical and satirical nature of his Erastianism. Some significant differences between Voltaire and the 'Scottish' Voltaire will also be examined. Chapter 6 will discuss one of the most misinterpreted essays, the 'Idea of a Perfect Commonwealth', in relation to his other political writings and the *History*. This enigmatic essay seems to be one of the best illustrations of compatibility between his consistent pursuit of politics as a science and his steadfast commitment to the spirit of scepticism. In Chapter 7, Hume's cyclical view of civilisation will be discussed. Although Forbes discards Hume's 'swinging pendulum' view of history as one element of his vulgar Whiggism, it will be made clear that Hume's cyclical view of history is far from being peripheral, but rather is central to elucidating the way in which Hume defends modern values within the intellectual and historical framework of Enlightenment as a shared sensitivity to the contemporary civilising process.

Chapter 8 has an approach distinct from the previous chapters. It concerns the early reception of Hume both as philosopher and as historian in late eighteenth- and early nineteenth-century Britain. The aim of this chapter is to revisit J. S. Mill's assessment that Hume's scepticism led him to political conservatism by examining other early responses to Hume's writings with the aid of recent scholarship. Some might think that analysing Hume's contemporary and later receptions to his writings has little relevance for our understanding of his own social philosophy. Considering that Mill's evaluation of Hume still predominates among commentators in some ways, however, it is not inappropriate to counterpoise his reputation as a conservative thinker with a different Hume without running into another extreme.

In short, my strategy in this book is two-pronged. On the one hand, through changing the very concept of the Enlightenment into a less agenda-oriented one, I will demonstrate that Hume's keen awareness of the instability of civilised societies – a result of his scepticism regarding human reason and progress – does not necessarily tarnish his avowed backing of civilisation; rather, Hume remains loyal to the values of modernity precisely because of his comprehension of their fragility. On the other hand, by reconsidering his allegedly 'conservative' aspects, I will not only claim that Hume's contributions to Enlightenment discourses deserve more attention, but also aim to illustrate that the distinction between the Moderate and Radical Enlightenment is not always as clear as Israel claims (2010: 18, 238). This is the reason I adopt such a somewhat oxymoronic concept as the 'Sceptical Enlightenment', which seems to be one possible way to conquer what Forbes terms the 'terrible campaign country'.

Notes

1. By contrast, the 'Academic' version reported by Cicero in his *De natura deorum* (*Of the Nature of the Gods*) suggests that sceptics can accept some plausible appearances as a basis for decision or action, even if lacking ultimate theoretical justification. Aside from interpretive difficulties in the distinction between two schools of scepticism (Striker 2010), Hume broadly adopts the latter form of mitigated scepticism in the first *Enquiry*.
2. For another example, Leslie Stephen commented that '[t]he translation of [Hume's] heretical scepticism into politics is a cynical conservatism; and Hume [...] evidently inclines to the side of authority as the most favorable to that stagnation which is the natural ideal of a sceptic' (1876: II, 185).
3. All of these commentators deny the allegation that Hume was a naïve traditionalist, but eventually deem him to be a certain kind of conservative. What complicates matters is that Livingston's reading of Hume as a conservative is the American version. Actually, Livingston pays attention to Hume's endorsement of modern values such as democracy and liberty, which, according to Livingston, should be understood as historically (or rather *traditionally*) contextualised. For further argument on this point, see Chapter 3 in this book. McArthur also characterises Hume's politics as 'precautionary conservatism' as opposed to traditionalism (2007: chap. 6).
4. Rorty's understanding of Hume is based on Baier's (Baier 1991). As for 'Rorty's Humean Turn', see Williams 2003; Voparil 2006: chap. 4. Thanks to Akira Abe for his information on the relationship between Hume and Rorty. For another possibility of Humean and Smithean 'reflective sentimentalism', see Frazer 2010.
5. During the last stage of preparing the typescript, I found that McCormick (2013), actually published in August 2014, also emphsises the significance of the link between Hume's scepticism and politics, and criticises Miller, Whelan and McArthur from a similar perspective to mine. While I share this basic concept with her, my concern is rather more historical and wider in scope. As for the connection between Hume's scepticism and politics, see also Marshall 1954.

6. In another paper, Schmidt (2001) argues that the contents of the Enlightenment project are nothing but a 'projection' of the nineteenth- and twentieth-century ideological disputes. However, neither Schmidt nor Delacampagne (2001), in his reply to Schmidt, seem to raise the question of whether the phrase 'the Enlightenment project' itself is historically appropriate or not.
7. Gay also uses the metaphor of 'family' to describe French philosophes (1966–69: II, x); see also Israel 2011: 5–8.
8. This might be impacted by Habermas's 'Unfinished Project of Modernity', a part of the title of his acceptance speech on receiving the Theodor W. Adorno Prize in 1980. For criticism of MacIntyre's term 'Enlightenment Project', see Wokler: 2012: 260–78.
9. Edelstein's definition seems to concur with Foucault's one of Enlightenment as an 'attitude' or 'a mode of relating to contemporary reality' (Foucault 1991: 39). In the light of my argument, it is important to note that Foucault clearly severs humanism 'always tied with value-judgment' from Enlightenment, defined as 'a set of events and complex historical process' (44).
10. It has also seemed necessary to account for certain alleged inconsistencies in Hume's thought; notably through the argument for his increasing conservatism with advancing age. Like Forbes (1963), I will reject this argument. This is not to deny that there was any intellectual development through his life and writings, but merely to assert that my primary concern lies in revisiting what Forbes calls the 'essential continuity of Hume's thought' (1975b: x).
11. I thank Jean-Pierre Grima-Morales for the information on Charles and Smith (eds) 2013.
12. Recently, Dennis C. Rasmussen (2014) has categorised Hume with Adam Smith, Voltaire and Montesquieu under what he terms the 'Practical Enlightenment'. His excellent research investigates from a more positive perspective than Israel's what these philosophers have in common. The term 'Practical Enlightenment', however, seems to be a mere paraphrase of Israel's 'Moderate Enlightenment' because the former basically follows the latter's groupings. It is also important to recognise even seemingly slight, but nonetheless significant, differences between Hume and these other thinkers.
13. On this point, see Norton 1965 (although I do not agree with his conclusion that Hume's project of the historical science failed as well as his philosophy did because both were insufficient to satisfy the goal he set out for himself, an experimentally-based science of man). See also Popkin 1965; 1976; Perinetti 2006: 1108–17.

14. Even Hume's essay 'Of Miracles' was read as a defence of the faith against the Enlightenment atheism (Popkin [1976] 1996: 20).
15. Yet Parusnikova seems to capture the distinctive feature of Hume's 'spirit of scepticism' by claiming that 'what makes him a postmodernist at heart is his *determination not to offer any convenient way out of skepticism and, as a consequence, not to offer any neat philosophical "package"*' (1993: 4).
16. Terence Penelhum emphasises as one of several influences of Bayle on Hume in his dealings with religious issues 'Hume's occasional resort to indirection and nominal reportage in his presentation of some of his key arguments' and 'the adaptation of a light and bantering manner while dealing with themes on which he felt very strongly' (2008: 331). On the difference between Hume and Bayle in their scepticism, see Ryan 2013.
17. On this score, LaVopa aptly points out in a review article on Israel's books that 'Hume saw [the construction of modernity] as a matter of practising rational critique within a disposition to live constructively with uncertainty' (2009: 734). Peter Gay also seems to give essentially the same assessment: 'Hume, therefore, more desicively than many of his brethren in the Enlightenment, stands at the threshold of modernity and exhibits its risks and its possibilities' (1966–9: I, 419).

2

'The Empire of the Imagination': The Association of Ideas in Hume's Social Philosophy

In the year 1735, the second son of a Scottish laird, having left the University of Edinburgh, disillusioned with his study of law but ambitious for success in literature and philosophy, was headed for La Flèche in France to complete his first book. He is the protagonist of this book, David Hume, who was later to become a highly acclaimed philosopher and historian, notorious during the eighteenth century and ever after for his controversial views. In his short autobiography 'My Own Life' written four months before his death and prefixed to the posthumous edition of his collected works, he describes how his first book, *A Treatise of Human Nature* (1739–40), 'fell *dead-born from the press*' (E 'My Own Life' xxxiv). Nevertheless, and despite the author's own official disownment of the *Treatise*, which he considered a 'juvenile work' (EHU Author's Advertisement), few works can be said to rival its influence on modern European philosophy. There are many appropriate starting points in the *Treatise* to investigate not only the philosophical Hume but also the historical Hume. I will commence with one of the claims which the author of this 'juvenile work' himself boasts of his originality: 'Thro' this whole book, there are great pretensions to new discoveries in philosophy; but if any thing can intitle the author to so glorious a name as that of an inventor, 'tis the use he makes of the principle of the association of ideas, which enters into most of his philosophy' (A 35; 661–2).

It has been generally acknowledged that Hume prided himself upon his adoption, not his discovery, of the theory of the association of ideas in the *Treatise*.[1] As Duncan Forbes points out, however, 'Hume's early enthusiasm for a new system of the moral sciences based on the principles of association waned' (1975b: 15). Certainly, in his last revision of the first *Enquiry*, Hume drastically shortened the section entitled 'Of the Association of Ideas': with the original eighteen paragraphs in the first edition reduced to just three (EHU 3.1–3[–18]; 23–4).[2] Concerning Hume's confused and confusing definitions of imagination, Norman Kemp Smith also claims that 'Hume's ascription of primacy to the imagination has no greater importance in the philosophy of the *Treatise* than that of being merely a corollary to his early doctrine of belief' (1941: 462–4). For these reasons, the significance of Hume's theory of imagination in his social philosophy has been much underestimated. The aim of this chapter is to demonstrate that Hume's continued interest in the theory of imagination and the association of ideas is essential for our understanding of his development of the 'science of MAN' into the moral, political and social fields.

There are other reasons why we should start our inquiry into Hume as an Enlightenment thinker with such a seemingly epistemological argument: this is closely related to the social and political significance and connotations of the theory of the association of ideas. Firstly, the psychological analysis of the human mind provided a new direction for the doctrines of progress (Spadafora 1990: chap. 4). Most eighteenth-century associationists argued for the possibility of further moral progress and even perfectibility of humankind by emphasising the malleability of human nature and the pedagogical role of this theory. Hartley's associationist theory was among the most important intellectual inheritances of the 'Age of Reason', and his (and partially Hume's) influence endured until the mid-nineteenth century. Secondly, Élie Halévy started his classical, voluminous work on the Philosophic Radicalism with detailed discussion of the associationist theory (1955: chap. 1). For philosophic radicals like James Mill, Jeremy Bentham and J. S. Mill, this theory provided an essential theoretical scaffold from which to construct their social and political reforms, although, for Mill the younger, this theory was also a nemesis because his father applied it for the education of his son ([1826] 1963–91: 138–43). Thirdly, 'associationism' also played a central role in nineteenth-century Britain especially for the literary and critical theory of the Romantics (Kallich 1970; Craig 2007). In spite of the significance of this theory, the contribution of Hume has often been regarded as peripheral or secondary at best. The reasons are clear: his influence over the later generations who took up this theory was exerted in a limited and negative way through his opponents' criticism of the *Treatise*. Besides, his interest in the working of the association of ideas has been alleged to wane after the *Treatise*, as Forbes argues. More importantly, despite his positive application of this theory to account for the diversity of social rules, institutions and manners, Hume never set out this theory for the purpose of social or pedagogical reforms (Chapter 7). To acknowledge this, however, should not reduce the significance of the associationist theory for Hume's social philosophy. Rather, in what follows, one of the central points is the difference between Hume and other eighteenth-century associationists in their understanding of the nature and connotations of this theory.

There is another historiographical reason for dealing with the theory of association of ideas. In the eighteenth century, associationist theory had sceptical and materialistic implications, and as we will see later, was connected to Epicureanism. If so, Hume's sanguine employment of this theory in the *Treatise* should not be considered solely as an expression of his philosophical attitude, but also to have important connotations for his social and political philosophy. Recently, intellectual historians have been rather reserved in 'making very much attempt to connect [Hume's handling of the historical and political vocabularies of his age] with his analysis of natural and moral philosophy' (Pocock 1985b: 126). If philosophical theories also reflected these vocabularies, it is also significant to investigate how Hume consciously used this 'value-laden' philosophical theory.

In what follows, I will first sketch the ideological implications of the eighteenth-century theory of the association of ideas. Second, I will contend that Hume's application of the associationist theory in Book 3 of the *Treatise* should be considered to have greater relevance to Hume's social and political philosophy than has so far been judged to be the case. Thirdly, I will show that Hume maintained the theoretical underpinning of the associationist theory to frame his argument concerning the origin of the rules of property. I will also argue that Hume's interest in the theory of association of ideas did not actually wane; on the contrary, it is deeply related to his support for moral causes and criticism of physical causes in the climate theory. And finally, the differences between Hume and the other associationists will be discussed. The underlying theme of this chapter is to depict the philosophical basis of Hume's Sceptical Enlightenment. In his understanding and treatment of the theory of imagination can be found many, if not all, important characteristics of the notion that we outlined in the previous chapter.

1 The Ideological Implication of the Theory of Imagination and the Association of Ideas

The so-called 'British empiricists' always face a serious question: how we can distinguish between correct experiences and wrong ones. Obviously, this fundamental question can be traced to Plato or Sophists in ancient Greek philosophy, and numerous modern philosophers have also confronted the same issue in one way or another.[3] The impact of Hobbes's 'train of thoughts' and John Locke's 'way of ideas', however, seems to provide us with a proper starting point for our understanding of one of the most significant elements of the eighteenth-century empiricism: the theory of the association of ideas (MacLean 1936; Wood 1992: 650; Wood 1994).

Although Locke has a more significant presence in the history of this theory than Thomas Hobbes, the latter should not be underestimated as one of the founders of the theory of association of ideas, especially in the British context.[4] In the *Leviathan* (1651), Hobbes explains all of our mental operations from a materialist standpoint: he traces all mental phenomena to senses and imaginations (or fancies) as their weaker forms (Russell 2008: 86). After discussing various kinds of imaginations such as memory, experience and dreams and the distinction between simple and compounded imagination, he goes on to discuss trains of thoughts, which are divided into '*unguided*' and '*regulated*' (Hobbes [1651] 1996: 20–1 [I.3]). This distinction was to permeate the work of all his successors. As Christopher Berry points out, '[f]rom its "modern" origins in Hobbes, imagination had been closely associated with fictiveness' (1994: 165).[5]

John Locke also distinguished 'a natural correspondence and connexion [of some idea] one with another' and 'another connexion of ideas wholly owing to chance or custom', and he called the latter simply 'Madness' ([1689/90] 1975: 394–401 [II.33]). In other words, he discerned that there were natural (correct) and unnatural (wrong) correspondences of ideas within the natural order. In *An Essay concerning Human Understanding* (1689/90) and more clearly in 'Of the Conduct of the Understanding' (1697), when he uses the term 'association of ideas', it chiefly means a prejudice or confused imagination to be remedied through education (Spadafora 1990: 166–9).

As many studies show (MacLean 1936; Yolton 1956; 1984;

Kallich 1970; Shcuurman 2001; Carey 2006: chap. 2), Locke's emphasis upon the role of ideas in metaphysics seems to his contemporaries and later generations to be a bold assertion of scepticism and relativism. Obviously the doctrine of association is of concern not only in metaphysics, but also in moral philosophy. Precisely for this reason, at the beginning of the eighteenth century, the third earl of Shaftesbury criticised his old tutor's philosophy as well as Hobbes's:

> 'T was Mr. Locke, that struck the home Blow: For Mr. Hobbes's Character and base slavish Principles in Government took off the Poyson of his philosophy. 'T was Mr. Locke that struck at all fundamentals, threw all order and virtue out of the world, and make the very ideas of these (which are the same as those of God) *unnatural* and without foundation in our mind. (Shaftesbury 1900: 40 [To Michael Ainsworth, 3 June, 1709])

Here, Shaftesbury criticises Locke's interpretation of the role of ideas not only as a philosophical theory, but also in its relation to the issue of morals.

The issue of the association of ideas, however, was much more complicated than it appears. As Isabel Rivers points out, there are fundamental differences between Locke and Shaftesbury concerning their understandings of 'revealed religion, the source of moral action, the meaning and function of philosophy, and the value of classical moralists' (2000: 89). Locke's well-known *tabula rasa* theory posits that we have no innate principles (including what Shaftesbury was to call the 'moral sense'). Because the sources of our ideas are either sensations or reflections, we can access our knowledge of moral principles only through the process of rational deduction, although he also regards the gospel as indispensable to providing us with the motives for obeying natural law. Importantly, the philosophers of 'Lockeanism' (Edmund Law, John Gay, David Hartley and Joseph Priestley) criticised those of Shaftesburianism (Francis Hutcheson, Lord Kames, Adam Smith and Joseph Butler) by dismissing the alleged moral sense as nothing but 'habits' formed as a consequence of the association of ideas (Rivers 2000: 127, 334–5). This is why, as Dugald Stewart explains, the introduction of the association of ideas into the issue of morality was traced back to John Gay's 'Concerning the Fundamental Principle of Virtue or Morality' which was prefixed to Edmund Law's English translation of William King's *De Origine Mali* (*On the Origin of Evil*) (1702). John Gay, an English philosopher and clergyman and a cousin of his namesake the dramatist, demonstrated that 'our Approbation of Morality, and all Affections whatsoever, are finally resolved into *Reason*, pointing out *private Happiness* [...] and that wherever this end is not perceived, they are to be accounted for from the *Association of Ideas*, and may properly be call'd *Habits*' (King 1731: xiv; see also Stewart [1792–1827] 1854–60, 1994: I, 382). In his preface to the collected works of Locke, Law acclaimed Locke because 'he most effectually eradicated all innate or connate *senses*, instincts, &c. [...] these same senses, or instincts with whatever titles decorated, whether stiled *sympathetic* or *sentimental*, *common* or *intuitive*, – ought to be looked upon as no more than mere HABITS' (Law 1777; I, viii–ix, quoted in Rivers 2000: 334). In short, these Lockean philosophers (negatively) developed the theory of the association of ideas so as to undermine the core of Shaftesburian moral theory.

On the other hand, Francis Hutcheson, one of the most important successors of Shaftesbury, deflected the criticisms of his opponents by his own application of this theory to buttressing his own moral philosophy. What Hutcheson means by 'imagination' or 'association of ideas' is the mental deformity caused by wrong education and customs that pervert the proper manifestation of our innate and moral senses. For example, there are many negative expressions in *An Essay on the Nature and Conduct of the Passions and Affectations*, 'strange *Associations of Ideas*', '*Confusion of Ideas*' ([1728] 1990: 9, 12 [I.1.ii]) or '*confused Association of Ideas*' (23 [I.1.iv]). In *An Inquiry into the Original of Our Ideas of Beauty and Virtue*, he identified the irrational association of ideas with prejudices ([1725] 1990: 85 [I.vii.3]). Against these harmful effects of prejudices, he entrusts the judgement of moral sense to discern the harmony with natural order. For Hutcheson, the association of ideas has a theoretical significance only to explain irrational and unnatural ideas and passions. On this point, despite the fundamental disagreements between Lockean and Shaftesburian philosophers, Francis Hutcheson can be considered a successor of the associationist theorists in terms of his understanding of how the association of ideas can be distorted by wrong custom.[6]

The intellectual sources of Hume's philosophy were not limited to Britain. It is notable that the young Hume sent the manuscript of the *Treatise* to Pierre Desmaizeaux (des Maizeaux), the Huguenot protégé, translator and biographer of Pierre Bayle and Saint-Évremond then exiled in London. Hume solicited his opinion of 'my System of Philosophy' (L I, 29; Mossner 1980: 119–20; Russell 2008: 72–4, 79, 331n.26; see also Thomson 2008: 140–55). The close connection between Hume and the Chevalier (Andrew Michael) Ramsay when the former was writing the *Treatise* in France should also be heeded.[7] Despite the difference in political and religious affiliations between Hume and Ramsay (friend and disciple of Archbishop Fénelon, Quietist and Freemason), this religious mystic helped familiarise his younger compatriot with various radical thoughts, which he later criticised (Mossner 1980: 93–5; Emerson 1997: 21–2). In Hume's letter of 1737 to Michael Ramsay, a cousin of the Chevalier Ramsay, the young philosopher recommends some other reading to help his friend since early youth comprehend his own *Treatise*:

> I shall submit all my Performances [a draft of the *Treatise*] to your Examination, & to make you enter into them more easily, I desire of [y]ou [...] to read once over le Recherche de la Verité of Pere Malebranche, the Principles of Human Knowledge by Dr Berkeley, some of the more metaphysical Articles of Baile's Dictionary; such as those [o]f Zeno, & Spinoza. Des-Cartes Meditations wou'd also be useful [...]. These Books will make you easily comprehend the metaphysical Parts of my Reasoning. (Cited in Norton and Norton 2007: 442–3; see also Mossner 1980: 626–7)

Aside from George Berkeley and Zeno, Hume mentions here four major modern European thinkers. Spinoza and Malebranche seem to have been especially influential on Hume in their philosophical treatment of imagination (on Bayle, see p. 67 and pp. 110–11). Although Hume's recommendation is not exclusively focused on his predecessors' arguments concerning imagination, these continental philosophers also tend to regard imagination as one of the fundamental causes that lead us to errors and fallacy. Broadly following Descartes's articulation between understanding and imagination (Descartes [1641] 2008: 52–3 [6th Meditation]), for example, Benedict de Spinoza acknowledges the fundamental differences between three types of knowledge, that is, the 'knowledge of the first kind, opinion or imagination' based upon symbols and reports, which is distinguished and distinguishable from the other two kinds of knowledge, reason and intuition (Spinoza [1677a] 1955: 113 [Pt. 2, Prop. 40, N. 2]). In a similar way to John Locke, he also described how to improve our intellect by distinguishing various types of perception or knowledge in his *Tractatus de Intellectus Emendatione* (*On the Improvement of the Understanding*) ([1677b] 1955: 8).

Despite such seemingly traditional treatments of imagination, these Continental philosophers gave the workings of imagination a central and more positive status among our psychological processes than their British predecessors allowed.[8] On this point, Spinoza is innovative in his application of the theory of imagination to the issue of religious superstition. In the *Tractatus Theologico-Politicus* (*Theological-Political Treatise*), he unequivocally affirms that 'the prophets were not endowed with more perfect minds than others but only a more vivid power of imagination' (Spinoza [1670] 2007: 27 [Ch. 2, 1]; see also Wilson 1996; James 1997: Part 2; Steenbakkers 2004; Russell 2008: 277). He also attempts to separate the teachings of Christ as a universal moral code from the distortions and misrepresentation infused by the ecclesiastics and theologians through his critical exegetics. It is interesting to add that Spinoza considers that because passion is 'a confused idea' (Spinoza [1677a] 1955: 185 [Pt. 3]), 'fear is the root from which superstition is born, maintained and nourished' and 'dread is the cause of superstition' ([1670] 2007: 4, 5 [Preface]). Along with his empirical and critical accounts of prophecy, beliefs in miracles and revealed religion, Spinoza's extensive analysis of religious superstition with the theory of imagination would not have failed to inspire the young Hume, who was later to write the chapter 'Of Miracles' in the first *Enquiry* (1748), the essays 'Of Superstition and Enthusiasm' (1741) and 'The Natural History of Religion' (1757) (De Dijn 2012; see also Popkin 1979: 66; Klever 1990: 55).

As Forbes points out, Malebranche's panoramic argument on imagination is also important for our understanding of Hume's version of the association of ideas (Forbes 1975b: 10n.2, 107, 130; see also Wright 1983: esp. 70–1, 205–7, 213–15; James 2005). Malebranche uses the phrase 'the connection of ideas' and gives a less materialistic account of the associationist theory in *De la recherche de la vérité* (*The Search after Truth*) than Hobbes (Malebranche [1674–5] 1997: especially 101–9 [Bk. 2, Pt. 1, Ch. 5]; see also 161–72 [2.3.1–2]). He also discusses the influence of animal spirits upon the imagination, based upon Descartes's dualistic ontology between the body and the mind as well as the influence of the 'air' upon the animal spirits. However, as the common assumption that 'Hume's theory of causation is occasionalism minus God' suggests (Lennon 1977: xxii), Malebranche's less materialistic analysis of the imagination is much closer to Hume's version than Hobbes's. Furthermore, his discussion of imagination is not only purely metaphysical, but also sociological. He asserted that '[s]trong imaginations are extremely contagious' in *De la recherche de la vérité* (Malebranche [1674–5] 1997: 161 [2.3.1]), and, as we will discuss below, this seems reminiscent of Hume's argument on the contagion of manners and customs in the *Treatise* (2.3.1.9; 402) and the essay 'Of National Characters' (1748).

In addition to these possible Continental sources and inspirations, a more positive (though satirical) development of the associationist theory was undertaken by Bernard Mandeville, a modern Epicurean and Hobbesian. In contrast with Hutcheson, who commits more positively to the political theory of Locke, Mandeville deployed Lockean philosophy to satirical advantage in his depiction of the artificial manipulations of the vulgar by politicians and moralists. He makes a good (though superficial) use of Locke's philosophical claims to prove that all the morality and the principles of honour are nothing but a product of imagination: 'there are no Innate Idea's, and Men come into the World without any Knowledge at all [. . .], and therefore it is evident to me, that all Arts and Sciences must once have had a Beginning in some body's Brain'; 'The Brain of a Child, newly born, is *Charte Blanche*' (Mandeville [1714/1729, 1732] 1988: II, 149 [158]; II, 168 [183]). What is important is his adaptation of Lockean 'way of ideas' in the field of social and political theory. To emphasise the influence of imagination in social rules when addressing the problem of the sovereignty of reason could sound either Sceptic or Epicurean.

To be more precise, the emphasis upon the artificiality and arbitrariness of social rules based on the fickleness of imagination concerns the philosophers' standpoint about the status of reason among the human faculties, and consequently about the status of human beings in the universe. As J. G. A. Pocock emphasises, the negative connotations of words such as opinion, imagination and fancy in the field of the history of political thought were typically introduced into the vocabulary of the 'Neo-Machiavellian' political economists at the end of the seventeenth and the beginning of the eighteenth century (1975: esp. 456–61; see also Phillipson 2011: 56). In spite of active controversies over the definition of republicanism, the language of reason and virtue form its core insomuch as the autonomy and self-government of citizens are emphasised (Scott 2002: 66–71). In Stoicism, human reason is also considered to be a divine endowment allowing us to discern the natural and eternal order of the universe (Brooke 2012: xii). However, the priority of reason should not be taken to be exclusive in either republicanism or Stoicism. To overcome the moral scepticism revived at the Renaissance was also a 'continuing ambition of modern natural law' since Grotius in his *De Jure Belli ac Pacis* (*Of the Law of War and Peace*) (1625) challenged Carneades, 'the representative of all scepticism' (Haakonssen 1996: 24–5; cf. Tuck 1999: 97–8, 102). As Jonathan Scott summarises, 'classical republicanism and natural law theory shared an appeal to the faculty of human reason which was Greek in origin, but frequently in the early modern period Christian in application' (Scott 2004: 26). These ancient and modern rationalists, in the broadest sense of the term, have been broadly apprehensive of the strong affinity between mere habits or customs and the association of ideas. This is because the notions of fancy and imagination are considered risk factors with the potential to undermine human reason and the natural order of the universe and to underline a much greater contingency of our moral rules. For this reason, this emphasis upon imagination and custom must have political implications, especially among the rationalist-oriented thinkers in seventeenth- and eighteenth-century intellectual discourses.

For Hume, like Mandeville, to demonstrate that social rules are much influenced by the operations of imagination serves his purpose of criticising those rationalists who presuppose that the universe has a rational structure and that the relationship things bear to each other within this structure can be discerned by reason. His emphasis upon imagination is aimed at underlining the greater contingency of our moral rules, and undermining claims for the existence of universal and immutable laws discernible through human reason. It is likely that Hume was well aware of the implications of his claim for the universal applicability of the associationist theory. In the *Abstract* he acknowledges that 'the reader will easily perceive, that the philosophy contain'd in this book is very sceptical, and tends to give us a notion of the imperfections and narrow limits of human understanding' (A 27; 657; see also Buckle 2007).

Unlike Mandeville's more sarcastic relativism, however, Hume believes that imagination has its own course of operation. As we will see below, Hume identifies some types of the workings of imagination as more general and universal, because it 'is a kind of ATTRACTION, which in the mental world will be found to have as extraordinary effects as in the natural' (T 1.1.4.6; 12–13). This is the reason Hume can firmly believe that the 'science of MAN' does not necessarily lead to total relativism (Brahami 2009: esp. 372–4). In what follows, we must bear in mind Hume's strategy on these two fronts, as well as his understanding of the two-pronged concept of imagination.

2 Property and Imagination in the *Treatise*

Before addressing the significance of the theory of association of ideas in Hume's moral and political writings, we must examine Hume's definition of imagination in Book 1 of the *Treatise*. Like his predecessors, Hume makes a basic distinction between the type of imagination that represents the fundamental workings of the association of ideas and that which consists merely of whimsical fancies:

> In order to justify myself, I must distinguish in the imagination betwixt the principles which are permanent, irresistible, and universal; such as the customary transition from causes to effects, and from effects to causes: and the principles, which are changeable, weak, and irregular [...]. The former are the foundation of all our thoughts and actions, so that upon their removal, human nature must immediately perish and go to ruin. The latter are neither unavoidable to mankind, nor necessary, or so much as useful in the conduct of life [...]. (T 1.4.4.1; 225)

He repeats this distinction in another place: 'the understanding, that is [...] the general and more established properties of the imagination' is distinguished from 'that singular and seemingly trivial property of the fancy' (1.4.7.7; 267–8). Hume here rephrases 'the understanding' as the 'general and more established properties of imagination'. He gives another, slightly different definition in a footnote of the *Treatise*. Here, imagination is divided into narrower and broader senses: the first is 'the faculty by which we form our fainter ideas', especially when it is opposed to the memory. The second is 'the same faculty, excluding only our demonstrative and probable reasonings', when opposed to reason (footnote 22 to 1.3.9.19; 117–18n.). This version was added to the proof sheet of the *Treatise* just before its publication (Norton and Norton 2007: 749). To provide a coherent definition of imagination in Hume's philosophy is not my purpose here. What is important is that Hume principally recognises two levels of imagination: one is more fundamental and indispensable, while the other is capricious and whimsical. As this boundary is not always clear, however, his notion(s) of imagination can appear Janus-faced. On this point, despite his new definition, Hume also seems to be conscious of the spectre of the traditionally negative connotations of imagination (Kemp Smith 1941: 459–63; Miller 1981: 26–34, 37–9).

Hume's vague definitions of technical words including 'imagination' are notorious (Traiger 2008: 58); nevertheless, we should pay more attention to the fact that Hume rarely uses the association of ideas to describe the processes of 'fancy'. For Hume, as we saw above, imagination has two different meanings: it is used both for the 'understanding' and for 'fancy'. Despite his ambiguous uses of the word 'imagination', and unlike Hutcheson, Hume almost never uses the term 'the association of ideas' to refer to a 'confused' imagination or fancy.[9] This is not a minor point, considering the fact that Locke and Hutcheson had used 'the association of ideas' in a negative sense, almost synonymous with 'prejudices' or creations of 'fancy'. To put it another way, Hume attempts to divorce the principle of the association of ideas from its negative connotations, and establish it as fundamental to the universal working of human understanding. On that account, Hume should be credited not only with the expansion of the theoretical potential of the associationist theory, but for a fundamental shift in its meaning and significance.

In his explanation of property in Books 2 and 3 of the *Treatise*, Hume seems to maintain the two different meanings of imagination. Hume maintains his belief in the importance of the more fundamental working of the association of ideas in his explanation of property, while he describes the trivial variations of particular cases with the emphasis on the frivolous and whimsical nature of fancy (Miller 1981: 71–3). In Book 2 of the *Treatise*, Hume remarks that property is a kind of relation between a person and an object, and that 'property may be look'd upon as a particular species of causation'. In this explanation, there is no room for whimsy or fancy. It is an immutable fact that 'the mention of the property naturally carries our thought to the proprietor' (T 2.1.10.1; 310). In Book 3 (in the section 'Of the rules, which determine property') Hume elucidates this point in a long footnote (footnote 73 to 3.2.3.7; 506–8n.). In this section, he picks up the four 'most considerable' laws of property: occupation, prescription, accession and succession. Keeping in mind the distinction between the two meanings of imagination, it becomes clear that Hume never doubts the validity of the 'natural propensity [of human nature] to join relations' between persons and objects, especially in each *simple* case of possession. In the case of accession, for example, he emphasises the relation between objects thought to resemble one another, and maintains that the mind 'finds a kind of fitness and uniformity in such an union' (footnote 75.2 to 3.2.3.10; 509n.). In this instance, property is explained not only by the relation of causation, but also by that of resemblance. As another example, Hume maintains that the right of succession is 'a very natural one', and the consent of the parent and the public interest are reinforced by 'the influence of *relation*, or the association of ideas, by which we are naturally directed to consider the son after the parent's decease' (3.2.3.11; 511). For Hume, these associations of ideas are 'the only links that bind the parts of the universe together, or connect us with any person or object exterior to ourselves' (A 35; 662). In this sense, the association of ideas is indispensable for all aspects of our common life. Hume clearly declares at the beginning of the longest footnote explaining the inheritance of property that '[t]his source of property can never be explain'd but from the imagination, and one may affirm, that the causes are here unmix'd' (T footnote 75.1 to 3.2.3.10; 509n.).

Problems arise when Hume starts to explain complex examples. In such real instances, 'as [various] circumstances may be conjoin'd and oppos'd in all the different ways, and according to all the different degrees, which can be imagin'd, there will result many cases, where the reasons on both sides are so equally ballanc'd, that 'tis impossible for us to give any satisfactory decision' (T footnote 75.13 to 3.2.3.10; 512–13n.). Elsewhere in the *Treatise*, he emphasised that even the interpretations of '*fundamental laws*' are 'the work more of imagination and passion than of reason' (3.2.10.14; 561–2). Hume examines some debatable cases and declares such disputes unsolvable, 'because the whole question hangs upon the fancy, which [...] is not possess'd of any precise or determinate standard, upon which it can give sentence' (footnote 73.4 to 3.2.3.7; 508n.; see also footnote 73.1; 506n.). In these sentences, imagination appears in the sense of fancy or whim.

In Hume's explanation of the particular laws of property, these two levels of imagination are almost always intermingled, if not confused. This explains why the role of imagination sounds very essential and basic in some places, while it sounds unstable and unsteady in others. Distinguishing the two dimensions of the workings of imagination in Hume's moral and social theory is essential to understand his claim regarding the diversity of social institutions and the universality of human nature. The principle of the association of ideas, according to Hume, 'is a kind of ATTRACTION, which in the mental world will be found [...] to shew itself in as many and as various forms' (T 1.1.4.6; 12). At the micro level, each operation of imagination invariably falls into one of three categories: resemblance, contiguity or causation. In its concrete manifestation, on the other hand, the number of its variations is infinite, and they are inevitably influenced by many trivial circumstances. Despite this conceptual distinction, his reservation in providing any clear-cut criterion to distinguish these two levels of imagination in each specific case gave his contemporaries the impression that his discussion of property is too sceptical, because he seemingly founds all the right of property on mere fancy. As mentioned in Chapter 1, Hume's scepticism about demarcation in the real world comes partly from the working of the general rule that is subject to overgeneralisation (2.2.5.13; 362). In Book 1 of the *Treatise*, Hume admits that reflection can amend '*general rules*, which we rashly form to ourselves' by distinguishing between essential and superficial circumstances:

> In almost all kinds of causes there is a complication of circumstances, of which some are essential, and others superfluous; some are absolutely requisite to the production of the effect, and others are only conjoined by accident. Now we may observe, that when these superfluous circumstances are numerous and remarkable, and frequently conjoined with the essential, they have such an influence on the imagination, that even in the absence of the latter they carry us on to the conception of the usual effect, and give to that conception a force and vivacity which make it superior to the mere fictions of the fancy. (1.3.13.9; 148)

This section ('Of unphilosophical probability') including the above citation has produced various interpretations of Hume's intention and different judgements concerning the success or failure of his argument (Immerwahr 1977; Livingston 1998: chap. 2). As Hume's appeal to the 'force and vivacity' as a criterion to differentiate essential from superfluous circumstances suggests, the double sense of the term 'imagination' seems to raise a difficulty similar to that at the heart of a long-standing controversy over his success or failure in distinguishing between fact and fiction (Kemp Smith 1941: 460).[10] More importantly, Hume's argument on 'the general rules' in Book 1 of the *Treatise* can be considered to parallel, in a sense, his discussions of 'the general points of view' in Book 3, where he tackles the same issue: how we can adjust and refine our judgement by forming more reliable standards through the working of sympathy and imagination (T 3.3.1.15; 581–2; Gautier 2005: chap. 2). While he focuses on the steadiness and stability of the general points of view in Book 3, Hume does not claim that the general points of view could provide us with a sheer objectivity of moral standard, but with a shared and common guideline of our moral judgement, which always leaves room for some degree of moral disagreement in complicated cases. Hence, we ourselves can never completely escape from the dual nature of imagination because the working of imagination is indispensable even for forming or correcting our moral judgements. After all, this issue has to bring us back to the 'Conclusion' of Book 1 of the *Treatise*. Here, Hume again turns to the problem that 'in some circumstances [two operations of imagination] are directly contrary [...]. How then shall we adjust those principles together?' (1.4.7.4; 266). He admits that this 'contradiction' or 'deficiency' 'proceeds merely from an illusion of imagination; and the question is, how far we ought to yield to these illusions' (1.4.7.6; 267). To put it another way, while he admits the difference of qualities of two imaginations, how far we should pursue that distinction is a question of degree. Finally, he concludes (willingly or resignedly) that 'I can only observe what is commonly done; which is, that this difficulty is seldom or never thought of' (1.4.7.7; 268). This attitude can be called a version of Humean naturalism; as we saw in Chapter 1, I will claim that this is an example of his scepticism about clear demarcation, which permeates through his entire writings.

This 'Humean' attitude brings us to reconsider the relationship between the working of imagination and the public interest. In

Book 3 of the *Treatise*, as we saw above, Hume spends many pages explaining the rules of property, such as possession and succession, from the working of imagination, or simply 'the association of ideas' (T 3.2.3.11; 511). In the *Appendix* he continues to describe how imagination fixes our rules. These arguments show that his stress upon the role of imagination is not necessarily secondary to his emphasis upon the public interest. Certainly, the public interest gives a common foundation for many social institutions and rules, including property, which are indispensable for our civilised life in larger societies. It is not obvious whether the operation of imagination is limited only to determining particular rules, or whether it can affect our judgement of public interest itself. In a footnote of the *Treatise*, Hume states that '[n]o questions in philosophy are more difficult, than when a number of causes present themselves for the same phenomenon, to determine which is the principal and predominant'. Here, he admits that 'motives of public interest' are the basis of 'most of the rules which determine property'; 'but', he continues:

> still I suspect that these rules are principally fixed by the imagination, or the more frivolous properties of our thought and conception. I shall continue to explain these causes, leaving it to the reader's choice whether he will prefer *those derived from public utility, or those derived from the imagination*. (footnote 71.1 to 3.2.3.4; 504n. Italics added)

Since the counterpart of this argument cannot be found in *An Enquiry concerning the Principles of Morals* (the second *Enquiry*), it is not clear whether Hume changed his opinion on this important point or not. The above citation from Book 1 of the *Treatise* on the problems of establishing general rules clearly shows, however, the difficulty Hume identified in distinguishing what is essential from what is superfluous concerning the peculiar content of social institutions and systems, including property rules. Moreover, although the public interest remains fundamental for Hume's account of justice, Hardin is right in pointing out that:

> Hume's psychological approbations [of the utility] are not likely to lead to a very detailed organization of society but are likely to leave very much of it indeterminate in the sense that we could not say what organization of society is commended by utilitarian considerations. (Hardin 2007: 158; see also Sabl 2012: chap. 1)

In this sense, the role of imagination in Hume's explanation of justice as an artificial virtue should not be underestimated. His main concern in the sections on property of Book 3 does not lie in sorting out these two levels of imagination by explaining particular cases, but rather in showing how haphazardly intermingled these two imaginations are in the real world. To repeat the point, the conceptual distinction between the association of ideas and fancy remains fundamental even in his account of private property as an artificial virtue, but this distinction does not provide any straightforward explanation of why, how and to what extent either of these two levels of imagination determine the content of specific rules.

If almost every institution in our social milieu is affected by the operations of imagination, Hume's explanation in relation to property can be applied to any other social institution. In the second *Enquiry*, he gives us the example of houses (which example he explicitly compares to the rules of property). There are various types of houses in the world, while their fundamental architecture is the same. This is because they are influenced by 'the finer turns and connexions of the imagination' (EPM 3.46; 203) at the particular or superficial level.[11] We can further illustrate this point by another example Hume gives of social institutions: the system of marriage, which is repeatedly referred to, both directly and indirectly, in his work. In Book 3 of the *Treatise*, he argues that the 'chastity' of women is one of the most important pillars sustaining our social institutions including private property (T 3.2.12; 570–3). As Hume demonstrates in the essay 'Of Polygamy and Divorces', marriage 'must be susceptible of all the variety of conditions, which consent establishes, provided they be not contrary to' the propagation of our species (E 181). In this essay he freely discusses the issue of polygamy and monogamy, and the right and wrong of divorces, but this does not by any means lead him to endorse complete sexual promiscuity; rather the opposite (Baier 1989: 47–8; see also Berry 2003; Baier 2010: chap. 9).

Hume's emphasis on the artificiality of justice and his proud application of the associationist theory in moral issues never failed to provoke strong criticisms of his alleged moral relativism among his contemporaries. Hume claims that many social rules and institutions are established through our consideration of public utility and that their particular rules are decided by the workings of imagination; these claims (especially the former) continue obscuring his distance from 'the selfish system of morals' (EPM App. 2.3; 296), although he actively acknowledges the existence of limited benevolence and natural virtues and his moral theory in broad terms could be placed in the camp of Shaftesburianism (Rivers 2000: 293).

Apart from his emphasis on public utility, another reason why his version of the associationist theory caused his contemporaries much uneasiness ultimately lies in Hume's thorough application of the theory of association of ideas to the issue of causality.[12] He does not explain our associations of ideas from causality, but conversely attributes the latter to the former: with the effect, according to his contemporary critics, of dissolving causality altogether. If this theory is used just to explain wrong customs or poetical imagination, it would cause no problem at all. James Beattie, the fiercest adversary of Hume, for example, expatiates on the subject without hesitation in his *Dissertations Moral and Critical.* He classifies the principles connecting various ideas into four categories: resemblance, contrariety, contiguity (vicinity) and *cause and effect* (1783: I, 99–108). However, this principle of association plays a central role in Hume's account of natural relations, which he explains as 'an association betwixt' two ideas (T 1.3.14.31; 170). Hume further argues that 'we are able to reason upon [causation], or draw any inference from it' 'only so far as it is a *natural* relation, and produces a union among our ideas' (1.3.6.16; 94). The same Beattie who believes the causal maxim as an axiom of common sense, on the other hand, critically rephrases Hume's (allegedly dangerous) tenet that 'what we call the power, or necessary connection' 'is merely a determination of my fancy, or your fancy, or any body's fancy, to associate the idea or impression of my volition with the impression or idea of the motion of my arm' in his *Essay on the Nature and Immutability of Truth* ([1771] 1778: 266; see also Manning 2002: 47–52). According to Beattie, if the bedrock of causality was nothing but the trivial workings of mere imagination (fancy), not only the issue of moral responsibility based upon our voluntary motives, but also the distinction between the eternal truth of morality and mere prejudices should disappear.

Despite these allegations, Hume's emphasis upon the role of imagination in the rules of property does not endorse his completely relativistic standpoint on this matter. Although he emphasises the diversities of particular laws and rules concerning property in human societies, he never forgets to reiterate the impossibility of 'ideas of *perfect* equality'. In other words, he believes a perfectly communist and egalitarian society to be unfeasible, because 'they are really, at bottom, *impracticable*; and were they not so, would be extremely *pernicious* to human society' (EPM 3.26; 194; though Hume admits that '[a] too great disproportion among the citizens weakens any state' (E 'Commerce' 265)). Hume's firm conviction on this point is explicable from his observation that we have a natural psychological propensity to form a connection between an object and a person related to it. Hume's consistent distinction between the two meanings of imagination through the discussions of artificial virtues, therefore, can be considered to reveal the way in which he was able to remain convinced of the fundamental uniformity of our mental processes (underpinned by the association of ideas) among the seemingly infinite diversities of our manners (varied by fancy). This variety in any large society operates only within the institution of private property, which is considered to be fundamental except for in cases of 'pressing emergence' (EPM 3.8; 186; see also Chapters 6 and 7 in this book).

On this point, Hume's account of property based on his understanding of imagination can be considered to fit in with the reality of our lives better than the Lockean labour theory of property (on this point, see also Moore 1976a: 114–15; 1976b: 36–9). In Book 3 of the *Treatise*, Hume attempts to find fault with Locke's labour theory of property. In the *Two Treatises of Government* Locke emphasised the role of labour as the sole ground for justifying our natural right of private property: 'In most of [products] ninety-nine hundredths are wholly to be put on the account of labour' ([1690] 1988: 296). In the *Treatise* Hume argues that '[s]ome philosophers account for the right of occupation, by saying that every one has a property in his own labour; and when he joins that labour to anything, it gives him the property of the whole' (T footnote 72 to 3.2.3.6; 505n.). Then he counts up three exceptional cases to criticise Locke's claim. According to Hume, the addition of labour to some goods is nothing but one of the causes to raise a new 'relation' between the owner and its object in our minds.[13] He also applies the theory of the association of ideas to criticise Locke's justification of the right of resistance. In his discussion of 'the late *revolution*', Hume touches on the issue of the right of revolution, and explains how we come to think it 'lawful and suitable [...] to dethrone' a tyrannical king and 'the remaining members of the constitution acquire a right of excluding his next heir'. He said that these judgements do not depend upon any abstract right of resistance, but are founded upon 'a very singular quality of our thought and imagination' (3.2.10.17–18; 564–5).[14] Surprisingly, Hume's basic explanation of this point remained unchanged through his life. In the *History of England*, as we will see in the next chapter (esp. p. 69 and pp. 81–4), he used the expression 'opinion' and repeated the same judgement.

3 Does Hume's Interest in the Theory of Imagination Wane?

If there are such theoretical potentialities in the theory of imagination, why does Hume mention it less frequently in his later writings? I claim that it is not a matter of content, but rather of style. To use Hume's own phrase, this change comes 'more from the manner than the matter' (E 'My Own Life' xxxv). However, this does not necessarily mean that he lost his confidence in his general application of the theory of imagination to moral and social issues. In fact, in a letter to Henry Home (Lord Kames), Hume notes that his correspondent's *Essays upon Several Subjects concerning British Antiquities* (1747) borrowed from his own conceptualisation of comparative jurisprudence: 'You do me the honour to borrow some principles from a certain book: but I wish they be not esteemed too subtile and abstruse' (L I, 108; Forbes 1975b: 12n.1). Ian Simpson Ross, the biographer of Lord Kames, confirms that Hume here 'alluded [...] to the importance he attached to imagination and custom, as well as the account he gave in the third book, 'Of Morals', concerning property and government' (Ross 1972: 54; see also 206 and 265). Hume was aware that Kames had devoted much attention to the psychological aspects of the comparative jurisprudence and 'the true old Humean philosophy' (Ross 1995: 412–13; see also Raphael 1977; Skinner 1979).

In the letter to Kames, Hume's wording 'subtile and abstruse' is noticeable. In the first *Enquiry*, which he was to publish a year later, he contrasts 'the easy and obvious philosophy' with 'the accurate and abstruse' one. He comments that 'ADDISON, perhaps, will be read with pleasure, when Locke shall be entirely forgotten' (EHU 1.3–4; 7), although he neither exclusively exalts the easy philosophy nor denounces the abstruse one. In this book he simply displays a partial interest in the theory of association to explain the basic principles of poetry (*à la* Addison's 'pleasures of imagination') and historical narratives, though this section was to be largely shortened in the 1777 edition.[15] The fact that he published the first *Enquiry* as a separate book is another factor that has perhaps contributed to the lack of recognition of the presence of the associationist theory in his work as a whole.

In the second *Enquiry*, however, Hume does not renounce the theory of imagination. He repeats the same point about 'the right of succession or inheritance' or the 'acquisition of property by accession' from 'the relations and connexions of the imagination' (EPM footnote 65 to App. 3.10; 309–10n.). Clearly, Hume believes that these detailed explanations are too abstruse for the general reader. Thus, he avoids giving an extensive account of 'the variations, which all the rules of property receive from the finer turns and connexions of the imagination, and from the subtilties and abstractions of law-topics and reasonings' (3.46; 203). Although he does not directly mention his earlier characterisation of imagination as subtle, he just intends not to repeat the lengthy commentary on the legal disputes already given in his juvenile work. Hume also emphasises that, while the separation and constancy of possession is required by 'obvious, strong, and invincible' necessity, he considers that the rules assigning particular objects to particular persons are based upon 'very fine connexions and turns of imagination' (footnote 65 to App. 3.10; 310n.).

The theory of the fundamental and universal working of imagination is also maintained in Hume's later accounts of property. It can be found more clearly in his 'Dissertation on the Passions' (1757) than in the second *Enquiry*. He mentions several principles that 'are not commonly much insisted on by philosophers':

> The first of these is the *association* of ideas, or that principle, by which we make an easy transition from one idea to another. However uncertain and changeable our thoughts may be, they are not entirely without rule and method in their changes. They usually pass with regularity, from one object, to what resembles it, is contiguous to it, or produced by it. (DP 2.6)

Hume goes on to explain the working of the passions. As in the original version of the *Treatise*, property is considered important as a cause of pride: '*property*, as it gives the fullest power and authority over any object, is the relation, which has the greatest influence on these passions' (2.30). In a footnote to this sentence, he gives us an account of property, arising from the theory of the association of ideas, in a concise and succinct way.

> That property is a species of *relation*, which produces a connexion between the person and the object is evident: The imagination passes naturally and easily from the consideration of a field to that of the person to whom it belongs. [...] Property therefore is a species of *causation*. [...] It is indeed the relation the most interesting of any, and occurs the most frequently to the mind. (footnote 3 to 2.30)

Hume utilises many sentences from Book 2 of the *Treatise* in the 'Dissertation on the Passions'. By computer collation, Beauchamp, the editor of the Clarendon edition of the 'Dissertation', has demonstrated that there is a considerable carry-over of passages from the *Treatise* to the 'Dissertation'. The content of the footnote just quoted is basically a repetition of the *Treatise* (2.1.10.1; 309–10). However, there are several indications that this footnote is not a passing addition for Hume. The above footnote is one of the newly written sentences (which approximately comprise only 27.5 per cent of the 'Dissertation') (DP intro, li). Furthermore, Hume took the trouble to add this footnote after the 1760 edition. It seems to suggest that, in his later writings, the associationist theory is still essential and fundamental to his explanation of the psychological origin of property.

There are additional circumstances to consider. In the middle of the eighteenth century, the general application of the associationist theory to the science of human nature was not Hume's intellectual monopoly. To cite several examples, in France, Condillac's *Essai sur l'origine des connaissances humaines* and *Traité de sensations* were published respectively in 1746 and 1754. Helvétius's *De l'esprit*, which develops Locke's epistemology in a more materialistic (and atheistic) direction than Condillac's version, was published in 1758. In England, David Hartley published the *Observations on Man, his Frame, his Duty, and his Expectations* in 1749. In Scotland, George Turnbull published *The Principles of Moral Philosophy* in 1740 – coincidentally, the same year Hume published Book 3 of the *Treatise* – with the same publisher (John Noon) with whom Hume published the first two volumes of the *Treatise*. We might also add La Mettrie's *L'Histoire naturelle de l'âme* (1745) and *L'Homme machine* (1748) for their mechanistic and physiological explanation of the passions, although he did not clearly develop the theory of the association of ideas in his writings (Thomson 2008: chaps. 6 and 7).[16]

As we saw above, the use of this theory had moral and political, as well as philosophical, implications for Hume's contemporaries. As James Moore (1994; 2007) points out, Hume's emphasis upon utility and artificiality of justice led his contemporaries to designate him as Epicurean. Hume's recourse to the working of imagination in his account of property also led many critics to believe that he belonged to the Epicurean school, together with Hartley and Priestley, a strong exponent of Hartley's associationism (Priestley 1775). For example, Lord Monboddo in his *Antient Metaphysics* inquires critically: 'Whether the Metaphysics that have prevailed in Britain, from Mr. Locke down to Mr. David Hume and Dr. Priestley, are a-kin to this Philosophy of Epicurus' (Monboddo 1773–92: II, Preface v; see also II, 3). According to Monboddo, who wanted to reintroduce innate ideas into the constitution of human nature *à la* Shaftesbury (Rivers 2000: 155), Hume's philosophy shows that all our intellectual knowledge or ideas can be reduced into mere external stimuli:

> Thus, I think, I have shown, that Man has knowledge much superior to that of the Brute, not only in degree but in kind. What has led men to think otherwise, is, first, the confusion of Sensations and Ideas, which Mr Locke first introduced, and Mr David Hume has much improved upon. (Monboddo 1773–92: II, 98)

For this reason, Hume and other 'associationists' have been accused of being Hobbesian or Epicurean.

Actually, Hartley's version strongly inclines towards physiology: his system depends upon the parallelism between physiological vibrations and the association of ideas in the mental world (Oberg 1976). A similar theory to Hartley's, perhaps an intellectual predecessor, is Condillac's *Essai sur l'origine des connaissances humaines*, where he argues for the 'connexion of ideas' (liaison des idées) (Condillac [1746]1756: 45–50 [Pt. 1, Sec. 2, Ch. 3]).[17] In this piece, Condillac's physiological bent is as clear as his declared intellectual debts to Locke.[18] In a footnote, he supposes that 'the physical cause of the perception of the mind is the concussion of the fibres of the brain'. Another person who held similar views to Hartley was Turnbull, though his work preceded the former's. In *The Principles of Moral Philosophy*, independently of Hume,

Turnbull describes the association of ideas as 'the law of habits'. At the same time, he emphasises '[t]he dependence of genius, temper, and mental abilities upon the temperature of the body, air, diet, and other such physical causes' and he refers his readers, for the details of this mechanism, to 'the Chapter on the association of ideas' in his book (1740: 75; Forbes 1975b: 3–5; Mossner 1989: 113; Berry 1997: 84).[19] These physiological inclinations are one of the reasons why Lord Monboddo warned his readers of the dangers caused by 'all the Materialists, from [Epicurus] down to Mr David Hume', because 'Epicurus has endeavoured to prove the mortality of the Mind, by showing [...] that it is inseparable from the Body, and must subsist or perish with it' (Monboddo 1773–92: II, 227). As is clear from these examples, the principles of association which some of Hume's contemporaries began to adopt on moral and social issues, was generally condemned as materialism.

Despite Monboddo's criticism of Hume as a materialist, however, there is a big difference between the theories of association put forward by Hume and other associationists. Although there is no textual evidence that Hume intended to directly criticise the physiological version of the associationist theory in his writings after the *Treatise*, it would not be inappropriate to assume that Hume was aware of the differences between his own associationism and Hartley's physiological version (Berry 1997: 79–80).[20] For example, Hartley clearly adopted Newton's 'doctrine of vibrations' and claimed his own science of the human mind to be part of natural philosophy (1749: I, v; I, 354). On the other hand, Hume's reservations about physiological explanations were already evident in the *Treatise*. He admitted that many impressions 'depend upon natural and physical causes', but he determined to 'confine [himself] to those other impressions, which I have called secondary and reflective', because he did not want to be involved 'into the sciences of anatomy and natural philosophy' (T 2.1.1.2; 276). It is not only because these fields are not his specialty, but because these arguments are not necessarily indispensable to his 'science of MAN'; he goes on to say that '[n]othing is more requisite for a true philosopher, than to restrain the intemperate desire of searching into [the further original, but obscure] causes' (1.1.5.6; 13). Although Hume was arguably an Epicurean in the sense that he undermines the rationalistic doctrine of the immutability of moral truth by emphasising the role of utility and agreeableness and the influence of imagination on morality, he is not a materialist. Rather, he is consistently sceptical concerning the ultimate causes of our mental world. In the introduction of the *Treatise* he flatly claims that 'any hypothesis, that pretends to discover the ultimate original qualities of human nature, ought at first to be rejected as presumptuous and chimerical' (intro 8; xvii). Later in the same work he reiterates that '[t]o explain the ultimate causes of our mental actions is impossible' (1.1.7.11; 22), or 'my intention never was to penetrate into the nature of bodies, or the secret causes of their operations. [...] I am afraid, that such an enterprize is beyond the reach of human understanding' (1.2.5.25; 64; see also Long 2013: 213). In the first *Enquiry* the same point is repeated: 'no philosopher, who is rational and modest' has ever pretended to discover 'the ultimate cause of any natural operation' (EHU 4.12; 30; see also DNR 4.14; 163–4). He must have felt that those who pretend to be able to attribute our mental activities solely to the materialistic understanding of human nature could not have shared such scepticism.[21] Despite his associating Hartley with Hume in the *Elements of the Philosophy of the Human Mind* ([1792–1827] 1854–60, 1994: I, 382–3), Dugald Stewart elsewhere correctly appreciates this difference by arguing that Hume's works 'are perfectly free from those gratuitous and wild conjectures, which a few years afterwards were given to the world with so much confidence by Hartley and Bonnet' ([1821] 2000: II, 164–5; see also Stephen 1900: I, 155–7; Fontana 1985: 88–90). More generally, as Peter Jones correctly points out, materialism is 'a view inimical to Hume's Ciceronian humanism, with its irreducible reference to man' (1982: 17).

Almost ten years after the publication of the *Treatise*, Hume was to return once again to the issue of 'physical causes' in the essay 'Of National Characters' (1748).[22] His criticism of physical causes in this can be considered closely related to Hume's own understanding of the associationist theory. Importantly, his defence of moral causes and criticism of physical causes does not necessarily indicate a contrast between the social institutions and natural environment (Berry 1997: 84). He argues that '[b]y moral causes, I mean all circumstances, which are fitted to work on the mind as motives or reasons, and which render a peculiar set of manners habitual to us'. According to him, these causes are 'the nature of the government, the revolutions of public affairs, the plenty or penury in which the people live, the situation of the nation with regard to its neighbours, and such like circumstances' (E 198). Hume's explanation is a little misleading. In spite of his wording 'circumstances', his real point does not lie in the distinction between the natural environment and the social milieu. For example, he asserts that 'the neighbourhood of the sun inflames the imagination of men, and gives it a peculiar spirit and vivacity' (208). Hume here does not straightforwardly deny any influence of the natural environment; he merely gives priority to the intervention of the working of imagination over physiological or neurological mechanisms. In the last part of this essay, he attempts to explain from moral causes some phenomena which seem to be determined by physical causes: 'people in the northern regions have a greater inclination to strong liquors, and those in the southern to love and women' (213). Hume here does not make a direct recourse to institutional or political differences, but he draws our attention to the mental and psychological operations that influence human behaviours. If so, the distinction between physical and moral causes does not lie simply in the difference between the natural and social environment, but in whether such differences in national characters can be explained from exclusively physiological processes, or from psychological ones. For Hume, this seems significant in order to distinguish his own position not only from one of Montesquieu's 'rash and crude Positions' (L II, 133; see also Sebastiani 2013: chap. 1),[23] but also from another version of the associationist theory which Condillac and Hartley expounded.[24] Although Hume's previously clear references to the theory of imagination become less conspicuous in his later writings on its appearance, Hume has not lost his earlier pride in its universal applicability and its theoretical validity for the 'science of MAN'.

Although most of his contemporaries (except for Dugald Stewart) usually paid less attention to the differences between Hume and the other associationists on this question, some radicals did not completely lose sight of the importance of the Humean version of associationism in moral and political issues. William Godwin, for example, who criticises the overstated influence of physical causes in moral theory, states that:

> Every thing that [...] permanently distinguishes the character of one man from that of another, is to be traced to the association of ideas. But association is of the nature of reasoning. The principal, the most

> numerous and lasting of our associations, are intellectual [...] built upon the resemblances and differences of things [...]

As Hume insisted in the essay 'Of National Characters', Godwin here claims that people sometimes show very different characters even 'under the same or nearly the same external circumstances' (Godwin [1795] 1993: 34).[25] Godwin refers directly to the essay in the next section of the same chapter, which bears exactly the same title as Hume's (41; see also [*Variants*] 1993: 56). To reiterate how limited are the influences of physical causes and how considerable are those of moral causes on our manners is of much importance for Godwin the reformer. This is because, if the differences between the wise man and the fool, or the civilised man and the savage are explicable from moral, that is, artificial causes, then a person can control and ameliorate his situation by comparing 'the successive perceptions of his mind, and upon these depend the conclusions he draws and the conduct he observes'. In that case, he concludes, 'physical causes [...] sink into nothing, when compared with the great and inexpressible operations of reflection' (35).[26] Hume himself does not usually present his version of the associationist theory as a direct way to improve our manners through reflection. Nonetheless, the distinction between the psychological and physiological versions of the associationist theory is of much importance for Godwin, who deems Hume to be the most important precursor of the former:

> It may perhaps be useful to consider how far these reasonings upon the subject of liberty, are confirmed to us by general experience as to the comparative inefficacy of climate, and the superior influence of circumstances, political and social. The following instances are for the most part abridged from the judicious collections of Hume upon the subject. (Godwin [*Variants*] 1993: 56 (Editions 2–3))

Although the materialistic implication of the associationist theory was so strong in the eighteenth century that many critics have continued to identify Hume with other associationists, the late eighteenth- and nineteenth-century radicals (like James Mill) were clearly aware of the potential significance of the associationist theory for their reformist and educational purposes, and the contributions made by Hume to this issue (Buckle 2011: chap. 1). On this score, Hume's bold application of the associationist theory can be regarded as one of the significant turning points in the history of this theory. While Hume's emphasis upon imagination and custom could now be interpreted as conservative, it is still possible to show that even these aspects did have theoretically radical implications among his contemporaries and the generations that followed.

In conclusion to this chapter, more attention should be paid to Hume's consistent interest in the imaginative workings of human nature, especially in relation to his scepticism. Despite his confidence in the universal applicability of the associationist theory, he continued to be sceptical about the possibility of demarcating the workings of the two (trivial and essential) levels of imagination. This gives his overall arguments a *tone* of moral and cultural relativism. While abiding by his empirical observations, which had a strong implication of Epicureanism for his contemporaries, he is also dubious concerning the possibility of discovering the ultimate causes of our mental actions. Although the overt presence of his theory of imagination and association of ideas might be lessened in his later writings, his deep concern with the variety and changeability of human customs and manners retains its strong hold on him in another form – opinion, which, in Book 1 of the *Treatise*, is often used interchangeably with a 'belief' or 'A LIVELY IDEA RELATED TO OR ASSOCIATED WITH A PRESENT IMPRESSION' as a natural product of imagination (T 1.3.7.5; 96; see also 1.3.8.15; 105). As we will see in the next chapter, the notion of opinion is brought to the fore in his political and historical writings, which should be no surprise considering the significance and centrality of belief to his philosophy.

Notes

1. For the general significance of Hume's theory of imagination for his science of man, see Wright 1983: esp. chap. 5.
2. These deleted parts mainly concern his views on the workings of imagination in historical writings. After the second edition of the *Essays, Moral and Political*, Hume also withdrew the essay 'Of the Study of History', which contained his important observations on historical writing and its relationship with imagination and sentiment. On the role of imagination in Hume's historical writings, see Costelloe 2013 (although he does not consider the reasons for Hume's deletions).

3. In Epicurus, this appears as the issue of 'presentation' or *phantasia* (Epicurus 1994: 9–11[49–50], 34 [5.XXII–XXIV], 73–4 [1121d–e], 84 [68.203–11]; see also Steintrager 2012: 168–9, 171).
4. On Hobbes as Epicurean, see Mayo 1934: chap. 7; Wilson 2008: chap. 7.
5. Descartes can be considered to allude to the issue through his distinction between imaginations caused by the soul (volition) and by the body, and his explanation of the ways in which the mental processes including imagination are caused 'according as nature or habituation has diversely joined each movement of the gland to each thought' in *Les passions de l'âme* (*The Passions of the Soul*) ([1649] 1989: 29–30 [Pt. 1, Art. 20–1]; 43–4 [1.44]).
6. On the way in which Shaftesbury and Hutcheson address the issue of moral diversity, see Carey 2004; Kail 2013.
7. As for the Chevalier Ramsay, see Cherel 1926; Henderson 1952; Jacob 2006: 99, 224–5. Ramsay was a mystic and a Catholic apologetic, but his universalism and syncretism was not irrelevant to the eighteenth-century deistic movement in France (Betts 1984: 235–7). John Laird suggests that Hume's division of reason into three kinds – derived from knowledge, proofs and probabilities – is indebted to a footnote of Ramsay's *Travels of Cyrus* (*Les Voyages de Cyrus*) (1727) through Andrew Baxter's *Enquiry into the Nature of the Human Soul* (1733) (Laird 1932: 90n.1; see also Wright 2003: 129–31). As Tolonen emphasises (2008: 23–8), Ramsay is also important for the origin of Hume's interest in the idea of politeness (L I, 19–21).
8. Thanks to Amy Schmitter for making this point in her helpful comments on the earlier version of this chapter.
9. In some exceptional cases, Hume means the term 'the associations of ideas' in the traditional sense, that is, just as prejudices or preconceptions (T 2.3.8.2; 433; EPM 4.7; 207). These seem to be just more examples of his occasional vague usages of the terms 'imagination' and 'fancy'.
10. This difficulty is also augmented by what Douglas Long terms 'cognitive momentum' of imagination (2013: 204): 'the imagination, when set into any train of thinking [...] carries on its course without any new impulse' (T 1.4.2.22; 198). On the 'inertia of the imagination' and a similar idea in Malebranche, see also Forbes 1975b: 10n.2.
11. I thank Christopher J. Berry for reminding me of this point.
12. For the significance of Hume's theory of causation as his methodology of the social sciences, see Sakamoto (forthcoming).

13. Note that Hume does not necessarily deny that the labour invested into producing some economic goods can be considered one of the changes that produce the right of occupation; but he only admits the fact 'in a figurative sense' because the labour itself does not have any intrinsic value. Incidentally, Francis Hutcheson also criticised Locke's labour theory of property as 'some confused imagination that property is some physical quality or relation produced by some action of men' ([1755] 1990: I, 318; see also I, 346).
14. Hume's theory of imagination also refers to the issue of colonisation: how (it is supposed) a country might legitimately acquire colonies (T 3.2.3.8; 507; see also T footnote 73.4–5 to 3.2.3.7; 507–8n.). On this point, see Armitage 2000: 180. These issues had previously been raised by the legal theorists Grotius and Pufendorf (Norton and Norton 2007: 913).
15. Hutcheson, for example, used 'imagination' and 'innate sense' interchangeably ([1728] 1990: 114, 127). See also Whiter 1794 and Archer 1983.
16. For more on the physiological account of imagination in modern philosophy (especially in Gassendi, Hobbes, Locke and La Mettrie), see Steintrager 2012: 168–82.
17. Yet, there is also a difference between Hartley and Priestley who both believe in the existence of a 'cause of causes' and French materialists who flatly deny it (Garrett 2006: 166–9).
18. Unlike Helvétius, however, Condillac criticises materialism and espouses the doctrine of the immortality of the soul ([1746] 1756: 43; Berry 1997: 79).
19. Hume's *Treatise* and *Abstract* were mistakenly attributed to Turnbull by the *Bibliothèque britannique* (Mossner 1980: 125). On Turnbull, see Norton 1975; Broadie 2009: 108–23.
20. Hume possessed copies of Hartley's *Observations* and Condillac's *Essai* (Norton and Norton 1996: entries 600 and 296, respectively).
21. John P. Wright also emphasises 'the context of an established psychophysiological theory' in Hume's theory of imagination, but he rather considers that Hume 'modifies' it in terms of experience (1983: 191). On the historical contexts of the physiology and materialism in eighteenth-century England, Scotland and France, see Yolton 1984; Wright 2000; Yolton 1991, respectively.
22. Hume probably borrowed the abbé Dubos's definition of the physical and moral causes in his *Réflexions critiques sur la poésie et sur la peinture* (*Critical Reflections on Poetry, Painting, and Music*) (1748 [1719]: II, 96), to which Hume refers in his so-called 'Early

Memoranda'. As for the influence of Dubos's *Réflexions* on Hume, see Berry 1997: 79–80; Jones 1978; 1982: 93–106; Perinetti 2006: 1117–20. As for connections among Dubos, Montesquieu and Fontenelle through the salon of Mme de Lambert, see Broadie 2012: 174n.18. For the debate on national characters in the French and the Scottish Enlightenment, see Vyverberg 1989 and Sebastiani 2011; 2013, respectively.

23. Montesquieu's physiological inclination is also clear from his excitement over the experiment with the tongue of a sheep ([1748] 1989: 233 [3.14.2]). As for Hartley's philosophy in the context of the free will debate, see Harris 2005a: chap. 7.
24. See also Hume's comment on Helvétius's *De l'esprit* in a letter to Adam Smith (NL 52).
25. As for general discussions on the possible influence of Hume on Godwin in both metaphysics and social philosophy, see Long 2008; Philp 1986: 147–9, 153–4; 2014: 219–20. Godwin disagrees with Hume on the issue of luxury ([*Variants*] 1993: 328). He also criticises one of Hume's theses that the exposing of children 'might rather render those [ancient] times more populous' (E 399) (Godwin [1801] 1993: 200).
26. The associationists, such as Destutt de Tracy, who emphasise the physiological structures and operations of the body in our formation of complex ideas and judgements have to confront a dilemma (whether consciously or not): because their physiological determinism allows no role for independent volition, to what extent can these structures be ameliorated by the reforms of social environment and public education? On this point, see Head 1985: 38.

3

'What is Established'?: Hume's Social Philosophy of Opinion

In the history of social and political philosophy, Hume has been characterised variously: as one of the forefathers of conservatism preceding Edmund Burke (Miller 1981; Livingston 1998); as a champion of (economic) liberalism together with Adam Smith (Hayek 1967); or as one of the precursors of the utilitarianism espoused by Jeremy Bentham (Rosen 2003: 48–57). The very variety of interpretations built up around Hume's social and political philosophy demonstrates how difficult it is to adequately explain his thought by reference to any one of these characterisations. This chapter will not aim to place Hume within any of these 'isms', but to make clear how and why such a variety of interpretation occurs by exploring the significant role that the concept of 'opinion' plays throughout Hume's political and historical writings. Hume refers to the notion of opinion on numerous occasions in his political essays; I will argue that he also uses it as a benchmark in the *History of England*. The concept of opinion is used both to exonerate the first two Stuart monarchs from blame, and to defend the Revolution settlement. For Hume, the notion of opinion was appropriate for both of these purposes, not in spite of, but because of its changeability.[1] As Richard B. Sher correctly argues, 'Hume's moral and political thought may now seem moderate and impartial, as it did to Hume himself, but from the Scottish Presbyterian viewpoint of his own day it looked very much like a series of potshots at cherished principles' (1985: 66). To analyse the way Hume develops the thesis that every government is founded on opinion in order to both criticise and fundamentally modify the Whig ideology will help us to understand why some of his contemporaries regarded his claim as dangerous. Touching on Hume's thesis of opinion, Forbes timely asserts that 'the ruthless application of experimental method to moral subjects was dangerously avant-garde – Hume's friends seem always to have realized this better than Hume himself – yet it was at the same time a post-revolutionary, establishment political philosophy' (1975b: 91). The thorough analysis of the Humean notion of opinion will serve to provide a unified interpretation of Hume's criticism of both the ancient constitutional myth and the doctrine of resistance in the *History*. The following discussion will demonstrate the way in which Hume's analysis and deployment of opinion, similar to his understanding of the workings of imagination, expresses the 'spirit of scepticism' in his political and historical writings.

Hume's emphasis upon 'opinion' can be found throughout his moral, social and political writings. One of his most well-known theses is that '[i]t is therefore, on opinion only that government is founded' (E 32), which appears in the 1741 essay 'Of the First Principles of Government'. This maxim has resonances in many contemporaries and later generations. In France, Saint-Lambert – who also wrote the article 'Luxury' (Luxe) for the *Encyclopédie* of Diderot and d'Alembert – mentions Hume in the section 'De l'opinion' of his *Analyse de l'homme et de la femme*: 'There is, says M. Hume, no government where opinion is not the main force: the monarchy and the republic support themselves only by it' (1797–1801: I, 128–9).* In the nascent United States, James Madison used in the *Federalist* No. 49 almost the same expression that 'all governments rest on opinion', which Sheehan considers to be influenced by Hume (Sheehan 2005: 39). In his *Letters from a Farmer in Pennsylvania*, for another example, John Dickinson, one of the Founding Fathers, wrote that '[s]ome of the best writers have asserted, and it seems with good reason, that "government is founded on opinion"', citing Hume's essay (1768: 120). In Britain William Godwin echoed '[a]ll government is founded in opinion' in his *Enquiry concerning Political Justice* ([1793] 1993: 63).[2] This radical did not mention its source, but his intellectual debt to Hume is clear (see note 25 in Chapter 2). The variety of political standpoints of those quoting Hume's maxim evinces both its impact and its ambiguity. As a preliminary step for understanding the thrust of Hume's own notion of opinion, it would be helpful to investigate the possible original sources of the theory of opinion that Hume deploys.

* 'Il n'y a, dit M. Hume, aucun gouvernement dont l'opinion ne soit la force principale: la monarchie, la république ne se soutiennent que par elle'.

1 Hume, Temple and Others on Opinion

C. B. Macpherson and others have already pointed out that a very similar phrase to Hume's appears in William Temple's 'An Essay upon the Original and Nature of Government' (written in 1672 and published in 1679),[3] but a closer and more detailed investigation and comparison has yet to be done (Macpherson 1943: 49–50; Laursen 1992: 185; Castiglione 1994: 108, 113n42). Although Hume's evaluation of Temple as a writer in the *Essays, Moral and Political* was rather negative (E 'Civil Liberty' 91), he is among those who receive a more favourable evaluation in the *History*: 'Of all the considerable writers of this age, Sir William Temple is almost the only one, that kept himself altogether unpolluted by that inundation of vice and licentiousness, which overwhelmed the nation' (H VI, 544). Hume also comments that '[t]his man, whom philosophy had taught to despise the world, without rendering him unfit for it, was frank, open, sincere, superior to the little tricks of vulgar politicians' (VI: 219–20).

Seemingly, there is no special relationship between the Restoration-period English diplomat-essayist and the mid-eighteenth century Scottish philosopher-historian. Temple's thought has been summarised as 'a scepticism toward science, a rejection of the idea of progress, an attraction to the Epicurean ethic, and a championship of the ancients' (Steensma 1970: 23). Aside from their mutual attraction to Epicureanism, Temple's philosophy seems largely incompatible with Hume's. However, his influence on Hume and the similarities between them appear much greater than have generally been presumed. C. B. Macpherson, for example, calls Temple 'the Hume of the seventeenth century'; arguing that he unconsciously incorporated the inductive method of the new science in his investigations (1943: 44). Despite Macpherson's claim, the significance of Temple's political thought has been much undervalued and the extent of his direct influence on Hume remains unclear. Hence it seems appropriate to briefly examine here some considerable affinities between Temple and Hume.[4]

Firstly, Hume's advocacy of the superiority of the modern world is not as straightforward as it seems. As we shall see in Chapter 7, Hume vindicates the cyclical view of history in some significant points in both his essays and in the *History*. Nor was Temple a straightforward champion of the ancients, although he was ranked on that side in the *querelle des anciens et des modernes*. The image of Temple as a champion of the ancients in the quarrel should also be qualified in various important ways, bringing Temple closer to Hume. As Clara Marburg rightly suggests, 'Temple's quarrel with the moderns [...] was, in a sense, an expression of horror at the arrogance of the ignorant who were drunk with the idea of the limitless possibilities of man's power to understand' (1932: 6). On this point, Hume's denial of Hobbes's reductionist materialism is in some ways akin to Temple's contempt for the natural sciences. More generally, Hume's interventions in the quarrel should be considered more ambivalent and nuanced than previously thought (Jones 1982: 94).[5]

Secondly, both authors seem to share a somewhat elusive political and religious standpoint. In spite of his opposition to the Commonwealth and his service to Charles II, Temple was a life-long friend of Johan de Witt (1625–72) – Grand Pensionary (*raad-pensionaris*) of the States of Holland – and William of Orange (later William III of England), and continued to seek the alliance with the Netherlands against the French 'universal monarchy' scheme. Although his sister claimed his firm belief in Anglicanism, Temple was often criticised as a sceptic or atheist because of his religious tolerance (Davies 2004),[6] and as an Epicurean for his defence of Epicureanism in his essay 'Upon the Gardens of Epicurus' (Temple 1754: II, 190–1).[7] Homer Woodbridge, a biographer of Temple, emphasises his 'sceptical indifference to party' (1940: xi) – one of Hume's creeds in his political writings. The similarity between the political situation of Temple and that of Hume is also noteworthy. When Temple published 'An Essay upon the Original and Nature of Government', he must have keenly felt the instability of the English government after a series of political tumults that saw the Civil War, the Commonwealth era and the Restoration in just thirty years. Hume, as we will see later, also knew only too well the latent volatility of the British political situation after the two Jacobite Rebellions (1715 and 1745) and felt the continued necessity to consolidate the political legitimacy of the settlement that had followed the Glorious Revolution of 1688.

Temple's cautious attitude toward hasty political reforms also prefigured Hume's in many ways. In the essay 'A Survey of the Constitutions and Interests of the Empire, Sweden, Denmark, Spain, Holland, France, and Flanders' (1671), Temple compares government to an old tree: 'So as the breaking down an old frame of government, and erecting a new, seems like cutting down an old oak', the shade of which 'the son or grandson (if it prospers) may enjoy' (1754: II, 14). For another example, in the essay 'Of Popular Discontents' he analyses how our 'restless humour' causes factions, political commotions and revolutions (II: 370). Temple also gives princes and great ministers four pieces of advice to secure their safety: along with introducing the industrious and parsimonious habits within the country and preventing dangers from abroad, the other two are to avoid 'all councils or designs of innovation, in ancient and established forms and laws, especially those concerning liberty, property, and religion' and 'to choose and favour that which is most popular, or wherein the greatest or strongest part of the people appear to be engaged' (II: 371–2). Similar arguments, as we will see below, can be easily found in Hume's writings.

The arguments in the 'Essay upon the Original and Nature of Government' exhibit more significant parallels with Hume's view of human nature and the origins of government. Temple criticises both the Hobbesian view of humans as selfish and belligerent and the Stoic view of man as sociable and sheep-like in the state of nature. According to him, the former would have made it impossible for these bestial beings to unite through any form of social compact, while the latter would have felt no necessity to do so; thus, both characterisations fail to account for the historical formation of societies (1754: II, 38–9). Temple's empirical view of natural men seems much closer to Hume's in his account of justice as an artificial virtue in the *Treatise*, where he admits 'a limited generosity' along with self-interest in our human nature, while criticising both the simply egoistic and the extremely altruistic views of human nature (T 3.2.2.13–16; 492–4).

Upon the basis of his own understanding of human nature, Temple develops what can be called 'the patriarchal theory of society' that demonstrates how 'the father, by a natural right, as well as authority, becomes a governor in this little State'. His account is much more empirical and secular than that presented in Filmer's *Patriarcha*, published the year after the publication of Temple's essay (Filmer [1680] 1949; Woodbridge 1940: 142–4). István Hont correctly points out that Temple's 'theory of the paternal origins of political authority was built upon these skeptical [humanist] foundations and should not be confused with the quite different idiom of Sir Robert Filmer (Hont 2005: 195n.12).

On the other hand, Hume considers that wartime chieftains must have been the origin of the civil authority in tribal societies and that this seems 'more natural than the common one derived from patriarchal government, or the authority of a father, which is said first to take place in one family, and to accustom the members of it to the government of a single person'. Nevertheless, he admits that '[t]he state of society without government [...] must subsist with the conjunction of many families, and long after the first generation' (T 3.2.8.2; 540–1), and he emphasises the significance of the role of family in which parents inculcate fundamental moral codes in their children (3.2.2.4; 486).[8] From these particular examples, we can deduce wider affinities between Hume and Temple in terms of what can be variously called empiricism, naturalism or their consistency in providing a secular and descriptive analysis of the human world.

Having considered the affinities between both authors' views of human nature and the origins of government, we now come to Temple's central point in the 'Essay upon the Original and Nature of Government'. In this essay he declares:

> when vast numbers of men submit their lives and fortunes absolutely to the will of one, it should be want of heart, but must be force of custom, or opinion, the true ground and foundation of all government, and that which subjects power to authority. *For power, arising from strength, is always in those that are governed, who are many: but authority, arising from opinion, is in those that govern, who are few.* (Temple 1754: II, 34)

This is because 'authority arises from the opinion of wisdom, goodness, and valour in the persons who possess it' (II, 35). Along with these opinions about the moral and intellectual qualities of rulers, Temple asserts, '[f]rom all these authority arises, but is by nothing so much strengthened and confirmed as by custom'. Significantly, while emphasising the advantage of established government, Temple also indicates how a new authority could debase 'the old, by appearance or impressions of contrary qualities in those who before enjoy it', and how '[t]his induces a general change of opinion concerning the person or party like to be obeyed or followed by the greatest or strongest part of the people'. Despite his seemingly conservative argumentation, the general tenor of this essay is thoroughly empirical or even pragmatic: 'So as in effect all government may be esteemed to grow strong or weak, as the general opinion of these qualities in those that govern is seen to lessen or increase'. In the same vein, Temple criticised the fashionable contract theory of Thomas Hobbes and Richard Hooker by emphasising the role of opinion: 'From this principle [of opinion], and from the discovery of some natural authority, may perhaps be deduced a truer original of all governments among men, than from any contracts' (II, 36–7).[9]

Despite Temple's and Hume's criticism of Hobbes's contractarianism on the subject of the formation of political society, it would be important to note that Hobbes shares a certain degree of empiricism similar to that of Temple and Hume. In particular, these two authors' observations on why political authorities can hold power over the populace are much akin to Hobbes's implication in his *de facto* theory of sovereignty: a thesis that 'obedience is owed to those with *de facto* authority, even if their rule is not *de jure*' (Parkin 2007: 72).[10] After the Revolution, this thesis provided some Tories such as William Sherlock with one of the ideological options to reconcile with the new regime without adopting the Whig principle (Dickinson 1977: 37–8; Parkin 2007: 383–8). But we should not jump to the conclusion that such de factoism automatically entailed advocacy of Toryism or monarchism, much less absolutism. Unlike Sherlock's more providential version, the *de facto* tendency in Hobbes should be attributed more to his empirical statement than to any normative claims. In Hume's case, it can be attributed to the issue of the cost-effectiveness of changing a nation's constitution, as well as to his empiricism.

Another point to note is that Hobbes provides 'a missing link' between imagination and opinion in Hume's philosophy. Although the Scottish philosopher gives few clear indications of the theoretical connection between imagination and opinion, Hobbes is more explicit concerning this linkage in *The Elements of Law* (1640) and *De Cive* (1642). According to him, the power in politics is nothing but a matter of belief: 'the acknowledgement of power is called HONOUR'. The origins of honour range from beauty, strength and riches to authority. The pleasure we receive from the various signs of honour is the passion called glory 'which proceedeth from the imagination or conception of our own power'. This glory is called 'false' when it proceeds from 'fame and trust of others, whereby one may think well of himself, and yet be deceived'. Or it becomes 'vainglory [*inanis gloria*]' when it is based upon 'the fiction (which also is imagination) of actions done by ourselves, which never were done' ([1640] 1969: 34 [I.8.5]; 36 [I.9.1]). In *De Cive*, Hobbes claims that this vainglory is one of the main sources of conflict in the state of nature ([1642] 1997: 26 [I.4]); see also Tuck 1997: xxiii). In a much later chapter Hobbes again asserts that '[p]roperly speaking, HONOUR [*HONOR*] is nothing other than the opinion one has of the union of *power* and *goodness* in another person. [...] Thus Honour is not in the person honoured, but in the person who honours' ([1642] 1997: 175–6 [XV.9]). According to Hobbes, glory is a passion with a cognitive component of imagination and it plays a critical role in his account of the state of nature because of its essential subjectivity. Based upon the empirical observation of human nature he conducted the introspective analysis before Locke,[11] and made clear the link between imagination, honour and opinion in the field of politics. Despite Hume's criticism of Hobbes's materialism and a lack of direct textual evidence, the former would have taken note of the latter's argument on this point.

As Gunn (1993; 1995) elaborates, the notion of opinion has much wider significance in eighteenth-century British and French political thought. Some other possible predecessors to Hume's notion of opinion should be surveyed. Despite the negative connotations Locke gives to the association of ideas (Chapter 2) and Hume's criticism of his social contract theory, he sometimes gives a positive sense to the term 'opinion' in his political and philosophical writings. In the *Two Tracts on Government*, a manuscript written around 1660, for example, Locke emphasises that, however different in its atmosphere and ceremonies, decent and orderly religion must always be 'suited to the present opinion of the age' (1967: 147; see also 134–59; Nakagami 2003). In *An Essay concerning Human Understanding*, he lists 'the Law of Opinion and Reputation' along with two others: 'the Divine Law' and 'the Civil Law' ([1690] 1997: 352–7 [II.xxviii.7, Para. 10–12]; Carey 2004: 62–8). In the *Two Treatises of Government* Locke argues against an expected criticism that 'the People being ignorant, and always discontented, to lay the Foundation of Government in the unsteady Opinion, and uncertain Humour of the People, is to expose it to certain ruine [...]' ([1690] 1988: 414 [II.xix.223]). Although he replies to this by claiming the 'slowness and aversion in the People to quit their old Constitutions', he does not deny the point that his theory of social contract is to place the foundation of government in opinion. Viewed in this light, Locke's political theory (at least on this point) can be considered much closer to that of Temple and Hume, despite their criticism of his views.[12]

Hume was probably long familiar with Shaftesbury's *Characteristicks of Men, Manners, Opinions, Times* before writing the *Treatise*, because he possessed a copy of this book as early as 1726 (Mossner 1980: 31; Stewart 2005: 37–9). Compared with Locke, however, Shaftesbury's influence on Hume seems more limited on this point. This is because he essentially follows the traditional and negative connotations attached to the word 'opinion', though he added a philosophical twist. In 'The Moralists, a Philosophical Rhapsody', for example, a person, who appears in one of the correspondences between Philocles and Palemon, boldly claims that '[t]here can be no such thing as real valuableness or worth; nothing in itself estimable or amiable, odious or shameful'. He went on to argue that '[a]ll is opinion. It is opinion which makes beauty and unmakes it. [...] Opinion is the law and measure. Nor has opinion any rule besides mere chance, which varies it as custom varies [...]' (Shaftesbury [1711] 1999: 'The Moralists' 328). Philocles himself partly concedes such a claim: 'in short, if we may depend on what is said commonly, "All good is merely as we fancy it. [...] All is opinion and fancy only"'. Nevertheless, Philocles/Shaftesbury does not intend to yield to fancy; what matters is which or what opinions we should follow ('The Moralists' 335). His solution is thoroughly Stoic (Cary 2004: 129–35). In the 'Miscellany IV' he clearly argues that 'the fancy more consistent and the good more durable, solid and within my power and command, then the more such an opinion prevails in me, the more satisfaction and happiness I must experience' (Shaftesbury [1711] 1999: 'Miscellany IV' 423). For sentimentalist Shaftesbury, there is a sense in which everything we perceive is an internal phenomenon in our minds, and only for this reason we have to admit that 'opinion is all in all' ('The Moralists' 336). Not in spite of, but rather because of this, Shaftsbury believes we must learn how 'to regulate fancy and rectify opinions, on which all depends' ('Miscellany IV' 423). Hume is unlikely to accept a Shaftesburian Stoical solution on the issue of opinion.[13] Furthermore, Shaftesbury takes up this notion in a conventional way when discussing moral and aesthetical topics, while Hume utilises it in a more objective manner in his political writings.

Shaftesbury's influence on Hume in this issue, if any, is therefore likely to be limited or negative.

Pierre Bayle, who considers himself to be a 'historian of opinions' (historien des opinions), was another possible influence for Hume in his critical investigations of the authority and influence of opinion. John Robertson argues that, for Hume, Bayle could be one of the important 'exponents of a sceptical, Epicurean approach to morals and sociability' (2005: 259). As we saw in Chapter 2, the young Hume clearly mentioned Bayle's *Dictionnaire historique et critique* in a 1737 letter to Michael Ramsay (and as early as 1732 he had wrote to this old friend that 'I thank you for your trouble about Baile' (L I, 12; Stewart 2005: 35)), despite some debates over whether or to what extent Hume could have read any of Bayle's work at first hand before he wrote the *Treatise* (Pittion 1977) and over the dating of Hume's so-called 'Early Memoranda' which contains his occasional mentions of Bayle (Hume 1948; Stewart 2000; Sakamoto 2011b). In his *Pensées diverses sur la comète de 1680* (*Various Thoughts on the Occasion of a Comet of 1680*), Bayle discredits the maxim that 'generally established opinions are true' and instead claims that 'the antiquity and generality of an opinion is not a mark of its truth' in order to demonstrate the absurdities of superstitions concerning the bad influences of comets. While his treatment of vulgar opinion is consistently critical, Bayle admits as an empirical observation that 'our mind readily takes the antiquity and generality of an opinion as one of these external marks' of the supposed truth ([1682] 2000: 64, 130). Although he does not explicitly extend this theory to his politics, Bayle's thesis of 'a society of Atheists' perhaps led Hume to recognise how greatly and easily we are influenced by opinion, reputation and worldly honour in a much wider context. We will explore this aspect of Hume's thought further in the following chapters.

2 Hume's Political Science of Opinion

Obviously, the examples given here of the discussions of Hobbes, Locke, Shaftesbury and Bayle on the topic of opinion and imagination are neither exclusive nor exhaustive, but are selected to enhance our understanding of Hume's notion of opinion. These would suffice to evince his possible accessibility to various intellectual sources. Be that as it may, as far as Hume's argument in the essay 'Of the First Principles' is concerned, the similarities between Temple and Hume are more than mere coincidence. Hume undoubtedly took the starting point of 'the First Principles' from Temple's 'An Essay upon Original and Nature'; in the opening sentences of the essay Hume repeats almost verbatim one of Temple's claims (quoted on p. 63):

> Nothing appears more surprizing to those, who consider human affairs with a philosophical eye, than the easiness with which the many are governed by the few [...]. When we enquire by what means this wonder is effected, we shall find, that, as FORCE is always on the side of the governed, the governors have nothing to support them but opinion. It is therefore, on opinion only that government is founded; and this maxim extends to the most despotic and most military governments, as well as to the most free and most popular. (E 32)

In spite of the aforementioned similarities, Temple does not fully develop his thesis that 'every government is founded on opinion': leaving it to Hume to fully explore its implications with his own account of the role of opinion or 'imagination' in the *Treatise*.

Based on Temple's argument, Hume's originality in the essay 'Of the First Principles of Government' lies in his division between the opinion of public interest and the opinion of right, which is subdivided into opinion of right to power and to property. By including 'property' in the subcategory of the opinion of right, Hume critically modified Harrington's supposedly materialistic view that 'power follows property' as a driving force for social change (Harrington [1656] 1992: 60; see also E 47). At least according to *The Commonwealth of Oceana*, however, this power is supposed to reside purely in physical possession of a piece of land. The equal division of land among heirs will thus redistribute the associated power accordingly. In contrast to Harrington, Hume contends that a gap remains between economic and political power. This is because political power does not rest directly upon the real balance of property, but rather upon the 'opinion' held about it: 'A Government may endure for several ages, though the balance of power, and the balance of property do not coincide' (E 35). For Hume, power consists not only of its physical manifestation in the ownership of property; it also has psychological, cultural and historical elements (Moore 1977: 816).

Hume also argues that 'antiquity' functions as one possible driving force in achieving the support of opinion for a claim to power: 'Antiquity always begets the opinion of right' (E 33). Hume has generally been considered to attach importance to 'long possession' in his discussion of political legitimacy. Antiquity or long-term possession of the reins of authority is, however, just one of the foundations that Hume considers produce political legitimacy and authority in the popular psyche. Hume's underlying argument in Book 3 of the *Treatise* is that all claims to legislative authority, including 'original contract, long possession, present possession, conquest, or succession' are based on the importance attached to these concepts by the human imagination, or opinion, rather than possessing any inherent validity. Hume also states that to determine the bounds to the legislative power 'is the work more of imagination and passion than of reason' (T 3.2.10.14; 560–1; Stewart 1992: chap. 5). The theory of imagination, developed in Book 1 of the *Treatise*, here provides him in Book 3 with theoretical means to explain 'that famous *revolution*' and criticise the Lockean idea of a right of resistance (as we shall see later, he was to repeat the same point in the *History*). On the issue of loyalty to a monarch, Hume explains that the right to succession is susceptible to 'the slightest properties of the imagination', in which the monarch and the prince are strongly related (T 3.2.10.10–12; 559–60; Stewart 1992: 172–3n.8). The 'slight' nature of imagination does not indicate its weakness; rather, according to Hume, it provides scope for contingency in uncertain situations such as the Glorious Revolution. This is precisely because the workings of imagination are heavily influenced by many trivial circumstances, as Hume admits elsewhere in the *Treatise* (T footnote 75.13 to 3.2.3.10; 512–13n.; footnote 73.4 to 3.2.3.7; 508n.). Hume demonstrates how we can come to think it 'lawful and suitable [...] to dethrone' a tyrannical king and 'the remaining members of the constitution acquire a right of excluding his next heir'. He says that these judgements do not depend upon any abstract right of resistance, but are founded upon 'a very singular quality of our thought and imagination' (3.2.10.18; 565). When seen in this light, it is clear why in the essay 'Of the First Principles' Hume places most emphasis, not upon the mere longevity of each regime, but upon the effect that this has upon the opinion of the people.

A similar theory informs another category in Hume's classification of opinions – the opinion of interest. Hume sometimes emphasises '[t]he general interests or necessities of society' (E 'Original Contract' 481) as the fundamental reason for their allegiance to government. However, his emphasis on public interest does not mean that objective utility provides any clear-cut standard by which to judge whether any particular institution is right or wrong in real terms. His discussions in the essay 'Of the First Principles of Government' clearly show that public interest exists as nothing but an opinion. Importantly, when he appeals to public interest in his political writings, interest itself is perceived as neither neutral nor indifferent. While Hume frequently appeals to the public interest in political essays, the concept must inevitably take shape through the workings of 'opinion' in each time and place. Although Hume often emphasised the utilitarian foundation of political institutions when viewed on an ontological level, he did not consider that all contemporary political debates could be settled solely on the grounds of exclusively utilitarian considerations. 'It may farther be said', Hume argues, 'that though men be much governed by interest; yet even interest itself, and all human affairs, are entirely governed by *opinion*' (E 51). While he admits that any political institution, manners or custom has its own intrinsic pleasantness or utility, he claims that '[p]articular customs and manners alter the usefulness of qualities' (EPM 6.20; 241).[14] This does not necessarily mean that opinion alone could change any fundamental sense of utility; Hume notices that opinion *can* influence our perceptions and understandings of the public interest in one way or another, and to a certain degree (T 2.3.1.9; 402; Gunn 1993: 21). It should also be remembered that while he endeavours to clarify the three types of opinion in the essay 'Of the First Principles', he provides no evaluative hierarchy among them.

The Humean notion of opinion, in this sense, is generally descriptive. This can and should be distinguished from his normative appeal to 'general opinion', which he often uses as justification for moderation. The latter will be discussed below. For Hume, to recognise the central role of opinion in our everyday social and political life it was necessary to depart from the traditional (negative) connotations of the word 'opinion' as *doxa*, which should be eradicated or suppressed to reach the truth. Hume as 'anatomist' of human nature thus develops the thesis that every government is founded on opinion mainly to delineate the mechanism of how various governments can stand as they are (Phillipson 2011: 56). On the other hand, the Humean notion of opinion should be distinguished from the more democratic and normative concept 'public opinion' (opinion publique), which has often been thought to be increasing in popularity in his contemporary France (Ozouf 1988: S3–S4). Aside from the issue of the historical validity of this notion,[15] the almost total absence of the exact phrase 'public opinion' in Hume's writings remains distinctive. The single example of its use appears in the *History* (III, 386), but here it still lacks any democratic or positive connotations.

In addition, Hume's assertion of opinion as a basis for government is neither mutually exclusive nor incompatible with either his political science, or his preference for institutional analysis. In the 1741 essay 'That Politics may be Reduced to a Science' he claims that in order to establish politics as a science, one must explore each form of government as a system, and determine which type could attain a more predictable political administration (see Chapter 6). The point of this essay lies in his observation that the influence of particular forms of government is great and they have so little dependence 'on the humours and tempers of men' that we can draw a conclusion as highly reliable in politics as in 'the mathematical sciences' (E 16). We should pay attention to Hume's wording when he emphasises this point in the essay. He never denies the influence of opinion, but criticises those who 'think, that human affairs admit of no greater stability, than what they receive from the casual humours and characters of *particular men*' and those who place great importance on the dependence of political affairs 'on the humours and education of *particular men*' (14, 24. Italics added). Thus, what he rejects in this essay is just the influence of 'particular men', not of the collective opinion of the people. His point is that it would be possible to estimate the inherent merits of each political system without taking into account the particular talent or genius of its administrator. From the simple fact that he arranged the one next to the other in the *Essays, Moral and Political*, it is clear that Hume does not think these two essays – 'That Politics' and 'Of the First Principles' – were contradictory.

The true nature of Hume's notion of opinion, nevertheless, remains somewhat elusive and indeterminate. If opinion is a basis of government, what is the determinant factor of opinion? Hume does not explain the determinants of opinion – those factors by which it is canalised or changed. In the *Treatise* Hume explains that 'the great uniformity we may observe in the humours and turn of thinking of those of the same nation' arises more from 'sympathy, than from any influence of the soil and climate' (T 2.1.11.2; 316–17). In the 1748 essay 'Of National Characters' – where he uses the expression 'contagion' rather than sympathy – his notion of national characters is neither exclusively politically nor economically oriented: he mentions government, religion and geographical or climatic conditions among the determining factors. According to Hume, opinion is far from an independent variable; it should be thought of as the intersection of a variety of factors: as he admits elsewhere, '[o]ur opinions of all kinds are strongly affected by society and sympathy' (DP 2.33). Hume admits that the political institutions exert a strong influence on opinion (Forbes 1975b: 319). At the same time, his various explorations of the causes and effects of opinion demonstrate his belief that opinion can influence government as well as other factors and vice versa. If so, attention need not be devoted to the obsolete problem of which is the determinant factor of opinion in Hume's political philosophy (Miller 1981: 122, 126).[16] Rather, we must be aware that the plasticity and indeterminacy of Hume's notion of opinion is central to his system of 'the science of MAN' and his Sceptical Enlightenment.[17]

Exactly because of this plasticity, Hume never concealed his concern about the possibility of drastic changes in opinion or the consequences of such shifts. Hume's repeated comments on the instability of limited monarchy – especially that of contemporary Britain – betray his strong apprehension (E 35–6, 51–3, 527). Even well established social conventions are always susceptible to the influence of fanaticism, absurdity and barbarity. In the context of this troubling aspect of opinion, Hume's seemingly growing apprehension in his old age about the movement of contemporary opinion is entirely explicable. Although Hume in later life appears to have become increasingly aware that reality is in rapid flux, this does not mean that he changed his standpoint concerning the nature of opinion (Hampsher-Monk 1992: 150). Rather than being caused by a shift in his thought towards conservatism, this is an expression of his consistent awareness of the transient nature of opinion. As we will see below, this is also the case in the *History of England*.

3 Changeability of Opinion in the *History*

Despite Hume's repeated emphasis on 'opinion' in his political analysis, its significance in his *History of England* has been little discussed (O'Brien 1997a: 83).[18] One reason could be that, as is the case with much of his philosophical terminology, he conveys the same notion by different expressions or uses the word 'opinion' as part of longer phrases. In the following example, he juxtaposes this word to 'the principles of the times': 'Elizabeth continued to be the most popular sovereign that ever swayed the scepter of England; because the maxims of her reign were conformable to *the principles of the times*, and to *the opinion, generally entertained with regard to the constitution*' (H IV, 145. Italics added). Although more consideration is necessary to determine whether all were used to mean the same notion with the same weight, close attention to the notion of opinion and its variants will provide us with a different perspective on the *magnum opus* of Hume the historian.

Firstly, our attention to the role of opinion in the *History* brings us back to the issue of its relevance to imagination. The process of gradual development in the rule of law narrated in the *History* can be considered to be a slow realisation of reason as the 'general and more established properties of imagination' (T 1.4.7.7; 267–8), or a historicised version of the installation of the general points of view that are indispensable to our stable and impartial judgements regarding property (T 3.3.1.15; 581–2). In contrast, the rude and barbarous ages are characterised not only by cruelty and violence but also by 'revolutions [...] so much guided by *caprice*' (H I: 3. Italics added) – another and a troublesome aspect of imagination. In this sense, as Claude Gautier (2005) correctly argues, Hume in the *History* attempts to demonstrate to his readers the way we can achieve a more balanced and stable viewpoint based on long-term interests. At the same time, Hume's narrative of English history might be a story of convoluted development in manners and constitution, but it is far from progressivist or triumphalist. On the contrary, he repeatedly emphasises the fluctuations of political institutions, as well as the restless nature of people's thinking (V, 353; see also V, 236 and E 494–5; Spencer 2005: 131–2). Even after the supposed perfection of liberty, the possibility of humanity's return to barbarism always lurks (H II, 519; see also Livingston 1990: 134). For example, after the introduction of 'the triennial law' Hume emphasises the increasing threat of the volatility of political opinions: 'No danger remains, but what is inseparable from all free constitutions, and what forms the very essence of their freedom: The danger of *a change in the people's disposition*, and of general disgust, contracted against popular privileges' (italics added). 'To prevent such an evil', he recommends that we 'contain ourselves within the bounds of moderation' (V, 355). Thus the fickleness of opinion always pulls us back to sudden disorder and confusion, which seems to be the inevitable consequence of his empirical observations of human nature.

Secondly, in the *History of England*, Hume's notion of opinion plays a pivotal role in his well-known apologia for the first two Stuart monarchs, which is a common justification for characterising him as a Tory historian (E 'My Own Life' xxxvii).[19] The gist of his argument is that these monarchs had simply followed the established practice of their predecessor Queen Elizabeth who had, in turn, 'only supported the prerogatives, transmitted to her by her predecessors' (H IV, 354). In Hume's view, 'the two first Princes of the House of Stuart' might be regarded as incompetent to judge correctly the contemporary political climate, but 'were not exposd [sic] to so much blame as Party Zeal has commonly thrown upon them' (L I, 461; see also I, 264); and any naïve allegation that they had encroached on the ancient constitution is unfounded (H V, 543), although Hume does not deem them to be completely without guilt ('Their violations of law, particularly those of Charles, are, in some few instances, transgressions of a plain limit, which was marked out to royal authority' (V, 570, Note [W]; Forbes 1975b: 272–4)). The key to reconciling Hume's support for the settlement after the Glorious Revolution with his defence of the first two Stuart monarchs lies in understanding his analysis of the shift in the opinion of the people that took place between the two periods.

> On the whole, we must conceive that monarchy, on the accession of the house of Stuart, was possessed of a very extensive authority [...]. But, at the same time, this authority was founded *merely on the opinion of the people*, influenced by ancient precedent and example. It was not supported either by money or by force of arms. [...] *By the changes*, which have since been introduced, the liberty and independence of individuals has been rendered much more full, intire, and secure; that of the public more uncertain and precarious. (H V, 128. Italics added; see also E 'Protestant Succession' 509)

Hume makes two points in this passage: firstly, the absolute government of the House of Tudor and of (at least) the first two Stuart kings basically depended upon the people's willing obedience to their sovereignty, and more specifically on the aristocratic provision of troops and supplies for war. On this point, according to Hume, England was more vulnerable to the rapid change of popular opinion than other European countries with established standing armies. Second and more importantly, he emphasises the various changes that took place over the seventeenth century and the influence these events had over popular thought about liberty. In one of the Tudor volumes, Hume repeats the same point as follows: 'But when Charles I. attempted to continue in the same course [as Henry VIII], which had now received the sanction of many generations, *so much were the opinions of men altered*, that a furious tempest was excited by it' (H III, 326. Italics added).

Thirdly, appreciating his assessment of the shift in opinion is crucial to understanding the nature of Hume's defence of the Revolutionary settlement as 'the most perfect and most accurate system of liberty that was ever found compatible with government' (H II, 525). By depicting the advent and establishment of 'the regular plan of liberty' in the form of changing constitutions and practice through time, rather than in terms of any formal or a priori principle, Hume not only indicates that the concept of civil liberty itself is laden heavily with convention, but also he dexterously presents his argument for the institutionalised realisation that the maintenance of political liberty is a criterion of legitimate government, even if this principle was not upheld in previous constitutions (Wertz 2000: 77). For example, he insisted that 'in all the historical plays of Shakespear [sic], where the manners and characters, and even the transactions of the several reigns are so exactly copied, there is scarcely any mention of *civil Liberty*' despite the claims of some 'pretended' historians that it had been an issue of major importance (H IV, 368 footnote [f]). While Hume showed that the establishment of the rule of law is certainly the most veritable indicator for the realisation of political liberty at the constitutional level, he argued that it is necessary to wait for people to accept it as reasonable and proper. Throughout his narratives of the Stuart dynasty, Hume often brings our attention to the fact that 'the situation of affairs and *the dispositions of men became susceptible of a more regular plan of liberty*; the laws were not supported singly by the authority of the sovereign' (V, 40. Italics added). In other words, the popular conception that Elizabeth 'did not infringe any established liberties of the people' shows that 'her particular exertions of power *were conceived to be* nothing but the ordinary course of administration' (IV, 355. Italics added). Hume acknowledges elsewhere that liberty can emerge only when it is attended with 'a certain turn of thinking' (E 'Commerce' 265). Unlike an a priori appeal to liberty, this is a very characteristic way for Hume to vindicate the value of liberty, which enables him to avoid composing a 'saints and sinners' history.

Another point to be considered here is the distinction between opinion and manners, although this is not always clear in the writings of Hume and his contemporaries (Gunn 1995: 190). Hume stipulates that manners can shape opinion, but there is a significant time lag between the change of manners and the change of opinion in his narratives of the *History*. As Hume claims, 'the manners of the age were a general cause, which operated during this whole period, and which continually tended to diminish the riches, and still more the influence, of the aristocracy, anciently so formidable to the crown'. He also acknowledges that 'the farther progress of the same causes begat a new plan of liberty' (H IV, 385), but there is a long way to go to produce the consequence.[20] His emphasis on the changes of opinion between the Tudors and the Stuarts is more worthy of attention because of the relatively rapid shift that Hume describes taking place. Hume explained this sudden change from the psychological mechanism as 'the nature of novelty' in the 1741 essay 'Whether the British Government inclines more to Absolute Monarchy, or to a Republic'. The force of novelty means that a political and religious ferment excited by a new sect 'always spreads faster, and multiplies its partizans with greater rapidity, than any old established opinion' (E 50). As we have seen above, the real or physical balance of property between the people and the crown is not the same as the opinion about it, and there can be a gap between them. It is this gap that constituted the tragedy of Charles I that Hume the historian tried to reveal to his readers. 'Unhappily, [Charles I's] fate threw him into a period, when the precedents of many former reigns favored strongly of arbitrary power, and *the genius of the people* ran violently towards liberty' (H V, 543. Italics added. Cf. Temple 1754: II, 95). The tragedy would not work without either the changing opinion toward a new age or the King who was unaware of it.

4 Hume's Criticism of the Myth of the Ancient Constitution

As is well known, Hume reiterates the virtue of obedience to established practices in the political essays and the *History*, which seems initially to have ample affinity to his view of convention or his alleged theory of spontaneous order (Hayek 1967; Hamowy 2005: esp. chap. 2; Petsoulas 2001: chap. 4). Hume's appeal to established practice, on the other hand, seems initially to sit ill with his oft-forgotten criticism of the myth of the ancient constitution, which comprises one of his main themes in the *History*. The above discussions of Hume's notion of opinion in the *History* will serve to clarify the way in which his seemingly conservative appeal to established practices is compatible with his criticism of ancient constitutionalism.

Now let's start with the latter point. According to the Tudor volume of the *History*, a single ancient constitution should not be presupposed; rather, the existence of plural constitutions throughout English history should be accepted:

> By the ancient constitution, is here meant that which prevailed before the settlement of our present plan of liberty. There was a more ancient constitution, where, though the people had perhaps less liberty than under the Tudors, yet the king had also less authority [...]. But there was still a more ancient constitution, viz. that before the signing of the charters, when neither the people nor the barons had any regular privileges; and the power of the government, during the reign of an able prince, was almost wholly in the king. (IV, 355 footnote [l]; see also II, 525)[21]

Hume basically adopts the same position as the Tory historian Robert Brady had taken in the seventeenth-century debate over the belief in the ancient constitution. Brady and other contemporary critics of this myth emphasised the modernity of the English constitution and denied the claims of their adversaries to the existence of a free and independent Witenagemot, or national Anglo-Saxon council, before the Norman Conquest (Pocock 1957; Forbes 1975b: chap. 8; Pocock 1985b: 135). As Mark Spencer acutely argues, however, Hume's criticism of ancient constitutionalism is addressed to both the Whig belief in the continuity of an English liberty originating in the Saxon past, and against 'the Tory historical argument' that emphasises the absolute power of the English kings on allegedly historical grounds (2005: 133). Hume himself takes neither position.

The gist of Hume's appeal to the multiplicity of the English constitution rather lies in his consistency in the emphasis on the particular circumstances surrounding the framing of each constitution. The clearest expression of this point appears in the sentence, to which is annexed Hume's view of the multiple constitutions cited above:

> In the particular exertions of power, the question ought never to be forgotten, *What is best*? But in the general distribution of power among the several members of a constitution, there can seldom be admitted any other question, than *What is established*? [...] If any other rule than established practice be allowed, factions and dissentions must multiply without end: And though many constitutions, and none more than the British, have been improved even by violent innovations, the praise, bestowed on those patriots, to whom the nation has been indebted for its privileges, ought to be given with some reserve, and surely without the least rancour against those who adhered to the ancient constitution. (H IV, 355)

Until the 1773 edition, 'what is established' read 'what is usual' (Forbes 1975b: 271). When this substitution is noted, it becomes clear that Hume is not referring only to the institutional aspects of social practices; rather the notion of 'established practice' becomes relevant only after they are generally accepted among the people. The following passage states the point even more explicitly: 'In each of these successive alterations, the only rule of government [...] is the established practice of the age, and the maxims of administration, which *are at that time prevalent, and universally assented to*' (H II, 525. Italics added). These examples demonstrate that Hume identifies four distinct phases of the English constitution, not only in its institutional terms, but also as the general assumptions, that is 'opinion', surrounding the framing of each constitution.

For his contemporaries, however, the existence of plural constitutions is nothing but an oxymoron. Richard Hurd, one of his contemporary critics, repeatedly attacked Hume over this point:

> To tell us, that this constitution has been different at different times, because the regal or popular influence has at different times been more

> or less predominant, is only playing with a word, and confounding *constitution* with *administration*. According to this way of speaking, we have not only had *three* or *four*, but possibly three or four score, different constitutions. (Hurd [1759] 2002: I, 180)

Hurd's critique showed his and his contemporaries' premises; for them the constitution must be one and only (Wexler 1979: 73; Spencer 2005: 135–6). On this point, at least, Edmund Burke is much closer to Hurd than Hume. Despite his criticism of mysticism in ancient constitutionalism, Burke's principle of prescription can still be considered to presuppose the continuity and seamlessness of political constitution.[22] On the other hand, Hume has no need to appeal either to such antiquity or to the continuous growth of a single constitution. In addition to this, Hurd criticised Hume's inarticulate wordings: 'But here I suspect the historian to be playing tricks with us. For what, might one ask him, is this *antient* practice, and *antient constitution*?' (Hurd [1759] 2002: I, 177). Perhaps as a result of such criticisms, Hume changed the original phrase 'ancient practice' (in the first 1759 edition) into 'established practice' in later (after 1763) editions of the *History*, although the phrases the 'ancient constitution' or 'ancient practices' are still sometimes used. This criticism rather betrays the distinctive nature of Hume's view of constitutions: for him, as we just saw, any political constitution cannot stand without people's general assumptions of its legitimacy on which they act, and these assumptions change significantly through the ages.

Despite his contemporaries' criticisms, Hume's appeal to 'what is established' has a practical application to the contemporary issue of how to defend theoretically the constitutional situation established by the Glorious Revolution: what he calls 'the most perfect and most accurate system of liberty that was ever found compatible with government' (H II, 525). As many commentators have pointed out, his basic aim in many of his political and historical writings was to provide with theoretical underpinning the settlement of the Glorious Revolution of 1688, which was still considered precarious in the middle of the eighteenth century (Forbes 1975b: 263–4; Dickinson 1977: chap. 4). Importantly, Hume saw no need for the claim of authority to date from time immemorial, unlike Burke, nor was political authority a mathematical problem in which the strength of popular belief in the sovereign's legitimacy could be computed by an assessment of the longevity of the monarchy (Wolin 1954: 1003–4). Seemingly paradoxically, Hume even emphasises the recentness rather than the longevity of government in the 1752 essay 'Of the Coalition of Parties': 'The true rule of government is the present established practice of the age. That has most authority, *because it is recent*: It is also *best known*, for the same reason' (E 498–9. Italics added).[23] If Hume's aim was simply to nurture attachment to the constitution among his contemporaries, why did he risk destabilising the sense of unity and solidarity created by such attachment, by arguing for the recentness of the contemporary constitution? What is important for Hume is that a political practice is fully established, and accepted by as many people as possible. If following the established practices expressed in the constitution settled after the Glorious Revolution had brought public security and happiness during the last fifty years, or more correctly, if the population considers this to be the case, Hume believes, this is reason enough to continue to support the present establishment. Hume's view of opinion supports neither appeals to antiquity, nor the continuous growth of a single constitution, but the general assumptions surrounding the framing of four successive but different constitutions. For this reason, in the very last paragraph of the second volume, having brought the history of England up from the invasion of Julius Caesar to the accession of Henry VII, Hume criticises 'those who, from a pretended respect to antiquity, appeal at every turn to an original plan of the constitution' (H II, 525), and reiterates his doctrine of obedience to what public opinion assumes to be established.

In the *History* Hume also gives a curious example of recently established regimes that were nevertheless successful in arousing popular support. After the execution of Charles I in January 1649, the young prince whom the Scottish parliament proclaimed as a new king, tried to combat the force of Cromwell's army several times during 1650 and 1651. However, the Scots, English Presbyterians and Royalists who supported Charles II were unable to muster sufficient military force, while many militias arose in support of the new parliamentary cause. What attracted Hume's interest in this particular situation was the fact that, at this stage, only two years had passed since the execution of the former king: 'Such is the influence of established government, that the commonwealth, though founded in usurpation the most unjust and unpopular, had authority sufficient to raise every where the militia of the counties' (H VI, 35; see also E 512; cf. Temple 1754: II, 36–7). This example is not only the proof that established governments, even if they are new, have a strong influence on people's opinion; it is also indicative of the plastic nature of opinion.

These arguments make clear Hume's position that the authority of a regime depends on its imprint on public consciousness rather than deriving from any innate quality. He also recognises the capacity of a government to establish its authority over a very short period of time. He has been alleged to emphasise the effect of time and custom in his political writings. If Hume and other anti-Jacobite theorists did so on the basis of these two points – time and custom – *alone*, however, they would have 'completely failed' in defending the Revolution settlement and the Hanoverian succession. This is because the duration of the regime established thereby was still far shorter than the Stuart monarchy had held sway (McLynn 1983: 171). This is why he emphasises not the continuity, but 'what is established', and recognises the capacity of a government to establish its authority over a very short period of time. In this way, Hume's focus on the people's perceptions of political legitimacy provides a basis both for his criticism of the ancient constitutional myth, which betrays his opposition to naïve traditionalism or anachronism, and at the same time his support for the upholding of 'what is established' as a guiding thread for human society (Haakonssen 1996: 113–15; 2009: 357).

5 Hume's Reservation of the Right of Resistance

Hume's criticism of the myth of the ancient constitution is inseparable from his criticism of the idea of an original contract. While the theory of the ancient constitution might sound conservative, many historical studies have now shown that in eighteenth-century political thought the theory of the ancient constitution served to support calls for radical innovation. This is because the revolutionaries of the seventeenth and eighteenth centuries originally claimed that the reforms they demanded were aimed not at innovation but at a return to the first principles of the nation (Arendt [1963] 1990: 43; Harris 1993: 301). Hume's contemporaries easily connected the idea of the ancient constitution with the claim for the existence of an original social contract (for example, Burke [1791] 1992: 124).[24] Hence the claim that the ancient constitution destroyed by tyrants should be restored, which was transformed into the complaint that it had not yet been fully restored by the Glorious Revolution. Hume and the Court Whigs were thereby placed in a complex situation in which they were able to appeal neither to contract theory, nor to the myth of ancient constitution.[25] Both theoretical justifications of authority had been hijacked by their opponents; the former to justify endless rebellion and the latter to give undesirable pretexts to radical reforms (Dickinson 1995: 142). Considering this situation, it is clear how effectively Hume's appeal to established practices enables him simultaneously to avoid questionable appeals to antiquity in the *History* and to characterise the existence of any social contract as fanciful and anachronistic in his political essays.

Hume's attack on the abuses of social contract theory is also epitomised by his reservation of the doctrine of resistance. In the *History*, when he narrated the tragic death of Charles I, he argued that 'the doctrine of resistance' should be concealed 'from the populace'. His reasoning is supported by his thesis that as government is '*always founded on opinion*, not on force', it is dangerous to weaken reverence toward authority by instructing people in the doctrine of the right of resistance (H V, 544. Italics added). What matters here, however, is not this seemingly conservative aspect of Hume's attitude, but rather his method of limiting the legitimacy of this doctrine. He tries to do so through the argument that the proper range of justified resistance can be neither theoretically determined nor fixed *beforehand* (Forbes 1975b: 96–101; Merrill 2005). This doctrine should not be discussed in the abstract, but only becomes relevant when situated in a particular historical context. When he narrates the political debate over the Exclusion Bill in the *History*, Hume presents through the mouth of the court party the same maxim (with almost exactly the same phrase) in the essay 'Of the First Principles':

> An authority, they said, wholly absolute and uncontroulable is a mere chimera, and is no where to be found in any human institutions. *All government is founded on opinion* and a sense of duty; and wherever the supreme magistrate, by any law or positive prescription, shocks *an opinion regarded as fundamental, and established* with a firmness equal to that of his own authority, he subverts the principle, by which he himself is established, and can no longer hope for obedience.[26] (H VI, 389–90. Italics added)

Hume was to repeat a similar point in the essay 'Of the Origin of Government' published in 1770, and to compare a 'sultan' who cannot impose new taxes on his subjects, and 'a French monarch' who cannot encroach on the lives and fortunes of his subjects (here he repeats the same point with the same phrase that the power of the civil magistrates, 'being founded on opinion, can never subvert other opinions, equally rooted with that of his title to dominion' (E 40)). When well-established practices are suspected of having been violated, this is the time to begin to resist. The right to rebel against a sovereign is one assumed only by the leaders of the dissidents of the specific time and place and their particular choice has no bearing on the question whether the right of resistance is to be regarded as universally right or wrong. This dependence on the particular context of political decisions means that none should be considered as representing a universal standard, but, at the most, as valid only in terms of the prevailing situation or retrospectively (Dees 1992: 221).[27]

Thus, Hume's position on the issue of the right of resistance leaves little room for strictly constitutional debate. This is simply because such a necessity cannot be provided for within a constitutional framework that takes as its basis the compliance of the sovereign and people with the principles laid out within it. This view is expressed in Hume's depiction of the discussions taking place among the members of parliament after the Restoration:

> They were probably sensible, that to suppose in the sovereign any such invasion of public liberty is entirely unconstitutional; and that therefore expressly to reserve, upon that event, any right of resistance in the subject, must be liable to the same objection. [...] If such an attack [made by the sovereign] was at any time made, the necessity was then extreme: And the case of extreme and violent necessity, no laws, they thought, could comprehend; because to such a necessity no laws could *beforehand* point out a proper remedy. (H VI, 174. Italics added)

That he positioned the right of resistance outside the constitutional framework does not necessarily mean that we have no way of accusing any political or legal coercion made by royal power or parliament. Hume's strictures against 'egregious' tyrannies in his historical narratives are thorough and serious. But Hume gives no clear substantial criterion about what is egregious and when resistance can be justified (Sabl 2012: 115–17). Characteristically,

Hume remains silent about or indifferent to this point; rather he is critical of 'a preacher or casuist, who should make it his chief study to find out such [exceptional] cases' (E 'Passive Obedience' 490–1). This is an expression of Hume's 'spirit of scepticism' about demarcation in particular cases (Chapter 1). As early as the *Treatise*, he makes the exact same point as in the *History*:

> But tho' this *general* principle [of resistance] be authoriz'd by common sense, and the practice of all ages, 'tis certainly impossible for the laws, or even for philosophy, to establish any *particular* rules by which we may know when resistance is lawful; and decide all controversies, which may arise on that subject. (T 3.2.10.16; 563)

Authority always lies in and stems from 'the practice of all ages'. No matter how we catalogue the abuses and sufferings found in each reign, this inventory alone provides no justification to subvert or overthrow any particular regime. Hence Hume's seemingly paradoxical position that the doctrine of resistance should not be promulgated, while admitting its theoretical validity (Merrill 2005; Gautier 2005: chap. 4, esp. 84–5, 173–6). Significantly, in the essay 'Of the Original Contract' he does not flatly refute both the social contract theory and the divine right theory: he asserts that '*both the* schemes *of practical consequences are prudent; though not in extremes, to which each party, in opposition to the other, has commonly endeavoured to carry them*' (E 466; see also Buckle and Castiglione 1991; Castiglione 1994). The problem is not necessarily the theories themselves, but rather the extent of their applicability. Hume's appeal to established practices is effectively used for limiting excessive applications of these speculative principles.

In these political arguments, the term 'general opinion' often takes on the role of justification. This is distinguishable from his descriptive analysis of opinion, while the latter clearly provides an important theoretical basis for the former. This is simply because what he calls established practice or 'what is established' exists only in the form of a widely accepted opinion. When he declares that '[t]he general opinion of mankind has some authority in all cases; but in this of morals 'tis perfectly infallible' (T 3.2.9.4; 552), Hume's concept of general opinion is more normative than descriptive. In the essay 'Of the Original Contract' he repeats the same point: 'in all questions with regard to morals, as well as criticism, there is no other standard' than 'an appeal to general opinion [...] by which any controversy can ever be decided' (E 486). Hume's seemingly conservative appeal to general opinion, however, does not legitimate Livingston's general claim that '[t]he good is what is housed in the deeply established prejudices, customs, and traditions that make up the substance of the moral world' (1998: 191), although I concur with his argument that for Hume 'tradition is *dynamic* and *open ended*' (1990: 134). Hume repeatedly warns of the danger of blindly accepting tradition or prejudices: for example, 'in all questions, submitted to the understanding, prejudice is destructive of sound judgment, and perverts all operations of the intellectual faculties' (E 'Standard of Taste' 240). As Christopher Berry correctly argues, Hume's notion of 'superstition' is not limited to religion, but is far more general; throughout the *History* he denounces examples of 'bad manners' that people unconditionally believed to be well established at the time (2009: 70–4). Although Hume seemingly shares with Burke an emphasis on the significance of established practices, the Scottish sceptic is not as strident as the Irish-born political writer and statesman, who claims that 'we cherish [prejudices] because they are prejudices; and the longer they have lasted, and the more generally they have prevailed, the more we cherish them' (Burke [1790] 2014: 90). What is important for Hume is not to recommend blind reverence for what is established, but rather to trust it as a current and tentative guide while simultaneously keeping a sceptical eye on its changeability and instability.

Hume's observation that every government is founded upon opinion has not been closely examined, especially in relation to his *History*, despite his frequent references to the notion of opinion there. This is partly because his analytical and descriptive understanding of the indeterminate nature of opinion did not offer any straightforward ideological standpoints. This is also partly because Hume's strategy of choosing generally accepted opinion as a guiding thread allowed his contemporaries to read Hume's position not only as representing a 'Tory' standpoint, but also as 'inconsistent'. Daniel MacQueen, a critic of Hume's *History*, for example, complained: 'Can you imagine yourself to be reading the same author?' ([1756] 2002: I, 116; Forbes 1975b: 291).[28] These contemporary criticisms (including Richard Hurd's) are rather indicative of the peculiarity of Hume's notion of opinion, which plays decisive roles in his historical narrative, as well as in his political writings. The tragedy of Charles I acquires meaning only when viewed against 'the fluctuating nature of the constitution, the impatient humour of the people, and the variety of events' (V, 236).[29] At the same time, Hume was not reluctant but rather eager to support the present Hanoverian establishment, but he never did it without destroying the fundamental doctrine of what Duncan Forbes calls 'vulgar' Whiggism – the myth of the ancient constitution. To understand the changeability of opinion, Hume believes, will serve effectively to confute anachronistic beliefs, exemplified by the myth of the ancient constitution. Hume has always been aware of the fallacy of anachronism throughout his writings: 'Man is [...] susceptible of many different opinions, principles, and rules of conduct. What may be true, while he adheres to one way of thinking, will be found false, when he has embraced an opposite set of manners and opinions' (E 'Commerce' 255–6). In the *History*, Hume repeats that 'it seems unreasonable to judge of the measures, embraced during one period, by the maxims, which prevail in another' (H V, 240). For this reason, Richard Sher is correct to point out that 'both as a political theorist and as an ideological propagandist, Hume was the sort of friend that conservative Whigs would have been glad to be without' (1985: 190).

Hume's notion of opinion should be considered to be one of his strategies to find a new basis of morality and politics that would accommodate a diversity of customs of beliefs. Certainly some early eighteenth-century writers and polemists recognised that moderation was one of the best ways to ease the volatile and turbulent nature of political opinions (Phillipson 1983: 223–5, 242). Hume follows the same line as his predecessors. His originality rather lies in showing that this goal can be achieved only through our meta-recognition of the very changeability of opinion. His justification in recommending the reading of history lies in its potential to provide us with opportunities to develop a habit of detached reflection, although he admits that such enlarged thinking is accessible only to 'a philosophical mind' (H VI, 142; see also 'Of the Study of History'). In short, Hume believed that to foster such an awareness through historical narratives of changing established practices – even though it sounds paradoxical – was the most effective, if not the easiest, way to keep our opinion of 'what is established' from easily degenerating into any political fanaticism.

Notes

1. For more on the significance of Hume's notion of opinion in his moral philosophy, see Hayashi 2013.
2. An unidentified author, 'Mons. B–de', of a tract that was allegedly translated from French into English and published under the title *Reflections on the Causes and Probable Consequences of the Late Revolution in France*, also claims that '[t]he maxim, that all government is founded on opinion, is undeniably just', without mentioning the name of Hume (B–de 1790: 20).
3. The edition I use here is a copy of the same edition Hume possessed (Norton and Norton 1996: entry 1243). Hume also owned the 1692 edition of Temple's *Memoirs of What Passed in Christendom from 1672 to 1679* (entry 1242). The fact that Hume owned the 1754 edition of Temple's works does not exclude the likelihood that he was familiar with them much earlier.
4. The biographical affinities between Temple and Hume could also be counted. Hume did not lead a life of scholarly detachment from the world, but participated in the military campaign during the War of the Austrian Succession as Secretary to Lieutenant General St. Clair (1746–8) and engaged in contemporary diplomatic intercourse as Secretary (later Embassy Secretary) to the English Ambassador in Paris, Lord Hertford (1763–5). This recalls Temple's own diplomatic roles, although Hume neither occupied as high a position, nor brought about such substantial results as Temple, who was instrumental in negotiating the Treaty of Breda and served as the English Ambassador to the Netherlands (1668–71). Although Hume does not mention the name of the Ambassador in the essay 'Of the Balance of Power', he must have admired Temple's prescient understanding of the balance of power in the triple alliance of 1668 between the Dutch Republic, England and Sweden, aimed at curbing the expansionism of France (E 338; Temple's name appears in H VI, 220–1). Temple's *Memoires* were among Hume's important historical sources in his narration of the foreign policy during the reign of Charles II (Temple 1692), along with the *Observations upon the United Provinces of the Netherlands* (1673), which Hume quoted in the essay 'Of Taxes' in the *Political Discourses* (Hont 2005: 277). As for Temple's analysis of the Dutch trade, see Hont 2005: 194–201.
5. Hume must have been well acquainted with the *querelle des anciens et des modernes* since his youth, as his library contained Perrault's *Parallèle des anciens et des modernes* (1693) and Wotton's *Reflections*

upon Ancient and Modern Learning (1694) (Stewart 2005: 39; Norton and Norton 1996: entries 961 and 1367, respectively).

6. Israel emphasises the connection between Saint-Évremond and Temple, who were acquainted both with one another and with Spinoza in The Hague in the later 1660s. They also shared a commitment to Epicureanism and Sinophilia (Israel 2006, 641–2; see also 248). The title of one of Temple's essays, 'Of Heroic Virtue' also evokes Hume's endorsement of the essentially pagan values of heroism in the *Treatise* (3.3.2.13–15; 599–600).
7. Mayo labels Temple a 'sceptical humanist' (1934: 92). Temple is quite unusual in his combination of advocacy of Epicureanism and antipathy to modern science (Marburg 1932: chap. 2), given the general connection between the revival of Epicureanism and the evolution of natural science in the seventeenth century (Wilson 2008).
8. Certainly, Temple and Hume are not unique in providing such evolutionary accounts of the growth of human society. Kramnick points out a similar argument in Bolingbroke: 'a significant anticipation of Hume's critique of contractual thinking' (1992: 93; see also 109). This could be deemed one of the intellectual legacies of Lucretius in his *De rerum natura* (*Of the Nature of Things*) (Book 5 on the account of the origins of human society) (Baker 2007: 281). Mandeville also gives an explanation similar in this sense to both Temple's and Hume's in the *Fable of the Bees* ([1714/1729, 1732] 1988, II: 231 [264]; Tolonen 2013: 70–81). Despite Kaye's admission of the direct link between Lucretius and Mandeville and his emphasis on the originality of Mandeville among the moderns (II: cxii–cxiii, n.1), however, Mandeville actually mentions Temple's 'Essay upon the Original and Nature of Government' in the second volume of the *Fable*: 'it is highly probable, that most Societies, and Beginnings of Nations, were form'd in the Manner Sir William Temple supposes it' (II, 191–2 [214–15]). On this point, it can be safely argued that Mandeville shares Temple and Hume's empirical and naturalistic approach to the formation and development of human society. Mandeville also (though critically) mentions Temple's *Observations upon the United Provinces of the Netherlands* (1673) in Remark 'Q' (I: 189 [207]).
9. It is also interesting to note that Walter Moyle in *An Essay upon the Constitution of the Roman Government*, written around 1698, divides power into imaginary and real, although he regards the former as occupying a role subordinate to the latter: 'Imaginary

power is authority founded upon opinion: real power is authority founded upon dominion and property' ([1723] 1969: 217).

10. According to Parkin, Anthony Ascham was the first person to formulate the *de facto* theory from Hobbes's works preceding the *Leviathan* (2007: 72, 88). See also Hardin 2007: 212–24.
11. Hobbes is not a naïve realist, but he considers that our sense-impressions or internal 'phantasms' follow the general laws of motion and that, based on this supposition, we can conjecture the external world of material objects following the same laws (Tuck 1997: xvi–xvii). Hobbes's rejection of matter-spirit dualism, or what Gaskin calls his 'one-world realism' in *De Corpore* [1655] is much closer to Hume's, if we take both to be sceptical realists (Gaskin 1994: xxv).
12. In a similar vein, Hobbes argues that '[r]eputation of power, is power; because it draweth with it the adherence of those that need protection' ([1651] 1996: 62 [I.10]), though he merely touches on the subject, along with many other kinds of power such as riches, friends, nobility, and so on.
13. In religious opinions, however, Shaftesbury is an advocate of diversity (Carey 2004: 135–4, 142–9).
14. '[Bentham] certainly thought that in his mode of applying the principle he was breaking new ground. He neatly distinguished his own approach in this respect from that of Hume when he said in a letter to Dumont in 1822 that Hume had used the principle [of utility] "to account for that which is – I to show what ought to be"' (Dinwiddy 1989: 39).
15. As Gunn emphasises, the prevalence of the democratic notion of 'public opinion' was much more limited even in mid eighteenth-century France than has often been considered to be the case, and Rousseau should not be deemed a major proponent of such a notion (1995: chap. 5; Rousseau [1762] 1997: 141 [IV.vii]; see also Chisick 2002). As for Rousseau's notion of opinion, see Shklar 1969: 75–102.
16. Éléonore Le Jallé argues the same point on Hume's notion of 'manners' (2001: 127).
17. Hume's notion of opinion could be better understood as a form of convention in a broad sense, and the recent studies by Russell Hardin and Andrew Sabl also repeatedly emphasise the nature of indeterminacy in Hume's political theory (Hardin 2007: 47, 158, 171, 227; Sabl 2012: 32). Despite its apparent closeness to this sense of convention, however, Hume himself chooses to use the word

'opinion' rather than 'convention' after the *Treatise*, especially in his arguments on constitution.

18. For more extensive and detailed analysis of Hume's *History* as a narration of common belief (croyance commune) or popular belief (croyance populaire) in authority and legitimacy, see Gautier 2005.
19. Livingston considers Hume's analysis of the Puritan Revolution in the *History* to be a parallel of Burke's *Reflections* (1984: chap. 12), but his discussion does not sufficiently accentuate Hume's criticism of the myth of the ancient constitution.
20. For the thesis that Hume reversed the causal relation between liberty and commerce in the *History*, see Sakamoto 1995: chap. 5; Sakamoto 2003: 99; Wootton 2009: 460–1. On Hume as a pioneer of economic history, see Stockton 1976.
21. Forbes pointed out that 'this note on the ancient constitution was added to the *History* in 1763' (1975b: 267).
22. According to Pocock, Burke 'rejects the empiricist mystique of the immemorial' while endorsing the prescriptive constitution (1989b: 225). Pocock terms this 'a partial rationalization of the traditional common-law doctrine' (229). As for the difference between common lawyers and Hume, see McArthur 2007: chap. 3.
23. Expressions similar to 'the present established practice of the age' are too numerous to list in the *History*: just to cite two, 'the universal established principles of the/that age' (H III, 467 Note [A]; V, 552 Note [G]). Gerald J. Postema correctly points out that '[w]hat is most fundamental to legitimacy', for Hume, is 'the fact of its present wide acceptance' (1986: 90).
24. For this reason, paradoxically, Janice Lee observes that '[i]n general, the conservative historians [of the late eighteenth century] made relatively little use of Burke and his more sophisticated repudiation of the ancient constitution myth' and that 'the conservatives' closest affinity lay not with Burke but with David Hume' (1985: 178).
25. Hume's defence of the early Stuart monarchs was where he departed from the Court Whigs, who seldom failed to invoke the tyranny of these kings in their claim that the ancient constitution had been fully restored by the Glorious Revolution.
26. The paragraph of the *History* cited above seems to paraphrase some sentences of Montesquieu's *Considérations sur les causes de la grandeur des Romains et de leur decadence* (*Considerations on the Causes of the Greatness of the Romans and their Decline*): 'It is an error to believe that any human authority exists in the world which is despotic in all respects. There never has been one, and never will

be, for the most immense power is always confined in some way [...]. [Montesquieu here used the same example of 'Grand Sinior' as Hume's] There exists in each nation a general spirit on which power itself is based, and when it shocks this spirit strikes against itself and necessarily comes to a standstill' ([1734] 1999: 210).

27. As for the analytical discussions from the perspective of the coordination theory, see Hardin 2007: 126–9; Sabl 2012: 103–7, 115–17.
28. As for a favourable opinion of Hume's 'contextualised' view, see a review published in *Göttingische Anzeigen von gelehrten Sachen* (Anon. [1755] 2002: I, 22–5).
29. In the same vein as Hume, Temple argues in 'Of Popular Discontents' that '[t]hese opinions and pretences divided the nation into parties, so equal in number or in strength, by the weight of the established government on the one hand, and the popular humour on the other, as produced those long miseries, and fatal revolutions of the Crown and nation, between 1641 and 1660' (1754 : II, 374; see also 'Essay upon the Original and Nature of Government' (II, 55–6)).

4

'Refinement' and 'Vicious Luxury': Hume's Nuanced Defence of Luxury

As we saw in the previous chapter, the images of Hume as a political philosopher and historian have often been deemed inconsistent and paradoxical. For his contemporaries, the apology for the Stuart monarchs is incompatible with the serious support of the Revolution settlement, both of which the notion of opinion enables Hume to do. Compared with his seemingly ambiguous standpoint in the *History*, his defence of luxury has been considered to be too optimistic. For example, Duncan Forbes who characterises Hume as a 'Sceptical Whig' evaluates him in the essay 'Of Refinement in the Arts' to be 'at his least sceptical: he had none of the doubts and misgivings which Adam Smith and all the other leading thinkers of the Scottish Enlightenment had about the all-round benefits of commercial civilization' (Forbes 1975b: 87–8). Such assessments are not confined to Hume scholars. A contemporary French reviewer of Hume's *Political Discourses* (1752) commented on his essay of luxury that '[t]his formidable sceptic seems at last to have changed his tone. He appears to be moved by the interest of his fellow-citizens: he wants to show them the route to happiness' (Anon. 1752: 244, quoted in and translated by Malherbe 2005: 54). Certainly Hume is one of the most resolute promoters of luxury (Sekora 1977; Goldsmith 1988; Berry 1994; Shovlin 2008). In the second *Enquiry*, published just before the *Political Discourses*, clearly mentioning the issue of luxury, he states:

> those who prove or attempt to prove, that such refinements rather tend to the encrease of industry, civility, and arts, regulate anew our *moral* as well as *political* sentiments and represent as laudable and innocent what had formerly been regarded as pernicious and blameable. (EPM 2.21; 181)

He regarded himself, no doubt, as one of those who undertook this task of promoting the potential benefits of luxury. However, when we closely re-examine *how* he attempts to 'regulate anew our *moral* and *political* sentiments', the answer is not so clear. It becomes still more complex when we take into account Hume's awareness of the negative effects of pernicious luxury in the very essay 'Of Refinement in the Arts'. If Hume admitted that luxury could produce bad effects in some circumstances, what after all is original in his defence of luxury?

To answer this question, it is useful to compare Hume's method of defending luxury with the approaches of other thinkers such as Mandeville, Montesquieu, Rousseau and Adam Smith. Together with them, Hume committed himself to the broader project of substituting Christian virtues with a more secular morality. In this programme, Hume was widely deemed 'Epicurean' among his contemporaries, but he is so in a peculiar way. His complete silence on the issue of the gap between reality and appearances – one of the features of Augustinian thought – is one of his distinctive features in the luxury debate. His originality also lies in his pointing out that 'a sense of honour' or 'a love of fame' plays a central role in promoting our sociability and in expanding the sphere of the 'conversable world'. In his emphasis on sociability, Hume was influenced by – or rather, he consciously adopted – Shaftesbury's defence of luxury, which provides Hume with a more sophisticated account of how to refine social intercourse through the enjoyment of luxury. On the other hand, it is also remarkable that Hume sufficiently acknowledges the possible negative effects of luxury; this aspect is also reasonably anticipated from his observation on how our sentiments of economic conceptions, including luxury, depend upon 'a change in the manners and customs of the people' (E 294). In analysing both the positive and negative effects of luxury, he maintains close attention to the inter-subjective psychological processes produced by changing circumstances.

The conclusion deduced from the following arguments on Hume's strategy will, I believe, not be ambiguous or undecided, although the term 'nuanced' might suggest so. Rather, I will show that he integrates various philosophical traditions and discourses in the way most appropriate to his empirical observation of human nature and his agenda for the secularisation of moral theory.

1 Hume's Political and Moral Defence of Luxury

This section traces Hume's argument concerning luxury, as it appears in the first half of the essay 'Of Refinement in the Arts', first published under the title 'Of Luxury', in the *Political Discourses* (1752). Like many contemporaries, he begins his discussion by pointing out the ambiguities inherent in the word 'luxury'. He evolves his own definition of luxury, and on that basis proceeds to criticise two extreme – libertine and ascetic – attitudes towards it. This allows him to qualify his own conception of luxury, which he defends in the discussion that follows. Refinement, the form of luxury he is prepared to accept as beneficial, must meet three conditions: (1) it does not require those who enjoy it to neglect other virtues such as benevolence, generosity or paternal duties; (2) it does not force one to forgo the pleasures of conversation with friends or; (3) to lose reputation (E 269; see also 279; EPM 9.25; 283–4; Stafford (ed.) 1997: 619). If luxury is redefined as 'refinement', then Hume can safely conclude that 'the ages of refinement are both the happiest and most virtuous' (E 269), and that the links between industry, knowledge and humanity are 'peculiar to the more polished, and what are commonly denominated, the more luxurious ages' (271).[1]

The expression 'commonly denominated' plays a central role in the efficacy of Hume's argument. The change of the title of this essay in the edition of 1760 from 'Of Luxury' to that which it now bears afforded him the possibility of stating his message without using the word 'luxury', which brought to the minds of so many of his contemporaries such negative connotations as effeminacy, decline, inequality and lack of virtue. Etymologically, the word 'luxury' (*luxuria* in Latin from *luxus*) denotes 'excess'. Hume's careful wording allows him to separate what he calls refinement from the negative connotations of the word luxury ('the finer arts, which are commonly denominated the arts of luxury' (E 256); 'refinement in the arts, or what they are pleased to call luxury' (H III, 76)).

Hume explains the influence of the introduction of luxury on the manners of people in both private and public life. In terms of private life, by enjoying new and splendid things, he argues that people achieve 'a relish for action and pleasure' (E 270). By engaging in their profession in order to acquire such things, he contends that they also acquire new vigour and spirit, in contrast to the indolence, inactivity and lethargy that had characterised their former ways of life. The objects of luxury are thus not only appreciated by the few who have a taste for them and the ability to acquire them, but also function to stimulate the industriousness of common people who are desirous of luxury. As Hume acknowledges, avarice is universal to human nature (E 'Rise and Progress' 113), but luxury is indispensable to unfold it thoroughly.

In terms of public life, once luxury awakens the spirit of industry and promotes commerce, Hume argues that it has a ripple effect, improving not only the knowledge of mechanical arts, but also refinement in the liberal arts. As for international relations, Hume emphasises a further merit which luxury brings about: it normally promotes imitation of prosperous neighbouring countries, a phenomenon, which he calls 'noble emulation' (E 'Rise and Progress' 135; see also 119). Provided a nation does not aim to become 'a monopolizer of wealth' (L I, 272), rather attempting to activate the spirit of industriousness in other nations ('If the spirit of industry be preserved', or 'as long as they all remain industrious and civilized' (E 'Jealousy of Trade' 330, 329)), imitation and emulation will bring out the capacity of each country to the full (Berdell 1996).

Moreover, according to Hume's analysis, we need not fear the allegedly inevitable enervation of the martial spirit. In the discourse of the age, it was often believed that luxury tended necessarily to make men corrupt and effeminate. This assumption rested upon the classical ideal of the rude but courageous people of the ancient republics. Hume dismisses such worries, and explains that 'a sense of honour' and discipline, if regulated well, could be an adequate substitute for the martial spirit, and as such is more suitable for 'ages of knowledge and refinement' (E 274, 276). A similar argument can be found in *A True Account of the Behaviour and Conduct of Archibald Stewart, Esq.*, which he published anonymously in 1747. In this pamphlet Hume depicted the uncultivated highlanders as 'ignorant of Discipline as the Low-Country Ploughman' and as having little knowledge of 'the Nature of Encampments, Marches, Ranks, Evolutions, Firing, and all the other Parts of military Exercise, which preserves Order in an Army, and render it so formidable' (TA 236 [6]). Although Hume's emphasis upon the development of military discipline and knowledge seems to be more suited to a standing army than to militia, he nevertheless upholds the view that the sense of honour and military discipline are not confined to the former, as he lays out a plan for the latter in the essay 'Idea of a Perfect Commonwealth'.[2]

Certainly Hume's discussion of luxury in the *Political Discourses* is oriented towards its economic implications, but his discussion of the term 'refinement' also moves beyond economics. Hume here emphasises two auxiliary phenomena which luxury brings out. The first of the two phenomena of which Hume speaks is the historical process, which produces alterations in people's manners and fosters new morals peculiar to the commercial age. The second is the process of continuous enjoyment of moderate luxury, which produces conditions favourable to the maintenance of morals. In the following, we shall discuss these two points in turn.

In the essay 'Of Commerce', which is placed directly before 'Of Refinement in the Arts' in the *Political Discourses*, Hume describes how 'the *pleasures* of luxury and the *profits* of commerce' awaken in those who already feel their own '*delicacy* and *industry*' (E 264). In the *History*, Hume repeatedly discussed the historical contingency of how the general 'manners of the age' shifted with societal change, giving rise to '[t]he habits of luxury' (H IV, 384). Those changes in manners are related to the historical emergence of what Hume refers to as the middling rank of men, 'who are the best and firmest basis of public liberty' (E 277) and who 'rose by slow degrees to their present importance; and in their progress made arts and commerce, the necessary attendants of liberty and equality, flourish in the kingdom' (H II, 109). According to Hume, this process is bound to occur steadily because '[t]he advantages, which result from opulence, are so solid and real', while '[t]he distinctions of birth and title' are 'more empty and imaginary' (V, 132).[3] Furthermore, when dealing with the Cromwellian era, he related the prevalence of democratic principles to the shift in attitudes meaning 'commerce has ever since been more honourable in England than in any other European kingdom' (VI, 148; see also E 93).

Hume argues that such a change of situation as that which took place in England following the Civil War, forms and fosters moral virtues peculiar to modern society; namely, industry, diligence, frugality and honesty, which appear more valuable than courage or military prowess. He emphasises the importance of commercial virtues in his second *Enquiry*: 'What need is there to display the praises of INDUSTRY [...]?' (EPM 6.10; 237). In contrast, in the earlier *Treatise of Human Nature*, with its catalogue of virtues, the commercial values play a less important role (T 3.3.1.24; 587; 3.3.4.7; 610). This suggests that, at this stage, Hume had not yet paid much attention to the full implications of the historical shift in morality.

Hume's unabashed defence of luxury in social interaction was bound to lead him onto more sensitive ground. In the essay 'Of Refinement' he remarks approvingly that '[b]oth sexes meet in an easy and sociable manner' (E 271) and emphasises the positive aspects of the increase in social interaction between men and women (the term 'commerce' had not only commercial, but also similar sexual connotations to 'intercourse' (Pocock 1985a: 540)). Traditionally, women and luxury had been seen as inextricably connected. Many eighteenth-century moralists and philosophers linked licentiousness and 'libertine love' closely to their discussion of the perils of a luxurious way of life, especially in their analyses of the corruptions of urban life (Berry 1994: 76–7).

Hume's way of defending this type of social intercourse is dexterous. Firstly, he concedes that 'libertine love, or even infidelity to the marriage-bed, be more frequent in polite ages, when it is often regarded only as a piece of gallantry'. Yet, he immediately goes on to remark, 'drunkenness, on the other hand, is much less common' (E 272). For Hume, the increase of infidelity is a kind of necessary evil and relatively less harmful than drunkenness.[4] Such a view must have been provocative to his contemporaries, especially since it appears consistently throughout his writings. In the second *Enquiry*, he contrasts French and Greek gallantry in order to highlight the latter's bad influence on public order and standards of decency. What Hume means by 'Greek gallantry' here is homosexuality and the marriage of half-brothers and sisters (EPM 'A Dialogue' 28–9; 334), while the French variety is 'that of amours and attachments, not that of complaisance' (48 footnote 93; 340n.2). He acknowledges the difficulty in choosing which form is more acceptable, but remarks that French gallantry is 'much more natural and agreeable' (32; 335). Why, then, does Hume consider love between man and woman less pernicious than other passions such as drunkenness? He explains in 'Of National Characters' that 'the passion for liquor be more brutal and debasing than love, which, when properly managed, is *the source of all politeness and refinement*' (E 215. Italics added; see also Susato 2007).[5] For Hume, the defender of civilisation in the modern world, social intercourse between men and women is a means to softening people's manners through the formalities of politeness involved in social interaction between the two sexes. As we will see in Chapter 8, these explicit remarks on libertine love sufficed both to strengthen his image as Epicurean (in its vulgar sense) and to provoke James Beattie.

To clarify the nature of Hume's contribution to the luxury debates, some comparisons with other philosophers will be useful. The defence of 'moderate luxury' in the *Political Discourses* is not Hume's intellectual monopoly: we can trace back its origins to Jean-François Melon (in the burgeoning field of political economy) (Hont 2006: 409–12), Joseph Addison (in 'polite' essays) ([1771–2] 1965: I, 235–6; Manning 2002: 67) and many others. Among them, Francis Hutcheson criticises the extremely rigorous notion of luxury as defined by Mandeville, and vindicates the enjoyment of moderate luxury by virtuous men. He remarks in his *Letters to the Dublin Journal* that 'the utmost improvement of Arts, Manufactures, or Trade, is so far from being necessarily Vicious, that it must rather Argue Good and Virtuous Dispositions' (Hutcheson [1726] 1997: 394).[6] Similarly to Hume, at least on this point, Hutcheson asserts that the enjoyment of moderate luxury by those who are fully virtuous is beneficial rather than harmful. However, Hutcheson merely demonstrates the compatibility of moral virtues with the enjoyment of luxury. On the other hand, as we will see below, Hume takes a step further by claiming that the enjoyment of luxury should be regarded as a condition favourable to the maintenance of morals. Although he calls these pleasures not 'virtuous' but just 'innocent', he considers that they can foster a new form of morality in commercial and refined nations. To put it another way, Hume emphasises the mutually facilitative relation between economic activities, our enjoyment of luxury, and the further refinement in our morality and knowledge (as Maurer (2012) and Sagar (2013) argue in detail, a broadly similar strategy to Hume's was taken by Archibald Campbell, who emphasised the love of esteem as a true self-love, though within the framework of providential order).

Hume's general vindication of commercial societies in the *Political Discourses* can be contrasted with Montesquieu's arguments on luxury in *De l'esprit des lois* (*The Spirit of Laws*). Despite his famous thesis of *doux commerce* ([1748] 1989: 338 [4.20.1]), Montesquieu basically differentiates commerce (or economic commerce) and luxury, and argues that only the former exists in republics, while the latter is permitted in monarchies (98 [1.7.2]; 340 [4.2.40]). Montesquieu often expresses sympathy towards the Spartan and Roman republics because of the consistency of their spirit of constitution with the lack of luxury: 'There was none [of luxury] among the Romans; there was none among the Lacedaemonians' (98 [1.7.2]; see also 48 [1.5.6]; Rawson 1991: 227–31, 238). Hume's point is, on the other hand, that luxury which cannot be separated from various aspects of commercial activities has no intrinsic negative effects in civilised societies, regardless of their political constitutions (Wootton 2009: 464). In the *Essays, Moral and Political* he sometimes admits that commerce flourishes better under republican governments than under absolute ones: 'Commerce, therefore, in my opinion, is apt to decay in absolute governments, not because it is there less *secure*, but because it is less *honourable*' (E 'Civil Liberty' 93). Nevertheless, Hume considered the France of his day, to be not an absolute monarchy, but a civilised one, where he believed the rule of law to be established to a certain degree. He assumed manners and customs in modern civilised countries, whether France or Britain, to be fundamentally different from those in the ancient republics. The fault line lies not between monarchy and republic, but between ancient and modern worlds. According to Hume in the *Political Discourses*, the 'ancient policy [of Sparta and Rome] was violent, and contrary to the more natural and usual course of things'. While he admits that such a violent policy 'may *sometimes* have no other effect than to render the public more powerful,' he argues, 'it is certain, that, in the common course of human affairs, it will have a quite contrary tendency' (E 'Commerce' 259–60). Contrasted with Montesquieu's preoccupation with the systematic classification of political constitutions, Hume's defence of luxury in modern society was fundamentally buttressed by his empirical understanding of human nature, and his phraseology regarding our economic activities in the *Political Discourses* aims to be thoroughly universal: 'Riches are valuable *at all times*, and *to all men*; because they *always* purchase pleasures, such as men are accustomed to, and desire' (276. Italics added). Although he distinguishes between innocent and vicious luxury, Hume does not systematically attach a specific type of luxury to any particular form of government.

This is not the place for an extensive comparison of Hume and

Voltaire on the issue of luxury; it will be sufficient to note that the two philosophers shared many intellectual sources (Bayle, Saint-Évremond, Melon and Mandeville[7]). More significantly, Voltaire's poem *Le Mondain* (1736) and the *Défense du mondain ou l'apologie du luxe* (1737) predated Hume's 'Of Refinement in the Arts' by over fifteen years. It is not improbable that Hume knew the verse and the controversy that followed its publication, because it coincided exactly with his youthful stay in La Flèche in Anjou while writing *A Treatise*. In some points, Voltaire's *Mondain* is more religiously provocative than Hume's essay, caricaturing the savagery of Adam and Eve in the allegedly pristine paradise (Voltaire 1968–: XVI, 295–313). This is partly because Voltaire did not intend to publish this verse (or, at least so he claimed) and, as he repeatedly insisted, it was merely a *badinage* (Maison 2003: 275). Still, Voltaire's emphasis in *Le Mondain* is on defence of the earthly enjoyment of personal consumption; in the *Défense* he underlined the socio-economic effects of consumption. The basic tenet on which this piece hinges is heavily reliant on Melon's *Essai politique sur le commerce*, published a year or two before *Le Mondain* (see his *Lettre de M. de Melon*) (Morize 1909: 111–29; Mason 2003: 283; Hont 2006: 412–18). Both verses seem to lack the moral dimensions that can be found in Hume's essays and the second *Enquiry*, as we will see below.[8]

Much later, in 1764, Voltaire repeats basically the same points made in the article on 'Luxe' in his *Dictionnaire philosophique*. This article is significant in itself because he seemed to intend a direct criticism of Rousseau. An unpublished note on the text, thought to have been written by Voltaire despite the lack of any decisive evidence for its identification,[9] remarks that 'every enemy of luxury should believe with Rousseau that the state of happiness and virtue for man is, not of the savage, but of the orang-outang' ([1764] 2010: 202; 1878: XX, 18n.1). This comment has two points in common with Hume's 'Of Refinement'. Firstly, Voltaire here states that a great inequality in fortunes is not the consequence of private property (as claimed by Rousseau) but of 'bad laws'. It reminds us of Hume's claim that the disorders in ancient Rome were actually caused not by luxury but by 'an ill modelled [sic] government' (E 276). Secondly, Voltaire recommends moralists to 'address their sermons to the legislators' because 'it is in the order of possible things that a virtuous and enlightened man may have the power to make reasonable laws' ([1764] 2010: 202; 1878: XX,

18n.1). This seems to have a more direct resonance with Hume's affirmation that 'the magistrate, who aims only at possibilities', should take the measure that is least pernicious to society (E 280). Moreover, in the article on 'Abeille' in the *Questions sur l'Encyclopédie* (1770), Voltaire again took up Mandeville's *Fable of the Bees*. He concluded it by claiming that 'it is very true that a well-governed society takes advantage of all the vices, but it is not true that these vices are necessary for the happiness of the people. They make very good remedies with poisons, but it is not poisons which make us live' (Voltaire 1968–: XXXVIII, 44–6).* It seems interesting to compare this with Hume's very similar phrases in 'Of Refinement'. To say that without a vicious luxury 'the labour would not have been employed at all', argues Hume, 'is only to say, that there is some other defect in human nature [...], for which luxury, in some measure, provides a remedy; as one poison may be an antidote to another. But virtue, like wholesome food, is better than poisons, however corrected' (E 279). Neither such a moral twist, nor the realism concerning policy-making that appears in Voltaire's later writings were found in *Le Mondain*. Certainly, the parallels between these works of Hume and Voltaire might be considered mere verbal similarities. Nevertheless, and apart from the possibility of mutual direct influence,[10] both swam with the same grand tide of secularisation. These two great infidels marked an intellectual watershed in the luxury debates in France and in Britain respectively.

2 Hume's Epicureanism and the Issue of Hypocrisy

It is not surprising that Hume's comprehensive and elaborate vindication of luxury attracted many contemporary criticisms, despite his cautious differentiation of his own position from Mandevillean libertine apologetics of luxury. This is mainly because, as we saw above, Hume included among the positive effects of luxury, not only the economic, but also the moral spheres. Many critics of Hume did not fail to discern the lurking danger of Epicureanism in his works on both morals and luxury. According to James Moore, Hume's moral theory – especially his theory of justice – can be

* 'Il est très vrai que la société bien gouvernée tire parti de tous les vices; mais il n'est pas vrai que ces vices soient necessaries au bonheur du monde. On fait de très bons remèdes avec des poisons, mais ce ne sont pas les poisons qui nous font vivre'.

considered Epicurean in some significant points. After distinguishing the 'more authentic or faithful reading of the great Epicurean moralists of antiquity' from the 'frivolous, popular tradition in which Epicureans were perceived to be lovers of sensuous pleasures', Moore sums up the characteristic themes of the former as 'the convention to abstain from the possessions of others', 'the argument that virtues are approved because of their usefulness and agreeableness', 'the idea that sympathy reinforces our approval of qualities which are useful and agreeable', and so on (1994: 27).[11] Although James A. Harris (2009) gives a rather negative evaluation of the usefulness of Epicureanism as a framework to characterise Hume's moral philosophy, it seems possible to be Epicurean without accepting its metaphysical and physiological understandings of human nature and the world. Rather, one of the characteristics of Hume's Sceptical Enlightenment lies in the combination between his consistent scepticism about the ultimate causes of our perceptions and his general acceptance of the social and political implications of Epicureanism (Chapters 1 and 2).[12] In a broader context, Hume's moral theory in general can be considered an intellectual attempt to secularise and demystify the operations of our morality without using any religious foundation. Paul Russell (2008) aptly terms Hume's irreligious and sceptical programme the 'Lucretian mission'. To discuss the issues of the Epicurean tradition as a whole is beyond the scope of this book and I owe much to Moore's and others' recapitulation of the points under discussion. It suffices here to point out that Hume's moral theory is generally, not exclusively, classified as one much closer to the Epicurean rather than the Stoic tradition. In what follows, I will trace how and why his contemporaries saw Hume as an Epicurean.

Although Hume refuses to identify his own position with those of Hobbes or Mandeville, the Humean defence of luxury in the essay 'Of Refinement' can be characterised as Epicurean because he declares that luxury 'has no natural tendency to beget venality and corruption' (E 276). Similar statements can be found in the essay 'Of the Pleasures' by the famous *libertine-sceptique* and French exile in England, Saint-Évremond. Hume owned the English translation of his collected works published in 1714 (Norton and Norton 1996: entry 444), whose editor and translator was Pierre Desmaizeaux, whose importance to the young Hume was mentioned in Chapter 2. Saint-Évremond declares: 'Let us endeavour only to Enjoy it with Moderation; and be assured that it is an

Error to Condemn Pleasures as *Pleasures*, and not as they are, Unjust and Unlawful' (Saint-Évremond 1714: III, 138–45; Morize 1909: 30–54; Moore 2002: 381).[13] These bold claims clearly echo the saying attributed to Epicurus that '[n]o pleasure is a bad thing in itself, but the things which produce certain pleasures entail disturbances many times greater than the pleasures themselves' (Epicurus 1994: 32 [Principal Doctrines, VIII]).[14]

Considered from this angle, it becomes clear that Hume's defence of luxury is not isolated from his more general vindication of worldliness in our moral evaluations. Hume's definition of virtue in the *Treatise* and the second *Enquiry* promotes a strongly secular understanding of moral virtues: he summarises the nature of virtues as characteristics 'useful or agreeable to themselves or others'. This typology of morality is one of the points that attracted much criticism from his contemporaries. James Balfour, Professor-to-be of Moral Philosophy at Edinburgh University, severely censored Hume's definition of virtue, because it contains not only the qualities of the mind, 'but the properties of the body, beauty, strength, and just proportion: nay, even external things, dress, riches, and indeed, by a necessary consequence, pleasures of every kind' (Balfour 1753: 116–17). More significantly, he continues:

> Our author's scheme of morality is, in effect, no other than the antient scheme which excluded religion, which Epicurus first reduced to some form, and clothed with a tolerably decent dress; he referred all to self-love and immediate enjoyment; but he excluded the grosser pleasures of sense, and introduced the virtues as subordinate ministers to the happiness he proposed. (123)

Balfour concludes that 'there is no other difference, but that the Epicureans used the word pleasure, where our author adopts that of virtue' (163; Sher 1990: 109–12). Here again, Balfour's understanding and usage of Epicureanism contains its somewhat vulgar aspects. To emphasise this might blur the distinction between the 'frivolous and popular' Epicurean tradition and the more 'authentic' one, an error that James Moore attempts to avoid. Nevertheless, Balfour is not completely off the mark in his attempt to encapsulate Hume's overall agenda in his moral theory. Hume not only accords with Epicurus in criticising wanton enjoyments of licentiousness; to highlight the innocuousness of pleasures is also essential for Hume who regards useful and agreeable qualities as sound objects of our moral evaluations.

In the eighteenth-century intellectual milieu, Hume's claim for the innocuousness of pleasures was closely related to a particular historical issue: namely, the cause of the collapse of the Roman Empire. Montesquieu, for example, pinpointed the Epicurean as one of the causes corrupting the Romans in the *Considérations sur les causes de la grandeur des Romains et de leur décadence* (1734) (Voltaire has a similar view. See Chapter 5). Contrasted with his panegyric to the Stoic (Montesquieu [1748] 1989: 465–6 [5.24.10]; 145 [2.7.16]), his attitude towards Epicureanism is hostile: 'I believe the sect of Epicurus, which was introduced at Rome toward the end of the republic, contributed much toward tainting the heart and mind of the Romans' (97). As Richard B. Sher points out, Adam Ferguson introduced the moralistic rhetoric of the civic humanism from Montesquieu into the discourse of the moderate literati of Edinburgh, among whom Christian Stoicism had previously been dominant (Sher 1985: 199–201, 237; 1990: 200–2). Ferguson counts himself among the modern Stoics, along with Montesquieu (1792: I, 8). In his *History of the Progress and Termination of the Roman Republic*, he emphasises the debauched and selfish nature of Epicurean moral doctrine (1783: II, 112–14). Despite the grouping of the Scottish Enlightenment thinkers around particular issues and their generally shared positive evaluation of commercial society, we should not undervalue the qualitative differences among its members.

On the other hand, Hume's endorsement of the Epicurean view of the innocuousness of pleasure would result in his support for this ancient philosophical tenet as socially, politically and even historically innocent. In the essay 'Of Refinement' Hume argues that the real cause of the decline of the Roman state was not luxury but 'an ill modelled [sic] government, and the unlimited extent of conquests' (E 276; see also McArthur 2007: chap. 4, esp. 96–100). Hume's strong claim on this point, although seemingly made in passing, attracted his contemporaries' attention. An anonymous writer wrote in *The Quintessence of Modern Philosophy Extracted from Ten Late Essays* as follows, mocking Hume's claims:

> III. To show, that Luxury is a most innocent Thing, and never ruined any State: – In which the Errors of the wisest Historians, and gravest Political Writers, that ascribed the Ruin of the *Roman* Commonwealth

> to this Cause, are confuted; and in which it is clearly proved, that they knew nothing of the Matter. (Anon. [c.1755])

Unsurprisingly, some eighteenth-century thinkers considered that Hume's endorsement of Epicureanism amounted to licentiousness and debauchery. John Brown, an English clergyman and essayist, who was critical of Hume's philosophical and religious positions, illustrated his own sense of the crisis he feared could result from Hume's irreligious and allegedly licentious philosophy. In Section 12 of his *Thoughts on Civil Liberty*, Brown listed some 'Enemies to their Country [Great Britain]' such as 'the noble Author of *Characteristics*' (Shaftesbury), Mandeville and Bolingbroke, who, Brown judged, attacked the Christian religion or opened the door to licentiousness. Brown continued to chastise the fourth person without mentioning his name:

> The last of these patriot Worthies, by which the present Age stands distinguished, is the Author of "Essays philosophical and moral:" Who, disdaining the vulgar Practice of a particular Attack, *undermines* all the *Foundations* of *Religion*, *revealed* and *natural*; and with a Pen truly *Epicurean*, dissolves at once all the *Fears* of the *Guilty*, the *Comforts* of the *Afflicted*, and the *Hopes* of the *Virtuous*. (Brown 1765: 102–3)

Brown's criticism of Hume's alleged Epicureanism does not completely exempt itself from the vulgar notion of that tradition. Nevertheless, what is important is that Hume as a defender of luxury has been almost always considered to belong to the Epicurean camp.[15]

Closely related to Hume's version of Epicureanism, here is another curious characteristic of his defence of luxury, though eclipsed by his bold defence of luxury; he never mentions one of the crucial issues in the luxury debate: the widening gap between reality and appearances in civilised societies. To put it another way, in his 'economic' essays, Hume never acknowledges the possible aggravation of vanity as a result of luxury or the potential consequences for society. In contrast, this is one of the central points for Mandeville, Rousseau and partially for Adam Smith.

Mandeville clearly states that 'it is impossible we could be sociable Creatures without Hypocrisy' ([1714/1729, 1732] 1988: I, 349 [401]). Elsewhere, he exemplifies this point more succinctly:

> It is this which encourages every Body, who is conscious of his little Merit, if he is any ways able, to wear Clothes above his Ranks, especially in large and populous Cities, where obscure Men may hourly meet with fifty Strangers to one Acquaintance, and consequently have the Pleasure of being esteem'd by a vast Majority, not as what they are, but what they appear to be: which is a greater Temptation than most People want to be vain. (I, 128 [130–1])

As E. J. Hundert points out, Mandeville here adhered to one of the Augustinian perspectives, the gap between reality and appearances in civilised societies – this is what Hundert calls 'theatricality', which was considered potentially destructive because of the threat it posed to social hierarchies (Hundert 1992: 95; see also Hundert 2005: 144).

Augustinianism, including the issue of theatricality, has sometimes been considered to be allied with Epicureanism. According to Pierre Force, the 'Stoicism' and the 'Epicurean/Augustinian' traditions constitute the grand intellectual frameworks for political discourses in the eighteenth-century British and French intellectual contexts and 'Augustinians and Epicureans have a common enemy, the Stoic' (2007: 59). This is because Augustine's depiction of the fallen human nature and its powerlessness in front of God's grace accords with the Epicurean criticism of the Stoic virtues based upon self-command. This Epicurean/Augustinian framework, Force claims, is one of the important intellectual counterbalances of Stoicism in the eighteenth century, although, as I will argue later, the extent to which this dichotomy is appropriate for representing Hume's position in the luxury debate is questionable.

Hundert correctly points out that one of Mandeville's contributions to the luxury debate is that he 'abandoned entirely the effective, and originally Platonic, corollary of this view, that is, that public theatrics were necessarily destructive of the political body and the social fabric' (2005: 151). Hence Mandeville's (in)famous thesis: 'Private Vices, Publick Benefits'. Even so, it should be admitted that according to his moral framework, hypocrisy remains one of the private vices, which is rooted in our vanity or 'self-liking' and reinforced by education: 'In all Civil Societies', Mandeville avers, 'Men are taught insensibly to be Hypocrites from their Cradle' ([1714/1729, 1732] 1988: I, 348–9 [402]).

Jean-Jacques Rousseau sublimated this issue into the quintessence of his overall criticism of civilisation, possibly through

Montesquieu, who attributed to 'the author of The Fable of the Bees' the following sentence: 'The more men there are together, the more vain they are, and the more they feel arise within them the desire to call attention to themselves by small things' (Montesquieu [1748] 1989: 97 [1.7.1]). Dennis C. Rasmussen appropriately adopts the phrase of 'the empire of opinion' from Rousseau's *Lettre à M. d'Alembert sur les spectacles* to represent the Rousseauean criticism of the worsening tendency of this Augustinian theatricality in civilised society (Rasmussen 2008: 12–13; see also 30–5, 76–83; Starobinski [1957] 1988; Shklar 1959: chap. 3). This is most distinctively exemplified in a sentence of the *Discours sur l'origine de l'inégalité* (*Discourse on the Origin of Inequality*): 'the Savage lives within himself; sociable man, always outside himself, is capable of living only in the opinion of others [. . .]' (Rousseau [1755] 1997: 187 [II.57]). The distinction between reality and appearances is one of the recurring themes in Rousseau's writings. He repeats Mandeville almost verbatim, and Smith translates the sentence to include in his 'Letter to the Authors of the *Edinburgh Review*': 'To be and to appear to be, became two things entirely different, and from this distinction arose imposing ostentation, deceitful guile, and all the vices which attend them' (Smith [1756] 1982: 252; Rousseau [1755] 1997: 170 [II.27], quoted in Rasmussen 2008: 69; see also Rousseau [1762] 1990–2010: 383).

Compared to Rousseau, Adam Smith's commitment to the issue of the 'empire of opinion' or Augustinian theatricality is less unconditional (Rasmussen 2008: 12–13). Although Smith less frequently uses negative terms such as 'hypocrisy' or 'dissimulation' in discussing the issue, the distinction between praise and praise-worthiness is one of Smith's preoccupations in his *Theory of Moral Sentiments*, and he terms those people who desire to be praised, rather than to be praise-worthy, 'hypocrites of wealth and greatness, as well as of religion and virtue' ([1759] 1982: 64 [I.iii.3.7]). Like Rousseau, Smith explains this mechanism with reference to vanity: 'To be observed, to be attended to, to be taken notice of with sympathy, complacency, and approbation, are all the advantages which we can propose to derive from it. It is the vanity, not the ease, or the pleasure, which interests us' (50 [I.iii.2.1]). Smith admits that there are 'two different roads' – one of wisdom and virtue, the other of wealth and greatness, 'equally leading to the attainment' of 'the respect and admiration' of others' (62 [I.iii.3.2]), and that the majority of humankind usually prefers the former to the latter. Nevertheless, Smith's approval of vanity as the engine of commercial societies is far less unequivocal than Hume's. Along with his emphasis on the virtue of self-command, the issue of the gap between reality and appearances can be traced back to his Stoicism, with which the Augustinianism can easily ally, *pace* Force (Sagar 2013: esp. 806–13).[16] In short, a concern over the issue of hypocrisy in civilised societies is shared by Mandeville, Rousseau and partially by Smith (Force 2007: 46). Although Smith views this process rather less negatively, all three believe that in civilised and commercial societies we are prompted to an endless search for novelty and vanity because the pressure of the market tends to reinforce our dependence upon the opinions of others (Hundert 2005: 230).

Considering the shared issue of the development of hypocrisy in civilised societies, it seems significant to note how sharply Hume distanced himself from Mandeville, Rousseau and Smith with his silence on this point. The general tenor of Hume's arguments in the essay on luxury is distinctive for the (almost) complete absence of the issue of possible increase of hypocrisy in commercialised societies. Despite his debt to Mandeville in some significant points (Tolonen 2013: chap. 4),[17] Hume in his 'economic' essays hardly ever uses the words such as 'pride' or 'vanity' in negative senses. In the essay 'Of Refinement' he never mentions the words 'hypocrisy' or 'dissimulation'. The word 'vanity' occurs only once in this essay: 'They flock into cities [...]. Curiosity allures the wise; vanity the foolish; and pleasure both' (E 271). This sole reference to vanity is not only passing, but also innocuous, compared with the ways in which Mandeville, Rousseau and Smith mention the same word. For Hume, the growing intensity of social intercourse in civilised societies provides us, not with an increased risk of hypocrisy, but rather with favourable conditions under which we may ameliorate our morality.

3 A Sense of Honour and the Rules of Good Breeding

According to Hume, luxury has no intrinsic tendency either to degenerate human morals or to promote hypocrisy among the members of refined societies. Rather, the increase of social communication through enjoying luxurious goods, Hume maintains, can be a very effective means both to harness our greed and develop polite manners: 'Nor can any thing restrain or regulate the love of money, but a sense of honour and virtue: which, if it be not nearly equal at all times, will naturally abound in ages of knowledge and refinement' (E 276). Hume believes that luxury tends to promote a 'spectatorial' basis for honour and reputation. In other words, it increases the number of onlookers evaluating our behaviour. The emergence of this new type of honour is conditioned by refinement, the product of innocent luxury, which Hume argues was most commonly found in commercial societies. This view contrasts with that of Montesquieu, who restricts this sense of honour to aristocrats. In fact, Hume also regards the sense of honour referred to by Montesquieu favourably, as preserving 'all ideas of nobility, gentry, family' and stabilising the existing social order (E 'Public Credit' 358). Nonetheless, what Hume calls 'a sense of honour' in the essay 'Of Refinement' is quite different from the inherited honour of the landed aristocracy.

A similar notion of a sense of honour appears in the second *Enquiry*. Although Hume does not use the phrase 'a sense of honour' in this book, he refers to a notion coextensive with it, namely 'the love of fame', which plays a central role in his moral theory (EPM 9.10; 276). 'The love of fame' is not intended to signify the wish to acquire wealth or temporal reputation, rather it is pride based upon the perceived praiseworthiness and creditability of one's character. Hume deems absurd and nonsensical the successful acquisition of the 'worthless toys and gewgaws' of worldly wealth if it requires sacrificing one's good character (9.25; 283).

More importantly, Hume's discussion of the 'rules of good breeding' in the *Treatise* is consistent with his position in the essays 'Of Commerce' and 'Of Refinement', and the second *Enquiry*. Certainly, Hume in the *Treatise* seems provocative, *à la* Mandeville, by admitting the positive workings of pride; one of the vices according to Christian morality. Yet, unlike Mandeville's, even in the *Treatise*, Hume's explanation of the formation and mechanism of politeness and good manners has no paradoxical connotation. This is because the establishment and development of the rules of good breeding is, for Hume, not hypocrisy which tends to augment the gap between reality and appearances, but a desired and necessary social skill to avoid anti-social contradictions and oppositions that would arise from any display of naked pride or ambition. To acquire this skill consequently contributes a more sophisticated satisfaction of our pride 'in an oblique manner':

> we establish the *rules of good-breeding*, in order to prevent the opposition of men's pride, and render conversation agreeable and inoffensive [...]. That impertinent, and almost universal propensity of men, to overvalue themselves, has given us such a *prejudice* against self-applause, that we are apt to condemn it by a *general rule* wherever we meet with it [...]. (T 3.3.2.10; 598)

Hume considers praiseworthy 'a genuine and hearty pride, or self-esteem, if well conceal'd and well founded' as something that is 'essential to the character of a man of honour' (3.3.2.11; 598). In order to develop this skill, '[t]he intercourse of sentiments, therefore, in society and conversation' (3.3.3.1; 603) is absolutely essential. Here there is no room for Mandevillean paradox (cf. Mandeville's comment on 'Good Manners': 'instead of extinguishing, they rather inflame the Passions' [1714/1729, 1732] 1988: I, 79 [73]).[18] This is also an important dividing line between Hobbes and Hume. According to Hobbes, there is no sociability in our human nature; even when people get together, 'it is still evident that what they primarily enjoy is their own glory [*gloria*] and not society'. Hobbes reduces '[e]very pleasure of the mind' to 'either glory (or a good opinion of oneself), or ultimately relates to glory'. Unlike Hume, Hobbes never admits the possibility of the general rules of society having been spontaneously produced by the working of imagination and sympathy. For Hobbes, who recognises that 'no large or lasting society can be based upon the passion for glory' ([1642] 1997: 22–4 [I.2]), the only means with which to overcome the endless conflicts produced by vainglory is the establishment of absolute sovereignty.

The issue of honour in Hume's moral theory is also deeply linked with the controversy over the possibility of 'a society of Atheists' first ignited by Pierre Bayle. In his *Pensées diverses sur la comète*, Bayle argues that a society without religion could not only exist but could also operate on moral principles, as much as or even more so than Christian societies. This is because, as the philosopher of Rotterdam argues, atheists 'are restrained by the harsh law of honor, which exposes them to infamy when they succumb to the natural inclination' (Bayle [1682] 2000: 200). Bayle repeatedly emphasises the significance of 'the desire to be praised', 'the love of a fine reputation' and 'the fear of "what will people say?"'. Interestingly, Bayle illustrates this point by citing as examples 'the chastity of women' and 'a matter of honor' (212, 202, 200–4, 215), just as Hume does in his explanation of artificial virtues in the *Treatise* (T 3.2.12; 570–3).[19] The criticism that Hume directed towards Mandeville is grounded in his belief in the naturalness and sanity of the aspect of human nature that leads people to want not only to show off their property and emulate others, but also to avoid what are perceived to be indecent and antisocial behaviours. According to Hume, as well as Bayle, vanity is not a private vice, nor politeness a dissimulation.

On the other hand, Hume considers that the ascetic way of life led by priests is pernicious to human societies because of the mechanisms produced by '*artificial* lives' (EPM 'A Dialogue' 52–7; 341–3). Such a lifestyle, according to Hume, consists of a vicious cycle of hypocrisy and insincerity. Despite his complete silence on the issue of hypocrisy in his discussions of commercial societies, Hume willingly adopts the critical discourse concerning clergy and religious hypocrisy from Mandeville and Shaftesbury (Chapter 5). In the *History*, especially in his depiction of the advancement of the puritans, Hume developed the logic of 'the artificial lives' in more detail:

> when the enthusiastic spirit met with such honour and encouragement [...]; it was impossible to [...] confine, within any natural limits, what was directed towards an infinite and supernatural object. Every man, as prompted by the warmth of his temper, excited by emulation, or supported by his habits of hypocrisy, endeavoured to distinguish himself beyond his fellows, and to arrive at a higher pitch of saintship and perfection. (H V, 441–2)[20]

Because of such a self-deception, a pernicious and unbounded sort of emulation occurs and prevails among the religious sects. This is exactly the type of emulation Hume believes society should endeavour to avoid, along with pernicious political factions. Interestingly, Hume's use of the terms 'hypocrisy' and 'dissimulation' both in the *Essays, Moral and Political* and the *Political Discourses* are almost exclusively confined to the well-known footnote in the essay 'Of National Characters', in which he criticises the occupational mentality of the priest (E 199–201). Hume's silence on the long-established issue of the increasing hypocrisy in polished societies and his longstanding criticism of priests because of their other-worldliness can be considered not only compatible, but also mutually reinforcing points.

4 Hume's Shaftesburian and Ciceronian Defence of Luxury

The distance that Hume put between himself and Mandeville on the augmentation of hypocrisy among luxurious societies let the Scottish philosopher approach the position of Shaftesbury that Mandeville criticised, despite the considerable tendencies towards Epicureanism evident in Hume's defence of luxury.

The similarity between Hume and Shaftesbury on the issue of politeness has been pointed out, despite their seeming or real differences on other points (as for Hume's own criticism of Shaftesbury, see, for example, T footnote 50 to 1.4.6; 254n.; EPM 1.4; 170–1). For example, Iain Hampsher-Monk argues that '[t]here are strong parallels between Shaftesbury and Hume in their moral naturalism, their arguments about refinement and their case for sociability' (2002: 91). Shaftesbury emphasises how much higher pleasures are natural affections, such as love, generosity, benevolence, and so on, compared with private and selfish affections, much less unnatural affections. Despite his claims concerning the artificiality of justice, Hume never denies the existence or the excellence of some natural virtues (Moore 1976: 24–30, 38). To confirm this point emphatically (learning the lessons of the *Treatise*), Hume underlined the innateness of our social virtues of humanity and benevolence in the second *Enquiry*.

The similarity on the issue of luxury between Hume and Shaftesbury is no more evident than in some key sentences in the latter's *Inquiry concerning Virtue or Merit* (1699). Here, Shaftesbury defends our capacity to feel natural and kind affections through 'an enjoyment of good by communication, a receiving it, as it were, by reflection or by way of participation in the goods of others, and a pleasing consciousness of the actual love, merited esteem or approbation of others'. According to Shaftesbury, most enjoyment of luxury, or even what Shaftesbury calls a 'debauch', carries with it 'a plain reference to society or fellowship'. If it loses any connections with 'all society or fellowship', Shaftesbury asserts, it would not be called by that very word, but be described just as 'a surfeit or excess of eating or drinking'

([1711] 1999: 204, 212; Hont 2006: 395–9). Along the same lines, Hume in the essay 'Of Refinement' argues that 'it is impossible but [people] must feel an encrease of humanity, from the very habit of conversing together, and contributing to each other's pleasure and entertainment' (E 271).

To demonstrate the positive mental effects caused by the enjoyment of natural and kind affections, Shaftesbury frequently testifies to the differences 'between solitude and company, between a common company and that of friends, the reference of almost all our pleasures to mutual converse, and the dependence they have on society either present or imagined'. For Shaftesbury, as well as for Hume, the place where refined and sophisticated people get together is the best to cultivate and develop our natural affections: 'the ostentation of elegance, and a certain emulation and study how to excel in their sumptuous art of living,' Shaftesbury asserts, 'goes very far in the raising such a high idea of it as is observed among the men of pleasure' ([1711] 1999: 202, 212). It seems almost unnecessary to mention that similar declarations are easily found in Hume's writings. In the essay 'Of the Rise and Progress of the Arts and Sciences' he asserts that '[a] noble emulation is the source of every excellence' (E 135). The positive cycle of sophistication of our tastes and learning is one of the central points in his essay 'Of Refinement':

> The more these refined arts advance, the more sociable men become [...]. They flock into cities; love to receive and communicate knowledge; to show their wit or their breeding; their taste in conversation or living, in clothes or furniture. (E 271)

Vivid contrasts between 'indolence, indifference [and] insensibility' (Shaftesbury [1711] 1999: 214) and 'industry, knowledge, and humanity' (E 271, 272) underlie both the former's *Inquiry* and the latter's essays. As Shaftesbury asserts that 'as they grow busy and employed, they grow regular and good' (Shaftesbury [1711] 1999: 214), Hume repeats that '[i]n times when industry and the arts flourish, men are kept in perpetual occupation, and enjoy, as their reward, the occupation itself, as well as those pleasures which are the fruit of their labour' (E 270).[21] As we saw in the previous chapter, Shaftesbury's solution to avoid fickle fancy and to maintain more consistent opinion is thoroughly Stoic in the sense that it depends heavily upon self-restraint; a strategy that Hume would have been unlikely to countenance.[22] In the present context, however, Hume clearly shares Shaftesbury's defence of luxury against the charges of bigotry and enthusiasm by promulgating the positive effects of the modest enjoyment of luxury.

Another, but related, point to note is that certain aspects of Hume's understanding of economic behaviour have been considered to have much to do with his version of the Stoic.[23] This was depicted earlier in one of the four sequential essays on happiness, 'The Stoic'. Through the mouth of the supposed Stoic, he tells us that nature urges the human being, 'by necessity, to employ on every emergence, his utmost *art* and *industry*' with which she originally endows us (E 146). His emphasis on the virtue of industry as a means to attain happiness in this essay anticipates his later claims in the several 'economic' essays: 'The great end of all human industry, is the attainment of happiness. For this were arts invented, sciences cultivated, laws ordained, and societies modelled, by the most profound wisdom of patriots and legislators' (148). Hume's Stoic warns us not to indulge ourselves in the 'luxurious pleasures' (150), which is significant considering the fact that 'The Stoic' directly follows 'The Epicurean'. However, this does not contradict, but rather corresponds to, his balanced view of the positive cycle of 'action, pleasure, and indolence' in the *Political Discourses*. Hume carefully emphasises that 'no one ingredient can be entirely wanting, without destroying, in some measure, the relish of the whole composition' (270). Eugene Rotwein points out, after admitting Hume shows a greater preference for the Epicurean and the Stoic than the Platonist viewpoints, that '[t]here would likewise seem to be no doubt that as between the positions of the Stoic and the Epicurean it was the former's emphasis on meaningful striving that Hume regarded as more ultimately significant for human well-being' (Rotwein 1970: xcvii).

However, what has not been fully investigated (especially in the field of the history of economic and political thought) is where Hume's version of the Stoic comes from, and how this is different from our common image of the Stoic. Adam Potkay is correct in pointing out that Hume's understanding of the Stoic is neither ascetic, nor indifferent to the suffering of others, much less based on providentialist metaphysics. He sums up the point as follows: 'Hume's "The Stoic" condenses Cicero's borrowing from Panaetius, with an added dash of Hutchesonian benevolence' (although the adjective 'Hutchesonian' might be replaced by 'Shaftesburian') and terms Hume's version 'a "soft" or moderated Stoicism' (2000: 78; see also Siebert 1990: 188).

More importantly, Hume's borrowing from Cicero takes us back to the issue of the theatricality, though not in the Augustinian, but in the Ciceronian version. Again, Potkay asserts that 'Hume's Stoic – and Hume's own moral theory – subscribe to a fundamental tenet of Cicero's "decorum"' (Potkay 2000: 69; Jones 1982: 41). Cicero, who highlights the role of *decorum*, that is, seemliness or propriety, actually detailed the art of conversation in which he recommended us to avoid 'to commend yourself, particularly if you do so untruthfully, or to imitate the "boastful soldier", arousing the ridicule of your listeners'. He also mentions the size and splendour of the house appropriate to one's social position (Cicero 1991: 52, 53–4). The viewpoint of others is considered here a catalyst, not to promote hypocrisy in our communication, but rather to nurture civility. This type of theatricality is that which Hume believes should be encouraged.

It would not be unexpected to find in Hume's defence of luxury some elements of both Epicureanism (the innocuousness of pleasures themselves) and of (Ciceronian) Stoicism (the significance of the *decorum*), once we understand which aspects Hume focuses upon within these ancient intellectual schools of thought. As Hume's work demonstrates, the adoption of, and adaptation to, strands of these (sometimes seemingly incompatible) intellectual 'traditions' are not necessarily mutually exclusive (Moore 2007: 133–4; see also Leddy and Lifschitz 2009: 5–10; Kavanagh 2010). Rather than being a passive recipient of the teachings of either philosophical camp, Hume appropriates aspects of each philosophy according to his own agenda. As we saw in Chapter 2, Hume's commitment to Epicureanism is decisively conditioned by his strong doubt of its confidence in materialism. In addition to this, in the context of the luxury debate, Hume's version of Epicureanism is distinctly severed from its Augustinian concomitant, which, according to Pierre Force, has been frequently allied with the former. Nevertheless, the Epicurean claim concerning the innocuousness of pleasures (and its irreligious tendencies) seems to be completely in tune with Hume's moral and economic theory.

On the other hand, Hume is consistent in his denial of the Stoic's asceticism and teleological cosmology, which seems incompatible with what he believes to be the 'true philosophy'. Some of the points for which he criticises the Stoic can be found in the first *Enquiry*: 'It is certain, that,' Hume argues:

> while we aspire to the magnanimous firmness of the philosophic sage, and endeavour to confine our pleasures altogether within our own minds, we may, at last, render our philosophy like that of EPICTETUS, and other STOICS, only a more refined system of selfishness, and reason ourselves out of all virtue, as well as social enjoyment. (EHU 5.1; 40; see also Rivers 2000: 248; Brooke 2012: 175–80)[24]

In spite of this fundamental criticism, some (Ciceronian) aspects of late Stoicism are not only appropriate, but also convenient for Hume's purpose of keeping himself from the gloomy, Augustinian, view of the fallen human nature, which prevailed among the 'modern' moral philosophers, such as Mandeville, Rousseau and Smith. On this point, Hume's version of the Stoic has something in common with Hume the Sceptic. Adam Potkay finds in Hume's essay 'The Sceptic' the same understanding that 'a necessary condition of our happiness is that it is reflected back to us in the agreeable eyes of others' (2000: 64). Actually, Hume's Sceptic preaches moderation and sociability: 'To be happy, the passion must neither be too violent nor too remiss', and 'the passion must be benign and social' and 'cheerful and gay' (E 168). He here seems to anticipate the basic tenet of 'Refinement in the Arts' by saying that '[i]t is certain, that a serious attention to the sciences and liberal arts softens and humanizes the temper [...]' (E 170). His prescription for happiness in the essay 'The Sceptic' does not fundamentally differ from Cicero (Rivers 2000: 250–5; Moore 2007: 135):

> the happiest disposition of mind is the virtuous; or, in other words, that which leads to action and employment, renders us sensible to the social passions, steels the heart against the assaults of fortune, reduces the affections to a just moderation, makes our own thoughts an entertainment to us, and inclines us rather to the pleasures of society and conversation, than to those of the senses. (E 168)

According to Hume, either the Stoic or the Sceptic, what matters is the presence of a spectator through whom we can cultivate our moral sentiments.

5 The Distinction between Vicious Luxury and Refinement

Since many contemporaries and scholars have taken Hume to be an ardent advocate of luxury, they often overlook the fact that he deals with the vicious form of luxury in the latter part of the essay 'Of Refinement'. This discussion occupies around one-fifth of the entire essay. Hume states that 'wherever luxury ceases to be innocent, it also ceases to be beneficial; and when carried a degree farther, begins to be a quality pernicious, though, perhaps, not the most pernicious, to political society' (E 278–9). Since Mandeville's *Fable of the Bees*, the ambiguity of the word 'luxury' has been a cliché, but Hume never uses this ambiguity to negate the distinction between innocent and vicious luxury. Throughout his writings, from the *Treatise* onwards, this distinction remained consistent. He claims that '*prodigality, luxury, irresolution, uncertainty*, are vicious, merely because they draw ruin upon us, and incapacitate us for business and action' (T 3.3.4.7; 611). The second *Enquiry* concludes with the following remark:

> And in a view to *pleasure*, what comparison between the unbought satisfaction of conversation, society, study, even health and the common beauties of nature, but above all the peaceful reflection on one's own conduct: What comparison, I say, between these, and the feverish, empty amusements of luxury and expense? (EPM 9.25; 283–4; see also E 'Delicacy of Taste' 5)

These negative views of luxury in Hume have been little commented on, but Saint-Lambert heeds the point in the article 'Luxury' (Luxe) in the *Encyclopédie*:

> This luxury must then continue to grow in order to foster the arts, industry, and commerce, and to bring nations to that point of maturity that is necessarily followed by their old age and ultimately their destruction. This opinion is quite widely held, and even Mr. Hume shares it. (Saint-Lambert [1764] 1965: 208)[25]

Although Hume never presents his distinction between innocent and vicious luxury as a historical or causal process, the presentation of the advantages and disadvantages of luxury by

Saint-Lambert is basically in accord with Hume's arguments in the essay 'Of Refinement'.

In a different and rather more critical way, the marquis de Mirabeau also recognised the significance for Hume of this distinction in his *L'Ami des hommes* (1756–70). While praising the Scottish philosopher together with Melon, Mirabeau, who supported the revitalisation of agriculture and feared the depopulation of modern commercial European countries, expectedly refutes Hume's distinction between 'the innocent and the vicious luxuries' (le luxe innocent et le luxe vicieux).[26] This physiocrat claims that 'from the beginning to the end of his treatise, [Hume] confounds luxury with politeness, industry and arts. I agree with him of all good effects that he attributes to the latter; but, in my sense, the luxury is not it' (Mirabeau 1756–60: I, 124. I use (in part) the translation by Malherbe 2005: 62).* Mirabeau was well aware that Hume's strategic defence of luxury hinged on his rewording 'luxury' to 'refinement', although the latter's 'vicious' luxury is not so different from what Mirabeau defines as 'luxe': 'Luxury is the *abuse of wealth*' (III, 194).†

On the surface, the difference between Hume and Mirabeau appears merely a trivial and verbal dispute; there are two main reasons why this is not the case. Firstly, they differ in their accounts of the concrete content of luxury. Hume conceptually distinguishes between prodigality by lords and refinement. In the second *Enquiry* he criticises the 'liberality in princes' that often converts 'the homely bread of the honest and industrious' into 'delicious cates for the idle and the prodigal' (EPM 2.20; 181). In the *History* he repeatedly depicts how the 'rustic hospitality' among the barons maintained a 'great number of idle retainers, ready to any disorder of mischief' (H II, 179; see also I, 463–4; Sabl 2012: 66–8). In stark contrast to Hume, Mirabeau in the final volume of *L'Ami des hommes* (1760) takes a favourable view of 'splendour or pomp' (le faste) as 'the *hierarchical* spending' (la dépense *hiérarchique*), while criticising Hume's definition of innocent luxury. The marquis clearly has Hume in mind when he argues that the 'sincere panegyrists' (panégyristes de bonne-foi) of luxury made mistakes in 'confusing pomp and luxury' (confondant le

* 'Du moins il me semble que d'un bout à l'autre de son Traité il confound le luxe avec la politesse, l'industrie & les arts. Je demeure d'accord avec lui de tous les bon effets qu'il attribue à ces dernier; mais, à mon sens, le luxe n'est pas point cela'.

† 'Le luxe est *l'abus des richesses*'.

faste et le luxe) (Mirabeau 1756–60: III, 193). Hume in turn seems to react to Mirabeau's defence of princes' hospitality when Hume took the trouble to insert some sentences in 'Of Refinement' after the 1768 edition (after the 1770 edition they have been moved into a footnote): he claims that the prodigality 'is much less frequent in the cultivated ages' because idleness as a source of prodigality has less opportunity to exert itself among industrious societies. Moreover, he retorts against Mirabeau by simply repeating the latter's phrase: 'Prodigality is not to be confounded with a refinement in the arts' (E 632). Interestingly, this was the sole fundamental addition to the essay 'Of Refinement' after its publication in 1752, though he made some minor revisions of expressions and changed its title from 'Of Luxury' after the 1760 edition. For Hume, the prodigality of princes is merely a feudal and fully outmoded style of expenditure.

Secondly, and more significantly, there is an essential difference between Hume and the French physiocrat in that the latter discriminates between luxury and 'politeness, industry and arts' *qualitatively*, while Hume considers the difference between innocent and vicious luxury to be a matter of degree. For this difference, Mirabeau lightly concludes that 'it is easy for the government to stop, even to extinguish [luxury] without harming the arts and industry' (1756–60: II, 174),* while Hume insists on its impossibility. Hume's strategy is to advise legislators to choose the courses of action that are the least evil for society overall, rather than attempting to recommend social reformation in a fruitless quest for perfection. In the last few passages of 'Of Refinement', Hume proposes an imaginary state in which all people are relieved from suffering, including that produced by the harmful effects of vicious luxury. Hume argues that, even if we could banish only vicious luxury from society, this would not help to eradicate the other social ills caused by 'some other defect in human nature' (E279); rather the situation would become worse. Such a theoretical construct serves to highlight the incommensurability of exclusive economic benefits with morality as well as the impossibility of such a state in reality. In the real world, Hume considers that 'the magistrates, who aim only at possibilities' can never 'free [men] from every species of vice' and are obliged to 'cure one vice

* '[. . .] il est aisé au gouvernement de l'arrêter, de l'éteindre même, sans nuire aux arts et à l'industrie'.

by another'.[27] Hence he alleges that even extreme luxury might be a remedy for 'indolence, selfishness, inattention to others' to a certain degree, but he does not commit himself to the question of whether the advantages produced by luxury could compensate for other moral deficiencies thus created. Hume called it 'a *philosophical* question, not a *political* one' (E 279–80). In another essay, 'Of Money', he replies to the question of which mode of living, the simple or the refined, is the most advantageous to the state or public, as follows: 'I should, without much scruple, prefer, the latter, *in a view to politics at least*' (E 293. Italics added).

Such reservations about Hume's defence of luxury are inevitable because he admits that the distinction between vicious and innocent luxuries is not absolute (unlike Mirabeau) but a matter of degree. This is clear from his own definition of vicious luxury: '*when carried a degree farther*, [luxury] begins to be a quality pernicious' (E 279. Italics added). Refinement does not have to, but can, if taken to extreme, degenerate into morally vicious forms of luxury. This means that these two forms of luxury are often overlapping in the real world, even if conceptually distinguishable (see Chapter 1). The man who is a slave to luxury will disregard his duties and fall into immorality, resulting finally in a general state of unhappiness. If this disregard of moderation becomes collective, Hume warns that political and economic repercussions will follow, for people will no longer regard one another with the same care or recognise the interdependency holding the society together. Actually Hume reveals the negative effects of excessive luxury and its 'unnaturalness' in the essay 'Of Public Credit':

> In this unnatural state of society, the only persons, who possess any revenue beyond the immediate effects of their industry, are the stockholders [...]. These are men, who have no connexions with the state, who can enjoy their revenue in any part of the globe in which they chuse to reside, who will naturally bury themselves in the capital or in great cities, and who will sink into the lethargy of a stupid and pampered luxury, without spirit, ambition, or enjoyment. (E 357–8; see also Shaftesbury [1711] 1999: 214)

In the essay 'Of the Populousness in Ancient Nations' Hume also warns against the dangers caused by 'extravagant luxury, irregular expense, idleness, dependence, and false ideas of rank and superiority' in the capital cities of vast monarchies (E 448).

Such criticisms of luxurious and rootless lives were often found in 'republican' writings in the eighteenth century. What is important here, however, is that Hume retains the basic tenet that moderate luxury tends to augment the vigour and action of people, while criticising the excessive luxury, which is futile and prompts only indolence and inactivity.

Now let us examine Hume's view of the process of degeneracy caused by the vicious form of luxury. Some light is shed on it by Hume's description of misers: 'A griping miser, for instance, praises extremely *industry* and *frugality* even in others, and sets them, in his estimation, above all the other virtues' (EPM 6n.26; 234n.). The misers, who repeatedly appear in Hume's texts, are often caricatures (see the essay 'Of Avarice'), but the aforementioned comment is based on neither caricature nor exaggeration. As we have seen, Hume believed that when commercial nations flourish, their members acquire characteristics such as frugality or industry, which further their economic activities. As he shows in 'Of Interest', there are many more misers among merchants, whereas 'among the possessors of land, there is the contrary' (E 301). Thus, the virtues of people in a commercial state, if extended beyond their capacity or usefulness, may turn into vices (selfishness), just as love, if taken beyond a certain level, 'renders men jealous, and cuts off the free intercourse between the sexes, on which the politeness of a nation will commonly much depend' (E 'National Characters' 215). Hume does not consider that the sense of honour or a love of fame vivified by the increase of luxury and social intercourse can inevitably and automatically save us from the danger of falling into vice posed by luxury.

Yet, that vicious luxury can sometimes boost our selfishness and inattention to others is not the whole story: these harmful effects are also produced by social sympathy. Interdependency realised through sympathy will succeed only by having 'a duly limited object', but may produce narrow-mindedness in a limited circle (EPM 5n.22; 225n.). The same regard for others which makes for morality also makes for '[p]opular sedition, party zeal, a devoted obedience to factious leaders', which Hume saw as some 'of the most visible, though less laudable effects of this social sympathy in human nature' (EPM 5.35; 224). Moreover, '[h]onour is a great check upon mankind: But where a considerable body of men act together, this check is, in a great measure, removed' (E 'Independency of Parliament' 43), which may under-cut societies' ability to sustain refinement (Herdt

1997; Herdt 2013). The same considerations apply to economic and political relations among neighbouring states. While he advises the legislators to discard the jealousy of trade, Hume acknowledges such jealousy as 'reasonable and well-grounded' (E 'Balance of Trade' 315) because 'nature has implanted in every one a superior affection to his own country' (EPM 5n.22; 225n.). Thus, patriotism in a reasonable measure is beneficial to the nation, but if such feelings were nurtured too much, public welfare would be considerably impaired in the long run. This can be the case even if we can find the seemingly opposite statement in 'Of Refinement': 'Factions are then less inveterate, revolutions less tragical, authority less severe, and seditions less frequent' (E 274).

Even his arguments against the contemporary concern over the alleged decline in the martial spirit are not unconditional, but indirect and oblique. As we have seen above, he does not subscribe to the view that the increase of luxury necessarily enervates the martial spirit, and, in 'Of Refinement', illustrates this by reference to the military strength of France and England. However, Hume carefully excludes Italy from what he calls the 'refined' countries. Like many of his contemporaries (Dennis 1711: 18–25; Brown 1757–8: II, 42), though for different reasons, he considers Italy to be an 'effeminate' nation. Whilst others attributed this alleged effeminacy to the indulgence of the Italians in luxury, Hume attributes it to 'an ill modelled government' (E 275–6), which had failed to keep the harmful effect of luxury in check. As we saw earlier, an increase in luxury is not necessarily beneficial to either an individual or a nation, but must be carefully controlled by self-examination and the ruler respectively. In the *History* Hume depicts the situation of the Dutch, who were regarded as the most commercial nation in the late seventeenth century, as follows:

> By a continued and successful application to commerce, the people were become unwarlike, and confided entirely for their defence in that mercenary army, which they maintained. After the treaty of Westphalia, the States, trusting to their peace with Spain, and their alliance with France, had broken a great part of this army, and did not support with sufficient vigilance the discipline of the troops which remained. (H VI, 258)

We find a similar opinion in *A True Account of the Behaviour and Conduct of Archibald Stewart*. In this pamphlet, Hume claims that the surrender of the town in the face of the Jacobite Rebellion of 1745 was not Archibald Stewart's personal fault, but an inevitable result of general negligence in not maintaining fortifications or keeping proper vigilance and discipline: 'When Men have fallen into a more civilized Life, and have been allowed to addict themselves entirely to the Cultivation of Arts and Manufactures, the Habit of their Mind, still more than that of their Body, soon renders them entirely unfit for the Use of Arms [...]' (TA 236 [7]). These passages reveal that Hume does not think that the devotion to commercial activities automatically leads to the cultivation of a martial spirit. Rather, it is the increase of military knowledge, including the formation of discipline and honour, if effectively exercised, which could compensate for the lack of martial spirit. That is to say, if a nation ceases to be vigilant, the increase of commerce, far from promoting the martial spirit, can produce its decay. Such a stalemate can only be resolved when industry is accompanied by '[k]nowledge in the government' manifested by '[l]aws, order, police, [and] discipline' (E 273).[28] That is not to say that Hume believed that, as Mandeville argued, the clash between the needs of an individual and those of a state, or between morality and political effectiveness, must necessarily lead to a paradox. In the essay 'Of Commerce' Hume certainly admits the truth of the maxim that 'the greatness of a state and the happiness of its subjects' are generally 'inseparable with regard to commerce'. Yet, he also recognises that this maxim 'may possibly admit of exceptions' and that there are some circumstances, which produce quite different or even contrary effects (255). He also well understands that judgements about when people are considered to have violated the three conditions set for the moderate and beneficial enjoyment of luxury would differ from society to society: Hume summarily states that '[t]he value, which all men put upon any particular pleasure, depends on comparison and experience' (E 276). How luxury affects particular societies varies as he noted in 'A Dialogue':

> A degree of luxury may be ruinous and pernicious in a native of SWITZERLAND, which only fosters the arts, and encourages industry in a FRENCHMAN or ENGLISHMAN. We are not, therefore, to expect, either the same sentiments, or the same laws in BERNE, which prevail in LONDON or PARIS. (EPM 'A Dialogue' 41; 337; see also E 419)

The assumption that the manners of the Swiss were exceptionally simple was seemingly common among Hume's contemporaries (Kapposy 2002: 227–31). What is rather significant about this assessment is that it leads us back to Hume's general theory of opinion, discussed in Chapter 3. On this point, Hume is not only realistic, but even sceptical about the positive effects of luxury. To put it more precisely, he does not dogmatically believe in the inevitability of the positive effects of luxury. Rather, he clearly acknowledges in the essay 'Of Commerce' that '[l]iberty must be attended with particular accidents, and a certain turn of thinking, in order to produce that effect' (E 265). As exemplified by this statement, Hume always recognises much room for contingency in the relationship between economic development and changing opinions about morals and liberty, while firmly asserting that modern civilised societies are generally more conformable with 'the more natural and usual course of things' than the ancient ones (E 259).

These considerations of Hume's assessments of negative luxury seem to make him closer to other Scottish Enlightenment thinkers. Nevertheless, there is a significant difference between Hume and other Scots. Most notably, Adam Smith and Adam Ferguson emphasise the devastating effects produced by the advancement of division of labour in commercial societies. We can find similar arguments in Millar, Dunbar and even Lord Kames (Berry 2013: 174). On the other hand, Hume has been deemed exceptionally optimistic or negligent on this point. Some might interpret this as partly due to his over-optimism about the merits that commercial society brings about, or partly because he finished publishing almost all his major writings before the 1760s and he could not have a chance to see the harsh realities of the Industrial Revolution. However, another and more plausible interpretation is possible. As we saw above, Hume is not reluctant to admit that luxury can produce various negative effects if its enjoyment goes beyond the proper limits; but he sees no necessary *causal* link between the advancement of luxury and its negative effects. Actually he does not fail to notice the oppressive situation of the poor (see Hume's comments on the poor in the deleted essay 'Of the Middle Station of Life' (E 546)). He also explains the differences between 'a day-labourer' and 'a man of quality' from a moral cause, that is, the different social positions in which they find themselves (T 2.3.1.9; 402) – a point that Adam Smith was to adopt as the difference between 'a common street porter' and 'a philosopher' in the *Wealth of Nations* ([1776] 1982: 28–9 [I.ii.4]). For these reasons it is unlikely that Hume failed to show his usual perceptiveness only on this occasion. What is conspicuously absent in his arguments on luxury is the causal understanding that the advancement of economic activities *regularly* produces moral and intellectual torpor among the labourers. The same can be said about his understanding of the relation between the advancement of luxury and the decline of martial spirit. Moreover, this is also applied to what Hume calls a 'jealousy of trade'. As Mankin remarks, '[j]ealousy the vice may be transformed into jealousy the tractable psychological impulse and fed into the machine of social relation' (2005: 67), but vice versa. In this sense, a 'noble emulation' is always contiguous with the devastating economic jealousy (Hont 2005: 115–25). Hume's judgement on these points is characteristically open-ended. Neither the degree of optimism, nor the historical development of real commercial societies, but this seems the biggest point to differentiate Hume and other Scots.

For Hume, who attempts to give a thoroughly secular basis for our morality, the prodigality of princes should be criticised because such an economically wasteful mode of consumption is completely outmoded and morally enervating; the freer intercourse of the sexes can be permissible because of its relatively less harmful effects than drunkenness and because of its positive effects in promoting communication. More fundamentally, the gist of his argument lies in his observation on the favourable situation in which luxury acts to cultivate our morality in modern societies. The only feasible, if neither the best nor the sole, way to 'regulate anew our *moral* as well as *political* sentiments' is to direct our attention toward conversation and various social intercourses through enjoyment of worldly pleasures, not vice versa. This is, Hume believes, the most appropriate way to help prevent sudden pandemics of both religious and political enthusiasm (exemplified in his depiction of the simple and ascetic prevailing manners during the Civil War) and possible degeneration into superstition (as he portrayed in the medieval volumes of the *History*). It might also (hopefully for Hume) contribute to expelling an economically unproductive state of mind. This conclusion is more than words on paper for Hume. In the 'Letter to a Physician', which he wrote when he was around twenty but seemingly never posted, he compared his mental distemper to 'a Coldness & Desertion of the Spirit' of 'the French Mysticks & [...] our Fanatics' (L I, 17; see also Wright 1983: 190–1, 236–7; 2003). Finally, however, he found the way out of this mental dysfunction: 'as there are two things very bad for this Distemper, Study & Idleness, so there are *two things very good, Business & Diversion*'. Then the young Hume resolved to seek 'a more active Life' (L I, 17. Italics added) and began to work as a clerk in Bristol. His recommendation for an active and sociable life is the very lessons learned from his own life experience.

Hume seems much less overconfident, nevertheless, of the plausibility of the claim that the development of luxury could immediately alleviate political factions and religious bigotry. This is partly because strengthening the love of worldly things in our minds and activities does not always entail eradicating political estrangements and struggles; rather it can sometimes reinforce them. This is also partly (and more significantly) because Hume judges religious bigotry itself to be the chief enemy of his strategy of sound secularisation through the enjoyment of luxury, due to the very vicious workings of religious hypocrisy.

From an optimistic perspective, Hume's strategy of luxury could be expected to indirectly contribute to the cultivation of the morals of a people by means of conversation. In his view, however, this would only be possible if institutional approaches were in place to prevent other devastating social effects of political factions and religious bigotry. Hence, as we will see in the following two chapters (Chapters 5 and 6), how to tame the 'tyranny of priests' and how to 'refine the democracy' were the two most vital targets of Hume as a defender of refinement and politeness.

Notes

1. Hume does not refer to 'humanity' as necessarily involving religious sensibilities (although they are not necessarily lacking either), as did some of his contemporaries. John Brown, a critic of Hume, identified two types of humanity. The one, which arises from 'Courage tempered by pure Religion', is 'regular, extensive, and consistent'. The other, which arises from 'Effeminacy', is 'partial, irrational, and confined'. It is clear which of these Brown thinks most highly of (Brown 1757–8: II, 40).
2. Hume did not conceal his apprehensions about the possible dangers of a standing army in his other writings; in one instance he

referred to them as suffering from 'mortal distemper' (E 'Perfect Commonwealth' 647; the paragraph including this expression was omitted after the 1770 edition). Andrew Fletcher has already pointed out the significance of military discipline for militias (1997: 24–9). For further discussion of this issue and of Hume's apprehensions regarding the standing army, see Robertson 1985. Hume, like Smith, observed that improvement in military knowledge and weapons contributed to reducing the misery of soldiers in the field (H II, 230). On this point, see Berry 1997: 147–8 and note 28 in this chapter.

3. In this book, Hume cites the historical changes recorded by Raphael Hollingshed (Holinshed), the Elizabethan chronicler, who pointed out the increase in the number of chimneys, the changes in building materials and the fact that people were able to stay up later at night (H III, 464 and 480 Note [U]; see also H IV: 383).
4. Drunkenness is one of the themes relevant to the luxury debates (Mandeville [1714/1729, 1732] 1988): Remark (G), esp. 89–92 [86–91]).
5. For a more general discussion on the issue of gender in the Scottish Enlightenment, see Sebastiani 2013: chap. 5.
6. I am indebted to Carl Wennerlind for bringing to my attention the works cited here. See also Hutcheson [1728] 1990: 10; [1725] 1990: 227–8 [II.vi.ii].
7. There is no definite biographical evidence that Voltaire knew well Mandeville's *Fable of the Bees* when he wrote *Le Mondain*, but, as Morize maintains, the internal (textual) evidence seems to demonstrate that he knew it, at first hand or second (Morize 1909: 72–111; Mason 2003). Wade is more sceptical on this point, and he claims that the influence of the *Fable of the Bees* should be limited to the *Défense* ([1947] 1967: 22–56).
8. Wade seems to confirm the same point by arguing that Voltaire in *Le Mondain* is 'a mundane moralist' who admits luxury as a source of personal enjoyment; the emphasis is placed here not on 'moralist' but 'mundane' ([1947] 1967: 32). He also asserts the lack of the moral dimension in the *Défense* (34). Voltaire mentions the issue of luxury in his *Observations sur Mm. Jean Lass* [John Law], *Melon et Dutot, sur le commerce, le luxe, etc.* (1738), but his arguments in this piece contain little of note, at least in terms of the present context (1968–: XVIIIa, 239–57).
9. This note is not included in the Oxford edition of *Œuvres complètes de Voltaire*. Yet, Robert Wokler judges that this '*is* one of [Voltaire's] own compositions' (2012: 285n.41).

10. Voltaire possessed two copies (1753–56 and 1758 editions) of Hume's *Essays and Treatises on Several Subjects*, which includes the *Political Discourses* as the fourth volume. He also left marginal comments on some essays (Voltaire 1968–: 545–7 [entries 777, 778]).
11. In addition to these three points, Moore points out two: the distinction between justice and the natural virtues, and the state of nature. To respond to the critical comments by Norton (2005), Moore further elaborates his argument in Moore 2007 (this 'polemic' is deeply related to another pending issue – the influence of Hutcheson on Hume (Turco 2007) but it seems possible to separate this from Epicureanism in Hume to a certain extent, not completely). See also Moore 2002; Taylor 1989: 344–7; Tuck 1999: 37.
12. Hume's endorsement of Epicurean morality and his reserve concerning its physics seem to be preceded (in a sense) by Jacques Abbadie, an exiled French Protestant and the author of *L'Art de se connaître soi-même* (1692). For more on Abbadie, see Nakhimovsky 2003.
13. Hume cites Saint-Évremond in the *Treatise* (T 3.3.2.12; 599) as well as in the second *Enquiry* (EPM 6.9; 237, and EMP 7n.36; 252n.).
14. A more intelligible version of this Epicurean maxim is found in *De l'esprit des lois*: 'it is not the liquor, but the vessel that is corrupted' (this sentence has no footnote regarding its source). Montesquieu's point here, however, is not to show the harmlessness of luxury, but to demonstrate that '[t]here are few laws that are not good when the state has not lost its principles' ([1748] 1989: 121 [8.1.11]).
15. In his *L'Ami des hommes* the marquis de Mirabeau criticises Hume's argument on luxury with Melon's comments that 'the system of Epicurus is as dangerous in politics as faulty in physics' (Le systême d'Epicure est aussi dangereux en politique, qu'il est fautif en physique) (1756–60: II, 141) without directly mentioning the name of Hume in this context.
16. This does not necessarily mean that all aspects of Smith's moral theory can or should be understood solely as those of a Stoic. Thomas Reid, for example, criticised Smith's moral system not only as 'a Refinement of the selfish system' but also as 'what Cicero says of the Epicurean' (Reid [1984] 1997: [318] 66; [1965] 1997: [34–5] 81). The Epicureanism of Smith's moral theory was emphasised by István Hont in the series of Carlyle Lectures entitled 'Visions of Politics in Commercial Society: Comparing Jean-Jacques Rousseau and Adam Smith' in the University of Oxford (5 February to 12 March 2009).
17. For example, Mandeville's listing of luxurious goods and qualities

([1714/1729, 1732] 1988: I, 342 [393]) bears a close resemblance to Hume's as the causes of our pride (T 2.1.2.5; 279; see also Finlay 2007: chap. 5).

18. Mikko Tolonen recently argued that Hume was influenced, not by Mandeville in the *Fable of the Bees*, but by his 'revised' vision in *Part II* of the *Fable*. I basically agree with Tolonen's elaborate interpretation that Hume aims at 'a Mandevillean goal, the circle of refinement' (2013: 178) in a sense, but significant differences in tone and emphasis between them still remain. Furthermore, the closeness between Hume and the author of Part II of the *Fable* in their understandings of civil society seems to be a different matter from the issue of which Mandeville Hume makes a target for criticism.
19. As for Bayle's influence on Hume, see Robertson 2005: chap. 6, and on Hume's irreligious aims in the *Treatise*, see Russell 2008: chap. 20.
20. Hume gives a more detailed account of this psychological mechanism in a footnote of the *History* (V, 572 Note [AA]). He also utilises the same mechanism to explain why modern chivalry produced its singular and extravagant rules of conduct in his unpublished manuscript 'Historical Essay on Chivalry and Modern Honour': 'And in this Case of an imagin'd Merit, the farther our Chimera's hurry us from Nature, & the Practice of the World, the better pleas'd we are, as valuing ourselves upon the Singularity of our Notions, & thinking we depart from the rest of mankind only by flying above them' (Hume 2012: 205–6 [3]). Although the asceticism of the Puritans was antithetical to the gallantry of the chivalric manners prevalent in the court of Charles II, the escalation in unworldly behaviour among Puritan groups during the Civil War, Commonwealth and Protectorate periods recalled the self-absorption of self-proclaimed knights in the age of chivalry. Although most commentators suppose that Hume wrote this essay long before his publication of the *Treatise*, Sakamoto suggests 'a new possibility namely, that *A Dialogue* [in the second *Enquiry*] was not the echo of the juvenile work but was written at the same time as the historical essay on chivalry' based on the fact that the watermark of this manuscript is the same as Hume's so-called 'Early Memoranda' that Sakamoto postulates was written in the late 1740s (2011b: 164n.39). Cf. Stewart 2005: 34–5; Wright 2012.
21. It has to be admitted that Shaftesbury is here emphasising the contrast between the working class and the upper class (in favour of the former). Hume stresses the importance of the middle class, and tends

to undervalue the moral capacity of the lower class (See the essay 'Of the Middle Station of Life').

22. For Shaftesbury's anti-Epicureanism, see Klein 1994: 60–9.
23. There is no wonder in this connection, considering Shaftesbury's intellectual debts to Cicero in his notion of politeness (Klein 1994: 44–7).
24. Hume also uses the expression 'those refined reflections', though not naming the Stoic, in the essay 'The Sceptic' (E 173), which reminds us that he calls Montesquieu's philosophy 'its false Refinements' (L II, 133). As for the negative usages of 'refinement' in Hume's philosophy, see Livingston 1998: 217–25.
25. John Shovlin argues that Saint-Lambert was critical of Hume's optimistic discussion of luxury and gave a more balanced view, although Shovlin somehow omits the above mention of Hume by Saint-Lambert (2008: 218).
26. In a letter to the abbé Morellet, Hume severely condemns the physiocrats as 'the most chimerical and most arrogant that now exists, since the annihilation of the Sorbonne' (L II: 205). As for the difference between Hume and the French physiocrats, see Deleule 1979: chap. 4. On Mably's republican criticism on Hume's economic writings, see Wright 1997: 58–64,
27. For Hume's critical attitude toward utopian perfectionism in economic matters, see Velk and Riggs (1985). Danford (1990) rightly pays attention to Hume's concluding comments in 'Of Refinement'.
28. There is a small but significant difference between Hume and Smith on this issue. In these contexts the former rarely evokes the superiority of the standing army, despite his repeated emphasis on the technological advance in artillery, while the latter has no serious worries on that point (Robertson 1985: 66–7, 216–17).

5

Taming 'the Tyranny of Priests': Hume's Advocacy of Religious Establishments

Hume has long been known as a fierce critic of religion, but his position on religious issues within Enlightenment discourse is rather ambiguous. This ambiguity is closely related to his scepticism (or, more properly, agnosticism in this context).[1] On the one hand, Hume's scepticism has been considered lukewarm compared with more adamant and clear-cut atheism among certain of his contemporaries. As Diderot attests, when Hume told Baron d'Holbach that '[he] did not believe in atheists, that he had never seen any', he was surprised by the baron's reply that there were fifteen atheists among the eighteen guests in the baron's house at that moment; the baron added that 'the three others haven't made up their minds' (cited in Mossner 1980: 483). When Edward Gibbon visited Paris in 1763, he remarked that he could not 'approve the intolerant zeal of the philosophers and Encyclopedists, the friends of Holbach and Helvétius; they laughed at the scepticism of Hume, preached the tenets of atheism with the bigotry of dogmatists, and damned all believers with ridicule and contempt' (Gibbon 1961: 145; on the similar contrast between Hume and the French philosophes testified to by their Italian contemporary Alessandro Verri, see Mazza 2005: 216, 230). E. C. Mossner was right to point out that the French philosophes could not understand his agnosticism and they were inclined to think that Hume 'had not entirely thrown off the shackles of bigotry' (1980: 485). From Hume's viewpoint, however, bold atheists have 'a double share of folly' because they are not content to espouse the principle in their hearts, but also they are 'guilty of multiplied indiscretion and imprudence' in professing it to the public (DNR 1.18; 139). As we saw in Chapter 2, Hume's scepticism about the ultimate causes or qualities of human nature was completely consistent with the characteristic self-concealment of his personal belief in his posthumously published work: *Dialogues concerning Natural Religion* (1779). According to him, both atheism and materialism are dogmatic in that they are confident in their ability to grasp the ultimate causes of the nature of things, no matter how lukewarm his agnostic position appeared to the French philosophes.

On the other hand, Hume's anti-religious sentiments constitute an important dividing line between him and other Scottish Enlightenment thinkers, especially the Moderates such as William Robertson, Hugh Blair and Adam Ferguson. These men, in turn, were criticised by the more orthodox evangelicals among the Scottish Presbyterian clergy for keeping company with the great infidel: 'This intimacy of the young [Scottish] clergy with David Hume', affirms Alexander Carlyle, a member of the Moderate party too, 'enraged the zealots on the opposite side, who little knew how impossible it was for him, had he been willing, to shake their principles' (Carlyle [1910] 1990: 288–9). Although these moderate literati defended Hume and Lord Kames when they were impeached for their allegedly irreligious writings (the former's *Treatise*[2] and the latter's *Essays on the Principles of Morality and Natural Religion*) in the General Assembly of the Church of Scotland in May 1755 and 1756 (at the latter time the prosecution was confined to Hume) (Ross 1972: chap. 5; Mossner 1980: chap. 25), there was a deep rift between the members of the Moderates who were clergy and/or university professors, and Hume who was deprived of the opportunity to get an academic post because of his alleged atheism.[3] As we will see below, the first edition of Volume 1 of the *History of Great Britain*, provoked some criticism, especially among the clerics, for Hume's depiction of the puritans as enthusiasts (H I, xiv–xvi; Phillips and Smith 2005: 303–4). Even before publishing the *History*, Hume's scepticism in the *Treatise* was sufficiently destructive as to provoke the accusation of 'Heresy, Deism, Scepticism, Atheism &c &c &c' (L I, 57; Fieser 1995; Rivers 2001; Stewart 2003). Even in France, those who held a generally favourable opinion of Hume also thought that he carried his criticism to extremes. Montesquieu in a letter to Hume, for example, comments on his description of the clergy in the essay 'Of National Characters' that 'you maltreat the ecclesiastical order a little' (cited in Mossner 1989: 260).

Two major points can be drawn from these considerations. Firstly, Hume, at least on religious issues, should not be placed with several other Scottish Enlightenment thinkers in the category of the Moderate Enlightenment. Secondly, an exhaustive analysis of Hume's personal religious beliefs is not necessarily imperative for our understanding of the nature and intellectual origins of his criticism of false religions; for our present purpose, it will suffice to confirm that Hume retains his agnosticism in his published works on religion.

Despite these qualifications, Hume's view on religious institutions deserves a much deeper investigation, because it has also been reputed among scholars that Hume advocated a religious establishment in the *History*; he allegedly acknowledges the merits of a state subsidy to the clergy. He is also claimed to have taken a more favourable attitude towards superstition in the *History*. The relationship between this stance and his notorious anticlericalism, therefore, has been an issue of concern. One of the aims of this chapter is to offer a more coherent understanding of Hume's criticism of priesthood and his advocacy of a religious establishment. I will also point out that the stances of Hume and Smith, despite their alleged dissimilarities in religious policy, were rooted in the same core belief that a magistrate must take the most appropriate measures in order to keep the possible disturbance caused by religion to a minimum. Finally, I will discuss the similarities and differences between Hume and another infamous 'infidel' – Voltaire. The characteristics of Hume's Sceptical Enlightenment will be clarified by juxtaposing the great infidels of the French and Scottish Enlightenments.

1 Hume's Alleged Conservatism on Religious Issues

As a preliminary step, we must examine the reasons for Hume's alleged conservatism on religious issues in the *History*. There are two pertinent issues here: Hume's favourable view of superstition and his support for a national church. As for the former, J. G. A. Pocock recognises that Hume shifted his attitude toward superstition and began to acknowledge its stabilising effect by satisfying the senses of the vulgar through the splendour of various ceremonies. Actually, Hume conceded:

> The splendour too and pomp of worship, which that religion [Catholicism] carefully supports, are agreeable to the taste of magnificence, that prevails in courts, and form a species of devotion, which,

> while it flatters the pampered senses, gives little perplexity to the indolent understandings, of the great'. (H I, xvi–xvii; these passages were deleted after the second edition of the first volume of the *History of Great Britain* (Hume [1754] 1970: 98))

Elsewhere, he argues that 'the pomp and splendour of worship which belonged to so opulent an establishment, contributed, in some respect, to the encouragement of the fine arts, and began to diffuse a general elegance of taste, by uniting it with religion' (H III, 137). He repeats the same point: 'That delicious country, where the Roman pontiff resides, was the source of all modern art and refinement, and diffused on its superstition an air of politeness' (H I, xvii).

Based on these testimonies, Pocock concludes that '[i]f civil liberty were the management of an opulent society in which property was mobile and thought politely free, it had no reason to quarrel with superstition, the religion of senses'. He even assesses that Hume is here envisaging 'an alternative Enlightenment, in which cultic Christianity would have remained intact' (1990: 209–11). Donald T. Siebert, based on more detailed investigation of Hume's various works, also points out that 'later in the *History* Hume moves from ridicule of liturgy to an endorsement of ritual as a means of insulating worshipers from the consequences of unchecked spiritual zeal'. According to him, Hume 'was surprisingly moderate in his condemnation of Catholicism. [...] Superstition [...] is simply preferable to enthusiasm as a religion for the multitudes' (1990: 110, 94). Even among 'liberal' readings of Hume, this interpretation is not rare (Stewart 1963: 283). Even his contemporaries discerned the ambivalence in Hume's attitude toward clergy and religious establishments between his essays and the *History*. As early as the 1790s, one critic, who alleged Hume's support for the ceremonies of the Church of England, his preference for Episcopacy over Presbyterianism, and his lenient treatment of William Laud, the Archbishop of Canterbury, concluded as follows:

> Had Mr. Hume been serious in his opinion, he might have deserved an answer. But on turning over his Essays, we are surprized by the most stupendous and unblushing contradiction. [...] What are we to think of a professed infidel defending the barbarous insolence of the priesthood? (Garden [1791] 2002: II, 194–5)[4]

What complicates the situation is that his Erastianism has been considered to be one of his allegedly Tory biases in the *History*. On this point, Duncan Forbes is right to insist that '[t]he spotting and listing of attitudes that look like "Tory" attitudes, for example, Hume's approval of the established Church of England [...], does not add up to a discovery of the historical Hume' (1975b: 126–7). In fact, the endorsement of a complete civil control of religious establishment and clergy was not unusual, but common among the Enlightenment thinkers and their predecessors: Machiavelli, Hobbes, Voltaire and Rousseau (to name just a few) basically advocated Erastianism. Thus, it would be pointless to receive Hume's support of a national church as a proof of his political conservatism without inquiring into the nature of his Erastianism and how to reconcile it with the general tenor of his anti-religious views.

In order to address these issues, we need to place Hume's anticlericalism in a much broader context. For Enlightenment thinkers including Hume, criticism of priesthood and false religions was not merely an institutional issue; it was fundamentally rooted in concerns about the denial of Providence and reward or punishment in the future life. Through the process of secularisation in early eighteenth-century Europe, as some recent studies show, the various forms of Epicureanism (especially Lucretius and Horace) and Spinozism (through *Traité des trois imposteurs*, for example) exerted much influence over the radicals and libertines who were eager to undermine the established system of religion (Israel 2001: 5, 340–1, 623–7; Robertson 2005: 221–5; Jacob 2006; Thomson 2008: chap. 5; Leddy and Lifschitz 2009: 1–11).[5] Hume also owes much of the content of his arguments on religious and moral issues to predecessors including Bayle and Mandeville.

Although his anti-religious attitudes and their connotations were already evident in the *Treatise*, he developed them fully in the first volume of the *Essays, Moral and Political* (1741). Along with political essays including 'Of Parties in General' and 'Of the Parties of Great Britain', the essay 'Of Superstition and Enthusiasm' develops a typological analysis of two aspects of false religions – superstition and enthusiasm. When he published the third edition of the *Essays* in 1748, in a footnote to the essay 'Of National Characters' he severely criticises the negative effects of the priesthood on society. This provoked some counterarguments among the clergy, including that of Alexander Gerard (1762).[6]

For the purpose of this chapter, however, it is necessary to define and distinguish between Hume's targets in his various writings: his morphology of two false types of religion on the one hand, and his criticism of priests in general on the other. In the 1741 essay 'Of Superstition and Enthusiasm', Hume contrasts these two types of 'false' religion: superstition arises from '[w]eakness, fear, melancholy, together with ignorance', while enthusiasm is founded upon '[h]ope, pride, presumption, a warm imagination, together with ignorance' (E 74). His point is that religious enthusiasm, when it abates in the long run, can be amenable to civil liberty (78–9), a theme that he was to develop in the *History* much later. In a footnote to the 1748 essay 'Of National Characters', on the other hand, Hume's target is quite different from his taxonomy of false religion: he directs his criticism at the priesthood *in general*.[7] Strictly speaking, the two arguments, both of which were heavily influenced by his radical predecessors, should not be completely separated because they relate to the same issue: the status of religious institutions in civilised societies. Nevertheless, this distinction helps us to appreciate why Hume's endorsement of a religious establishment and positive view of superstition in the *History* does not necessarily contradict his life-long harsh criticism of churches and priests.

The differences in scope and objectives of each argument should be heeded. His life-long antipathy to priesthood and false religions is clearly revealed in the footnote to 'National Characters' noted above. On this basic tenet, Hume founded his comparative analysis of false religions – and even his partial acknowledgement of their comparative merits. In the following two sections, I will demonstrate that Hume's treatment of 'enthusiasm and superstition' and his criticism of priesthood can be traced back to the different strands of arguments of the third earl of Shaftesbury, Mandeville and some Whig journals respectively – despite the differences between Mandeville and Shaftesbury in moral theory, there were many similarities between their 'theologico-political views' (Primer 1975: 128; on Shaftesbury, see Klein 1994: chap. 8). On that basis, it will be made clear that Hume's pragmatic and sardonic Erastian strategies in the *History* should be separated from his occasionally flattering remarks on the Church of England as a middle way between superstition and enthusiasm: two arguments that have previously been loosely grouped together.

2 Enthusiasm and Superstition

Hume's criticism of religion was first set out in the *Treatise* and developed in full in his *Essays, Moral and Political*. There are many examples of critical comments on religious factions and priesthood throughout Hume's writings. What is significant is that Hume's arguments on religious issues have much to do with his analysis of imagination. It is needless to pose the question of how he distinguishes between superstition or enthusiasm and sound opinion. This is not because such conceptual distinctions are meaningless for him; they do exist in a similar way to his distinction between innocent and vicious luxury. For Hume such differences are mostly a matter of degree. However, the consequences produced by religious opinions are quite different from those of luxury, because '[g]enerally speaking, the errors in religion are dangerous' (T 1.4.7.13; 271–2). As we saw in Chapter 4, Hume discerns the acceleration of heated passions and imagination in the devastating operations of 'religious hypocrisy'. According to him, hypocrisy has a socially dangerous characteristic that tends to fall away from what he calls 'the ordinary course of nature in the constitution of the mind' (T 3.2.2.8; 488; Siebert 1990: 101–3, 125–6; Herdt 1997: 198–201). He makes a similar point using the term 'artificial lives' in 'A Dialogue' of the second *Enquiry*, where he selected Diogenes as an ancient and Pascal as a modern example. Those who 'depart from the maxims of common reason' are 'in a different element from the rest of mankind' (EPM 'Dialogue' 57). He succinctly analyses the reason in the first *Enquiry*:

> The *imagination* of man is naturally sublime, delighted with whatever is remote and extraordinary, and running, without controul [sic], into the most distant parts of space and time in order to avoid the objects, which custom has rendered too familiar to it. A correct *Judgment* observes a contrary method, and avoiding all distant and high enquiries, confines itself to common life, and to such subjects as fall under daily practice and experience [...]. (EHU 12.25; 162)

According to Hume, except for 'the embellishment of poets and orators', the frenzy of imagination should be severely restricted, particularly when it comes to religious orientations, because it could jeopardise the practicability of moderate judgement based on our experience of common life (Herdt 1997: 113–14). In the essay 'Of Superstition and Enthusiasm' Hume notes 'a warm imagination' along with hope, pride and ignorance as the sources of enthusiasm. Once 'the imagination swells with great, but confused conceptions' in spiritual elevation, it goes beyond the reach of our ordinary course of human nature and rejects reason or morality as fallacious guides (E 74). Hume not only severely criticised the disturbing effects caused by irregular or extraordinary religious behaviours and practices, but also closely analysed their mechanisms and operations.

On the other hand, superstition is also a product of human imagination. Although the connection between imagination and superstition is made less explicit in 'Of Superstition and Enthusiasm', Hume uses superstition as a parallel to justice in the *Treatise* and the second *Enquiry*; although he contrasts the frivolity and uselessness of the former with the absolute necessity of the latter (EPM 3.38; 199). As we saw in Chapter 2, imagination is an indispensable component of his account of justice, especially in his account of particular rules of private property. He goes on, rather sardonically, to compare the obligation to honour a promise to the ritual commitment involved in '*transubstantiation* or *holy orders*'. Both bind us only by 'a certain form of words, along with a certain intention' and exert a strong influence on the course of our life, although superstition lacks the basis of public interests for which justice (including keeping a promise) exists (T 3.2.5.14; 524; see also Guimarães 2009: esp. 361–3). In the 'Natural History of Religion', he estimates that barbarous people motivated by fear and hope would attempt to discover the 'unknown causes' by employing the imagination (NHR 2.5).[8] Despite its lack of public interest, superstition has no less great an influence over mankind than enthusiasm. Seen in this light, Hume's understandings of enthusiasm and superstition in his later works are a continuation of his analysis of imagination in the *Treatise*. This is because a starting point of Hume's discussion is to presume that we are ineradicably entangled with various types of beliefs and opinions to different degrees. One of Hume's main and consistent themes is how to cope with the disturbing and devastating effects of these social pathologies, but there is no naïve triumphalism concerning the supremacy of reason over religious dogma in Hume's thought.

As far as religious anomalies are concerned, Hume's analysis has many intellectual sources. According to Tom Beauchamp, Hume could have known John Trenchard's *Natural History of*

Superstition, which is likely to have inspired the title and part of the contents of Hume's 'Natural History of Religion' (Beauchamp 2007: 218, 225), despite the former's more physiological leanings (Trenchard 1709: 36).[9] As I pointed out in Chapter 2, Benedict de Spinoza's criticism of miracles and prophets based upon his argument concerning imagination in the *Tractatus Theologico-Politicus* (1670) could also have influenced Hume's anti-religious attitude (see also Addison [1711–12] 1965: 287–90; Trenchard and Gordon [1720–1] 1995: I, 849–64).

In addition to these relatively recent intellectual sources and other materials, and not to mention ancient sources such as Epicurus, Lucretius or Horace (Quintus Horatius Flaccus),[10] Hume seems to borrow his dichotomy between superstition and enthusiasm more directly from Shaftesbury's *Characteristicks*, which Hume possessed as early as 1726 (Mossner 1980: 31). Throughout this work, the contrast between – or sometimes the combination of – enthusiasm and superstition as forms of corrupt or false religions can be found, although in passing (Shaftesbury [1771] 1999: 'A Letter concerning Enthusiasm' 11). Shaftesbury distinguishes between the psychological mechanisms underlying these two conditions in a manner that resembles Hume's claim in the essay 'Of Superstition and Enthusiasm' (Jaffro 1998: 170–2; on the difference between Hume and Shaftesbury, see also 171): 'in religion the enthusiasm which works by love is subject to many strange irregularities, and that which works by fear to many monstrous and horrible superstitions' ('Miscellany II' 355). In the *Miscellaneous Reflections*, explaining the development of early Christianity in ancient Rome, Shaftesbury linked enthusiasm with 'the high speculations of philosophy' while superstition was connected with 'the grossest ideas of vulgar ignorance'. The former 'which ran upon spirituals', Shaftesbury argues, is quite different from the latter: 'which ran upon external proportions, magnificence of structures, ceremonies, processions, choirs and those other harmonies which captivate the eye and ear' ('Miscellany II' 377). As we saw in Chapter 4, Hume shares the Shaftesburian mission of defending the sober enjoyment of pleasures accompanying an increase in social intercourse. It is no surprise to find that Hume completely corresponds to Shaftesbury in his criticism of the pernicious effects of false religions: 'the most evidently ruinous and fatal to the understanding is that of *superstition*, *bigotry* and *vulgar enthusiasm*' ('Miscellany IV' 467).[11]

Still, there is another possible intellectual source of Hume's dichotomy between superstition and enthusiasm. A fact that has generally gone unnoticed is that an essay in *The Old Whig*, an English journal, pre-empted many of Hume's arguments on this point. Duncan Forbes points out that Hume's essay 'was giving a political dimension to an essay in *The Old Whig* of 9 March 1738 [No. 157], on the parallel between Superstition and Enthusiasm, which is in many ways remarkably similar to Hume's more famous one'. In the footnote added to these sentences, however, Forbes admits without identifying the authorship of this essay that 'I have taken this from the précis in the *Gentleman's Magazine* (vol. 8, 148): I have not seen the original version in *The Old Whig*' (1975b: 214). Significantly, the essay that appeared in *The Old Whig* was itself a précis of several earlier essays written by Gilbert Burnet in the 1720s.[12] Gilbert Burnet, the second son of his namesake, the bishop of Salisbury, published a series of essays in *The Free-thinker*, edited by Ambrose Philips (Moore 2004),[13] including one essay actually entitled 'Of Superstition and Enthusiasm'. In fact, this is the original on which the précis Forbes mentions is based.

Taking into account the entire series of essays written by Burnet, it can be said that his treatment of the causes and effects of superstition and enthusiasm anticipated Hume's basic points. Burnet expressly identified the causes of superstition as stupidity, ignorance and ill temper of mind, while defining enthusiasm as 'a kind of an overweening, and groundless Persuasion of being the particular Favourite of Heaven; of being inspired from thence with every wild Fancy, that happens to spring up in a warm and distempered Brain' (Philips 1740: I, 101–2). He also detailed the devastating effects of such states of mind on arts and knowledge, morality and religion; and, unlike Hume, he classified enthusiasm into contemplative and active forms (I, 258–63; II, 101–2). According to Forbes, 'what Hume had to add was the political dimension, and the historical examples' (1975b: 214): Hume's originality lies in linking Burnet's arguments to the relationship between enthusiasm and liberty in English history. Burnet argued that enthusiasts could emerge from their states of delusion precisely because their self-obsession might eventually lead them to more sober self-judgement (Philips 1740: II, 195; cf. E 77), although he did not associate this effect of enthusiasm with the mentality of puritans, as Hume did later in the *History*. In Hume's historical narrative, the idea of the spirit of liberty establishing itself through the religious frenzy of puritans is of paramount importance (H IV, 145–6).

Forbes's comment that Hume merely added to Burnet's essays a political dimension and historical illustration seems to underestimate the ingenuity of the Scottish philosopher. Hume mastered the argument of the original essays, but also thoroughly expanded the pathology of false religions to a far greater extent than Burnet. For Hume, enthusiasm is not only a religious phenomenon, but also a political and even a philosophical matter, as evinced in his discussions on the 'artificial lives' in 'A Dialogue'. The observations of such startling but recurrent phenomena continue to arouse the interest of Hume as the scientist of man. Furthermore, according to Hume, the boundaries between superstition and enthusiasm are often blurred: for example, 'the STOICS', he asserts, 'join a philosophical enthusiasm to a religious superstition' (NHR 12.22).

Clearly, his careful and advanced analysis of superstition and enthusiasm permeates his many writings (Pocock 1982; Livingston 1998: chaps. 3 and 5). In *A True Account of the Behaviour and Conduct of Archibald Stewart, Esq.*, the pamphlet which he published anonymously just after the '45 Jacobite Rebellion (Mossner 1962; Box et al. 2003), he vindicated Stewart, the previous Provost of Edinburgh, who was accused of dereliction of duty (negligence of the defence of the city) upon the invasion of insurgent troops. In the postscript to this pamphlet, Hume classified the adherents of both the Whig and Tory parties into the 'religious' and the 'political' (Stewart 1992: 246–9, esp. n.15). In contrast with the political Whig – 'that of a Man of Sense and Moderation, a Lover of Laws and Liberty, whose chief Regard to particular Princes and Families, is founded on a Regard to the publick Good', he asserts, '[t]he religious *Whigs* are a very different Set of Mortals, and in my Opinion, are <as> much worse than the religious *Tories*; as the political *Tories* are inferior to the political *Whigs*'. Hume's message is clear. The adjective 'religious' here connotes personal characteristics such as 'Dissimulation, Hypocrisy [,] Violence, Calumny, Selfishness', which are explicitly resonant with his depiction of the priesthood in the footnote to the essay 'Of National Characters' discussed above. What is important is that Hume ranked the religious Tory above the religious Whig, although he regarded neither positively. He explained the reason as follows: 'it seems to me, that a Zeal for Bishops, and for the

Book of Common-Prayer, tho' equally groundless, has never been able, when mixt up with Party Notions, to form so virulent and exalted a Poison in human Breasts, as the opposite Principles' (TA 251–2 [postscript 5–6]). If we can roughly match the dichotomy between superstition and enthusiasm with that between religious Tory and Whig, Hume is consistent with his observation in the essay 'Of Superstition and Enthusiasm' in which he states that '*superstition is favourable to priestly power*' while enthusiasm 'naturally begets the most extreme resolutions' and 'produces the most cruel disorders in human society' though it soon exhausts itself (E 75, 77). As we will see below, this dichotomy survives up until the *History of England*, where it provides him with an important framework for his historical and theoretical understanding of the religious issues in British history.

3 'Priests of all Religions are the Same'

The main argument of the essay 'Of National Characters' published in 1748 is to criticise the 'climate theory', which accounts for the differences of national characters by geographical and climatic factors; instead, as we saw in Chapter 2, he tries to explain the diversity of manners from moral causes. Related to this issue, he mentions in a famous footnote to this essay an empirical fact that each profession tends to shape a distinctive personality, and compares clergy's and soldier's vocational characters. In addition, his depiction of priests is unsparingly critical: 'The ambition of the clergy can often be satisfied only by promoting ignorance and superstition and implicit faith and pious frauds' (E 198, 200n.3). Importantly, his aim here is not the typology of religious sects, but the analysis of the common characteristics of priests. Such a criticism should be placed in the broader context of the discourse of 'priestcraft', which had become important in late seventeenth-century and early eighteenth-century England, especially in the political discourses of the radical Whigs, such as *The Independent Whig* (Trenchard and Gordon 1994 [1720–1]: 6–10) and *Cato's Letters* (Trenchard and Gordon 1995 [1720–3]: I, 29–31). As Mark Goldie remarks, James Harrington's coinage of the word 'priestcraft' covered Protestant clericalism, while the word 'popery' had been traditionally associated only with Roman Catholics (Goldie 1987: 212–13; 1993). The word 'priestcraft' was, however, gradually applied to all forms of Christian religion.

When seen in this light, it is easy to separate Hume's general anti-clericalism from his taxonomy of false religions.

In order to delineate Hume's point a little more finely, however, it might be helpful to select one phrase from 'Of National Characters' as a guiding thread. Hume said that '[i]t is a trite, but not altogether a false maxim, that *priests of all religions are the same*' (E 199).[14] This phrase is significant because, in a footnote to the essay 'Of Superstition and Enthusiasm', he did make a clear distinction between 'priests' who are 'the Pretenders to Power and Dominion' and '*Clergymen*, who are set apart *by the laws* to the care of sacred matters and, to the conducting our public devotions with greater decency and order'. He adds, 'There is no rank of men more to be respected than the latter' (E 617n.1, 619). He considerably rewrote several paragraphs of the text to which this footnote was attached, and consequently deleted this entire footnote after the 1770 edition.[15] Along with this omission, John B. Stewart uses the fact that Hume dropped the Church of England from the list of false religions in 1770 (E 617) as proof of a softening in his attitude toward its clergy (Stewart 1963: 283; 1992: 280). Neither does this necessarily support his claim, however. If we take into account both his support of the maxim that priests of all religions are the same in the essay 'Of National Characters', and his deletion of the distinction between wicked priests and respectable clergymen in 'Of Superstition and Enthusiasm' in 1770, it is possible that Hume had a gradual change of mind on this point – moving toward a position opposed to Stewart's claim. After publishing the *Essays, Moral and Political*, he seems to have lost his respect for clergymen, and finally concluded that 'priests of all religions are the same'. One possible reason why Hume starts to criticise priests publicly in 1748 is the affair of the Edinburgh University chair in 1745. Placed at a disadvantage in that election because of his alleged 'accusation of Heresy, Deism, Scepticism, Atheism &c', he even published *A Letter from a Gentleman to his Friend in Edinburgh* in 1745 to defend his eligibility for the chair of Ethics and Pneumatical Philosophy. Just after his candidacy for the professorship was rejected at the meeting of the Town Council of Edinburgh, he complained in a letter that 'by the cabals of the Principal, the bigotry of the clergy, and the credulity of the mob, we lost it' (L I, 62; See also Sher 1990; Emerson 1994; Stewart 1995 for the details of this affair). Furthermore, as we will see below, in 1751 Hume anonymously published a broadside squib called the *Bellmen's Petition*, in which he mocked the sextons' grasping claims to raise their stipends.

Hume does not give the source of the phrase 'priests of all religions are the same', but it clearly derives from John Dryden's poetic political satire *Absalom and Achitophel* originally published in 1681 (the very term 'priest-craft' appears in the first line of this verse).[16] This satire was written against the backdrop of the Popish Plot and the Exclusion Bill Crisis. Not coincidentally, this phrase had much resonance in the context of the Deist debate in Britain before Hume picked it up. One of the most interesting examples of its use is George Berkeley's in *Alciphron, or the Minute Philosopher*. In one passage, Berkeley's imaginary enemy, Alciphron, rants: 'priests of all religions are the same: wherever there are priests there will be priestcraft'. Berkeley's aim was to refute such free-thinkers as Alciphron (representing thinkers like Shaftesbury and Collins) and Lysicles (standing for Mandeville), but Hume might well have been attracted to the haranguing of Berkeley's 'minute philosopher', who acutely identified 'these three pursuits of ambition, avarice, and revenge' as the true interests of the priesthood (Berkeley [1732] 1993: 27–8). As Hume cited Berkeley's dialogue in a footnote to 'Of National Characters' in a different context (E 209n.11), there is no doubt that he read this dialogue with much attention.

Hume's critical analysis of the pernicious effects produced by the clergy, however, seems more directly influenced by Mandeville, against whom Berkeley was writing. One of Mandeville's projects in *Free Thoughts on Religion* was to expose the ways in which 'clergy-men are made of the same mould, and have the same corrupt nature with other men', and consequently are liable to the same temptations (Mandeville [1720] 1729: 299; see also 291). While he tried to explain the priesthood according to his view of human nature as essentially selfish, he warned that the pernicious effects could be augmented in the case of clergy: 'because they have greater opportunities [of their encroachments], and are less mistrusted' (306; see also 303–4). Hume not only repeated the Mandevillean concern about the opportunity for the selfish nature of mankind to manifest itself among the priesthood in 'Of National Characters', but he also emphasised the peculiarity of the profession and its attendant dangers in a clearer way than Mandeville. Hume wrote:

> all wise governments will be on their guard against the attempts of a society, who will for ever [sic] combine into one faction, and while it acts as a society, will for ever [sic] be actuated by ambition, pride, revenge, and a persecuting spirit. (E 201n.3)

Mandeville also argued for 'the clergy carefully restrain'd from doing mischief to the society, and the publick [sic] every way guarded against them, as if they were the worst of men' ([1720] 1729: 307–8). Here, Mandeville is dealing with clergymen in general: 'When I advise the laity to keep the clergy in awe, I mean all clergy-men and religious teachers in general, and would by no means exclude the dissenters' (271). Although he did not use Dryden's phrase in *Free Thoughts on Religion*, he explained in the second volume of the *Fable of the Bees* the character of Horatio as the person who seems 'to be of the Opinion, which is express'd in that trite and specious as well as false and injurious Saying, Priests of all Religions are the same' (Mandeville [1714/1729, 1732] 1995: II, 16 [xvii]).[17]

The keynote of this dictum is the dangers of the connection between religion and politics. Even if Hume did not repeatedly use the same phrase in his later writings, the gist of it can be easily found throughout his published works. In 1751, when he was plausibly working on a draft of the *Dialogues concerning Natural Religion*, Hume anonymously published a sheet of satire called *Bellmen's Petition*. In concert with the real petition to increase the stipends of ministers and the salaries of schoolmasters in Scotland, the bell ringers were supposed to appeal to raise their payrolls in this broadside. Although the contextual settings of this squib are local and Scottish, his ridicule is not directed towards a specific type of Christian religion. Along with many laughable claims, the sextons aver that 'the Cause of Religion is as intimately and inseparably connected with the temporal Interests and worldly Grandeur of your Petitioners, as with any of these Ecclesiastics whatsoever' (Hume [1751] 1997: 5). It is evident from the satire that Hume agrees with the Scottish landowners (to which group he belonged) in their unwillingness to raise the stipends of ministers (Emerson 1997: 11). The issue of how to regulate or tame the arrogance of priests by secular interests is the very topic that Hume was to pick up in the *History of England*.

4 Hume's Sarcastic Defence of National Church and his Anticlericalism in the *History*

As we saw in Chapter 3, one of Hume's purposes in the *History* is – through experimental analysis of the historical shifts in commonly held opinion – to undermine dominant Whiggish political prejudices exemplified by the myth of the ancient constitution and the gratuitous criticism of the first two Stuart monarchs. Yet Hume was not only condemned as a Jacobite for this attempt, but he also attracted much criticism for his religious opinions. Some contemporaries noticed the seeming discordance between Hume's alleged apology for the Stuart monarchs and his irreligion. For example, the earl of Charlemont, one of Hume's friends, remarks that '[Hume's] History is as dangerous as in politics, as his [Philosophical] Essays are in religion'. '[I]t is somewhat extraordinary', he continues, 'that the same man who labours to free the mind from what he supposes religious prejudices, should as zealously endeavour to shackle it with the servile ideas of despotism' (Hardy 1812: I, 236). Although the earl mentions Hume's infidelity in the first *Enquiry* here, those of the *History* were also sufficiently provocative for his contemporaries. In a letter to his friend and publisher William Strahan, just after publishing the first volume of the *History of Great Britain* on the Stuart monarchs, Hume remarks: 'I see it is your Opinion, that the Enmity of the Clergy chiefly has hurt me. Others say, it is the Imputation, however absurd, of Jacobitism. Perhaps, it is both together' (Klemme 1991: 660). As exemplified in his anonymous pamphlet, Hume recognised that the religionist, whether Whig or Tory, would be prone to being inflamed with rage at his depiction of religions in the *History*.

It should be noted at the outset that Hume's apparently complimentary remarks regarding the Church of England were initially triggered by the contemporary criticism of his depiction of puritans as enthusiasts in the first volume of the *History of Great Britain* (published in 1754), dealing with the Stuart monarchs. Responding to these criticisms, Hume withdrew several passages devoted to characterising puritans as enthusiasts and Catholics as superstitious from the later editions of this volume.[18] He also inserted an exculpatory statement in a footnote to the second volume of the *History of Great Britain* published in 1756 (this note appears only in this edition). It should be remembered that around this time Hume was under the Highflyers' campaign of persecution in the General Assembly against him. Hume here distinguishes between 'true' and 'false' religion, and argues that '[e]very institution, however divine, which is adopted by men [...] will be apt, unless carefully guarded, to degenerate into one extreme or the other'. He here treats religion not in an ideal form, but as it exists in this world, and again utilises the dichotomy of 'superstition and enthusiasm' to define the two forms of false religion. For Hume, the problem is not how to realise 'true religion', but how to cope with the possible degeneration of religion into superstition or enthusiasm.[19] After discussing both possibilities of degeneration in actual religions, Hume remarks that '[t]he church of England itself, which is perhaps the best medium among these extremes, will be allowed, at least during the age of archbishop Laud, to have been somewhat infected with a superstition, resembling the popish' (Hume 1756: 450). The draft version of this footnote reads 'Of all the Sects, into which Christians have been divided, the Church of England seems to have chosen the most happy Medium [...]' (Mossner 1980: 306–7).[20]

When Hume advocated the Church of England in the Tudor volumes of the *History* published two years later (1759), he followed the same line by presenting a moderately flattering picture of the Church of England: 'OF ALL THE EUROPEAN CHURCHES, which shook off the yoke of papal authority, no one proceeded with so much reason and moderation as the church of England'. In order to prevent the most harmful effects of false religions, Hume argues, the best way is to steer a middle course between the two extremes of superstition and enthusiasm. Hume depicts 'the fabric of the secular hierarchy', 'the ancient liturgy', 'many ceremonies' and 'the distinctive habits of the clergy' in a positive light. His point is that, through such means, the Church of England 'had preserved itself *in that happy medium*, which wise men have always sought, and which the people have so seldom been able to maintain' (H IV, 119–20. Italics added). When Hume endorses the revival of ancient ceremonies by Laud, he is writing with this balance between enthusiasm and superstition in mind (V, 459–60). Thus, Hume in the *History* continues to develop the dichotomy of superstition and enthusiasm recognised by Burnet (and Shaftesbury). His vindication of the Church of England as the balanced medium between these two extremes, however, did not sound original or revealing to his contemporary readers, as the celebration of *via media* Anglicanism, as a bulwark both against Popery and against the rational or deistic dissenters, was something of a cliché by that time (Young 1998: 197–8). It should also be noted that Hume actually locates the Church of England, not beyond, but *within* the framework of false religions by admitting it as a 'happy medium' between superstition and enthusiasm.

On the other hand, Hume never withdrew from his criticism of priesthood in general. As mentioned above, he published the second volume of the *History of Great Britain* at the end of 1756, and just a few months after appears the *Four Dissertations* which contains 'The Natural History of Religion'. Certainly he seems to have a more favourable view of ancient polytheism than of monotheistic religion intolerant of heresy, but, unlike some contemporaries, he never connects these tolerant ancient religions with Catholic superstition; rather his contrast lies between ancient polytheism and modern Christianity in general. Moreover, the most fundamental tenet of this essay lies in his observation that religious belief 'springs not from an original instinct or primary impression of nature [...]. The first religious principles must be secondary' (NHR intro). This essay provoked fierce criticism from Richard Hurd, whom Hume called one of 'the Warburtonian school' (E 'My Own Life' xxxvii), and Warburton himself judged in a letter to Andrew Millar, the publisher of the *Four Dissertations*, that the aim of 'The Natural History of Religion' was 'to establish naturalism, a species of atheism, instead of religion' (quoted in Mossner 1980: 325).

It is still less known that Hume anonymously contributed a short piece of advertisement to Charles Smith's *A Short Essay on the Corn Trade and Corn Laws* in 1758, just after he published two volumes of the *History of Great Britain*. The published version of this advertisement is much defanged, but the draft version discovered by David Raynor and attributed to Hume abounds in Humean diatribe against the priesthood in general:

> Cou'd our Dealers in spiritual Ware show us, from the very Nature of their Commodity, that their Traffic was as little lyable [sic] to Abuses as that of the Corn Merchant, we shoud [sic] entertain the same favourable Opinion of them. But the Case is plainly the Contrary. They all aspire to be monopolists: They sell their Quack Powder, for which they pretend to have a Patent, at most enormous Prices. (Raynor 1998: 22)[21]

At least from this draft, there is no evidence that Hume moderated his distrust of the priesthood. What is important is that his diagnosis of the Anglican Church as occupying the middle ground between superstition and enthusiasm should be contextually and theoretically separated from his pragmatic and sardonic support of a religious establishment in general.

Hume's best-known defence of religious establishments in the first Tudor volume of the *History* was published in 1759, the year after Charles Smith's book. He reflects on the reasons 'why there must be [...] a public establishment of religion in every civilized community'. His argument starts in a serious mood, but it soon becomes clear that his endorsement of a religious establishment is heavily ironic. Here he is talking about 'every religion, *except the true*' that has 'a natural tendency to pervert the true [religion]'. The merit of religious establishments, for Hume, is 'to bribe [clergy's] indolence, by [...] rendering it superfluous for them to be farther active' (H III, 134–6. Italics added). To this dismissive tone of voice is added another characteristic of Humean argumentation of this issue: his application of the theory of unintended consequences. Hume explicates the historical evolution of religious establishments as follows:

> *in the end*, the civil magistrate will find, that he has dearly paid for his pretended frugality, in saving a fixed establishment for the priests [...]. And in this manner ecclesiastical establishments, though commonly they arose at first from religious views, prove *in the end* advantageous to the political interests of society. (H III, 136. Italics added)

The phrase 'in the end' is used twice in these short sentences. He emphasised that a religious establishment turned out to be politically beneficial only in hindsight. Hume skilfully utilises this logic not only in his account of the good but ironic effects of religious enthusiasm leading to political liberty in English history in the essay 'Of Superstition and Enthusiasm', but also of religious establishment here. This tactic is ingenious, because he never praises the role of 'false' religions in and of themselves. It does not necessarily follow from his acknowledgement of the political liberty unintentionally produced by religious enthusiasm that Hume positively appreciated religious fanaticism. In the same vein, his recognition of the unintended positive results of the existence of religious establishments does not mean that Hume took an invariably favourable attitude to the roles of national churches in civilised societies.

More importantly, Hume never mentions the salvation of souls in his discussion of the role of the clergy. On this point, his Erastianism is obviously quite different from, for example, William Warburton's self-justifying and latitudinarian version. Warburton emphasised the significance of an 'alliance' between church and state, based on the division of roles between spiritual and secular matters. He does not advocate the total independence of the clergy from civil government, as this would create '*imperium in imperio*', but he argues that the civil establishment should not interfere with spiritual matters (Warburton 1748: 67; see also Young 1998: chap. 5). On the other hand, when he asserts that '[t]he union of the civil and ecclesiastical power serves extremely, in every civilized government, to the maintenance of peace and order' (H I, 311), Hume's advocacy of such a union has nothing to do with any spiritual role for religion in society. While he is willing to acknowledge the presumptive virtues of 'true' religion for fostering peace and order in society, the central aim of his Erastianism is just to prevent social disorders and conflicts caused by religion. This is the reason he regarded the establishment of the Church of England by Henry VIII as a wise precaution: in placing himself as the head of secular power over the ecclesiastical body, he had prevented the possibility of religious confrontation. 'Henry was able to set the political machine in that furious movement, and yet regulate and even stop its career: He could say to it, Thus far shalt thou go and no farther' (H III, 244; allusion to Job 38: 11). Although he here cites the Anglican Church as an example, Hume repeats the same point in general terms. As early as the essay 'Of Parties in General', he acknowledged the complete separation of the civil and ecclesiastical powers as one of the causes of religious wars (E 60–3). In the essay 'Idea of a Perfect Commonwealth', where he chose the Presbyterian Church as an established church,[22] he also stated that '[w]ithout the dependence of the clergy on the civil magistrates, and without a militia, it is in vain to think that any free government will ever have security or stability' (E 525). Thus, his pragmatic and sardonic support of an established church should be distinguished from his rather flattering comments on the Church of England as the medium between superstition and enthusiasm.

Naturally, such Erastianism based on anti-clericalism is

influenced by Hume's predecessors' (notably Mandeville and Shaftesbury's) arguments. As we saw above, Mandeville warned that 'the publick [sic] every way guarded against' the clergy ([1720] 1729: 307–8). In *A Letter concerning Enthusiasm* (1708), Shaftesbury, a defender of toleration and free thinking, also insisted that 'as a notable author of our nation expresses it, a people should have a "public leading" in religion' (this notable writer is Harrington) ([1711] 1999: 11). This might bring him closer to other advocates of an established church among the seventeenth-century and his contemporary thinkers (like Hobbes, Harrington and Rousseau). However, Hume is quite different from Harrington and Rousseau who argue for a role of a national church in promoting the state ideology (Harrington [1656] 1992: 38; Rousseau [1762] 1997: Book 4, chap. 8, 'Of Civil Religion' 142–51 [IV.viii]; Champion 1992: chap. 6) – their views of the national church are more Machiavellian. In contrast, Hume never expects such a politically positive role from established churches, at least in this context. His emphasis is rather placed upon how to curtail (or even emasculate) the ecclesiastical influence through its subsidisation: it is about how to tame the possible zeal of the most powerful enemy by corralling it (NHR 9.3). Hume's ironic tone underlying these arguments also lacks Hobbes's seriousness concerning state control of religion (Hobbes [1651] 1996: chap. 42, 'Of Power Ecclesiasticall'; Tuck 1992). Considering the claim in his *Bellmen's Petition*, where he mocked the sextons' appeal to increase their salaries, the emphasis of Hume's argument in the *History* is not to positively claim Erastianism in any sense, but merely to caricature the selfishness and lust for power of the priesthood. The tone of this argument had been consistent since the essay 'Of National Characters'. In fact, throughout the *History* his criticism of clergy in general is not even remotely qualified: 'The epithet of the ignorant and vicious priesthood was commonly applied to all churchmen, addicted to the established discipline and worship' (H V, 301). Some of his contemporaries detected his intention in the *History*. Oliver Goldsmith, an Irish-born playwright and novelist, argues that '[w]ith regard to religion, [Hume] seems desirous of playing a double part, of appearing to some readers as if he reverenced, and to others as if he ridiculed it' (Goldsmith [1771] 2002: I, 343–4).[23]

As we have seen, it is not an easy task to gain a complete picture of Hume's assessment of the Church of England from his sporadic comments in the *History*. This is exactly because the Church of England was, and is, a national church in England. For this reason, Hume's view of an established church in general has been frequently confounded with his occasional excuses for the Anglican Church. Obviously, it has served to reinforce the image of Hume as a Tory historian. When each argument is analysed in its particular context, however, it becomes clear that his criticism of priests in general is the keynote throughout all of his writings, and that his ironical support of an established church is in fact the inevitable outcome of his anti-clericalism.

5 Hume's *Dialogues* and Smith's *Wealth of Nations*

If we exclusively focus on Hume's advocacy of religious establishment in the *History*, it would be natural to assume that Hume and Smith held opposite views on the matter. The contrast has been made between Smith's 'laissez-faire' approach in the *Wealth of Nations* and Hume's allegedly Tory, 'interventionist' and authoritarian approach to religious institutions (Davie 1994: 14; Fieser 2002: I, xvii; Jordan 2002: 708–10). In the *Wealth of Nations*, Smith refers to Hume's argument for the religious establishment (H III, 135–6) made by 'the most illustrious philosopher and historian of the present age'. He goes on to make a far less orthodox claim: that the system that the Independents attempted at the time of the Civil War was the most suitable 'where the society is divided into two or three hundred, or perhaps into as many thousand small sects, of which no one could be considerable enough to disturb the publick tranquility [sic]'. This is because, the author of the *Wealth of Nations* claims, it maintained competition among various religious sects. Smith seems to apply the famous logic of an 'invisible hand' to religious institutions (Smith [1776] 1982: 793 [V.i.g.8]).

Upon careful reading, however, it will be clear that Smith's position is much closer to Hume's than has been supposed by later commentators. I do not argue that there are no differences between the two philosophers, but rather that in many respects Smith owes his theoretical framework on religious institutions to Hume's arguments in the *History*. The following comparison between the two Scottish philosophers will also be helpful in further ascertaining the nature of Hume's ironic Erastianism in the *History*.

Firstly, just before the long quotation from Hume's *History*,

Smith clearly acknowledged the Humean thesis that paying a stipend to the clergy of an established church serves to enervate their activities (Smith [1776] 1982: 788–9 [V.i.g.1]). Smith has no reason to oppose Hume on this point, because both philosophers share the same premise: even the clergy behave according to their self-interest. They concur that the 'protectionist' policy applied to religious matters can sap the energy of the clergy, who are not forced to prove their worth. Smith also admitted Hume's historical description of religious establishment as an unintended consequence by claiming that the independent provision of the clergy 'has, perhaps, been very seldom bestowed upon them from any view to those effects' (791–2 [V.i.g.7]). These sentences might appear to be intended as a criticism, but again they are rather a confirmation of Hume's argument.

Secondly, we must attend to the premise of Smith's support for the Independents. He made the hypothetical supposition that 'if politicks [sic] had never called in the aid of religion, had the conquering party never adopted the tenets of one sect more than those of another', the new magistrate would have dealt with all the religious sects indifferently (Smith [1776] 1982: 792 [V.i.g.8]). At the same time, however, he conceded that such a rational religious policy was what 'wise men have in all ages of the world wished to see established; but such as positive law has perhaps never yet established, and probably never will establish in any country' (793 [V.i.g.8]). Smith seems to understand fully that his presupposition is quite unlikely, at least in the light of the actual history of modern Europe (791 [V.i.g.7]),[24] and that Hume had never supposed the same premise. It seems also unlikely that Hume in the above context of the *History* believed that magistrates should establish one dominant religious party as the established church if there were innumerable contending religious parties in one society.

Thirdly, and more importantly, Smith's supposition that civil magistrates 'would probably have dealt equally and impartially with all the different sects' (792 [V.i.g.8]) is almost the same as Hume's argument in the *Dialogues concerning Natural Religion*, written around 1750, but posthumously published. Smith, who refused Hume's request to publish his *Dialogues* after his death in 1776, must have known its content much earlier than the publication of the *Wealth of Nations*. Hume, in the voice of Philo, shows a seemingly different opinion on religious establishments:

> the utmost a wise magistrate can propose with regard to popular religions, is, as far as possible, [...] to prevent their pernicious consequences with regard to society? [...] If he admits only one religion among his subjects, he must sacrifice, to an uncertain prospect of tranquillity, every consideration of public liberty, science, reason, industry, and even his own independency. If he gives indulgence to several sects, which is the wiser maxim, he must preserve a very philosophical indifference to all of them, and carefully restrain the pretensions of the prevailing sect [...]. (Hume [1779] 1947: 223)[25]

Here Hume uses the phrase 'carefully restrain', which might sound 'interventionist'. However, his point is not that a magistrate should actively intervene in religious matters, but rather that he should vigilantly preserve a mildly competitive form of coexistence among the various sects. Although the above quotation still seems to contradict his support for a national church in the *History*, this is not necessarily so, if each passage is viewed in the context of the situation he is discussing. As he argues that 'if [a magistrate] admits only one religion among his subjects' it would produce devastating effects over public liberty and industry, it might be natural to think that Hume is considering a situation in which other religious sects are not tolerated. However, his support of religious establishments in the *History* clearly does not entail the persecution of dissenting sects; rather, he recommends the policy of toleration (H V, 459; V, 575–6, Note [FF]; on Hume's idea of religious tolerance, see below). Such an attitude of complete indifference towards all sects in the *Dialogues* is an ideal, but unfeasible, policy (especially in the European context) for Hume, as well as for Smith.[26] Smith in the *Wealth of Nations* renders more sophisticated the Humean perspective that different situations require different treatments. 'In a country where the law favoured the teachers of no one religion more than those of another', Smith argues, what a civil magistrate has to do is just 'to keep the peace among them'. But, he continues, 'it is quite otherwise in countries where there is an established or governing religion' because '[t]he sovereign can in this case never be secure, unless he has the means of influencing in a considerable degree the greater part of the teachers of that religion' (Smith [1776] 1982: 797 [V.i.g.16]).

It should also be heeded that Smith shares Hume's harsh criticism of 'the corporation spirit' (Berry 2009: 98–9). As we have seen, Hume lumps clergy and corn merchants together as 'monopolists' in his anonymous advertisement for Charles Smith's *Short Essays on the Corn Trade*. In the *Wealth of Nations*, Smith clearly echoes Hume in linking the two: 'The laws concerning corn may every where [sic] be compared to the laws concerning religion': 'The clergy of every established church constitute a great incorporation' (Smith [1776] 1985: 539 [IV.v.b.40]; 797 [V.i.g.17]). In the *Theory of Moral Sentiments*, Smith repeatedly criticised 'the factious and party zeal of some worthless cabal' who taught 'to imagine, that by sacrifices, and ceremonies, and vain supplications, they can bargain with the Deity for fraud, and perfidy, and violence' (Smith [1759] 1982: 170 [III.5.13]; see also 155–6 [III.3.43] and 176–7 [III.6.12]).

Taken as a whole, Smith's argument in the *Wealth of Nations* reflects both Hume's argument on religious establishments in the *History*, and his 'indifference' policy in the *Dialogues*: Smith supports Hume's 'indifference' policy in a theoretical situation where politics and religion can be peacefully separated, while he is willing to accept Hume's argument on religious establishments in the *History*. Thus, both philosophers jointly attempted to execute what Paul Russell (2008) calls the 'Lucretian mission', which was to displace the harmful influences of false religion in civilised societies. It is for good reason that Smith was often associated with Hume, especially on religious issues (Winch 1996: 185–91, 217; Phillipson 2010: 280–1).[27] Smith's affectionate depiction of Hume on his deathbed – published as *A Letter to Strahan*, appended to Hume's 'My Own Life' – also brought upon him 'ten times more abuse than the very violent attack [he] made upon the whole commercial system of Great Britain' (Smith 1982b: 251; see also Horne 1786). Although Smith probably wanted to have more discretion than Hume on the issue of religious belief, such a topic was still too sensitive and controversial in the late eighteenth century to warrant Smith's attempts to distance himself from the infamous Hume. Even in the early nineteenth century, Smith's view of atonement in the *Theory of Moral Sentiments* still drew criticism from William Magee, archbishop of Dublin, who lamented that he did not completely escape 'the infection of David Hume's society; and it added one proof more [...] of the danger, even to the most enlightened, from a familiar contact with infidelity' (cited in Raphael 1969). Smith's view of institutional religions can be considered as another proof of this infection.

6 Voltaire and 'the Scottish Voltaire'

The relationship between Hume and Smith concerning their criticism of priesthood leads us to consider the similarities and differences between Voltaire and Hume. This is because the maxim that legislators should maintain 'philosophical indifference' to a multitude of religious sects, which Hume shares with Smith, seems to be more directly inspired (or at least shared) by Voltaire. Hiroshi Mizuta points out that 'Smith's idea about the plurality of religious sects [...] seems to have been taken from Voltaire's *Lettres philosophiques* (letter 6)' (Mizuta 2000: 266). In fact, Voltaire claims that '[i]f there were only one religion in England, there would be danger of tyranny; if there were two, they would cut each other's throats; but there are thirty, and they live happily together in peace' (Voltaire [1733] 2003: 26; 1877–85: XXII, 99–100).

In a broad sense, it would not be unreasonable to follow Henry May in terming Voltaire another Sceptical Enlightenment thinker; nor would it be incorrect to deem Hume to be the 'Scottish Voltaire'.[28] As exemplified in the *Questions sur les miracles* (1769), Voltaire undermined the validity of testimonies on miracles, utilising the historical Pyrrhonism he learned from Bayle and other clandestine sources, as Hume did in his 'Of Miracles' (1748). Voltaire also insists on the dependence of the 'essential interest' (intérêt essentiel) of the clergy on the civil society ('Droit canonique' in the *Questions sur l'Encyclopédie* (Voltaire 1968–: XV, 547)). The attacks on established Christianity mounted by these two 'great infidels' often contained an ironic twist: in Voltaire's words, '[s]uch derision is a powerful barrier to inhibit the bigots from going too' ([1763] 2000: 25; 1968–: LVI(c), 155). Because of these sarcasms in their anti-religious writings, both are challenged by religious authorities in varying degrees, while defending religious tolerance and spreading more secular morality.

More significantly, the two great infidels shared another common enemy: the alliance between materialism and atheism (Roe 1985). Voltaire regarded the materialist views of baron d'Holbach and Diderot with antipathy ('Dieu. Réponse au *Système de la nature*' (1770) (1968–: LXXII, 143–63); 'Dieu, Dieux' in the *Questions sur l'Encyclopédie* (XL, 421–57, esp. 438–43)). As we saw at the beginning of this chapter, Hume was not necessarily hostile to these French materialists, while nonetheless in his philosophical writings, keeping them at a certain distance. In a broad sense, both Hume and Voltaire were forced to take a two-pronged strategy against orthodox Christianity and modern atheism.

In addition to this, despite his predominantly deistic orientation, Voltaire's sceptical tendencies were evident to the extent that some of his contemporaries and commentators deemed him to be not a deist, but an agnostic or even an undercover atheist (Besterman 1976: chap. 17). Voltaire sometimes emphasises the limit of our knowledge and reason, as exemplified by his claim that 'nature is a chimera' (la nature est une chimère) in *Les Oreilles du comte de Chesterfield et le chapelain Goudman* (1755) (Voltaire 1968–: LXXVI, 76; Roe 1985: 70).[29] Such elusiveness seems to approach him to Hume, who concludes his 'Natural History of Religion' by saying that '[t]he whole is a riddle, an enigma, an inexplicable mystery' (NHR 15.13). Among Hume scholars, there are some who term Hume's religious position 'attenuated deism' (Gaskin 1988; cf. Russell 2005/2013: § 10–11).[30]

It is with reason that Voltaire seems to consider Hume as a comrade against priesthood and religious bigotry. In a letter to d'Alembert, he includes Hume in a list of the same persuasion as himself (such as Confucius, Lucretius, Cicero, Julian, Collins, Shaftesbury, Middleton and Bolingbroke) (D8536; all the following references to Voltaire's letters are cited from Voltaire 2013, followed by the letter numbers of Besterman's edition of *Correspondence and Related Documents*, 2nd edn). Throughout his letters Voltaire applies the appellation 'athée' to Hume only twice. One is only to distinguish him from John Hume the poet (D9043); another is in mentioning others' evaluation of Hume: 'I like this Hume all the more because he was qualified as atheist in the *Journal encyclopédique*' (D11490; see also Pomeau [1954] 1969: 388).*[31]

Nevertheless, there are some essential differences between them. Although these should not be exaggerated, even slight differences can sometimes make a big difference. As we will see below, Voltaire seems to discern these differences in religious issues with Hume. It would be almost impossible to convincingly compare the evasive Scottish philosopher with such a prolific, encyclopaedic

* 'Ce Hume me plait d'autant plus, qu'il a été qualifié d'athée dans le journal Enciclopédique'.

and notoriously less systematic writer as Voltaire in a limited space. For all that, it is not futile to summarily contrast the two great infidels in order to clarify the diverse ways in which their contemporary thinkers tackled religious dogmatism. Such comparisons will also serve to further delineate the characteristics of Hume as Sceptical Enlightenment thinker.

First of all, Voltaire not only probably knew some of Hume's religious writings, but also criticised them on certain points. Voltaire's plausible mention, or rather critique, of these works appears in the article on 'Religion' in the *Dictionnaire philosophique* (1764). Voltaire argues that the earliest religion must have been monotheistic, criticising the claim of '[a]nother much more scholar [than Warburton] who is one of the most profound metaphysicians of our times' ([1976] 2004, 350; 1968–: XXXVI, 471; cited in Malherbe 2005: 69). Despite the editor's estimation that this might allude to Fontenelle's *De l'origine des fables* (Voltaire 1968–: XXXVI, 471–2n.13), Malherbe maintains that this is Hume's opinion on the historical priority of polytheism to monotheism in the 'Natural History of Religion' (2005: 69), which was translated into French for the first time in 1759 (Fieser 2003). They do share a fundamental point in terms of their psychological analyses of 'fear' (angoisse) as the origin of our evolving a concept of God to explain puzzling natural phenomena. Voltaire claims that 'a rude tribe' (une bourgade) tended to conceive the first image of God from an analogy of their chieftain. After several tribes had been integrated into a larger one, he argues, they would have had a polytheistic religion for the first time. The difference lies principally in their understandings of the anthropological origins of our religious beliefs. Voltaire here estimates that our primitive reasoning would proceed from simple to complex, while Hume went from imperfect to perfect (Malherbe 2005: 69). Much later, argues Voltaire, after a certain level of civilisation was realised, some philosophers would have reached a more rationalistic deism. However, the difference between the two authors is not completely on the theoretical level. For Voltaire's part, there seems to be another reason to insist on the monotheistic origin of religion, unlike Hume's (Gay 1966–9: I, 413).[32] Despite his formula 'écrasez l'infâme', he seems never to abandon his belief in deism or what he rather liked to call 'theism' in his later years (Pomeau [1954] 1969: 204). While admitting the diversity of human customs and manners as Hume does, he emphasised the simplicity, universality and omnipresence of the natural law throughout his writings, though not in any Judeo-Christian sense. For Voltaire, the pristine religion must be exempt from all kinds of superstitions later added by priests and politicians, and the primitive monotheism must be one of the indirect, if not the direct, historical proofs of his insistence on the 'pure religion'.

Secondly, despite his criticisms of miracles and Leibnitzian providentialism, Voltaire somewhat naïvely supports the argument for regarding God as the 'great designer' (suprême fabricateur) (*L'Histoire de Jenni ou le Sage et l'Athée* (1775) (1968–: LXXVI: 97)); a position which Hume was to devastatingly confute in his posthumous *Dialogues concerning Natural Religion* (1779). Voltaire, who died in 1778, had no chance to read this work, but his repeated reliance on the analogy of 'watch' (montre, horloge) and 'watchmaker' (horloger) was made to look banal, if not completely outmoded (Sec. 2 of 'Causes finales' in the *Questions sur l'Encyclopédie* (1968–: XXXIX, 548–9; Wade 1970: 721), for those acquainted with Hume's argument.[33] Voltaire's conviction in a universal moral law is closely connected with his belief in the order and regularity of this world.[34]

When examining the two points discussed above, a gulf opens up between Hume and Voltaire in their understanding of the relationship between religion and morals. Admittedly, Voltaire sometimes appeals to the utilitarian foundations of morality. His arguments in the *Traité de métaphysique* (especially in chaps. 8 and 9), for example, reflected Mandeville's *Enquiry into the Origin of Moral Virtue* (1714) (Wade 1970: 345–6; Wade [1947] 1967: 45). Voltaire here states that '*the virtue and vice, the good and evil are, therefore, in any country what is useful or harmful to the society*' (1968–: XIV, 475).* While accepting Mandeville's arguments of pride as an engine of the development of our social instincts, however, he also acknowledges the existence of a natural benevolence that God has instilled in us (Wade [1947] 1967: 45–8). In the same vein, while emphasising the diversity of positive laws, Voltaire often derives the fundamental universality of justice directly from 'the supreme Intelligence' (l'Intelligence suprême) in *Le Philosophe ignorant* (1968–: LXII, 76), for example.

The similar connection between his moral theory and deistic

* '*La virtu et le vice, le bien et le mal moral, est donc en tout pays ce qui est utile ou nuisible à la société*'

creed permeates Voltaire's views of the role of religion in our societies. In the article 'Athée, Athéisme' in *Dictionnaire philosophique*, he clearly claims the indispensability of religions not only for the vulgar, but also for the governors (1968–: XXXV, 390); he not only admits some positive aspects of superstitions but claims that even bad superstitions are much better than nothing (388; see also *L'Histoire de Jenni ou le Sage et l'Athée* 1968–: LXXVI, chaps. 11–12; Wade 1970: 649). In the *Traité sur la tolérance* he asserts that '[w]herever a community has taken root, religion is essential' ([1763] 2000: 83; 1968–: LVI(c), 242). Although Voltaire's personal belief in the immortality of the soul fluctuates throughout his writings (Pomeau 1969: 405–6), he seems convinced of the utmost importance of the notion of reward and punishment in the next world as a security of universal moral law. Hence he opines in the *Épître à l'auteur du livre des trois imposteurs* that 'if God did not exist, it would be necessary to invent Him' (Voltaire 1877–85: X, 403).* The urgency of his need for deistic religion became more apparent and imminent in his later writings (Pomeau 1969: 390). *Le Philosophe ignorant* (1766), for example, appeals to 'a necessary, eternal and intelligent Being' (un Être nécessaire, éternel, intelligent) (1968–: LXII, 54) in his justification of the universality of moral laws. His deism seems even to become dogmatic after the 1770s, when he dared to ally himself with some enlightened clerics in order to oppose the modern atheism of d'Holbach and Diderot (Wade 1970: 747). In a letter written in 1761, while probably mentioning Hume's posthumously published essays 'Of the Immortality of the Soul' along with Warburton's *Divine Legation of Moses*, Voltaire comments that 'Mr Hume went much further than Bayle and Warburton' on this issue (Voltaire 2013: D10078).[35] This sounds neither critical nor negative, but he pays heed to 'such boldness' (de telles hardiesses) as the two British writers show, and the fact that the *Encyclopédie* covers the same material as Bayle did; he concludes that 'I am afraid that all these reasons hold back our booksellers'.†

Compared with Voltaire's propagandistic commitment to deism, Hume's notion of 'true religion' appears much attenuated or merely excusatory. While he sometimes appeals to the 'true

* 'si Dieu n'existait pas, il faudrait l'inventer'.

† 'M. *Hume* a été encore plus loin que Bayle et Warburton'; 'J'ai peur que toutes ces raisons n'aient retenu nos libraires'.

religion', whether he seriously believes in it or not lies out of our present concern. It would suffice to say that Hume's defence of 'true religion' plays neither reformatory nor salvific roles in his writings, unlike in Voltaire's. While Hume sporadically acknowledges the positive effects on our manners of even false religions including Catholicism (Siebert 1990: 89–95; Rasmussen 2014: 186), these effects are not spiritual or otherworldly in a true sense, but are rather derivative, indirect and unintended. We might recall that from the time of the essay 'Of Superstition and Enthusiasm' Hume was willing to acknowledge the positive, though unintended, effects of enthusiasm to produce political liberty. Similarly, he asserts that '[t]he advantages, attending the Romish hierarchy, were *but a small* compensation for its inconveniencies' (H III, 137. Italics added). These sporadic acknowledgements of the positive effects of false religions should be considered to stem from his perpetual concern to guard against dogmatic or partisan views. These partial concessions never detracted from his overall and life-long hatred of priesthood. Hume hardly recommends any religions because of their possible deterrence of crimes by the fear of eternal punishments in the afterlife; he rather seems to emphasise the opposite in the *Dialogues concerning Natural Religion*, where he questions through the mouth of Philo '[h]ow happens it then [...] if vulgar superstition be so salutary to society, that all history abounds so much with accounts of its pernicious consequences on public affairs?' (DNR 12.11; 220). Serjeantson seems correct to point out that 'Hume is concerned in general to discredit Warburton's broad assertion, made in Book II of the *Divine Legation*, that a doctrine of a future state is necessary to society' (2012: 286). As we saw above, Voltaire plausibly noticed this point.

Through these considerations, it becomes clear that Hume's moral theory has a much greater affinity with Bayle's 'atheists' country' thesis than Voltaire's, in the sense that his moral theory did not necessarily require support from any religious faith (Wade 1970: 649–50; Harris 2003: esp. 247–53; Robertson 2005: chap. 6). On the other hand, Voltaire criticises Bayle's thesis in the article on 'Athée, Athéisme' in the *Dictionnaire philosophique* (1968–: XXXIX, 385–91; see also the *Histoire de l'établissement du christianisme* (1777) (XXXI: chap. 25)). He reluctantly admits the existence of the ancient atheistic sects: the Epicureans, Sceptics and Academics. Following Bayle, Voltaire also accepts that all the Roman senators and even some emperors were atheists. Nevertheless, he insinuates that the rule of these atheists had adverse effects on our morals. For example, he attributes the cause of the fall of the Roman republic to the 'Senate of Rome, who were almost all consisted of atheists in theory and practice'. He goes on to argue: 'The epicureanism survived under the emperors: the atheists of the Roman Senate were factious during the age of Sylla and Caesar; they were servile atheists under August and Tiberius' (XXXV, 389–40).*[36] As we saw in the previous chapter, Hume does not believe in the alleged pernicious effects of Epicureanism on societies.

Voltaire's claim for the state and civil control of religion was also more sincere and serious than Hume's. Voltaire expected priests to play the role of moral preceptors for the vulgar under the perfect control and inspection of the state ('Prêtre' in the *Dictionnaire philosophique* ([1764] 2004, 346–7; 1968–: XXXVI, 461–2). In the article on 'Curé de campagne' in the *Questions sur l'Encyclopédie* he also insists upon the necessity of a state subsidy for the clergy, especially for the indigent but diligent country curates, in order to maintain the authority necessary to the position (1968–: XL, 331–7; Neserius 1926: 44–6). In spite of his severe criticism of organised religions, he believes that religious institutions are indispensable for the maintenance of political order and public tranquillity in civilised societies. On this account Voltaire's Erastianism can be considered much closer to those of Hobbes and Rousseau in that they saw potential for the use of the national church as an auxiliary means for political administration.

The Humean method of support for religious toleration can be further contrasted with the Voltairean. Hume's mentions of the principle of religious tolerance are scattered throughout the *History* (Stewart 1963: 284–7; Spencer 2002: 892–5; Dees 2005; Sabl 2009; Rasmussen 2014: 188–9), but his account is consistently political and realistic. Although, like other contemporary thinkers, he could have supported religious tolerance for humanitarian reasons (and he did so partly), Hume rather emphasises the long-term political effects of 'the paradoxical principle and salutary practice of toleration' (H V, 130). Through the mouth

* '[...] du sénat de Rome, qui était presque tout composé d'athées de théorie et de pratique'; 'L'épicuréisme subsista sous les empereurs: les athées du sénat avaient été des factieux dans les temps de Sylla et de César; ils furent sous Auguste et Tibère des athées esclaves'.

of Cardinal Pole in the debate with Bishop Gardiner during the reign of Queen Mary, Hume explains that the severe persecution of heresy '*commonly proves ineffectual to the purpose intended*; and serves only to make men more obstinate in their persuasion, and to encrease the number of their proselytes'. This is because persecution results in fostering religious zeal among the heretics, who are willing to sacrifice their lives as martyrs. Not only that, Hume argues, but 'the spectators, moved with pity towards the supposed martyrs, are easily seduced to embrace those principles, which can inspire men with a constancy that appears almost supernatural' (III, 432–3. Italics added). Interestingly, Hume uses the logic of unintended consequences here as well as in his support of a national church and his account of enthusiasm as a cause of political liberty. However, Hume concedes that it is unlikely that people in Tudor times could have recognised, much less practised, such a subtle principle (IV, 54), because they were unacquainted with 'the true secret for managing religious factions' (IV, 352). 'An unlimited tolerance', for Hume, is a 'true' remedy for such 'a disease dangerous and inveterate' as religious hostility exacerbated by persecution (VI, 322), but vulgar politicians had recourse to more hasty remedies, because 'the operations of this regimen are commonly gradual, and at first imperceptible'. The fact that religious persecution tends to yield results that are completely contrary to its intention was finally accepted 'by fatal experience, and after spilling an ocean of blood in those theological quarrels' (V, 130). Hume's promotion of toleration – like his support for a national church – is a political strategy calculated to enervate religious enthusiasm, rather than impassioned advocacy of freedom of religion. For this reason, he does not believe in the universal applicability of unlimited tolerance, and justifies the persecution of heretics only in the case 'where a theology altogether new, nowise connected with the ancient religion of the state, is imported from foreign countries, and may easily, at one blow, be eradicated, without leaving the seeds of future innovation' (III, 433; see also IV, 459 and 575–6 Note [FF]).[37] Although Voltaire also emphasises the absurdity and bad effects of religious intolerance, his general tone of argument is rather based upon his conviction of deism as the sole effective bulwark against any religious bigotry; he concludes his *Traité sur la tolérance* with an appeal to 'God of all beings, of all worlds, and of all ages' (Voltaire [1736] 2000: 92; 1968–: LVI(c), 251; Wade 1970: 749).

In sum, despite the similarities between their sarcastic tones in their anti-religious writings and the overlapping of their attitudes in opposition to religious bigotry and in favour of tolerance, one of the biggest differences between Voltaire and Hume lies in the fact that the former has attempted to provide us with his notion of deism (theism) as an ecumenical platform for sane and permissible religious comprehension – which has been considered to be a 'constructive' aspect of his deism. On the other hand, apart from his personal, and deliberately ambiguous, view of religion, or his occasional but highly disputed and puzzling claims (for example, our belief in 'the primary principles of genuine Theism and Religion' in NHR intro.), the 'true religion' Hume refers to in his published writings cannot be considered to play such positive or serious roles as Voltaire's appeal to deism. Hume's own stance toward deism is most clearly exemplified in the anecdote recorded by the earl of Charlemont. In his memoirs he said that he 'never saw [Hume] so much displeased, or so much disconcerted, as by the petulance of Mrs. Mallet, the conceited wife of Bolingbroke's editor':

> This lady, who was not acquainted with Hume, meeting him one night at an assembly, boldly accosted him in these words: – 'Mr. Hume, give me leave to introduce myself to you; we deists ought to know each other'. – 'Madam,' replied he, 'I am no deist. I do not style myself so, neither do I desire to be known by that appellation'. (Hardy 1821: I, 235; cited in Mossner 1980: 395)

If this episode contains some truth, Hume's mockery and exhaustive criticism of religions including Christianity seems to approach him more to the atheists such as d'Holbach. This French materialist has a similar understanding about the causes of religious superstition to Hume's and Voltaire's: fear and ignorance (1768: I, 1). Nevertheless, as emphasised at the beginning of this chapter, Hume is far from triumphalist in his belief in the effectiveness of reason and knowledge. As a contrast, d'Holbach concludes in *Le Christianisme dévoilé*: 'truth must at last triumph over falsehood. – Mankind, fatigued with their own credulity, will return to her arms. – Reason will break their chains. – *Reason*, which was created to reign, with undivided empire, over all intelligent beings' (Holbach 1766: 293; 1795: 238). Obviously, neither a similar argument, nor such a tone can be found anywhere in Hume's writings (Russell 2005/2013: § 11; Mazza 2005: 236, 238). Based on his 'science of MAN' with its emphasis on the roles of imagination and passions, this Sceptical Enlightenment thinker denied himself the luxury of optimism, except for occasional sallies.

7 Hume's Alleged Moderation Revisited

Having completed the comparison between Hume and Voltaire on religious issues, before concluding this chapter, I will review Hume's allegedly benign attitude toward superstition in the *History*. Certainly, in contrast with his emphasis on the positive (though unintended) effects of puritan fanaticism on political liberty in the essay 'Of Superstition and Enthusiasm', his attitude to puritans in the *History* became harsher. Accordingly, he seemingly adopts a softer attitude toward Catholicism and those with Catholic leanings as shown by his lenient treatment of William Laud (who though not a Catholic, was accused of it by some contemporaries).

Two points should be heeded here. Firstly, Hume is willing to admit in the *History* that the manners of the earlier periods he was dealing with were superstitious. His analysis lies in elucidating their ways of thinking and the principle of behaviour of these ages rather than in blaming their personal barbarity and ignorance. For example, Hume warns us that the strict measures taken by William Laud against the puritans, though admittedly motivated by 'the intemperate zeal of a sectary', 'is more to be regarded as a general imputation on the whole age, than any particular failing of Laud's' (H V, 460). He used the same reasoning for the Catholic monarch, James II, and insists that the religious bias found in his writings is excusable. This is because '[f]rom the grossness of its superstitions, we may infer the ignorance of an age; but never should pronounce concerning the folly of an individual, from his admitting popular errors, consecrated by the appearance of religion' (V, 155). Exactly the same opinion can be found in the essay 'Of the Standard of Taste': 'Of all speculative errors, those which regard religion, are the most excusable in compositions of genius [...]. No religious principles can ever be imputed as a fault to any poet' (E 247). Considering his awareness of the changeability in the standard of our moral judgements (Chapter 3), Hume's seemingly benign comments should not be taken as mere ideological or personal apologetics for the Archbishop of Canterbury or the notorious monarch, much less for the Catholic religion.[38] Rather, he attempts here to distinguish between the factors attributable to personal characters and the spirit of the age. These considerations suggest that Hume's seemingly sympathetic attitude toward superstition in the *History* is a part of his efforts to describe the historical narrative of the past ages in a detached way. In his understanding, ignorance and superstition were characteristics of the Middle Ages and even early modernity. It does not necessarily follow that such follies of the past should be forgiven, but, at least 'to a philosophical mind' (H V, 459), it would not be justifiable to indiscriminately attribute all of them to personal faults.

Secondly, and related to the first point, his apparently benign expressions regarding and judgements of Catholicism do not necessarily mean that his overall attitude to superstition became softer. Not in the *History*, but rather in the correspondence of his later life, he continues to express his concerns about 'a new and a sudden Inroad of Ignorance, Superstition and Barbarism' (NL 199; see also L I, 511–12; II, 310). Interestingly, the emphasis in these letters is placed more on superstition than on enthusiasm, although the distinction between the two became blurry in his later writings. Obviously, Hume deems the 'Wilkes and Liberty' affair as 'Licentiousness, or rather the frenzy of liberty' (L II, 191) and he frequently laments the abuses or excesses of liberty taken by the press. Donald Livingston considers Hume's attitude toward the 'Wilkes and Liberty' movement to be an anticipation of Burke's criticism of the French Revolution, because of the 'false theorizing in history, economics, and political philosophy' allegedly embodied in this extra-parliamentary movement (Livingston 1998: 278, 288). Nevertheless, it is not clear to what extent Hume assumed that these extra-parliamentary movements were influenced by false philosophy. Despite Livingston's elaborate argument, Hume himself nowhere clearly and directly states that the 'Wilkes and Liberty' movement was excited by any systematically applied philosophical tenet.[39] Rather, Hume's expressions seem to indicate that he attacked 'the violence of the Mob', 'the despicable London Mob' or 'the contemptible Populace of London' (L II, 213; II, 234; II, 241) not because their claims were too *rational*, but rather because they were too *irrational*. While the word 'frenzy' is almost a synonym for 'enthusiasm' in his writings, and Puritans' adherence to the spirit of liberty was explained as 'that epidemical frenzy which prevailed' (H V, 348), Hume used the phrases 'popular frenzy' (VI, 342, 348) in his description of the Popish Plot. In this affair, Hume argues, 'reason and argument and common sense and common humanity lost all influence over' the people (VI, 333). The phrase 'general frenzy for crusades' also appears in the *History* (II, 65). Remarkably, Hume thought that the Wilkes affair was part of a more general retrogression towards 'Superstition and Ignorance' or 'barbarism, ignorance, and superstition' (L I, 521; II, 111). Livingston's notion of 'barbarism of refinement' as 'a new form of barbarism – a form possible only in an advanced stage of civilization' (1998: 219) seems unsupported as Hume's own one, although it is largely based upon Livingston's careful but stretched readings of Hume's essay 'Of Simplicity and Refinement in Writing'. This is because Hume usually does not connect the words 'refinement' or 'false philosophy' with 'barbarism', 'ignorance' or 'superstition' (except just once in H II, 70). Hume's concern with the return of superstition came back to haunt him on his deathbed. In a letter to Wedderburn, Smith envisaged Hume, sick in bed shortly before death, calling on Charon to wait until 'I have the pleasure of seeing the church shut up, and the Clergy sent about their business' (Smith 1982b: 204; see also Schliesser 2003). This was Hume's lifelong attitude toward clergy and church. Another version of this story appears in one of Hume's last letters: 'If I live a few years longer, I may have the satisfaction of seeing the downfall of some of the prevailing systems of superstition' (L II, 451). Hume is not optimistic on this point, however, because he also knew that it would never happen for 'these many hundred years' (see also Hume's 1775 letter to Andrew Stuart appended to Baumstark 2003: 256–7). This attitude can be contrasted with d'Holbach's Coterie who, according to Alexander Carlyle's report of Hume's testimony, 'were of opinion that Christianity would be abolished in Europe by the end of the eighteenth century' (Carlyle [1860/1910] 1990: 292; quoted in Mossner 1980: 274).

Hume's concerns about the return of superstition in his letters do not contradict his attitude in the *History*, but rather provide proof of his consistency as Sceptical Enlightenment thinker. He certainly accepts the fact that the manners of the past English were superstitious and admits that only 'during a very religious age, no institutions can be more advantageous to the rude multitude than a religious one' (H V, 459). At the same time, however, he continues to be apprehensive about the recurrence of superstition and ignorance, precisely because he believes that his contemporaries had reached 'if not the best system of government, at least the most entire system of liberty, that ever was known amongst mankind' (VI, 531; he elsewhere calls the English government 'the most perfect and most accurate system of liberty' and 'the most perfect government' (H II, 525)). This apprehension is closely related to his view of the British constitution and civilisation, which will be discussed in Chapters 6 and 7.

To summarise, Hume's complimentary comments on the Church of England and his endorsement of religious establishments has been considered a part of his alleged Toryism, but these two arguments should be differentiated. His flattering comments on the Anglican Church were in reaction to the criticism of his depiction of puritans: Hume maintains that the Church of England provides a middle ground between superstition and enthusiasm, but still within the framework of 'false' religions. His sardonic endorsement of religious establishments rather derives from his recognition of the tyranny of priesthood in general. For both strands of his argument, Hume is heavily indebted to his predecessors, such as Shaftesbury, Mandeville and Burnet. Along with Hobbes, Harrington and Rousseau, he is keenly aware of the necessity of civilian control over religious institutions. The ironic and mocking manner of Hume's Erastianism, however, distinguishes it from the version given by these thinkers, in which the involvement of religious establishments in politics is thought to have positive ideological advantages.

Adam Smith further develops Hume's anticlericalism in the *Wealth of Nations*: his endorsement of the Independents' policy is much closer to Hume's 'indifference' policy in the *Dialogues*. At the same time, Smith, following Hume, also admits the institutional merits of the religious establishments in the contemporary European context. Both considered curtailing the pernicious effects of 'false' religions in civilised societies as an urgent task.

On the other hand, Voltaire seems to differ more from the so-called 'Scottish Voltaire' in his sincere emphasis on the role of religion in civilised societies. Despite his notorious call to 'écrasez l'infâme' and his fierce criticisms of religious superstition, Voltaire seems willing to prefer the moderate version of Christian religion to atheism, although he continued attempting to approximate the former to what he calls 'une religion pure'. Hume, the Sceptical Enlightenment thinker, never fully aligns himself with Voltairean deism. At least in terms of his support for the thesis of Bayle's 'atheists' country', Hume's secular moral theory seems rather closer to that of contemporary atheists.[40] Nonetheless, Hume's persistent criticisms of religions remain compatible with his agnosticism. Even when he provocatively opines that religious principles are nothing but 'sick men's dreams' in the 'Natural History of Religion', he expressly mentions 'the religious principles, *which have, in fact, prevailed in the world*' (NHR 15.6. Italics added). Thus, he deliberately preserves a distance between his sceptical and agnostic arguments and the arrogance and overconfidence of those atheists who pretend that they can prove that God does not exist.

Notes

1. On the influence of the Academics and Cicero on Hume's view of belief in God, see Fosl (1994). See also Price 1964; Rivers 2000: 250–5.
2. Advertisements for Hume's *Treatise* (with the author's name) appeared in two periodic journals in January and February 1756, which he never authorised: 'The advertisement at this precise moment of a work which had not been advertised for fifteen years and which was never again to be advertised during the lifetime of its author is hardly to be attributed to coincidence' (Mossner 1950: 42). What Mossner means 'at this precise moment' is the affairs over the publication of the *Five* (not *Four*) *Dissertations* including the essays 'Of Suicide' and 'Of the Immortality of the Soul'.
3. When Blair, Robertson, Wedderburn and Adam Smith published a short-lived journal, the *Edinburgh Review* (1755–6), Hume was ostracised from the project and 'his recent *History of the Stuarts* passed unnoticed in its reviews' (Mossner 1980: 338). Smith's involvement in this journal does not disrupt my claim in what follows that his view of institutional religion is much closer to Hume's than the moderate literati.
4. See also a comment of Alexander Carlyle, a friend of Hume, in his Autobiography: '[Hume] was branded with the title of Atheist, on account of the many attacks on revealed religion that are to be found in his philosophical works, and in many places of his History – the last of which are still more objectionable than the first, which a friendly critic might call only sceptical' (Carlyle [1860/1910] 1990: 285).

5. As Champion demonstrates, anticlericalism did not necessarily imply irreligion among the Republicans, deists and freethinkers (1992: 178–9).
6. Robert Wallace also wrote (but never published) a manuscript critiquing Hume's negative depiction of priesthood (Mossner 1980: 260–2).
7. Note, in this regard, the idea that had already appeared in embryonic form in 'Of Superstition and Enthusiasm', where he considered that 'in almost every sect of religion there are priests to be found' because 'superstition is a considerable ingredient in almost all religion' (E 75). See also an entry of Hume's 'Early Memoranda': 'No Religion can maintain itself in Vigour without many observances to be practic'd on all Occasions. Hence the Priests are stricter upon these than moral Duties without knowing the Reason. There is a secret Instinct of this kind' (Hume 1948: 503, entry 39).
8. On the influence of Lucretius on Hume's 'Natural History of Religion' and *Dialogues concerning Natural Religion*, see Baker 2007: 279–81.
9. Yet Trenchard dwells less on the contrast between superstition and enthusiasm than does Hume (1709: 47–8). Incidentally, d'Holbach was to adopt exactly the same title as Trenchard's nearly sixty years later (Holbach 1768).
10. A broader and shared framework for Hume's contemporaries' and predecessors' criticism of religion can be found, though not exclusively, in Robert Burton's *Anatomy of Melancholy*. This Oxford scholar, who published the first edition of this book under the telling pseudonym 'Democritus junior', argues that the cause of melancholy can be ascribed to imagination (he also uses the term 'phantasy', the etymology of which is Latin *phantasia* and of ancient Greek φαντασία) ([1621] 2001: 253 [Part 1, Section 2, Member 3, Subsections 1–2]). In this book, he argues that 'religion is twofold, true or false; false is that vain superstition of idolaters' (320 [3.4.1.1]). He repeatedly points to 'hope, fear, ignorance and simplicity' as the main causes of superstition. While making no clear distinction between superstition and enthusiasm, he also remarks on another form of false religion, that is, the extreme reaction to 'Anti-christ, human traditions, those Romish rites and superstitions' (370 [3.4.1.3]). Burton takes Socinians, Brownists, Barrowists and Familists as these instances. This suggests, however, not a direct influence from Burton to Hume, but rather that these arguments had many antecedents and were widely shared, as Burton's incessant references to ancient, medieval

and modern sources evince. This point was kindly suggested by Roger L. Emerson in a private communication.

11. As for Shaftesbury's attempt to convert enthusiasm into a heightened sociability, see Carey 2004: 149.
12. Although there is no attribution of this essay in *The Old Whig* (Chandler 1735–8), several parts of the same series appeared in the preceding issues (No. 146, 22 Dec. 1737, No. 155, 23 Feb. 1738, No. 156, 2 Mar. 1738), and an anonymous contributor to *The Old Whig* in issue number 103 (24 Feb. 1737) was aware of the authorship of 'the late ingenious Mr. Gilbert Burnet, Son of the Bishop of that Name' (These issues are not included in *The Old Whig* (2 vols) published in book form in 1739). *The Free-thinker*, in which Burnet's essays originally appeared, was published during 1718–21. The compilation was published in 1722–3 in three volumes, and, as far as I could confirm, republished in 1733, 1739, 1740 and 1742. In the preface to the 1740 edition, the authorship of 'the late Reverend Dr. Gilbert Burnet' of the papers on superstition and enthusiasm was also revealed.
13. Moore does not directly mention the relationship between Hume and Burnet concerning the essays on superstition in this entry, but it seemed evident that he was fully aware of it. After drafting the original paper that was revised and expanded to become the present chapter, the author was able to confirm that this was the case through a personal communication. The priority on this point should be given to James Moore.
14. Some contemporary writers who criticised Hume's argument that the priests of all religions were the same tried to repudiate it by denying its universal applicability, rather than by defending the priesthood in general. Alexander Gerard, for example, counters Hume's argument: 'because different religions are unlike in many circumstances, fit to operate on the character, priests of all religions cannot be the same' (1762: 16).
15. Green and Grose's edition wrongly recorded that this note remained till the 1760 edition of the *Essays and Treatises on Several Subjects* (4 vols) and was deleted after the 1764 edition (2 vols) (Hume 1992 [1882]: 146–7), and Eugene F. Miller, the editor of the Liberty Fund edition of Hume's *Essays* adopted this without any *Textkritik*. Actually this footnote remained until the 1768 edition (2 vols) and was deleted after the 1770 edition (4 vols).
16. Hume also remarks in the same footnote to 'Of National Characters' that by 'having got what ARCHIMEDES only wanted (namely,

another world on which he could fix his engine) no wonder [the clergy] move this world at their pleasure' (E 200n.3). An American anonymous writer pointed out that this remark came from Dryden's *Don Sebastian* (Anon. [1816] 2002: II, 79).

17. A similar expression is also found in the *Histoire des deux Indes*: 'the spirit of the priesthood is everywhere the same' (l'esprit sacerdotal est par-tout le même) (Raynal [and Diderot] 1780: I, 37; quoted in Muthu 2003: 112). Muthu attributes this sentence to Diderot.
18. These deleted sentences appear in Hume [1754] 1970: 71–3, 96–9; the preface of the Liberty Fund edition (H I, xiv–xviii). Hume wrote to John Clephane that 'I am convinced that whatever I have said of religion should have received some more softenings' (L I, 237). Mossner guesses from this letter that Hume decided to soften his treatment of religious matters (1980: 305–6), although he admits that Hume had not 'altered his views concerning the rights and duties of a historian'. John V. Price, on the other hand, criticises this reasoning because the dating of this letter (1756) is based upon the editor's estimation, and conclusive evidence is still lacking (Price 1990). In a letter to Strahan (dated 22 Mar. 1755 cited in the beginning of this chapter), however, after admitting Strahan's opinion that 'in case of reprinting, I shou'd soften all the Passages, which have given Offence', Hume clearly confesses that '[n]othing vexes me more, than to find how easily that was done' (Klemme 1991: 660–1). As for John Brown's attack on Hume's alleged change of attitude between the *Essays* and the *History*, see Brown 1757–8: II, 86–7.
19. The general tenor of his excuse is similar to Montesquieu's *Défense de l'esprit des lois* (*A Defense of the Spirit of Laws*) ([1750] 1777: 243–4).
20. Although Mossner conjectured the dating of this draft to 1756, Baumstark set it at 1755, based on the fact that Hume had intended to publish in 1755 the second volume of the *History of Great Britain*, into which this draft was meant to be incorporated. Baumstark also estimates that this draft, which was entitled by a son of Gilbert Elliot as 'Draft of Preface to a volume of D Hume's History', seems to have been composed as a footnote or endnote from the beginning (2008: 154n.366). See also Hume's request to the abbé Le Blanc to insert several paragraphs into the French translation of the first volume of the *History of Great Britain* (Hume 1970: 33–7). Some of the sentences which he requested be incorporated into the French

translation (35–6) are the same as those which appeared in the footnote mentioned above (Hume 1756: 450).

21. Detailed information on this manuscript appears in Raynor (2009: 186n.99). R. D. Sheldon (2004) accepts Raynor's attribution in the article on 'Smith, Charles (1713–1777)' of *ODNB*.
22. Although it seems to contradict his endorsement of the Church of England in the *History*, Hume simply believes that the type of religion must be suited to each political constitution. In the *History* he points out the affinities between a Presbyterian Church and a republican government, while episcopacy has an air of greater ornament that bears a closer resemblance to that surrounding monarchy (H V: 387; see also V, 558–9 Note [J]; E 611).
23. As for the contemporary Scottish and English readings of Hume's *History*, see also Towsey 2010a: chap. 8; 2010b; 2013; Allan 2013 respectively.
24. In reality, Smith supported the Church of England for the same pragmatic reason as Hume: the Lutherans and the Church of England preserving the episcopacy were 'from the beginning favourable to peace and good order, and to submission to the civil sovereign' (Smith 1985 [1776]: 807 [V.i.g.34]). Whether Smith actually applied the individualism of market behaviour to religion has been controversial (Ekelund Jr., Hébert and Tollison 2005; Leathers and Raines 2008).
25. See also Hume's dedication to John Home's *Douglas*, where Hume advocates 'the Liberty of Thought' as modelled on the coexistence of various philosophical sects in ancient times (Home 1757: 3). This dedication also appeared in the *Four Dissertations* (Hume 1757: ii). Hume's argument here sounds very similar to the ancient policy of philosophical and religious toleration that Shaftesbury depicted in *A Letter concerning Enthusiasm* (in Shaftesbury [1711] 1999: 11).
26. For Hume's depiction of the Independents, see H V, 442; VI, 40; E 76. He seems to criticise them at the time of the Civil War because they tried 'to impose a more perfect system of liberty on the reluctant nation' (V, 509). Nevertheless, it is not obvious whether he posits the unfeasibility of the Independents' religious policy as his own position or merely as what people believed at that time.
27. Ian Simpson Ross, biographer of Adam Smith, rightly does not discern any clash of opinion between them (1995: 283). For the affinity of religious sentiments between Hume and Smith, see also Rothschild 2001: 130 and 298–9n.76, and Boyd 2000: 107.
28. This cognomen was first used by Thomas Carlyle, not for Hume,

but for Francis Jeffrey. In his *Reminiscences*, Carlyle says that '[y]ou could not define Jeffrey to be more than a potential Voltaire; say "Scotch Voltaire"' ([1881] 2012: II, 66).

29. See also the article on 'Cartesianism' in *Questions sur l'Encyclopédie* (Voltaire 1968–: XL, 509). On Voltaire's scepticism, see Wade 1970: 758–63; Charles 2012; Pujol 2012; 2013.
30. On what Hume has in common on religious issues with other 'Moderate Enlightenment' thinkers including Voltaire, see Rasmussen 2014: 166–90.
31. The two philosophers never met. It is not easy to guess Hume's feelings or ideas on Voltaire and his works. A direct reference to Voltaire occurs in Hume's published works only once, and in passing: in the 1742 essay 'Of the Middle Station of Life' (E 551). Mossner seems right in pointing out that Hume 'was not completely enthusiastic over Voltaire' (Mossner 1980: 487; see also L 1: 207–8). Hume says that the evaluation that he was Voltaire's 'pupil' and his *History* 'an Imitation of his Siècle de Louis XIV' 'flatters very much', but he rejects the allegation (L I, 226). In addition, Hume might well have been provoked by Voltaire's derogatory description (in the *History of the War of 1741*) of the unsuccessful British Naval expedition to Brittany, which Hume joined under General St. Clair in 1746. On this point, see L I, 228n.1; Hume's 'Descent on the Coast of Brittany' (L I, 94–8); Meyer 1951, Mossner 1980: 200; Hume 2014: 112–27 (Appendix II). By contrast, Voltaire's appraisal of Hume as a philosopher and a historian is generally high and probably sincere throughout his letters. For example, 'I like the philosophy of Mr. Hume as much as his historical works' (J'aime bien autant encor[e] la philosophie de Mr Humes, que ses ouvrages historiques)' (D11939); 'This Hume [...] is a true philosopher' ('Ce Hume [...] est un vray philosophe') (D8881; see also D7499). As for the comparison between Hume and Voltaire the historians, see Mossner 1941 and Meyer 1958.
32. As Serjeantson argues, the subject of one of Hume's critiques in the 'Natural History of Religion' was the 'Cudworthianism' of Shaftesbury, Bolingbroke and the Chevalier Ramsay – an argument that 'ancient philosophers had perceived the unity of God in a form of primitive monotheism' (2012: 287).
33. In *A Letter from a Gentleman*, however, Hume asserts that his sceptical argument of causation in the *Treatise* is compatible with the Design argument (Hume [1745] 1967: 23–4; Wright 2006: 12).
34. This might sound odd, considering the fact that he was the author of

the *Candide* in which he severely criticised Leibnitzian providentialism. Nevertheless, what the *Candide* denies is not providence, but providentialism (Pomeau 1969: 313).

35. Theodore Besterman annotates to this letter that 'it would be interesting to know how Voltaire obtained his information' (*Correspondance de Voltaire*, 1972, cited in Voltaire 2013). Although Besterman somehow assumes that Voltaire here mentions '[Hume's] essay on suicide', the context of this letter rather suggests that he alludes to 'Of the Immortality of the Soul'. Voltaire probably found little difficulty in obtaining these two essays before their unauthorised publication in 1777. Based on his friends' recommendation, Hume had suppressed these two essays at the last minute before the intended publication of *Five Dissertations* in 1756 (the revised version of which, containing an additional essay to replace those removed, was to be published as the *Four Dissertations* in 1757). However, as William Rose, one of the editors of the *Monthly Review*, testified in 1784 that 'by some means or other, however, a few copies [of the *Five Dissertations*] got abroad, and have been clandestinely circulated, at a large price' (cited in Mossner 1950: 41). As for the proofs of the *Five Dissertations* with Hume's own annotations, see Hume 2014: 158, 193–4n.4.
36. Voltaire's attitude toward Epicureanism is more complex than it appears at first glance. In the very next article on 'Atomes' (in the *Questions sur l'Encyclopédie*) he allies Epicurus, Lucretius and Gassendi with Newton in their claims regarding the void in natural science, and called them 'true philosophers' (vrais philosophes) (1968–: XXXIX, 196–7; for a similar contrast, see also Sec. 2 of the article on 'Causes finales', 546). However, he did so only in contrast with Descartes and Leibnitz who support plenism. Voltaire finally criticises the Roman Epicureans because, unlike Newton, they attributed all the movements of atoms 'by chance' (par hazard) (198). He does so on the basis that what we call chance is nothing but 'the unknown cause of a known effect' (la cause ignorée d'un effet connu) in the article on 'Athéisme', in a similar way to Hume (EHU 6.1; 56).
37. In the latter note, Hume mentions Montesquieu's *De l'esprit des lois*, but he does not completely endorse Montesquieu's double standard on religious toleration. After his mention of Montesquieu, he adds that 'I own, however, that it is very questionable, whether persecution can in any case be justifyed' (H V, 576 Note [FF]; Sabl 2009: 515).
38. Robert Bisset, an early biographer of Edmund Burke, seems to have

discerned Hume's balanced criticism: '[Puritans'] theological absurdities [Hume] certainly ridicules, as he also does the high church bigotry. He exposes the superstitious mummeries of Laud, as well as the enthusiastic phrenzy of James Naylor or Praise-God-Barebone' (1800: I, 440–1).

39. In the same vein, on the issue of American independence, Hume refrained from drawing the conclusion similar to the one of Adam Ferguson's *Remarks on a Pamphlet Lately Published by Dr. Price* (1776).
40. Boswell reported in the final interview with Hume that he said 'flatly that the Morality of every Religion was bad' (quoted in Mossner 1980: 597).

6

How 'To Refine the Democracy': Hume's Perfect Commonwealth as a Development of his Political Science

One of the biggest intellectual challenges for Hume was to alleviate as far as possible, if not to completely eradicate, the adverse effects produced by religious and political dogmatism. In order to cope with the former, as we saw in the previous chapter, he recommends that magistrates take pragmatic and expedient measures when faced with false religions. Considering the situation of contemporary Europe, for Hume, Erastianism was likely the most feasible option, although organised religions are not necessarily indispensable for sustaining the order and tranquillity of civilised societies. The characteristic element of Hume's politics regarding religious issues lies in proposing the possibility of completely secular morality, while maintaining his agnosticism at a distance from French (self-proclaimed) atheists. Despite their accord in critiquing organised religions, Hume's position also differs from Voltaire's attempts to restore the 'pure religion' under the banners of deism or theism.

On the other hand, Hume's attitude toward political conflicts is a quite different story. Despite his intense criticism of factions, he considers that '[t]o abolish all distinctions of party may not be practicable, perhaps not desirable, in a free government' (E 'Coalition of Parties' 493; Forbes 1975b: 185–6; Spencer 2002: 880–2). The task for Hume is how to differentiate positive factions from dangerous ones, and how to maintain the former through constitutional mechanisms. Seen from this viewpoint, one of Hume's most enigmatic political essays takes on a particular significance – 'Idea of a Perfect Commonwealth', published in the *Political Discourses* in 1752. The significance he attached to this essay is beyond doubt; he placed it at the very end of the *Political Discourses*, and continued to do so after the *Political Discourses* was integrated into his *Essays and Treatises on Several Subjects* in

1753. For every contemporary reader of the multi-volume *Essays and Treatises*, the most convenient and comprehensible collection of Hume's works, this has always been the closing piece of the *Essays, Moral, Political and Literary* (a compilation of the *Essays, Moral and Political* and the *Political Discourses* after 1758). Nevertheless, its utopian settings have often prevented this essay from receiving the consideration it deserves, and with good reason. Since the publication of Adair's paper, Hume's plan for an ideal republic has been discussed mainly in terms of its influence on James Madison's essay *The Federalist* No. 10 (Adair 1965; Conniff 1980; Draper 1982; Morgan 1986; Spencer 2002). In addition, John Robertson has asserted that the essay proves Hume's commitment to civic tradition (Robertson 1983: 174). Those who comment on Hume's plan are rather rare; John B. Stewart and Donald W. Livingston still remain in a minority in discussing it at length (Stewart 1992: 281–90; Livingston 1990: 132–4; 1998: 199–216; see also Inuzuka 2004a: chap. 3; Sakamoto 2011a: chap. 7; McCormick 2013). Many commentators mention this essay only in passing, or dismiss it as mere satire (Conniff 1976; Letwin 1998: 89). The debate over the possible satirical bent of the essay reveals both its importance and its ambiguous place in Hume's political and historical writings, as well as in eighteenth-century political thought.[1]

This chapter aims to understand his plan for a 'perfect commonwealth' as a continuation of a stance within his political science that he adopted in the *Essays, Moral and Political* (1741–2): in particular, his plan was closely related to his pursuit of the regularity of political administration through the analysis of political frameworks, and his anxiety over the unstable nature of mixed monarchy, which is first clearly expressed in the essay 'That Politics may be reduced to a Science'. Both clearly stem from his more fundamental concerns about political conflicts. Two points should be heeded here. Firstly, while he argues in the aforementioned essay that 'consequences almost as general and certain may sometimes be deduced from [the laws and particular forms of government], as any which the mathematical sciences afford us', this seemingly bold claim should not be considered a deviation from Hume's 'spirit of scepticism' – as usual, he does not forget to qualify the claim with the words 'may sometimes' (E 14). Moreover, he starts his argument in the essay 'Of Civil Liberty' of the same *Essays, Moral and Political*, as follows:

> I am apt [...] to entertain a suspicion, that the world is still too young to fix many general truths in politics, which will remain true to the latest posterity. We have not as yet had experience of three thousand years; so that not only the art of reasoning is still imperfect in this science, as in all others, but we even want sufficient materials upon which we can reason. (E 87)

He goes on to admit his lack of knowledge of the possibility of future 'refinement, either in virtue or vice' of human nature or of 'any great revolution in [mankind's] education, customs, or principles' (E 87–8; Miller 1981: 142–4). In the essay 'Of the Original Contract' of the *Political Discourses*, he remains open to the possibility of exceptions: 'the science of politics affords few rules, which will not admit of some exception' (E 477). Hume's claim for politics to be a science, therefore, must be comprehended within his enduring scepticism.

Secondly, and conversely, Hume's scepticism does not lead him to complete nihilism. Although he is consistently cautious about radical and violent political reforms, this does not hinder him from pursuing the best theoretical model of government. In order to understand this point, a worthwhile comparison is with Adam Smith, who seems to share with Hume an opposition to extreme attitudes towards the concept of perfection in this world. Despite his general claims regarding free trade, Smith acknowledges that expecting its perfect realisation in Great Britain is 'as absurd as to expect that an Oceana or Utopia should ever be established in it' ([1776] 1982: 471 (IV.ii.43); Winch 1996: 144).

Hume's scepticism and his theoretical pursuit of a more steady and well-regulated constitution are not mutually exclusive. Somewhat similarly, to point out the relevance and continuity between this plan and his other political writings does not mean that Hume deemed all the proposals included in his plan for an ideal republic feasible; much less does it evince his willingness to put this plan into practice. To make such claims would be as pointless as to dismiss this essay out of hand because of its seemingly utopian setting. I will not aim to settle the separate – and arguably irrelevant – issue of whether Hume wrote this essay seriously or as a satire, but rather to investigate how Hume maintains his 'spirit of scepticism' in this enigmatic essay. His scepticism about the perfectibility of human nature and his awareness of the fragility of human institutions are particularly relevant here.

The argument consists of four points. Firstly, a brief examination of several political essays in the *Essays, Moral and Political* will reveal that one of the most critical points for Hume's politics lies in the increase in the regularity and predictability of our political conduct. Sudden bursts of political factions are naturally culpable, according to Hume, because they tend to shake the stability of political and social systems. The bitter lessons of the Jacobite Risings taught Hume the inveterateness of political factions afresh. Secondly, it will be argued that his concerns about political factions continued to be one of the central themes in his *Political Discourses*. Hume's plan can also be considered to reflect his life-long preoccupation with the dangers he perceived as a result of the growth of factionalism and the development of the system of public credit in Britain. Thirdly, his plan should be re-examined along with his view of the electoral system. Although it is seldom remarked on, Hume consistently supports the importance of frequent elections, while simultaneously apprehending the epidemic corruption in elections and the possible confusions caused by their frequency. From this perspective, Hume's 'Perfect Commonwealth' can be seen as an intellectual attempt to avert the advent of tyranny, which would result from the erosion of what he called 'a kind of independent magistracy in a state' (E 358). And finally, I will suggest that Hume's plan in the 'Perfect Commonwealth' should be interpreted not as a proposal for radical 'democratisation', but rather as a theoretical scheme to preserve authority and to improve liberty in an increasingly commercialised society. Although Hume is deeply sceptical about the implementation of radical reforms, this attitude need not be seen as incompatible with his intellectual quest for the best possible system of government.

1 Republics and Representation in the *Essays*

Hume's aim of providing a scientific analysis of political institutions is frequently manifest in his *Essays, Moral and Political*. In the essay 'That Politics may be reduced to a Science' he claims that in order to establish politics as a science, one must explore each form of government as a system, and analyse which type is most likely to achieve a more predictable political administration.[2] Hume's claim for politics as a science is closely related to his distinctions between 'the general passions and interests' and 'whim, folly, or caprice' in the essay 'Of the Rise and Progress of the Arts and Sciences'. In this essay, which is an enlargement of his more metaphysical arguments on probability in the *Treatise* (1.3.11–13; 124–55), he distinguishes between chance and cause, and argues that the general passions 'are always of a grosser and more stubborn nature, less subject to accidents, and less influenced by whim and private fancy'. Thus, it is not 'possible to *reduce* [those dependent on a few people] to any general maxims or observations' (E 112. Italics added). Despite this, he goes on to attempt to trace the development in the arts and sciences of more refined passions than 'universal passions' such as avarice or the desire of gain. This is because he believes that even what is considered 'chance' may 'be accounted for, in some measure, by general causes and principles'. Then he opines that 'it were a pity to abandon [such a curious subject] entirely, before we have found whether it [...] can be *reduced* to any general principles' (114–15. Italics added). Hume used the verb 'reduce(d)' twice in the first part of the essay 'Of the Rise and Progress' and not in 'That Politics'. What matters here is Hume's focus on the probability of our passions that 'operate on a multitude' (112). As we saw in Chapter 1, Hume's mitigated scepticism enables him to enquire 'such subjects as are best adapted to the narrow capacity of human understanding' (EHU 12.25; 162), which includes 'politics' as a part of 'moral reasoning'. As he himself claims proudly in the introduction to the *Treatise* (intro 5; xvi), Hume's politics must be considered an application of his 'attempt to introduce the experimental method of reasoning into moral subjects'. Despite his usual scepticism of the universal truth in politics, this does not necessarily hinder him from his pursuit of general rules and principles in politics.

Obviously, such an attempt is not unique to Hume: his attempts to establish politics on a more solid theoretical basis had several precedents. For example, Malebranche – one of the authors whom the young Hume recommended to a friend (see Chapter 2) – had made a similar point in his *De la recherche de la vérité* (*The Search after the Truth*): 'in morals, politics, medicine, and all the practical sciences, we must be satisfied with probability, not permanently but temporarily' (Malebranche [1674–5] 1997: 15 [Bk. 1, Ch. 3, II]). He goes on to insist that 'probabilities need not be utterly despised, because several probabilities joined together generally can produce as much conviction as can very clear demonstrations'. In the same vein, Hume declares that we can deduce 'consequences almost as general and certain' from 'laws and particular forms of government' 'as any which the mathematical sciences afford us' (E 16; see also Forbes 1975b: chap. 7).

Back to Hume's arguments in the essay 'That Politics', he made his general judgement that republican governments were superior to monarchies in terms of the stability of political institutions. It should be heeded that his focus on general passions in the essay 'Of the Rise and Progress' and this general maxim in 'That Politics' are closely linked with each other. According to Hume, the administration of any absolute government necessarily depends on the personal characteristics of its monarch, and thus should be considered precarious. Conversely, a republic can be managed even by 'bad men', if it includes 'particular checks and controuls' in its constitution (E 15–16).[3] As we will see, Hume was already showing strong interest in the possible reforms in republican government through various institutional checks in the *Essays, Moral and Political*. Like many of his proposals in the early political essays, this concept was incorporated into his 'Idea of a Perfect Commonwealth', published about ten years later.

Although he included the British constitutional monarchy as an example of a 'republican and free government' in the essay 'That Politics' (E 15), Hume, unlike some of his contemporaries, did not consider it to be perfectly balanced. As many studies have shown and we will see below, Hume considered the situation of the British mixed monarchy in the middle of the eighteenth century so precarious that it was unlikely to last (Pocock 1985b: 125–41). This remained true, despite his later comment that 'to their mutual felicity, king and people were finally taught to know their proper boundaries' after the Revolution (H VI, 476). The title of one of his essays is expressive of this view: 'Whether the British Government inclines more to Absolute Monarchy, or to a Republic'. Behind this theoretical dilemma lies his grasp of the contemporary situation in which Britain was placed. He stated that the tide 'is just beginning to turn towards monarchy' and clearly believed it preferable 'to see an absolute monarch [rather] than a republic in this island'. Hume's anxiety about the possible violent political thrust towards a republican government was equal to or greater than his apprehension regarding what he called 'the true *Euthanasia* of the BRITISH constitution', that is, an absolute monarchy (E 51–3).

In the essay 'Of the Independency of Parliament' Hume also remarks that if 'such genius as CICERO and TACITUS' saw the British government, they would say that '[s]uch government [...]

will not be a *mixed* government' (E 43). This judgement is due to the imbalance resulting from what Hume considered to be the disproportionate constitutional power of the House of Commons. Nevertheless, he considered that in the case of England, this weighting in the system of government in fact promoted constitutional stability. Hume explains 'this paradox' as a system of self-restraint; the House of Commons does not try to usurp the power of the Crown, 'because such an usurpation would be contrary to the interest of the majority of its members' (45). In turn, he defends the influence of the British Crown on the House of Commons, because of the monarchy's role in maintaining such self-imposed restrictions. In Hume's view, however, the safeguarding of the monarch's legislative power is insufficient to redress the imbalance resulting from the increasing power of the Commons (44).

In the same essay, he goes on to say that only a 'pure republic' can settle this imbalance fundamentally. This essay concludes:

> In pure republics, [. . .] the checks and controuls [sic] are more regular in their operation; because the members of such numerous assemblies may be presumed to be always nearly equal in capacity and virtue; and it is only their number, riches, or authority, which enter into consideration. (E 46)

This feature of republics explains Hume's selection of this type of government for his ideal commonwealth.

Another notable feature of his political essays in the *Essays* is Hume's strong support for representative government as opposed to direct democracy. Hume was critical of the tumultuousness of 'democracy without a representative', like that which had existed in the ancient republic of Rome. When the Roman republic expanded its territory and population by conquest, Hume argues, its elections, which were exclusively led by 'the city-tribes', engendered populism. He believed that the common city folk were 'cajoled by every one that affected popularity' and 'supported in idleness by the general distribution of corn, and by particular bribes, which they received from almost every candidate' (E 16).

As we will see below, Hume also hinted at his concern regarding the volatility of republican governments in the *Political Discourses*. In the essay 'Of the Original Contract' he insisted that the Athenian popular assemblies 'were always full of licence and disorder, notwithstanding the institutions and laws by which they were checked' (E 473). In the essay 'Of Some Remarkable Customs' he returned to the topic in more detail. According to Hume, ancient Athens produced only confusion because of its lack of 'any limitation of property', 'any distinction of rank' and 'controul from any magistracy or senate' (that is, an upper house of government) (368). Hume's warning against an Athenian model for a democracy is absorbed directly into his plan, where Hume excludes those from less wealthy classes from direct participation in political administration. In fact, giving them suffrage to elect their representatives is a device to absorb 'the force of popular tides and currents' ('Perfect Commonwealth' 528; almost the same phrase appears in E 'First Principles' 36) in order to prevent an upsurge of their political influence. He believes that the senators should be elected by and among 'men of fortune and education' (524).

In sum, a republican government is preferable to a monarchy in terms of the regularity and predictability of its administration only if it possesses a well-designed system of representation (Moore 1977: 825). Thus, the fundamental disadvantage of a limited monarchy lies in the checks that it establishes being dependent on the personal characteristics of the monarch – even what Hume terms 'civilized monarchy (monarchies)' (E 'Civil Liberty 94; 'Rise and Progress' 125) is not immune to this defect (on Hume's arguments on civilised monarchies, see Forbes 1975b: chap. 5, esp. 156–60). This is not the case in a well-regulated republic (not republics in general), which is free from the influence of any particular statesman (E 527).

For Hume, the project of framing an ideal republic was not just an isolated, abstract vision; rather it was tied to his contemporary political circumstance because he believed that the British people were doomed in one way or another to lose their extreme or 'unbounded' liberty, which they enjoyed under the limited monarchy. Hume's concern about the volatility of his contemporary situation is best exemplified in the closing paragraph of the essay 'Of the First Principles of Government' in the *Essays, Moral and Political*. In this essay, he appropriates Harrington's scheme concerning the distribution of land, and explains the historical process of how the balance of political power in the constitution derives from the balance of property. He argues that, based on the redistribution of property, the newly emerging class represented by the House of Commons had gradually begun to acquire a share of political power previously denied them. However, Hume thinks the 'weight [of the House of Commons] in the scale is unequal to the actual property and power of all whom it represents'. Considering the real state of affairs, Hume continues to argue that it is unlikely that such an imbalance could persist over a long period. 'Were the members obliged to receive instructions from their constituents, like the DUTCH deputies', Hume presumes, 'this would entirely alter the case'. If this happens, the influence of the Crown would be too fragile to stop it, because, he says, the royal 'influence, which at present is only exerted once in seven years, to be employed in bringing over the people to every vote, it would soon be wasted; and no skill, popularity, or revenue, could support it' (E 35–6). Then he predicted the advent of a 'pure republic' in Britain as follows:

> I must, therefore, be of opinion, that an alteration in this particular [that is, the influence of crown] would introduce a total alteration in our government, and would soon reduce it to a pure republic; and, perhaps, to a republic of no inconvenient form. For though the people, collected in a body like the ROMAN tribes, be quite unfit for government, *yet when dispersed in small bodies, they are more susceptible both of reason and order; the force of popular currents and tides is, in a great measure, broken.* (E 36. Italics added)

The significance of this sentence is clear because in this essay (published as early as 1741) Hume here presented what can be called a prototype of his plan for the organisation of a republic (Adair 1957: 352–3). In the essay 'Perfect Commonwealth', Hume was to propose a plan for a large representative body politic subdivided into small parishes in a similar way.

2 Hume's Analysis of Political Factions

Hume's focus on the improvement in the regularity and predictability of our political behaviour is also closely related to his concerns about political factions. He started the essay 'Of the Independency of Parliament' by claiming that '[p]olitical writers have established it as a maxim, that, in contriving any system of government, and fixing the several checks and controuls of the constitution, every man ought to be supposed a *knave*', though he cautiously added that this maxim 'should be true in *politics*, which is false in *fact*'. Interestingly, he repeats the significance of institutional 'checks and controls' here as well as in the essay 'That Politics'. Immediately after this declaration, he explains why politicians act as if they had no 'regard to public interest and liberty' and why 'faction, disorder, and tyranny' would abound without any institutionally preventive measures (E 42–3).

In the essay 'Of Parties in General' Hume analyses the 'real' differences between political factions by dividing the composition of their ideologies into principle, interest and affection. Hume, in his discussion of party opposition, argues against Bolingbroke's claim that 'the difference [between Whig and Tory] is now abolished, and [...] there are at present no other parties among us but court and country' (E 71–2). Bolingbroke, who was an opponent of the Walpole administration, proposed this simple distinction between court and country to discredit the attempts of the governing party to propagate the real or imagined association of the Tory party with the perceived danger of Jacobitism. In contrast, Hume reemphasises the importance of the distinction between Whig and Tory (61–2; Forbes 1975b: chap. 6). In the essay 'Of the Parties of Great Britain' he states that, to put it simply, the Whig political philosophy is based upon the principle of liberty, while that of the Tories possesses a 'compound nature', composed of adherence to principles – of the indefeasible rights of the monarch and the passive obedience of the subject – and affection for the House of Stuart (71). On this point, Hume had already remarked in the *Treatise* that 'a strict adherence to any general rules, and the rigid loyalty to particular persons and families' are 'virtues that hold less of reason than of bigotry and superstition' and 'the study of history confirms the reasonings of true philosophy [...] teaches us to regard the controversies in politics as incapable of any decision in most cases, and as entirely subordinate to the interests of peace and liberty' (T 3.2.10.15; 562).

Hume's critical comments regarding 'the founders of sects and factions' (E 'Parties in General' 55) have led some commentators to argue that he has a completely negative view of party politics, comparable with that of James Madison, for example (Morgan 1986; Arkin 1995). It should be emphasised, however, that Hume never regards party politics as such as exclusively dangerous (E 'Coalition of Parties' 493). On the contrary, he states that some kind of political contest is vital, and even asserts that 'the opposition of interests' is the 'chief support of the BRITISH government' ('Perfect Commonwealth' 525). In the *History of England*, Hume remarks that the parties of Court and Country 'are the real causes of its permanent life and vigour' (H V, 556 Note [J]; Spencer 2005: chap. 6).

What kind of political factions does Hume aim to prevent throughout his political writings? In the essay 'Of Parties in General' he clearly states that of all factions, those based on interest 'are the most reasonable, and the most excusable', while those stemming from principles and personal affection are 'the most extraordinary and unaccountable' and 'often very violent' respectively (E 59, 60, 63). In the contemporary British context, the opposition of parties can be dangerous only when it is concerned with problems of the nature of the constitution or of religion. In the first paragraph of the essay 'Of the Parties of Great Britain', for example, Hume asserts '[t]he just balance between the republican and monarchical part of our constitution is really, in itself, so extremely delicate and uncertain, that, when joined to men's passions and prejudices, it is impossible but different opinions must arise concerning it, even among persons of the best understanding' (64). Hume finds that these critical problems have produced many disturbances in British history, and that a mixed government has a significant difficulty in preventing arguments over the nature of the constitution or keeping the proper limits of political power. Rather than advocating a complete revision of the British constitution to eliminate any factions, Hume's strategy is to encourage party opposition that is grounded in 'interest' (and sober principles) as far as possible and is thus able to benefit, rather than destabilise, the country.

While maintaining this basic analysis of political parties in the *Essays, Moral and Political*, Hume had an important experience – the '45 Jacobite Rebellion – that prompted him to reconsider the seriousness of political factionalism before publishing the *Political Discourses*. We can trace the trajectory of his thoughts through the revisions of these political essays. 'Of the Parties of Great Britain' is one of the essays that Hume repeatedly revised, effacing several sentences.[4] In order to situate his reconsiderations within broader context, we need to examine the most significant change between the original version and the last edition of this essay; that is, his mention of Jacobitism. Before the Jacobite rebellion, he wrote: 'As violent Things have not commonly so long a Duration as moderate, we actually find, that the *Jacobite* Party is almost entirely vanish'd from among us [i.e. in Scotland]' (E 615–16). In this paragraph Hume appears optimistic about the elimination of the Jacobites' potential to cause disruption. A friend of his, who proofread the *Essays* to correct Hume's Scotticisms, had given him advice about the above paragraph. This friend warned that 'I doubt whether this is not too strongly expressed [...] yet the Jacobite Party seems far from being vanished' (Anon. 1741 or 42: 6–7).[5] In spite of this advice, Hume did not change his opinion, even daring to retain the passage when he published the second edition in 1742. In 1745, unexpectedly for Hume, however, rebellion broke out. Hume had learned his lesson – the obstinacy of personal attachment to the former royal family. In the 1748 edition of the *Essays, Moral and Political*, just after the rebellion, he omitted the paragraph cited above, and thereafter in the 1752 essay 'Of the Protestant Succession' he expressed the opinion that the recurrence of the Jacobite Rebellion was a danger: 'But the claims of the banished family, I fear, are not yet antiquated; and who can foretel[l], that their future attempts will produce no greater disorder?' (E 508). Thus, this event can be argued to have triggered Hume's realisation that party zeal, especially based upon personal attachment, was stronger and more dangerous than he had previously estimated. The '45 Rebellion brought him back to the analysis of the political parties of Britain, composing four essays on this topic, of which two ('Of the Original Contract' and 'Of Passive Obedience') were to be published in the *Three Essays, Moral and Political* (1748, and later added in the 1758 edition of the *Political Discourses*), and the others ('Of the Protestant Succession' and 'Of the Coalition of Parties' composed around the same time as the first two, but published in 1752) in the *Political Discourses*.

The mention of the Jacobites that occurred in the last few pages of the earlier version is notable by its complete absence from the last edition of the essay 'Of the Parties of Great Britain'. In the former, Hume states:

> A JACOBITE seems to be a TORY, who has no regard to the constitution, but is either a zealous partizan of absolute monarchy, or at least willing to sacrifice our liberties to the obtaining the succession in that family to which he is attached. (E 615)

Thus, although Hume did not identify all Tories with Jacobitism, he regarded the Jacobite philosophy as one strand of extreme Tory thought. In the 1768 edition this passage was omitted, leaving only the statement that a 'Tory' was '*a partisan of the family of* Stuart' (71): nowhere can we find the words 'Jacobite' or 'Jacobitism'.

The '45 Rebellion had another impact upon Hume; it rendered him keenly aware of another type of bigotry that can be caused by faction. In *A True Account of the Behaviour and Conduct of Archibald Stewart, Esq.*, the pamphlet which he published anonymously just after the rebellion, he vindicated Stewart, the previous Provost of Edinburgh, who was accused of dereliction of duty (negligence of the defence of the city) upon the invasion of insurgent troops. In the postscript of this pamphlet, Hume classified the adherents of both the Whig and Tory parties into the 'religious' and the 'political'. Furthermore, he ranked them hierarchically as follows: 'The religious *Whigs* are a very different Set of Mortals, and in my Opinion, are <as> much worse than the religious *Tories*; as the political *Tories* are inferior to the political *Whigs*' (TA: 252 [postscript 6]).[6] When Archibald Stewart was found not guilty, Hume came across some Whigs who severely criticised this judgement. These were the people whom Hume referred to as religious Whigs, who are characterised by 'Dissimulation, Hypocrisy[,] Violence, Calumny, Selfishness'. On the other hand, according to Hume, the political Whig is a person who is 'a Man of Sense and Moderation, a Lover of Laws and Liberty' (251 [postscript 5], 252 [6]), and therefore one who not only acquiesced to, but was delighted at the acquittal of Stewart. The difference between the political and religious adherents among the Whigs is not made entirely clear, but one criterion is personal character (see also Chapter 5, esp. pp. 141–2). Although in this pamphlet Hume does not specifically associate the religious party members with the clergy, he regarded the profession as having a tendency to promote bigotry and hypocrisy in 'Of National Characters' published at the same time (E 199–200n.3).

Hume apparently did not perceive any essential division within the Whig party at the stage when he published the *Essays, Moral and Political*. As John B. Stewart expounds, the *True Account* is in any case the earliest textual evidence that Hume clearly discerned that the Whig party was less monolithic than he had previously thought (1992: 246–9). His distinction between the religious and political Whig can partly explain his ambivalent attitude toward the Whig establishment: he preferred the political Whig to the political Tory, while severely criticising the religious Whig. Hume always believed that, since he had embarked upon the literary profession, he should try to moderate the 'PARTY-RAGE' through his 'Moderation and Impartiality in [his] Method of handling POLITICAL SUBJECTS' ('Advertisement' to the *Essays, Moral and Political* in Hume [1886] 1992: III, 41). This attitude was not changed but deepened after the '45 Rebellion by his reflection and continual correction of his own past opinions.[7] The events of '45 taught him anew the surprising tenacity of personal attachments to particular monarch(s) and highlighted the mixture of moderates and bigots in the ruling party.

3 Hume's Anxiety over Political Factions and the Role of Elections

By considering Hume's keen interest in republics with a representative system in the *Essays, Moral and Political*, and the plausible impact on Hume of the '45 Rebellion, we can now understand how critical these two issues continue to be for Hume in the *Political Discourses*.

Hume's anxiety over the instability of the British mixed monarchy, which tends to produce dangerous political factions, is closely linked to his preoccupation with the possible advent of a pure republic in Britain. In the essay 'Whether the British Government inclines', Hume clearly regards an absolute monarchy as preferable to the factionalism that he believed would result from the establishment of such a republic. After the publication of the *Essays, Moral and Political*, Hume's concerns about the internal precariousness of the British mixed monarchy did not change. Four essays coming before 'Perfect Commonwealth' in the *Political Discourses* were devoted to the issues inherent in the British mixed monarchy: 'Of the Original Contract', 'Of Passive Obedience', 'Of the Coalition of Parties' and 'Of the Protestant Succession'.

Hume's new attitude is found in these four essays where he (re)presents the conflict between Whig and Tory in terms of their theoretical oppositions. This arrangement in these essays and his removal of his original reference to the Jacobites from 'Of the Parties of Great Britain' reveals that he had distanced his conception of Jacobitism from his depiction of the mainstream political parties (E 479 and 501). Instead, he dealt separately with

Jacobitism as a problem concerned with the historical legitimacy of the Hanover line in the essay 'Of the Protestant Succession'. The identification of the Tory party with the Jacobites was a commonly used weapon in Court Whigs' arsenal of propaganda. This is exemplified by the fact that Hume himself was labelled a Jacobite after the publication of his *History*. At that time, as we saw above, he is likely to have been aware that he had once unwittingly committed himself to the same mistaken association.

Not only that, but his anxieties over the instability in the British mixed monarchy were augmented by his growing apprehensions over the possible emergence of an absolute monarchy caused by public credit. As recent studies have shown (Robertson 1993; Hont 2005: chap. 4; Sonenscher 2007), his view of public debt was firmly rooted in his understanding of eighteenth-century international politics: the appearance of 'fiscal-military states' in the seventeenth century had produced a close relationship between large-scale military expenditure, increased dependence on public credit and the eventual high taxation necessary for the repayment of public debt (Brewer 1989). Through the War of the Spanish Succession (1701–14), the War of the Austrian Succession (1740–8) and the Seven Years' War (1756–63), this system had become firmly established. Hume envisaged two possible endings to the projected crisis resulting from public debt in the essay 'Of Public Credit'. In the first scenario, the sovereign would declare voluntary bankruptcy by neglecting the creditors' demands for the payment of interest. Alternatively, procrastination on the part of the leadership would lead to most of the tax revenue being mortgaged for the redemption of national bonds: this would drain funds from national defence and leave the country 'at the mercy of the conqueror' (E 365). He put these two scenarios succinctly as follows: 'either the nation must destroy public credit, or public credit will destroy the nation' (360–1).

When the essay on public credit is closely read, it can be noticed that Hume mentioned the possibility of 'democratical frenzy' along with 'Jacobitish violence' because, he guessed, '[t]he immense greatness [...] of LONDON, under a government which admits not of discretionary power, renders the people factious, mutinous, seditious, and even perhaps rebellious' (E 355. This sentence was added in the 1770 edition).[8] This addition to the essay can be considered to demonstrate a renewal of Hume's concern that a republic was a possible (but not necessarily desirable) outcome of the crisis imminent in the contemporary British system of mixed government as a result of factionalism and public credit. This new dimension of his concerns was also augmented by Hume's awareness of some extra-parliamentary movements typified by 'Wilkes and Liberty', which had begun to undermine political authority itself (L II, 244–5; see also II, 180–1; Forbes 1975b: 187–9).

Ahead of his growing concern about the extra-parliamentary movement of the 1770s, however, Hume clearly showed much interest in the issue of elections. As early as the *Essays, Moral and Political*, he seems to call attention to the necessity of an elaborate setup for elections, mentioning the possible advent of a pure republic in Britain in the essay 'Whether the British Government inclines':

> If the house of commons, in such a case, ever dissolve itself, which is not to be expected, we may look for a civil war every election. If it continues itself, we shall suffer all the tyranny of a faction, subdivided into new factions. (E 52)

In another inkling of the possible advent of a large republic in Britain in the essay 'Of the First Principles of Government', as we saw above (p. 185), Hume suggested that two related points could possibly induce a complete change in the present constitution: an alteration of the degree of instructions from the constituencies, and the rapid decline in the king's influence caused by more frequent elections (35–6).

What has not been stressed is that Hume's mention of the possible advent of a republic in 'Of the First Principles' was closely related to contemporary discussions about the range and degree of instructions from the constituencies. This remains unnoticed partly because the original last paragraph, which immediately followed the passage cited above mentioning the 'prototype' of his plan, was omitted after the 1764 edition from the essay 'Of the First Principles'. Here, Hume mentioned 'the present political controversy, with regard to instructions', referring to an issue that had been under discussion in Britain since the early eighteenth century. Isaac Kramnick assumes that 'Hume's understanding of the nature of representation corresponds to Walpole's and forms a convenient link between Walpole and Burke' (1992: 127; see also 250), contrasting it with Bolingbroke's and the *Craftsman*'s more radical position that the people should have the right to instruct their members of parliament. However, Hume's point is not to positively support the Walpolean position, but rather just to reveal the unproductiveness of such a polemic.

> The question, then, is only concerning the degrees of weight [...]. But such is the nature of language, that it is impossible for it to express distinctly these different degrees [...]. Besides, how is it possible to find these degrees, considering the variety of affairs which come before the house, and the variety of places which members represent? (E 606–7)

Hume's conclusion here was that as long as it was impossible to determine the proper range and degree of the instructions exactly, this controversy would never result in any definite limitation (Letwin 1998: 80). This can be considered to be a good example of his scepticism on demarcation. More attention should be paid to the fact that Hume's first anticipation of a pure republic was clearly related to his interpretation of contemporary domestic politics. For Hume, this 'very frivolous' (606) issue could cause a total alteration of government (Forbes 1975b: 129, 134, 212–13).

Hume's interest in elections grows in the *Political Discourses*. In the essay 'Of Refinement in the Arts' he admits that 'corruption may seem to encrease of late years' and ascribed its cause to 'our established liberty'. However, unlike many of his contemporaries, he maintained a favourable attitude towards the effects of the increase of luxury, stating that 'this corruption or venality prevails much more among the electors than the elected; and therefore cannot justly be ascribed to any refinements in luxury' (E 277). Hume here considers the increasing corruption present in elections to be the result not of economic development, but of the frailty of political institutions. In the essay 'Of Public Credit' he states that when a society over-invests, leading to public debt, apathy among the people is the result and '[e]lections are swayed by bribery and corruption alone' (358). Hume's criticism of 'democracy without a representation' was already stated clearly in the *Essays, Moral and Political* ('That Politics' 16, 18), but these negative comments upon popular elections and the electors in the *Political Discourses* show his growing interest in the necessity of reform of the electoral system on a constitutional level.

4 Hume's Criticism of Utopians and his 'Perfect Commonwealth'

So far we have observed three points: Hume's consistent support of republics with representative systems as a more regular and stable form of government than monarchy (including the British mixed monarchy), his persistent worries about political factions, and his interest in elections in the *Political Discourses* as well as in the *Essays, Moral and Political*. We are now able to see how he continually attempts to give a theoretical solution to these issues in his 'Perfect Commonwealth'. Before entering into detailed discussions of this essay, it is important to distinguish between mere probability and expectation or hopefulness in Hume's political thought. As we saw above, he clearly believed that any sudden, violent and drastic change in the British political constitution would be the most *likely*, though he recognised that only 'projectors' would *expect* or *hope* their visionary plans to be realised: his firm conviction in the probability of some events should not be equated with a hope on his part for their actual occurrences. If so, Hume's keen awareness of any drastic change would be not only compatible with, but actually promote both his search for the theoretically best political system and his warnings against political projectors.[9]

There are three points to consider: (1) despite its seeming utopian settings, Hume clearly distinguishes his own plan from those of other utopian writers, retaining within the view of human nature he had expressed since the *Treatise*; (2) Hume's proposal for a large republic with a representative system seems to be a continuation of his pursuit of politics as a science and his theoretical solution to the issue of dangerous political factions peculiar to the British mixed monarchy; (3) the provision for a two-tier system of suffrage in his plan is an important institutional device for Hume, who was not a supporter of political participation or the concept of popular sovereignty.

The versions of the essay 'Perfect Commonwealth' that appear in the earlier editions of Hume's *Political Discourses* begin with a critique of 'political projectors', who attempt to realise any ideal political system by destroying the established one. Although his assertion that '[o]f all mankind there are none so pernicious as political projectors' was omitted from the 1770 edition (E 647), some commentators have used this opening statement to posit Hume's opposition to utopian writings as the focal point of the essay. What is important, however, is to explore the details in which Hume's own plan differs from those of the utopians he attacks. Unless this point is made clear, one would be liable to consider the rest of the essay as a mere parody of utopian writings. The most significant difference between Hume and the utopian theorists he criticises lies in their reliance on the mutability of our human nature as opposed to his assertion that human nature is essentially uniform and unalterable.

Following his criticism of political projectors, Hume makes it clear that he has many predecessors in his search for the best state of human society. Hume classifies the works of those authors into two main categories, represented respectively by Plato's *Republic* and Thomas More's *Utopia* and by Harrington's *Commonwealth of Oceana* (E 514). While the basic aims of all three authors is to design ideal political structures in theoretical terms, the key distinction lies in their respective views on human nature. As Hume pointed out, Plato and More proposed plans for which the changeability of human nature is a prerequisite. Both considered that the self-interested nature of man and the fundamental institution of private property that it gives rise to can be altered by educational measures. Hume had already criticised Plato's view of human nature as unrealistic in *A Treatise* (2.3.1.10; 402; see also Chapter 2 in this book), and in his plan for an ideal commonwealth dismisses it along with More's as 'plainly imaginary' (E 514).

Notably, Hume's criticism of Plato and More's optimism regarding human nature could be extended to some of his own contemporaries, although he did not make this connection himself. For instance, in his *Various Prospects of Mankind, Nature, and Providence*, Robert Wallace – who was Hume's friend but also his opponent on the question of whether the population of the ancient world was greater or less than that of the modern world – proposed 'the model of a perfect government' (Wallace [1761] 1969: 32; Robbins 1959: 204–6; Luehrs 1987). Wallace depicts an agrarian society without private property, and remarks that 'new maxims of education [are] to be introduced' in order to elevate human nature. This is because he considers the education of the young to be the most effective countermeasure against societal vices. Thus, Wallace, like Plato and More, believes in the changeability of human nature and the possibility of altering an institution as fundamental as private property through educational programmes. Belief in the malleability of human nature confirms the (allegedly) theoretical feasibility of utopian projects, regardless of the authors' opinions of the actual likelihood of their realisation. On the other hand, Hume argues that '[a]ll plans of government, which suppose great reformation in the manners of mankind, are plainly imaginary' (E 514; see also 279–80, 476–7). This is likely to explain why education is not integral to his 'Perfect Commonwealth', and Hume must have been proud of the actuality of his plan, contrasting it with the purely utopian visions of others, like those of Plato or More.

Hume seems to follow to a large extent the line Harrington takes in *The Commonwealth of Oceana*: Hume is relatively close in his philosophy to Harrington, compared with his distance from the optimism of Plato and More. For example, Harrington and Hume agree on the possibility of a republic existing on a large scale and the effectiveness of the bicameral legislature. In Harrington's system, however, harmony is achieved by the establishment of an 'equal commonwealth' based upon the division of property in the 'Agrarian Law' and the rotation of positions of authority. According to Harrington, these legal systems work to limit and contain the natural tension between rich and poor rather than proposing a fundamental change in human nature through education. He also emphasises the significance of public education to ensure popular support for his ideal republic (Harrington [1656] 1992: 197–9).

On the other hand, Hume strongly criticises the most central features in *Oceana*, describing as impracticable both the rotation system and the 'Agrarian Law' espoused by Harrington (E 515–16; H VI, 153; see also Shklar 1959: 664; Inuzuka 2004a: chap. 3; 2004b). In addition, according to Hume, Harrington's *Oceana* 'provides not a sufficient security for liberty' (E 515) because of the veto that the senators hold. In a letter to his nephew Hume wrote:

> [Ha]rrington is an Author of Genius; but chimerical. No Laws, however rigorous, [woud ma]ke his Agrarian practicable. And as the People have only a Negative, the [Senate] woud perpetually gain Ground upon them. You remember, that Montesquieu says, that Harrington establishing his Oceana in opposition to the English Constitution is like the blind Men who built Chalcedon on the opposite [Shore] to the Seat of Byzantium. (L II, 306–7)

Surprisingly, in spite of his criticism of Harrington's *Oceana* that Hume mentioned in the above letter, Montesquieu accords with Harrington and More in their endorsement of what Eric Nelson terms the 'ancient Greek model' of political thought. According to Nelson, there is 'a basic incommensurability between Greek and Roman values' in terms of their republicanism. According to Nelson, the former (exemplified by the views of Plato and Aristotle) tended to see justice as 'an arrangement of elements that accords with nature' that is 'a completely anti-Roman endorsement of property regulations' (Nelson 2004: 15). In his *Mes pensées* – which Hume was unlikely to have encountered – Montesquieu asserted that: 'I am not to be numbered among those who view the Republic of Plato as something ideal and purely imaginary, and the institution of which would be impossible' (Montesquieu 1949: 1036, translated and quoted by Nelson 2004: 169–70; see also Montesquieu 2012: 322 [1208]). As we saw in Chapter 5, the difference between Hume and Montesquieu on this point seems to explain their opposing evaluations of the Spartan model (Nelson 2004: 170; see also Rawson 1991).

I detailed above how Hume proposed an ideal commonwealth based upon his firm belief in the constancy of human nature and the necessity of private property as its corollary. This is the reason his discussions in the 'Perfect Commonwealth' are strictly confined to the theoretical structure of a political organisation, with mention of neither educational reforms nor property regulations. When he claims that 'one form of government must be allowed more perfect than another' (E 513), he does not set forth as a premise any peculiar or unusual social customs or at least what he believes to be so. For Hume, such supposition is not only unnecessary but should be avoided even in this kind of speculative theory. Therefore, his criticism of other utopians and philosophers whose models rely on changing such fundamental social structures as private property is also demanded by his science of man and his efforts to reduce politics to a science.

We come now to the point at which it is necessary to deal more carefully with the content of his plan. Hume proposes a large republic with a bicameral system through a two-stage election. To begin, this perfect commonwealth divides 'any territory of equal extent' to Great Britain and Ireland into 100 counties, subdividing each into 100 parishes. Each parish elects one county representative annually; these representatives then choose one senator from amongst themselves by ballot. The senators hold full executive authority, while the county representatives possess full legislative power. In order to avoid both the possible confusions caused by debates in a large assembly and the possible danger of 'combination and division' in the senate, Hume proposes that the senate should be dependent on the large assembly through a two-tier election, that the number of senators should be limited to 100, and the senate should be deprived of a veto (E 516–24).

In the main, Hume echoes the classical view of political theorists that republics tend towards instability, while he is distinctive in his concern for the regularity of republics' administrations and his criticisms of direct democracy. Furthermore, unlike those who considered republics unsuitable for the government of extensive territories (particularly after the collapse of Oliver Cromwell's regime), Hume argues that a large area would in fact act to reduce the inherently turbulent nature of this form of government by reducing the risk of factions seizing power (E 527–8).

In his plan, Hume carefully attempts to remove political oppositions before they come to full bloom, and to utilise only the salutary effects of factions: 'Separate this great body; and though every member be only of middling sense, it is not probable, that any thing but reason can prevail over the whole' (E 523). To illustrate how significant this point is for Hume, it is helpful to compare Hume's plan and Montesquieu's proposal for the federation of republics in *De l'esprit des lois* (Montesquieu [1748] 1989: 131–2 [2.9.1]). Superficially, Hume's idea seems similar to that of Montesquieu in terms of their assessment of the fragility of small republics and the solution to this problem. There are, however, some important differences to be noted. According to Montesquieu's system, each republic can dissolve the federation if it is inconvenient to remain a part of it (124 [1.8.16]; 132–3 [2.9.1]). Hume, by contrast, divides an existing, unified country into 100 counties, each of which is further divided into 100 parishes. This is because Hume's basic concern lies not in external threats to security, but rather in the settlement of domestic disputes, from which he considers that republics tend to suffer. The unification of small republics into an optional federation, which is at the heart of Montesquieu's proposal, on the other hand, contains no mechanism to prevent internal turbulence. Hence, Montesquieu retained the long-held belief that republics should have small territories, though Hume expressed the same opinion in his letters (L II, 306).

Considering the theoretical discussions over the internal structure of representative governments, it seems more interesting to compare Hume's plan with Rousseau's *Considérations sur le gouvernement de Pologne* (*Considerations on the Government of Poland*) (written in 1772, published only in 1782). This is partly because Rousseau proposes a more feasible reform plan in this manuscript than he had in the *Du contrat social* (*The Social Contract*), while keeping the central claims of his earlier work in view. More importantly, despite his strong support for direct democracy evident in *Du contrat social*, Rousseau in the *Considérations* extensively argues for the representative system (As Sonenscher points out, 'Rousseau certainly ruled out representative sovereignty, but he did not rule out representative government' (2007: 235)). In spite of the seeming contradictions between both philosophers not only in personality, but also in their ideas, there are (at least) three striking similarities between Hume's and Rousseau's reform plans.[10] Firstly, both endorse the significance of frequent elections. Rousseau argues that 'England [...] lost its freedom for having neglected' the frequent renewal of the Deputies (Rousseau [1782] 1997: 197 [7.3]; see also 200 [7.11], 201 [7.14]); he believes that frequent changes of representatives could reduce the opportunities to corrupt them (on Hume's support of frequent elections, see below). Secondly, in a very similar way to Hume, Rousseau proposes to 'increase the number of Deputies' and 'to decrease the number of the Senators' (206 [7.29]). This is because in his contemporary Polish constitution, he believes that 'the Senate has too much influence in the deliberations' in the Diet (206 [7.27]; see also 215 [8.10]). Thirdly, Rousseau even alludes to the possibility of having 'the Senators appointed by the Diet', in which he sees 'many benefits too obvious to require detailed description' (207 [7.33]). This is exactly what Hume proposes in his 'Perfect Commonwealth'. As a corollary of this, Rousseau also suggests that the lifetime position of the Senate should be limited only to the first rank including the Bishops and Paladins (208 [7.35]). A similar reform plan for the British House of Lords is proposed by Hume: 'Their seats not hereditary, but during life' (E 527).

It should be admitted that there are significant differences between Hume's and Rousseau's plans. Firstly, Rousseau, as well as Montesquieu, attempts to 'perfect the system of federative Governments, the only system which combines the advantages of large and small States' (Rousseau [1782] 1997: 194 [5.2]).[11]

He never proposes a large republic; he remains faithful to the well-established belief that republics should be small. Secondly, his reform plan for the Polish adopts the elective monarchy (213–15 [8.7–10]). This does not necessarily mean that he chooses a monarchy in any positive way (Rousseau [1762] 1997: 97 [III. vi.10]); he merely adjusts his plan to the existing constitution in Poland. Even so, the elective monarchy that Rousseau adopts here must be the last choice for Hume (E 'That Politics' 18; see also T 3.2.10.11; 559–60). Rather he is willing to admit that a hereditary monarchy, as exemplified in contemporary France, could be a civilised one which enables its subjects to enjoy a considerable degree of liberty (E 'Civil Liberty' 92–3, 'Rise and Progress' 125; Forbes 1975b: chap. 5). On the other hand, the author of *Du contrat social* insists that 'heredity in the throne and freedom in the nation will forever be incompatible' (Rousseau [1782] 1997: 213 [8.7]). Moreover, it should be noted that there are more fundamental differences in reasoning underlying the above-mentioned similarities. Rousseau's proposals all arise from his anxiety about the independence of the legislative power from the executive. In order to avoid corruption, he strongly believes that the limitation (not the elimination) of luxury and the institution of a national education system appropriate to form free men (189–93 [4.1–8]), as well as the aforementioned political reforms, are inevitable. On the other hand, as argued above, Hume's interest rather lies in the predictability and regularity of political administration by excluding the destabilising influences of particular persons (including monarchs). Although Rousseau's *Du contrat social* has exerted much influence over the later generations, and his *Considérations sur le gouvernement de Pologne* shows quite a few parallels with Hume's plan, Hume's 'scientific' approach to politics seems to enable him to conceive another idiosyncratic (but later becoming rampant) idea of a large republic.

Based upon these comparisons, Hume's rationale for proposing a large republic as an ideal political system becomes clearer. His worries are not 'republican' concerns about the loss of virtue and its consequent corruption. He is also on the road to being emancipated from the long-established belief that republics must be small. Hume's ideal large republic not only allows the existence of a regular administration, free from the influence of the personal characteristics of a particular monarch; it also serves to curb the political factions that tend to destabilise the political system.[12]

5 Hume's View of Election in his 'Perfect Commonwealth'

Hume's views of electors and elections in his 'Perfect Commonwealth' are also consistent with opinions expressed in his other writings. Let us firstly consider Hume's idea of the traditional 'forty-shilling freeholder' franchise. He made a key comment on this issue in one of the pre-Tudor volumes of the *History of England* published in 1761: 'This sum was equivalent to near twenty pounds a-year of our present money; and *it were to be wished, that the spirit, as well as letter of this law, had been maintained*' (H II, 452–3. Italics added). Some political writers had already expressed similar complaints about this traditional franchise. Hume's conversion rate echoes Jonathan Swift's in his 'Of Publick Absurdities in England', in which he argues that '[t]he good effects of this law [of Henry IV enacting the forty-shilling freeholders as qualification for franchise] are wholly eluded, partly by the course of time, and partly by corruption. Forty shilling in those ages were equal to twenty pounds in our's' (Swift [1730] 1778: 139; Colley 1981: 14).

A more immediate and possible inspiration for Hume is found in Josiah Tucker's proposal in his pamphlet, *A Brief Essay on the Advantages and Disadvantages which respectively attend France and Great Britain, with regard to Trade* (1749). In this pamphlet, Tucker suggested: 'Suppose, now, that *Twenty Pounds per Ann.* was the requisite Sum for a Freeholder and *Two Hundred Pounds* Stock in Trade for a Tradesman, to *qualify* them to vote'. By realising this proposal, Tucker asserts, 'the Manufacturing Part of our Nation would not be called from their Work, to run *roving* after ever Electioneering: A proper *Subordination* would be effectually introduced [...]' (Tucker [1749] 1753: 50–2). Although there is no evidence to prove that Hume read Tucker's proposal before (or even after) publishing the *Political Discourses*, Tucker's suggestion of 20 pounds for a freeholder is the same qualification as Hume makes in his proposed version of county elections in the final edition (1777). Furthermore, Hume gives the same conversion of forty shillings into contemporary value in the *History of England*, while Tucker's proposal of 200 pounds in property as a qualification for the franchise of merchants and traders is also equivalent to Hume's recommendation for town parishes in the editions from 1753–4 to 1768. In the *History*, as we will see below, Hume also praised Cromwell for the qualification of '[a]n estate of 200 pounds value' because '[t]he elections of this parliament were conducted with perfect freedom' (VI, 69). Tucker, whom Mossner describes as 'the genial clergyman and economist' (1980: 500), was one of Hume's close friends from around the 1760s onwards and seems to have shared Hume's sentiments about the turbulence engendered by frequent elections.

In addition to discerning the possible influence of these predecessors, it is possible to form some impression of Hume's own sentiments on the franchise through other essays in the *Political Discourses*. In the essay 'Of the Populousness of Ancient Nations' Hume remarks that the ancient Athenians 'whose *census* was less than 2,000 *drachmas* (about 60 *l. Sterling*)' – 'census' referring here to the registration by citizens of the value of their property – were not permitted to vote. Importantly, Hume adds that 'though such a government would to us appear *sufficiently democratical*, it was so disagreeable to that [Athenian] people' (E 415–16. Italics added). Because Hume described the limitation to sixty pounds in property as 'sufficiently democratic', it is unlikely that he imposed the limitation of '500 pounds in the town parishes' in his own plan in the belief that it embodied the spirit of Athenian-style democracy. Rather, he took a more pragmatic view, regarding this level as sufficient to prevent dissent among the common people while preserving political judgement for those he regarded as capable (516).[13]

As John B. Stewart correctly argues, '[a]pplied to the eighteenth-century English franchise, Hume's recommendations would have cancelled the effects of inflation on the county property qualification and standardized the borough qualifications' (1992: 285). Nevertheless, such measures to limit popular suffrage also seem grounded in Hume's recognition of the increasing power of the common people, and his distrust of the political ability of the less wealthy. Although the relationship of 'Perfect Commonwealth' to his other 'economic' essays is not made explicit in the text,[14] 'Of the First Principles of Government' and 'Of the Independency of Parliament' in the *Essays, Moral and Political* have suggested the connection between his historical understanding of the newly emerging middle classes and the resultant gap between their economic and political power, and the possibility of a pure republic in consequence. In his economic writings, Hume speaks highly of the middle ranks of men as 'the best and firmest basis of public liberty'

(E 277), noting the positive effects (including the increase of liberty and '[k]nowledge in the arts of government' (273)) produced by their commercial activities. Unlike Livingston's suggestion (1998: 212–14), however, there is no direct indication that Hume believes that engagement in commerce or industry inevitably raises the *political* ability of every individual. In the essay 'Of the Middle Station of Life' (which appeared only in the second volume of the *Essays* and was omitted after 1753), Hume remarked '[t]he middling Rank of Men have Curiosity and Knowledge enough to form Principles, but not enough to form true ones, or correct any Prejudices that they may have imbib'd' (E 616).

Undoubtedly Hume had no illusions about the right to vote or the right to political participation: he regarded neither as essential to the framing of a regular government. In the essay 'Of the Original Contract' he expresses a cynical attitude toward elections ('what is this election so highly vaunted?'), challenging the doctrine that the representation of the people is the exclusive foundation of all lawful government (E 472). Hume's discussions concerning representative government and the right to vote are completely unrelated either to any kind of chauvinism or to what Forbes called the 'vulgar Whiggism'; it is rather concerned with his consistent interest in political institutions.

Hume's growing negativity about electors is also reflected in his 'Perfect Commonwealth': in the later editions, he raised the requirements of the suffrage from those given in the earlier editions of the *Political Discourses*. The first edition read as follows: 'Let all the freeholders in the country parishes, and those who pay scot and lot in the town parishes, meet annually in the parish church, and chuse, by ballot, some freeholder of the county for their member, whom we shall call the county *representative*' (E 647). This qualification is different from the 'forty-shilling freehold', but regional variations in the necessary qualifications for the franchise were notorious in Hume's time. In one borough, Gatton (now near Reigate in Surrey), the form of suffrage established did come close to his original idea.[15] In subsequent revisions of his *Political Discourses*, he raised the requirements. The editions from 1753–4 to 1768 read: 'all the freeholders of ten pounds a year in the country, and all the householders worth 200 pounds in the town parishes' (647). In the final (1777) edition published during his lifetime, Hume gives the right to vote to 'all the freeholders of twenty pounds a-year in the county, and all the householders worth 500 pounds in the town parishes' (516).

Hume's revisions of the franchise in his designs for an electoral system can be cross-referenced with his mentions of the election of Oliver Cromwell in the essay 'Perfect Commonwealth' and in the *History* (Baier 2008: chap. 4, esp. 60–1). In the essay he proposed as one of the reform measures for his contemporary British government that '[t]he plan of Cromwell's parliament [the first and second editions read 'of the republican government'] ought to be restored, by making the representation equal, and by allowing none to vote in the county elections who possess not a property of 100 pounds value' (E 526. After the 1753 edition, it read 'a property 200 pounds value' (647)). In the *History of England*, originally published in 1756 under the title of the *History of Great Britain*, Hume admires the electoral system that Cromwell implemented as 'being so favourable to liberty' because:

> [Cromwell] deprived of their right of election all the small burroughs, places the most exposed to influence and corruption. [...] The lower populace too, so easily guided or deceived, were excluded from the elections: An estate of 200 pounds value was necessary to entitle anyone to vote. The elections of this parliament were conducted with perfect freedom. (H VI, 69)

As Forbes points out, the fact that Hume raised the qualification of the suffrage through his revisions of the *Political Discourses* should not simply be considered a proof of his growing conservatism (1975b: chap. 5), but rather as an important sign that Hume deemed his plan to be in need of some fine-tuning to meet the changing circumstances of the real world.

Such a restriction of the suffrage should be considered in relation to Hume's strong support of frequent elections, which it seems to contradict. Although his proposal for annual elections in his plan (E 516) was apparently not taken seriously among commentators, Hume's favourable opinion of frequent parliamentary elections is evident in the *Essays, Moral and Political* and the *History*. Since 1716 when the Septennial Act had replaced the Triennial Act of 1691, the Whigs had established an oligarchy of ministers in Parliament. Perhaps with this in mind, he states in the essay 'Of the Rise and Progress' that 'frequent elections by the people, are a considerable check upon authority' (117).[16]

Although Hume considers that more frequent elections could trigger drastic changes in the political constitution (E 35–6), this does not negate the consistent significance he attaches to frequent elections.[17] In the *History* Hume repeatedly emphasised the importance of the Triennial Law: 'nothing could be more necessary than such a statute, for completing a regular plan of law and liberty' (H V, 307–8). Nevertheless, his advocacy of the Triennial Law as 'everlasting guardians to the laws' is always weighed against his concerns about 'an immeasurable appetite for liberty'. This is because the introduction of this law could increase the risk of '[t]he danger of a change in the people's disposition, and of general disgust, contracted against popular privileges', which, in turn, might cause anarchy and result in the total loss of liberty under the 'peaceable and despotic rule of a monarch' (V, 355–6; see also VI, 190). This state is not what Hume called 'euthanasia' but rather 'a grievous despotism' (E 'Public Credit' 358; Hont 2005: 341–6). In order to cope with the potential dangers of the caprice and whims of popular opinion, the raising of the franchise – which is seen as complementary to shorter parliaments – is a necessary check to avoid possible tyranny.

Another merit of his own plan, Hume considers, is in that '[t]he representation is more equal' (E 526). Despite his critical comments on his contemporary 'disorderly elections' ('Original Contract' 472), he never denies the importance of equal representation. In the *History*, while mentioning the Agreement of the People drawn up and submitted to the Parliament by the Levellers, he claims that '[m]any parts of this scheme, for correcting the inequalities of the representative, are plausible; had the nation been disposed to receive it, or had the army intended to impose it', although other parts are 'too perfect for human nature' (H V, 532).

In his 'Perfect Commonwealth' he writes proudly of one of his remedies that it ensures '[t]he great dependence of the senators on the people by annual elections; and that not by an undistinguishing rabble, like the ENGLISH electors, but by men of fortune and education' (E 523–4). In this sentence, he emphasised both the merit of frequent (in this case annual) elections and the importance of a two-tier electoral system (in which the senators are not directly elected by the people, but by their representatives). In this scheme there is an indirect dependence between the senators and people through frequent elections, while the restriction of the election at the initial stage to the choice of 10,000 county representatives is another, though related, matter. These cross-references between his plan and other works help us to see his plan as a part of the evidence that Hume tackled the issue of elections in a large republic as seriously as his contemporaries and intellectual successors.

6 Liberty and Authority in Hume's 'Perfect Commonwealth'

Around the end of the 1760s, Hume became concerned about the consequence of the excess of liberty. Hume states in a letter written in 1768, when the influence of the affair of John Wilkes's outspoken opposition to the King began to cause major public disturbances: 'They roar Liberty, tho' they have apparently more Liberty than any People in the World; a great deal more than they deserve; and perhaps more than any men ought to have' (L II, 180). Elsewhere, he makes his point more clearly: 'Our Government [...] is too perfect in point of Liberty' (II, 216) or 'the English Government is certainly happy, though probably not calculated for Duration, by reason of its excessive Liberty [...]' (II, 261). However paradoxical it sounds, Hume says in a letter sent to his nephew in 1775 that '[One] great Advantage of a Commonwealth over our mixt [sic] Monarchy is that it [would] considerably *abridge our Liberty*' (II, 306. Italics added). Needless to say, this does not mean that Hume tries to *oppress* liberty, an accusation he levels at certain other proposed models of government. Those 'liberties' that Hume considers excessive are associated with licentiousness (II, 210). This is clear in the essay 'Of the Liberty of the Press', in which Hume states: 'there is as much liberty, and even, perhaps, licentiousness in GREAT BRITAIN, as there were formerly slavery and tyranny in Rome' (E 12). The connection between licentiousness and excess that is implied here makes it clear that this harmful form of liberty should be checked. Furthermore, to do so would serve to improve the kind of liberty that Hume tries to preserve, namely defending the rights of citizens by the presence of a well-regulated administration and the rule of law. This type of liberty is what Hume has in mind when he mentions Cromwell's election as 'being so favourable to liberty' and avers that '[t]he elections of this parliament were conducted with perfect freedom' (H VI, 69; see also E 526). By curtailing the 'liberty' of the uneducated lower classes that he considered incapable of independent judgement, while exploiting their guile, Hume believed the liberty of the nation as a whole to have been improved. For Hume, unlike many radicals of the late eighteenth century, improving liberty did not always mean promoting the expansion of suffrage.

Hume's preference for a republic rather than a monarchy also does not necessarily mean that he wishes to decrease authority. To mitigate the volatility of popular opinion, for Hume, is fully compatible with his insistence on the importance of authority – monarchical or otherwise – capable of ensuring the stable and regular administration of government. 'Authority, as well as liberty,' Hume argues in the *History*, 'is requisite to government; and is even requisite to the support of liberty itself, by maintaining the laws, which can alone regulate and protect it' (H V, 356). Rather, it can be assumed that he tries to enhance and stabilise political authority by selecting a large republic as the ideal form of government. All the measures discussed in his 'Perfect Commonwealth' were designed by Hume to ensure the selection of those he considered 'men of fortune and education' (E 524). Although there is no guarantee that men of such qualities will be selected, Hume goes on to evolve a system intended to preserve the authority of such people, whom he describes as 'a kind of independent magistracy in a state' in his essay 'Of Public Credit'. In the same essay, Hume expresses apprehension about the possible loss of 'all ideas of nobility, gentry, and family' (358). In fact, in his description of the perfect commonwealth, Hume proposes the enhancement of the authority of the House of Peers 'in order to bring [the present British government] to the most perfect model of limited monarchy' (526; Stewart 1992: 251–2). Although Hume presents the programme for improvement of the constitutional monarchy as less satisfactory than that for a large republic, in neither scheme does he dismiss the role of the upper classes. In his plan, by giving suffrage to the lower orders of society, power will reside in the hands of the 'men of fortune and education' that they will elect as representatives.

Thus, seemingly undemocratic measures could, for Hume, serve to consolidate what he considered the best balance between 'liberty' and 'authority' (Livingston 1990: 132). This can be considered to be the main reason Hume boasts of his own model as 'a form of government, to which I cannot, in theory, discover any considerable objection' (E 516). In contrast to this comment about the ideal system, Hume does not give the British government of his age the appellation of being 'the best system of government';

rather, he refers to it as 'at least the most entire system of liberty, that ever was known amongst mankind' (H VI, 531; cf. III, 525).

Hume's repeated assertion that any plan of a perfect republic should be only speculative does not necessarily undervalue the importance of his own plan. Rather, Hume's 'Perfect Commonwealth' was an expression of his long-standing but pressing concerns about the volatility of the British mixed monarchy and the possible advent of a pure republic. This can be demonstrated by the intricacy of his plans: along with his detailed discussion of the internal mechanism of a bicameral legislature, Hume clearly regarded the fine design of the electoral system as vital, particularly to prevent the descent of democracy into confusion in a large republic. His plan directly reflects both his approval of frequent elections and his concerns about corruption among electors, which are exemplified in his appraisal of the Triennial Bill and the Cromwellian franchise in the *History*. Moreover, his revision of the requirements of the franchise in his plan went hand in hand with his understanding of the Cromwellian franchise.

Hume occasionally achieves a degree of scepticism such that he seems to deny any value to pure speculation. In the essay 'Whether the British Government inclines' he stated '[t]he question is not concerning any fine imaginary republic, of which a man may form a plan in his closet' (E 52). In the *History*, referring to Harrington's *Oceana*, he simply dismisses '[t]he idea [...] of a perfect and immortal commonwealth' as 'chimerical as that of a perfect and immortal man' (H V, 531–2). 'But what is this general Subject of Speculation to our Purpose?' Hume states severely in a letter dated 1775, '[Republicanism] is only fitted for a small State: And any Attempt towards it can in our [Country], produce only Anarchy, which is the immediate Forerunner of Despotism' (L II, 306; the words in brackets are supplemented by the editor of L). Here, he seems to be relinquishing his own scheme for an ideal republic. However, his criticism seems to be directed, not against speculation itself, but rather against rash attempts to translate such speculation into practice (Stewart 1992: 283). This is because, unlike Harrington who expected Cromwell to accept his plan, Hume was sufficiently sceptical as to remark that '[i]f any single person acquire power enough to take our constitution to pieces, and put it up a-new, he is really an absolute monarch; [...] such a person will never resign his power, or establish any free government' (E 'Whether the British Government inclines' 52). Hume does not put forward his plan as a blueprint designed to appeal to any political movement. Throughout his writings Hume's attitude to the reality of politics on this point remains constant. Such ambivalence might explain why he chose a utopian setting in his plan ('in some future age, [...] either by a dissolution of some old government, or by the combination of men to form a new one, in some distant part of the world' (513)). This utopian style could be one way to make his exposure of the absurdities of hasty and violent reforms compatible with his presentation of a hypothetical and speculative model. Despite their utopian *setting*, however, the institutional proposals in his plan and his view of human nature are not utopian. According to him, it is vital to propose a plan that neither presupposes the changeability of human nature, nor involves any drastic educational programmes. As we saw above, this is because Hume considers his plan to be an extension of his theoretical pursuit of the scientific bases for politics. Admittedly, such a manoeuvre is far from easily understandable, but rather open to misconstruction. The abbé Le Blanc, a French translator of the *Political Discourses*, adds in a footnote to 'Perfect Commonwealth' the comment that '[w]hat's the good of these ideas of chimerical perfections? [...] Such writings would serve only to excite fanatical minds, and would be at best useless' (Hume 1755: II, 214).* A careful exegesis of the text reveals that Hume and Le Blanc shared the same point of view, although Hume remained widely misunderstood, even by his translator. More interestingly, even in the midst of his theoretical pursuit of a perfect commonwealth, Hume is so sceptical as to assert that '[i]t is needless to enquire, whether such a government would be immortal'; he never relinquishes his deeper scepticism on the 'immortality, which the Almighty seems to have refused to his own productions' (E 529) – this is our topic in the next chapter.

Notes

1. For the reception of this essay by his contemporaries and later generations, see Susato (forthcoming).
2. An expression similar to the title of this essay is found in a passage

* 'A quoi sevent toutes ces idées de perfections chimériques? [...] De semblables Ecrits ne laissent pas que d'échauffer des têtes fanatiques, & le mieux qui en puisse arriver est que ce soit en pure perte'.

of Swift's *Gulliver's Travels* (1726). The captain Gulliver, who reached Brobdingnag (the country of giants) after leaving Lilliput, gives lectures on the politics of Britain (including the issue of public credit) to the King of Brobdingnag. Despite Gulliver's efforts, the King concludes the British to be 'the most pernicious Race of little odious Vermin' ([1726] 2012: 189). The captain finally laments that 'I take this Defect among [Brobdignagians] to have risen from their Ignorance; by not having hitherto reduced *Politicks* into a *Science*, as the more acute Wits of Europe have done' (193; see the editor's note in 193–4n.15). This might not go beyond a mere coincidence. Considering the fact that Swift was one of Hume's favourite authors (Potkay 2001), however, it might be possible that this phrase remained in the latter's head when writing his essay 'That Politics'.

3. Caroline Robbins terms Hume a 'theoretical republican' (1959: 217–18; see also Claeys 1994: 253). However, Forbes argues that '[c]ertainly to describe Smith, as Rae does, as "always theoretically a republican," is not saying very much. The same could be said about Hume' (1975a: 195).
4. Another essay that suffered many deletions was 'Of the Liberty of the Press'. Compare this with his passage on the subject in the *History* (VI, 540. The paragraph concerning the liberty of the press was inserted after the 1773 edition). On the seeming shift in his attitude on this point, see Forbes 1975b: 183–4.
5. Fieser remarks that Hume retracted the sentence in question 'after the 1742 edition', but it was in fact retained in this (second) edition.
6. It is possible that Hume derived this distinction from Paul de Rapin-Thoyras's *Dissertation sur les Whigs & les Torys* (1711), despite his criticism of the latter's qualificatons as a historian. In this pamphlet (immediately translated from the French original published in the same year), Rapin classifies both Whigs and Tories into the 'Political' (or 'State') and the 'Ecclesiastical' (1711: passim, but esp. 46–51). Political Whigs are subcategorised into the 'Republican' and 'Moderate', while Political Tories are 'Arbitrary' or 'Moderate'. He repeatedly emphasises that 'the *Moderate Whigs and Tories*, are in most respects, of the same Opinion' (51), because they share common interests despite their difference in political principles (62–3). As Gautier accurately argues, there are many similarities between Rapin's and Hume's discussions and taxonomies of political parties (2005: 96–7n.1), although Gautier does not mention the possible relation between Rapin's *Dissertation* and Hume's *True Account*.

7. The reactions of certain readers of the *History of Great Britain* led Hume to acknowledge that historical comparison can be used as a litmus paper to detect the dangers of partisanship. In the volumes on the Tudor regime (published in 1759), he remarks that '[t]here are indeed three events in our history, which may be regarded as touchstones of partymen'. He goes on to argue: 'An English Whig, who asserts the reality of the popish plot, an Irish Catholic, who denies the massacre in 1641, and a Scotch Jacobite, who maintains the innocence of queen Mary, must be considered as men beyond the reach of argument or reason, and must be left to their prejudices' (H IV, 395 Note [M]). It is unsurprising that Hume's interpretation of these historical events provoked much objection from every side (especially as for the Marian controversy, see Mossner 1980: 413, 467).
8. Despite his extremely pessimistic tone in the essay 'Of Public Credit', Hume's partial (though unwilling) admittance of some advantages in public credit is significant, especially compared with Montesquie's defiance on this point (Winch 1978: 128). Hume argues as a partial merit of public credit the possibility that 'the first visible eruption, or even immediate danger, of public disorders [...] will make them fly to the support of government' (E 355). A similar idea is found in Swift's *The History of the Four Last Years of the Queen*: 'Whoever were lenders to the government, would by the surest principle be obliged to support it' (Swift 1758: 158–9; cited in Kramnick 1992: 41). Note that Swift's *History* was first published in 1758, and the above sentence in Hume's essay is added after the 1770 edition.
9. More generally, as Kalyvas and Katznelson point out, the Scottish Enlightenment thinkers' reliance on the theory of unintended consequences in their accounts of the origins of social institutions does not necessarily contradict their deep interests in constitutionalism and their pursuit of institutional solutions (2008: 64n.68).
10. Michael Sonenscher acutely suggests that Hume's 'Perfect Commonwealth' 'contained a plan for a system of gradual promotion [...] that was somewhat similar to the one that Rousseau set out in his proposals for a reformed Polish system of government' (Sonenscher 2007: 279), though he does not develop this comparison any further (see also 235–7). It is possible that Rousseau could have had a chance to talk with Hume about these issues during their short friendship. Naturally, there was no mention of the *Considérations sur le gouvernement de Pologne* in Hume's letters because Rousseau had not conceptualised the work at that time. However, the Scottish

philosopher knew something about Rousseau's *Projet de constitution pour la Corse* (*Plan for the Constitution for Corsica*): Hume said in a letter written in 1766 that Rousseau 'showed me the letter which he had received from the Corsicans, in which he is invited to [...] frame them a body of laws, and to be the Solon or Lycurgus of this new commonwealth' (L II, 14).

11. As Voltaire's endorsement of the same belief, see Voltaire 1994: 201, 222 and intro. xxxiv.
12. Tracy also advocated representative government in his *Commentary and Review of Montesquieu's Spirit of Laws*. Significantly, he did so by criticising Montesquieu's support for a federation of small republics for very similar reasons to those given by Hume (Tracy 1969 [1811]: 83). Tracy also explains, in a similar way to Hume, that 'the citizens at large cannot be supposed to know generally all those who are properly qualified for such a purpose [as to directly choose the deputies of the assembly] [...]; in which circumstances it would be a good expedient to choose from among the members of the primitive assembly some person worthy of confidence and capable of making a proper selection for the purpose' (121; cf. E 522). Tracy supported 'a legislative body composed of a great many numbers, each having influence in different parts of the territory, will more easily obtain the general confidence, and will more readily be obeyed' (124; cf. E 527–8). There is no evidence that Tracy read Hume's 'Perfect Commonwealth', and furthermore he rarely read books written in English. As for Tracy's acquaintance of *The Federalist*, Kennedy speculates that '[i]t is remotely possible that one of the editions Trudaine de la Sablière's translation, *Le Fédéraliste* (Paris, 1792, 1795), was known to Tracy' (1978: 171n.12). If so, it is also possible that Tracy knew Hume's 'Perfect Commonwealth' through the French translations or reviews of this essay.
13. John Adams, on the other side of the Atlantic Ocean, criticised Hume's plan as 'a complicated aristocracy' (1787: 369–70). See also Spencer (ed.) 2002: 35–7.
14. Roger Emerson correctly points out that Hume's plan, along with his essay on population, 'should be considered with the more clearly economic essays' (2009: 156).
15. 'Gatton enjoyed a liberal franchise. All freeholders and inhabitants paying scot and lot were entitled to vote, but they only amounted to seven' (May [1871] 1912: I, 223). See also Dickinson 1995: 31.
16. Smith also attests in the *Lectures on Jurisprudence* (A) that '[f]requency of the elections is also a great security for the liberty of

the people [...]'; 'The more frequent these elections are, the more dependent are the representatives' (Smith 1982a: 273 [v.8–9]; see also Winch 1996: 144).

17. In 1742 Hume wrote a letter to William Mure of Caldwell, where he mentioned his previous, now missing, letter that contained his view of some present political issues and says that '[f]or let all the Letters of my Epistle be regularly divided, they will be found equivalent to a dozen of No's & as Many Ay's. There will be found a No for the Triennial Bill, for the Pension Bill, for the Bill about regulating Elections, for the Bill of Pains & Penalties against L. Orford &c. There will also be found an Ay for the Standing Army, for Votes of Credit, for the Approbation of Treaties &c' (L I, 43–4). Hume's opinions shown in this letter are a little embarrassing because they are almost the opposite to his later views. Forbes cites Hume's comments in this letter as evidence of his indifference to (or superficial concerns about) the issues of the Triennial Bill, the public credit or the standing army (1975b: 127). However, we should be more careful about Hume's intention especially in this letter because we have no way of knowing whether this is a correct summary of his 'last letters'. Moreover, ironic expressions abound in this as well as other letters. Incidentally, an anonymous – Mossner judged very Hume-like – reply to the criticism of the essay 'A Character of Sir Robert Walpole', which appeared in *The Scots Magazine* in 1742, said that '[t]here are many instances [of the declension of liberty], tho', I hope, none fatal; such as, the increase of the civil list, votes of credit, and too large a standing army, etc' (1980: 144–5).

7

Human Society 'in Perpetual Flux': Hume's Pendulum Theory of Civilisation

As we saw in Chapter 1, Hume endorses the importance of a 'spirit of scepticism' in politics when he criticises Hobbes as a rationalistic dogmatist. In a letter to Montesquieu Hume also asserts that he 'kept on the sceptical and doubtful side' of the debate over the populations in the ancient and modern worlds (L I, 177; see also Box and Silverthorne 2013). Although he finally claims in the essay 'Of Populousness' that the population of the modern world was greater than that of the ancient, Hume's stance on the *querelle des anciens et des modernes* is more nuanced than is immediately apparent from the conclusion in this essay. Examples of such scepticism abound in his political writings, many of which are related to his view of civilisation. As Forbes appropriately points out, '[t]hat political civilization is a precarious thing is Hume's most general and most useful and lasting lesson of moderation' (1975b: 309). From this perspective, it should be reconsidered how Hume's view of civilisation is an indispensable and probably the most important aspect of his Sceptical Enlightenment.

Throughout his writings, Hume maintains a coherent conviction regarding the vicissitudes of a nation: that any country will experience a period of cultural progress followed by decline. In other words, he adopts a cyclical or pendulum view of history. In spite of the assumptions the term 'cyclical' or 'pendulum' often evokes, however, Hume's emphasis is placed not upon the claim that human history in any field inevitably follows a particularly determined pattern. On the contrary, as he repeatedly asserts, 'human society is in perpetual flux' (E 'Original Contract' 476), or '[n]othing in this world is perpetual; Every thing, however seemingly firm, is in continual flux and change' ('Immortality of the Soul' 597). For Hume, a blind belief in any sort of predetermined cycle within our history differs not at all from the faith in perpetual progress that he criticises. Nevertheless, Hume retains a faint underlying image of 'the rise, progress, perfection, and decline' (H II, 519), especially in the fields of the arts and sciences, without prescribing any particular route for this process in either case. It will explain his strong concern over the plausible decline of the arts in his contemporary Britain (NL 199).

Hume's version of the 'cyclical' view of history has been a thorn in the side of several commentators who have attempted to place him within the Enlightenment. This is because the strong belief in 'Reason and Progress', which is clearly wanting in Hume, has been considered one of the most evident intellectual features of the French philosophes. As a result, Forbes plays down Hume's own assertion of his cyclical view of civilisation because he argues that it 'can only apply to literature and the fine arts, and makes nonsense of Hume's whole notion of civil liberty and the progress of political experience and knowledge' (1975b: 315). Otherwise, it has been recognised as one of 'what was to be a consciously acknowledged fundamental disagreement between Hume and the politically idealistic French intellectuals of this later period' along with his (allegedly) anti-liberal doctrine (Bongie [1965] 2000: 55). Both interpretations, however, seem quite unsatisfactory; Forbes disregards Hume's belief in the parallel development of the arts and sciences and political governance and economy. Those who consider Hume's cyclical view of history proof of his 'Counter-Enlightenment' attitude fail to pay due attention to the other aspects of Hume's thought that make him very much the defender of modern values. Recent studies in the history of economic thought have also discussed Hume's conception of cyclical history in the context of the 'rich country-poor country' debate. Unfortunately, these analyses have interpreted Hume's controversial argument mainly from the viewpoint of the intellectual discourse in political economy: it is treated from the same angle as his specie-flow mechanism and free trade doctrine, thus separating it from the wider context of Hume's social and political philosophy.

The structure of this chapter is roughly two-fold. In the first half, we will consider the following points regarding Hume's cyclical view of history. Firstly, after examining some possible precursors of his cyclical view, Hume's definition of the 'coarse' and 'refined' arts will be elucidated, demonstrating that his cyclical theory is not confined to the fine arts and literature. Secondly, we will approach in an oblique way the perplexing point of whether

Hume's cyclical argument refers only to the particular situations in which it is invoked or whether it is a general characteristic of his thought. These considerations will enable us to clarify the meaning of Hume's references to the 'decline' and even 'death' of nations, which occur in various essays.

These considerations support my argument in the second half of this chapter that Hume's arguments in the economic essays of the *Political Discourses* do not contradict his pendulum theory. This perspective will allow us to perceive that, in the 'rich country-poor country' debate, the divide between the positions of Hume and Tucker is not limited to their views on international economic theory, but rather represents fundamental differences in the two thinkers' notions of civilisation. In the last section, we will explore the strategic purposes of Hume's notion of oscillating civilisation. Considering these points will explain the widespread misunderstanding of Hume's argument among scholars, as well as revealing how the constancy of his claims regarding the cyclical nature of history can be reconciled with his status as one of the champions of modern civilisation.

1 Hume's Cyclical View and its Predecessors

As recent studies show, the cyclical view of history was shared by many early modern political philosophers and Hume's contemporaries (Vyverberg 1958; Jones 1982: 93–102; Jack 1989: 193–200; Pocock 1990: 280; Mason 1996: 201–2). In addition to this, there had been many discussions and anxieties about the possible radical changes caused by the ever-increasing concern over the perils of public credit long before the French Revolution (Sonenscher 2007: 8–9). These preoccupations demonstrate that, far from a naïve belief in progress, the possibilities of decline and fall constantly occupied the thoughts of many eighteenth-century thinkers.[1] Aside from a few, such as Turgot and Condorcet, adamant apologists of progress were rather rare (Brumfitt 1972: 152). Seen in this light, Hume's cyclical view of civilisation is expressive of these Enlightenment concerns. At the same time, it is important to consider each particular case according to its individual context and intention, because the patterns they observed in the motion of history were by no means monolithic.[2]

The earliest indication of Hume's cyclical view of history can be found in his *Essays, Moral and Political*. In the essay 'Of the

Rise and Progress', which first appeared in the second volume of the *Essays* in 1742, after discussing the general incentives that promote the rise of arts and sciences in a nation, he progresses to the following 'fourth observation': '*That when the arts and sciences come to perfection in any state, from that moment they naturally, or rather necessarily decline, and seldom or never revive in that nation, where they formerly flourished*' (E 135). Another, similarly strong assertion is found in the second volume of his *History*, which was first published in 1761. Here he refers to cultural fluctuations on a grander scale: from the fall of the Roman Empire, through the Dark Ages, to the revival of the arts and sciences in the Renaissance (H II, 519–20).[3] Regarding these observations, Duncan Forbes comments that Hume 'falls back on the swinging pendulum of the classical historians and Machiavelli' (1975b: 315; as for those with a similar view to Forbes's, see Hont 2005: 288–9n.56). Obviously, investigating the origins of the cyclical view of history often leads us to ancient sources. According to Adam Potkay, Hume's story of the rise and decline of the arts and sciences in the above essay is nothing but a summary of a passage by the Roman historian Velleius Paterculus in his *Historiæ Romanæ* (c. AD 29) (Potkay 2000: 153–4):[4] 'Genius is fostered by emulation. [...] And, in the nature of things, that which is cultivated with the highest zeal advances to the highest perfection; but it is difficult to continue at the point of perfection and naturally that which cannot advance must recede' (Velleius Paterculus 1924, 1955: 45).

Yet, we can find more similar remarks in the work of Hume's more modern predecessors. Among others, William Temple, whose possible influence on Hume was discussed in Chapter 2, offers in 'An Essay upon the Ancient and Modern Learning' his version of the cyclical view of history – one which seems very close to that of Hume:

> Science and arts have run their circle, and had their periods in the several parts of the world: they are generally agreed to have held their course from *East* to *West*, to have begun in *Chaldea* and *Egypt*, to have been transplanted from thence from *Greece* to *Rome*, to have shrunk there, and after many ages, to have revived from those ashes, and to have sprung up again, both in Italy and other more *western* Provinces of Europe. (Temple 1754: II, 160; see also Levine 1991: 26)

In a very similar way, in the essay 'Of Civil Liberty', Hume traces the progression of the arts and sciences from the Persians and Egyptians, through the Greeks and Romans to the modern Western nations. Hume places rather more emphasis than Temple on the significance of liberty:

> It had been observed by the ancients, that all the arts and sciences arose among free nations; and, that the PERSIANS and EGYPTIANS [...], made but faint efforts towards a relish in those finer pleasures, which were carried to such perfection by the GREEKS [...]. It had also been observed, that, when the GREEKS lost their liberty, though they increased mightily in riches, by means of the conquests of ALEXANDER; yet the arts, from that moment, declined among them, and have never since been able to raise their head in that climate. Learning was transplanted to ROME, the only free nation at that time in the universe; and having met with so favourable a soil, it made prodigious shoots for above a century; till the decay of liberty produced also the decay of letters, and spread a total barbarism over the world. (E 89)

He again uses the simile of plants and soil at the very end of the essay 'Of the Rise and Progress' (137).[5] Although Temple was known as a defendant of the ancients in the *querelle des anciens et des modernes*, he shared with Hume a strong scepticism regarding the possibility of perpetual progress. Let us compare the following remarks, taken from Temple's 'An Essay upon the Ancient and Modern Learning' and Hume's *History* respectively:

> It were too great a mortification to think, that the same fate has happened to us, even in our modern learning, as if the growth of that, as well as of natural bodies, had some short periods, beyond which it could not reach, and after which it must begin to decay. It falls in one country or one age, and rises again in others, but never beyond a certain pitch. (Temple 1754: II, 169)

> But there is a point of depression, as well as of exaltation, from which human affairs naturally return in a contrary direction, and beyond which they seldom pass either in their advancement or decline. (H II, 519)

As these comparisons reveal, it is difficult to claim any inherent originality in Hume's cyclical view of civilisation, but to acknowledge this does not reduce its significance for Hume's thought. The aim of this chapter is to demonstrate the strategic value of his ideas of civilisation for critiquing both those who viewed history as a trajectory of perpetual progress and those who regarded human society as in a process of successive decline. Hume's pendulum argument neither stemmed from a pessimistic view of human nature nor was it mere rhetoric: rather it was deeply connected with his understanding of the universality and constancy of human nature. Before discussing this point, we need to address the lack of clarity of many of his references to his own viewpoint, which has caused much misunderstanding, not only among his contemporaries, but also among later scholars.

2 Hume's Cyclical View of Civilisation and 'the Constant and Universal Principles of Human Nature'

The first aspect of Hume's viewpoint to consider is the range of subjects to which he applied his cyclical view of history. Duncan Forbes, in an attempt to avoid the seeming contradiction between this cyclical view and his notion of the progress of commerce and political liberty, states that Hume's assertion in the passage reproduced above 'can only apply to literature and the fine arts' (1975b: 315). In fact, at the beginning of his essay 'Of the Rise and Progress', Hume makes a distinction between commerce on the one hand, and the arts and sciences on the other, stating that it is easier to trace the rise of the former, because it is founded upon a more general and universal human trait: 'avarice, or the desire of gain'. In comparison, the sciences and the fine arts are said to be founded upon less influential passions such as 'curiosity, or the love of knowledge' (E 113). In the *History* Hume upholds the similar division between 'the refined arts' and 'those vulgar arts of agriculture, manufacture, and commerce' (H II, 519). Upon this account, Forbes's division seems to be justifiable. However, the phrase 'the arts' encompassed a vast range of different meanings in the eighteenth century (Johnson 1960: chap. 13), and Hume's distinction between various types of art does not entirely square with modern terminology. As a first stage towards comprehending his definition, Hume in the essay 'Of the Rise and Progress' included under the heading of 'the arts', not only literature and liberal arts, but also the 'manual arts and manufactures' (E 124).

A more essential distinction among the various arts is, for Hume, not between economic goods and the fine arts, but between what he regards as 'coarse' and 'refined' arts. He stated that 'what is profitable to every mortal, and in common life', that is the coarser arts, 'when once discovered, can scarcely fall into oblivion', while '[t]he arts of luxury, and much more the liberal arts, which depend on a refined taste or sentiment, are easily lost' (E 124). Hume's distinction between the coarse and refined arts on the basis of whether they are profitable to the majority of humanity or are the exclusive preserve of those few with the leisure to practise them corresponds to his awareness that the more refined a form of art, the more prone it is to decline.

Hume's emphasis upon the distinction between the coarse and refined arts is consistent even in the essay 'Of Refinement in the Arts' in his *Political Discourses* (1752). Although this essay has often been regarded as one of his 'economic' essays, we should remind ourselves that the improvement of 'delicacy' and the refinement of 'taste' are central to his argument in this essay. Indeed, the very title of this essay shows that Hume's focus did not lie on a vindication of economic progress as an end in itself, but on its connection to the progress of the refined arts, including the liberal arts and even political knowledge (E 270–1, 273–4). In the essay 'Of Money', Hume applied the same cyclical framework with which he had described the rise and decline of arts and science to manufactures:

> Manufactures [...] leaving those countries and provinces which they have already enriched, and flying to others, whither they are allured by the cheapness of provisions and labour; till they have enriched these also, and are again banished by the same causes. (E 283–4)

It is hard to draw a clear line between Hume's view of the refined arts and the products of economic progress, since he regarded them as overlapping spheres and their development as interlinked.

The next point is whether Hume's cyclical view of history refers only to particular cases or whether it is intended as a generality. Hume took the liberty of applying his argument concerning the cyclical nature of achievement in the arts in various ways. His statements are particularly ambiguous in the essay 'Of the Rise and Progress', where he does not make a clear distinction between his discussion of specific art forms and 'the arts' in general. He moves from a discussion of individual art forms, such as painting and sculpture in a particular nation, to elucidate the general decline and revival of European history from a grander viewpoint. Thus, the reader is also uncertain whether his argument is intended to apply to one nation, or to European countries in general. It is the indistinctness of these points that has given rise to a generally negative interpretation of his pendulum theory among Hume scholars (as exemplified in Forbes). A similar latitude of argument caused Hume's contemporaries to misinterpret his claims in the essay 'Of the Jealousy of Trade', as we will see below.

For current purposes, however, we do not need to dwell on these questions. Hume's basic standpoint in the essay 'Of the Rise and Progress' is maintained throughout the several 'economic' essays in the *Political Discourses*. Hume's underlying assertion is that those factors that inspire the cultivation of the arts are precisely the same as those that prompt their endogenous retrogression. His work consistently emphasises the stimulatory influence of novel objects, often introduced from abroad. This stimulation prompts those who are exposed to it to try to obtain such objects, by trade or by imitation, which directly encourages innovation in industry (E 'Jealousy of Trade' 329–30; H II, 519; Hont 2005: 115–19). Hume's emphasis upon the significance of the sense of novelty produced by objects introduced from abroad is already evident in the *Treatise* (T 2.2.4.4; 352–3). At least theoretically, it could be argued that there are no limits to the human capacity for imagination, curiosity and emulation for the perfection of art forms, which means that it should be possible to keep the flame of innovation perpetually alight. Hume, however, never supported the idea that human imagination and desire expand linearly and infinitely. He explained why this is not the case in the essay 'Of the Rise and Progress', where he stated that his pendulum argument 'may, at first sight, be esteemed contrary to reason'. He went on to admit that '[i]f the natural genius of mankind be the same in all ages, and in almost all countries, (as seems to be the truth)', seemingly we can progress perpetually because of the continual accumulation of precedents (E 135). However, this is not the case in practice, as the accumulation of good models in each art will ultimately naturally discourage the emulation of precedents among newcomers by decreasing the stock of 'praise and glory' that they receive, as the 'posts of honour are all occupied'. The same thing will happen, he argues, if one nation imports their models of artistic achievement 'in too great perfection' from a foreign country, as 'this extinguishes emulation and sinks the ardour of the generous youth' (136). In short, the encouragement of industry and emulation in the arts will eventually produce standard models of excellence that, as a natural consequence, tend to absorb further motivation for progress.

Significantly, when he directly opposes the argument for the possibility of endless accumulation of human knowledge and advances in technology, Hume endorses the universality of human nature, stating that it 'seems to be the truth' that the natural genius of man is equal in all ages. In fact, this principle plays a significant part in developing his cyclical view of history. In the essay 'Of the Populousness of Ancient Nations' in the *Political Discourses* he states:

> Stature and force of body, length of life, even courage and extent of genius, seem hitherto to have been naturally, in all ages, pretty much the same. The arts and sciences, indeed, have flourished in one period, and have decayed in another: But we may observe, that, at the time when they rose to greatest perfection among one people, they were perhaps totally unknown to all the neighbouring nations; and though they universally decayed in one age, yet in a succeeding generation they again revived, and diffused themselves over the world. As far, therefore, as observation reaches, *there is no universal difference discernible in the human species*. (E 378. Italics added)

This passage shows how Hume demonstrates the compatibility of his principle of the universality of human nature with his cyclical view of history. He did not deduce the possibility of the constant accumulation of models from this principle. On the contrary, he derived it from his observation of the vicissitude of this world. Additionally, as Silvia Sebastiani points out, 'the opening of [the essay 'Of the Populousness'] about the corruptibility and mortality of the fabric of the world was an explicit quotation of Lucretius and an implicit response to Wallace, who labelled the Roman philosopher as "the unreligious poet"' (2013: 41; Lucretius 1997: 160 [5.826–7]). Again, however, Hume cautiously excludes '[t]hese *general physical* causes' from his considerations (E 378), which is completely consistent with what I call his 'modern Epicureanism without its materialistic foundations' in Chapter 1.

Again, William Temple made a similar point in 'An Essay upon the Ancient and Modern Learning', although he leaned more toward the climate theory by way of explanation: 'as to wit or genius, that, nature being still the same, these must be much at a rate in all ages, at least in the same climates, as the growth and size of plants and animals commonly are' (1754: II, 142). The opening sentences of the 'Essay upon the Original and Nature of Government' encapsulate his persistent view of human nature and history:

> The nature of man seems to be the same in all Times and Places, but varied like their Statures, Complexions and Features, by the Force and Influence of the several Climates where they are born and bred; which produces in them, by a different Mixture of the Humours and Operation of Air, a different and unequal Course of Imagination and Passions, and consequently of Discourses and Actions.[/] These Differences incline Men to several Customs, Educations, Opinions, and Laws, which form and govern the several Nations of the World [...] (II, 29)

The following comments on Temple's view of history by Clara Marburg can be applied to Hume without much modification: 'Temple, in his contemplation of the history of the world, could not believe in progress. For the very basic assumptions of his epicurean philosophy were that men in all ages and places are fundamentally alike [...]' (1932: 26).

More importantly, Hume could also resort to the argument of Temple's opponent, Bernard Le Bovier de Fontenelle. Hume seems indebted (although not exclusively so) to Fontenelle for his claim in the essay 'Of the Rise and Progress' that the arts always seek fresh soil (Jones 1982: 102).[6] Although Hume never directly mentions Fontenelle's *Digression sur les anciens et les modernes*, there are many striking similarities between Hume and Fontenelle's intellectual strategies to demonstrate the superiority of the modern to the ancient. As William Temple does for the opposite purpose, Fontenelle repeatedly asserts the universality of human nature: 'nature keeps in her hands a certain dough which is always the same' (Fontenelle [1688] 1742: 171).* Fontenelle's discussions lead to the analysis of the significant influences of 'moral causes' as determinative factors of manners: 'People clearly see that all the

* 'la nature a entre les mains une certaine pâte qui est toujours la même'.

differences, whatever they are, must be caused by external circumstances such as the age, governments and the situations of general affairs' (176).* This is almost the same definition of moral causes as Hume gives in the essay 'Of National Characters' (E 198). Hume and Fontenelle's belief in the superiority of the modern to the ancient does not necessarily mean that either's standpoint prefigured Hegelian dialectical theory of the evolution of human nature: that is, the idea that human nature itself was progressively elevated, as a result of humanity's progress throughout a rising spiral pattern of history (Berry 1982: 65, 124; Holthoon 2013: 154–5; cf. Hegel [1837] 1980: 65).

Hume's claim for the 'universal and constant principles of human nature' (EHU 8.7; 83) has long been a target of criticism for its 'unhistorical' conception. I will not enter here into the debate over Hume's alleged '(un)historicism': it will suffice to quote Forbes's brilliant argument on the compatibility of 'Hume's "sociological relativism" with his belief in the uniform principles of human nature' (1975b: 117). He claims that Hume's principles 'are to be regarded as abstractions from the concrete variety of human (=social) experience; Hume's "general psychology" is concerned with the function and mechanism, not the content of mind, which is various and supplied by social and historical circumstances' (118–19; see also Evnine 1993; Wertz 2000: chaps. 3 and 4; Le Jallé 2001: 134–5). This succinct explication is remarkably helpful in clarifying the following statement in the first *Enquiry*: 'the manners of men different in different ages and countries', he argued, nevertheless afford 'room for many general observations concerning the gradual change of our sentiments and inclinations, and the different maxims, which prevail in the different ages of human creatures' (EHU 8.11; 85–6). I hasten to add two points to Forbes's statement, however. Firstly, Hume's general and empirical, although tentative, observations indicate his opinion that any society is subject to the cyclical fluctuation in its civilising process. Forbes discards Hume's cyclical view of history as an element of his 'vulgar Whiggism'. Yet, Hume hardly maintains his view of the fluctuations in human societies to be deterministic in any sense: indeed, their content and period necessarily varies according to

* 'On voit clairement que toutes les différences, quelles qu'elles soient, doivent être causées par des circonstances étrangères, tel que sont le temps, les gouvernements, l'état des affaires générales'.

time and place (note the following phrase by Hume: 'All causes are not conjoined to their usual effects, with like uniformity' (EHU 8.12; 86)). Secondly, although Forbes mentions in passing the 'corrective' function of Hume's insistence on the similarity among nations as an antidote against 'the very common view of [the ancient] as super-human' (1975b: 118), he fails to note (at least in this context) the limits of Hume's 'sociological relativism'. Hume's universal principles do not only provide him with a theoretical basis to comprehend a wide variety of human customs, but also function as a ground from which he can dismiss the claims of some utopians or the reports of certain travellers as suspicious (T 2.3.1.10; 402). In accordance with his usual scepticism concerning the attainment of the truth in politics, as we saw in the previous chapter, Hume can believe neither the feasibility of a perfect communist society (EPM 3.24; 193), nor the veracity of a travel report about the country in which the inhabitants 'were entirely divested of avarice, ambition, or revenge, [and] knew no pleasure but friendship, generosity, and public spirit' (EHU 8.8; 84; see also Chapter 2 in this book). It seems interesting to add that Hume is willing to believe in the existence of some nations 'who entertained no sentiments of Religion' (NHR intro). This suggests the affinity between Bayle's thesis of an atheists' country and Hume's understanding of human nature (Chapter 5). It is perhaps a result of Forbes's own, rather prescriptive, concept of 'Whiggism' that he confines Hume's pendulum theory to the periphery by relating it only to the field of the fine arts. Nonetheless, this aspect of Hume's thought clearly had wider applicability and deserves closer attention.

3 The Metaphor of 'Death' in Hume's *Essays*

As the passages cited above demonstrate, the main point of Hume's cyclical view lies in his awareness that human societies exist perpetually within successive cycles of progress and decline. To convey this idea to his readers, he repeatedly likens the body politic to the body of an animal (E 'Whether the British Government inclines' 51, 'Public Credit' 363), although this metaphor was very popular at the time.[7] Hume's thought in relation to the fluctuations in the constitution of social institutions in general is consistently characterised by the maxim that '*the corruption of the best things produces the worst*' (E 'Superstition and Enthusiasm' 73). In the essay 'Of Superstition and Enthusiasm', he applied this concept to religion, and in the essay 'Perfect Commonwealth', to the body politic (529). To put it another way, if we employ Hume's metaphor of the tides ('Whether the British Government inclines' 51), a moderate tidal movement is preferred to a violent one. China, in Hume's mind, was a long-lived but flourishing country, not only because of its various geographical merits, but also because of its 'slow progress' checked by the homogeneity of religion, language and manners ('Rise and Progress' 122). In the essay 'Of Commerce', for the purposes of his remonstration against the jealousy of trade, Hume cited China as the most flourishing country without extensive foreign trade (264).

Taking into account these observations, we should note Hume's strong belief that contemporary Britain was on the downward slope of its own cycle. This aids us in understanding his reasoning in advocating the 'euthanasia' of the British government in the *Essays, Moral and Political*: he poses the question of '[w]hether the British Government inclines more to absolute Monarchy, or to a Republic'. His answer is that '[a]bsolute monarchy [...] is the easiest death, the true *Euthanasia* of the BRITISH constitution' (E 53) because, unlike the alternative, it is not preceded by major disturbances throughout the nation. Hume's references to the death or ruin of political bodies in the *Political Discourses* can be found in at least four places: in addition to the quotation reproduced in the previous section from the essay 'Of the Populousness', he mentions three types of 'death' in the essay 'Of Public Credit', and the 'necessary progress of human affairs' that 'human nature checks itself in its airy elevation' ('Balance of Trade' 341). With increasing frequency, in his letters and writings, he expressed his conviction that the British nation had already reached its peak of civilisation: 'I am only sorry to see', Hume grumbles, that 'the total Extinction of Literature in England, prognosticates a very short Duration of all our other Improvements, and threatens a new and a sudden Inroad of Ignorance, Superstition and Barbarism' (NL 199; see also H IV, 373 footnote [c]). In a diary recounting a journey with Hume some months before his death, John Home records Hume's opinion that 'a national debt must be the ruin of Britain' and that 'the two most civilized nations, the English and French, should be on the decline' (Home 1976: 16; this refers to a comment made by Hume on 24 April 1776).

Nevertheless, although he often uses the word 'death', in none of these cases does Hume mean to imply actual collapse or extinction: rather, he refers to cultural decline or to upheavals in the system of government. Even in the essay 'Of Public Credit', the various possible fates predicted to occur as a result of public credit do not necessarily involve the real death, or termination, of a nation (even in the case of the 'violent death' by conquest). In a letter written at a later date, Hume connects public bankruptcy, which he calls 'natural death', with 'the Restoration of the Government to the King, Nobility, and Gentry of this Realm' (L II, 210; II, 184; Pocock 1990: 197; Hont 2005: 347–8). Now it becomes clear that Hume's use of the word 'death', which caused unnecessary apprehension among his readers, does not mean the real dissolution of a nation, but merely indicates a halt or change of direction in its progress or a change in the system of government. Throughout the history of human civilisation, he argues, there have been 'interruptions in the periods of learning' as well as 'interruptions in political government and societies'.[8] He even suggests that such discontinuities 'would be rather favourable to the arts and sciences' because these intervals, by breaking the 'progress of authority' (E 'Rise and Progress' 123), create the opportunity for revival and renewal of innovation in the arts as well as governance. These understandings of Hume's cyclical view explain an important divergence between Hume and his contemporary, Josiah Tucker.

4 Hume and Tucker in the 'Rich Country-Poor Country' Debate

In the field of the history of economic thought, the debate that arose from Tucker's critique of Hume's essay 'Of the Balance of Trade' is known as a substantial part of the 'rich country-poor country' debate. According to István Hont, the controversy started when Tucker rebutted Hume's belief in the existence of constant fluctuations of commerce and defended the possibility of the continual advancement of the fortunes of a rich country. Hume responded to Tucker's criticism, and added another essay 'Of the Jealousy of Trade' to the 1758 edition of the *Political Discourses*. In this essay he conceded, or rather articulated, the point that a rich country can maintain its economic advantage by combining a cooperative foreign policy with encouragement for domestic industry, and that decline is not inevitable if technological progress and industriousness is sustained (Hont 2005: chap. 3, esp. 279, 293).

The conclusion of this debate, however, was rather unclear. In fact, Tucker himself expressed uncertainty regarding Hume's final standpoint: 'Tho' I cannot boast that I had the Honour of making the Gentleman [i.e., Hume] a *declared* Convert, yet I can say, and proved likewise, that in his Publications since our Correspondence, he has wrote, and reasoned, as if he was a Convert' ([1774] 1993: v). More recent commentators have also failed to reach a consensus as to what extent the two thinkers agreed or disagreed after their exchange. Hont argues that Hume and Tucker have, in reality, reached the same conclusion, namely that 'the international division of labor between rich and poor countries through sharing out the production of simpler products to the poor and of more sophisticated products to the rich countries' constituted the first stage of free trade (2005: 281). Within the context of the two authors' views concerning formation and development of international trade theory, I accept Hont's contention. However, I wish to emphasise here a point that falls outside the scope of Hont's argument: namely that Hume himself has no intention of implying that the poor country would remain indefinitely in the position of producing more basic products. For example, Hume states in a letter to Lord Kames that a poor country should 'at first' attempt simple forms of industry (L I, 271).[9] As Hont argues, attempts to create a simplistic division between the camps of optimists and pessimists regarding the issue of the potential of human societies for progress tends to cloud the analysis of the true position of the two writers (2005: 270n.5; 289n.57). While Hont is correct that the debate between Hume and Tucker should not be regarded in terms of this simplistic division, there are nevertheless important differences between the two thinkers that are not encompassed by Hont's arguments concerning their views on the mechanisms of international trade. The 'rich country-poor country' debate can be viewed as a part of much wider discussions within the Enlightenment discourse over the nature of civilisation.

Hume and Tucker differ on two points: one is Tucker's mistaken belief that Hume's concept of the constant fluctuations in the fortunes of nations entailed the inevitable ruin of a rich country. István Hont observes that the debate was initiated from 'comedies of error' based upon both Hume's obscure statement and Tucker's subsequent misunderstanding and overreaction (2005: 273). While this section owes much to Hont's research, my interest lies rather in probing into the aspects of Hume's position liable to prompt the misunderstanding that occurred. The other difference lies in their views regarding the possibility of the accumulation of models of excellence – this point will be addressed in the next section.

In the letter addressed to Lord Kames, responding to Tucker's argument, Hume proposed the question of 'whether these advantages [of a rich country] can go on, increasing trade *in infinitum*, or whether they do not at last come to a *ne plus ultra*, and check themselves, by begetting disadvantages, which at first retard, and at last finally stop their progress' (L I, 270). Hume answers his own question briefly in the same letter:

> the growth of all bodies, artificial as well as natural, is stopped by internal causes, derived from their enormous size and greatness. Great empires, great cities, great commerce, all of them receive a check, not from accidental events, but necessary principles. (L I, 272; see also E 340–1, 448)[10]

Here, we should note that Hume mentions merely the existence of 'checks' and the halting of growth rather than referring to any real death or end. The question to be explored here is whether Hume's belief in the constant flux of civilisation contradicts his argument in the *Political Discourses*, including that laid out in the essay 'Of the Jealousy of Trade'. In the *Political Discourses*, as we saw above, he maintains his earlier claims that '[m]anufactures, therefore gradually shift their places' (E 283). Similarly, in this passage he does not forecast the *inevitable* ruin of the country in which this shift takes place. Although even this statement was interpreted as pessimistic by his contemporaries, his point lies in illustrating the constant instability of the arts, even the arts of commerce and manufacturing, rather than the successive decline of nations.

Hume endorses in the essay 'Of the Jealousy of Trade' the view that most countries have their own staples based upon their particular geographical advantages, and acknowledges the importance in international trade of primary products, what he refers to as the 'coarse' arts. A country such as Britain, with a natural advantage in the production of primary products such as wool, should not be placed at a disadvantage due to the expansion of the trade of neighbouring nations: this is particularly true for countries with a natural diversity of staples (E 329–30).[11] In the case of technology and labour-intensive industries, what Hume called the 'refined' arts, however, more dynamic fluctuations are likely to occur (L I, 271). When he suggests that the spirit of industry, if well preserved, 'may easily be diverted from one branch to another' on demand (E 330), Hume does not deny that a rich country could lose some, or even most, of its revenue from manufacturing in future, but reiterated his belief that any country is vulnerable to the continual fluctuation of commerce.

It now becomes clear that the frameworks within which Hume and Tucker placed their discussions in the 'rich country-poor country' debate diverged, even when their conclusion was the same. Tucker claimed that rich countries would never lose their advantage, especially regarding the production of refined and elaborate products, if they maintain their industriousness. In contrast, Hume emphasised the fact that even if a backward nation was able to catch up with the rich nation, the inhabitants of the latter could shift their national power to other industries, or 'may lose most of its foreign trade, and yet continue a great and powerful people' (E 'Commerce' 264). Even after adding the essay 'Of the Jealousy of Trade' to the *Political Discourses*, Hume made no effort to remove from his work references to his conception of history as a cyclical process. Far from it, his pendulum argument continued to appear in his subsequent writings and letters. This does not mean, however, that the 'rich country-poor country' dispute arose solely from misinterpretations. There is another, and more essential, difference between the positions of Hume and Tucker.

5 The '*Ne Plus Ultra*' or the 'Threshold'?

The issue at stake in the 'rich country-poor country' debate ranged far beyond economic theory, to the views of the two thinkers on civilisation itself. Hume's notion of internal 'checks' is not exclusively economic-oriented, as shown in his many discussions of the factors at work within great cities and empires. Tucker's work manifests a similar awareness that this topic extends to the fields of politics, commerce and the arts and sciences. Both were well aware that the issue of the possibility of future progress was not purely theoretical, but had metaphysical, or even religious, implications. This is demonstrated by Tucker's inclusion of the discussion in more detail in his sermons than in his 'theoretical' essays ([1774] 1993: 47). Certainly, this is a sermon rather than a theoretical enquiry, but Tucker did not consider his economic and ecclesiastical claims to be mutually irrelevant, stating that the content of his sermons 'will throw such new and striking Lights on the Subject of Commerce, as will induce Men of a liberal Education to study it for the future as a *Science* [...]' (xiii).

Replying to Hume's notion of internal 'checks', Tucker stated that he did not intend to assert that progress must continue endlessly:

> no Man can positively define, *when*, or *where* it must *necessarily* stop [...] and therefore, 'till the *ne plus ultra* of all Advancements in Arts, Sciences, and Navigation, etc. etc. is clearly demonstrated [...], we may still be allowed to assert, that the richer manufacturing Nation will maintain its Superiority over the poorer one, notwithstanding this latter may be likewise advancing towards Perfection. (Tucker [1774] 1993: 41)

At first reading, Tucker seems here to be adopting a similarly sceptical view to that of Hume regarding the possibility of the continuous advancement of wealthy nations. However, Tucker's real intention is to argue that the continued progress of a rich country is possible, on the grounds that its perfection will be reached in an unknown and infinitely distant future. Tucker proposes here that human society has 'just got within the Threshold' rather than 'that we arrived at the *ne plus ultra* of useful Discoveries' (23). He bases his argument upon a comparison between the knowledge of a Goth living in the Dark Ages and that of a man of his own society, the advancements of which would have been unimaginable to the barbarian.

In contrast, Hume, as we have seen before, derives his theory of the inalterability of human nature from the flux and reflux of civilisation, including the rise and fall of the ancient empires and the long Dark Ages. He stated in the essay 'Of the Populousness' that 'as it must still be uncertain, whether, at present, it be advancing to its point of perfection, or declining from it, we cannot thence presuppose any decay in human nature' (E 379). Thus, Hume and Tucker extracted diametrically opposed opinions from the empirical observations of history.

Tucker's observations were, to his own mind, founded on empirical evidence. In his sermon emphasising 'the plan of lasting and extensive commerce', he described how the accumulation of the works of genius makes it possible to kindle a flame of emulation and progress 'from Generation to Generation throughout an almost endless Progression and Variety' ([1774] 1993: 29–30 [Sermon 2]). From these reflections, Tucker concluded that 'tho' it be true that Body Politic *may* come to an End, as well as the Body Natural, there is no physical Necessity that it *must*' (47). Tucker supported his conviction about the possibility of future progress by reference to the benevolent intentions of providence.

Hume picked up on this argument and turned it around to illustrate how the same logic could be applied to provide evidence for the existence of constant fluctuations in the fortunes of nations: Tucker 'draws an argument from the goodness of Providence; but I think it may be turned against him. It was never surely the intention of Providence, that any one nation should be a monopolizer of wealth' (L I, 272). As Hume points out, we can draw an opposing argument from Tucker's initial supposition: that is, it could be the intention of benevolent providence that each country should share equally in the benefits of commerce.

In such reasoning, Hume is at his strongest. For example, in the *Dialogues concerning Natural Religion*, he draws parallels between animals or plants and the human world to counter those who claimed the existence of God as the creator of a rationally designed world on the basis of the analogy between artificial machines and the human world (DNR 7.8; 177). In the *Dialogues*, it is certainly hard to pinpoint a particular character, Philo or Cleanthes (or even Pamphilus), as the author's spokesperson. When Cleanthes speaks of 'the nature of human society', however, his words are entirely consistent with the author's observation elsewhere: the state of human society 'is in continual revolution, between ignorance and knowledge, liberty and slavery, riches and poverty' (6.9; 172). In Section 8 of the 'Natural History of Religion', after discussing the progress from polytheism to monotheism, he did not forget to add the reflux to the opposite direction.[12] From these considerations, we can confirm that Hume's belief in the continual flux of civilisation ranged over those topics that his contemporaries would have placed within the purview of religion, although, as Roger Emerson points out, Hume 'refused to give [...] a rule about how religions and their cycles related to other cycles in politics and the arts' (2009: 140).

6 The Strategy of Hume's Cyclical View

Hume's pendulum argument allows him the scope to counter the historical visions of those who believed in the possibility of perpetual progress on the one hand, and the eschatologists and reactionaries on the other (Mossner 1941; 1949: 147). Concerning the former, he clearly refutes the argument of not only Tucker but also others, including the French statesman and philosophe Turgot, who claimed that there exist no limits to the progress of civilisation. Certainly, he admitted that painting, poetry and music are much more vulnerable to the vicissitudes of public life (Turgot 1973: 52). In this sense, it is not difficult to find expressions similar to Hume's even in Turgot's writings, and it can be said that belief in the possibility of progress is a matter of degree. Nevertheless, what is at stake here is precisely the way in which and the degree to which this belief is expounded by each philosopher. While conceding that these arts 'are a long time in reaching this point' of perfection, for example, Turgot finally asserts that '[b]ut although perfect in this respect [of giving pleasures to the senses] and in relation to style, [poetry] is capable of continuous progress in many other respects' (113; see also 55–6).

Such claims, when made by Turgot, were often connected with the optimistic and teleological view that it is possible, desirable and indeed likely, that the human race itself would continue infinitely to improve through the acquisition of knowledge and skills: an outlook towards which Hume showed no propensity.[13] In a letter responding to Turgot's suggestion that humans possess the capacity for perfection (perfectibilité) (Burton 1849: 163–4),[14] Hume answers negatively and sceptically, giving examples such as 'the Disturbances arising from foreign Wars, an incurable Evil, which often springs from the greatest & most unexpected Absurdity' (L II, 181). This comment demonstrates clearly his belief that the continual fluctuations he observes in the course of history depend not upon any chance, accident or 'unknown causes' (E 'Rise and Progress' 114), but arise from built-in checks to the progress of nations.

Another point worth mentioning is that Hume does *not* connect his view of civilisation to his theory of the association of ideas. At first glance, philosophers' views of civilisation have nothing to do with a philosophical and psychological theory of mind such as this. As David Spadafora elucidates, however, many proponents of the associationist theory claim that the progressive view of civilisation originates in Lockean epistemology (1990: chap. 4). They saw in the latter a promise for the continual amelioration of our knowledge through educational reform, provided it could give them a fundamental clue to the method of acquiring more accurate information and knowledge.[15] Hence, not a few associationists committed themselves to perfectionism in their views of human nature and civilisation, though in varying degrees. For example, George Turnbull underlined the significance of the law of habit that 'renders us capable of improvement to perfection' (1740: II, 197; Spadafora 1990: 147). As Alexander Broadie summarises, for Turnbull, 'the disposition to associate ideas is a part of our nature, and it makes its own distinctive contribution to the fulfilment of God's intention for us, that we flourish as human beings' (Broadie 2009: 117). Joseph Priestley also avers that '[t]he perfection of intelligent beings consists in *comprehension* of mind [...]. By this means happiness comes to be of a more stable nature' (1771: 4; Spadafora 1990: 231–52; Tapper 1996; Schofield 1997: 148). In his *Esquisse d'un tableau historique des progrès de l'esprit humain*, Condorcet also claims that Locke's 'method was soon adopted by all philosophers and, by applying it to moral science, to politics and to social economy, they were able to make almost as sure progress in these sciences as they had in the natural sciences'. As a result, he goes on to claim, Lockean philosophy established a permanent 'barrier between mankind and the errors of its infancy; a barrier that should save it from relapsing its former errors under the influence of new prejudices [...]' ([1795] 2012: 96–7). Finally, these developments feed into the foundation of 'Ideology' by Destutt de Tracy, who was deeply inspired by Locke's associationist and Condillac's sensationalist theory. Tracy claims that '[o]ur way of existence is completely artificial. We take from the nature, that is, our organization, only feelings and perfectibility: we owe all the rest to our industry'. And if '[h]abit is a second nature, the man is an animal of habit', he goes on to argue that 'in order that [the truth] has an influence upon our conduct, it must be habitual for us' ([1797] 1992: 137, 162).* The word 'habit' (habitude) here

* 'Notre manière d'exister est totalement artificielle. Nous ne tenons de la nature, c'est-à-dire de notre organization, que la sensibilité et la perfectibilité: nous devons tout le reste à notre industrie'; 'L'habitude est une seconde nature, l'homme est un animal d'habitude; [...] il faut, pour qu'une vérité influe sur notre conduit, qu'elle nous soit devenue habituelle'.

has shifted in its meaning, from an unconscious or unintentional tendency to an artificially controllable practice.[16] Compared with these affinities between the theory of mind and historical perfectionism that were drawn by some French philosophes and British associationists, Hume's reticence in referring to the associationist theory in his discussions of civilisation is conspicuous. This is probably because he focuses his attention on the empirical analysis of the operations of our mind as they are rather than on methods to improve them.

The restrictive aspect of Hume's belief in the universality of human nature is also relevant here. As we saw above, Hume's endorsement of this principle enables him to account for a wide range of human behaviours and social manners, but not to the degree claimed by the reformers and radicals of the late eighteenth and early nineteenth centuries. Hume neither dreamed of using the associationist theory in any systematically educational or reformatory way (note his reticence regarding educational reform in 'Perfect Commonwealth'), nor would he believe that such an effort could work well, given his own understanding of human nature.

On the other hand, Hume took issue on several fronts with the arguments of those who regarded history as a process of perpetual decline. In the population debate, for example, Hume opposed Montesquieu and Wallace's claims regarding the continual depopulation of Europe. However, Hume's conviction that there was a larger population in the modern world than in the ancient should not be considered a simplistic and optimistic glorification of modern civilisation. As we have already seen, he maintained strongly from his observation of the continual fluctuations of populations worldwide that 'we cannot thence presuppose any decay in human nature' (E 378). As Tomaselli correctly points out, population growth was, for the philosophers in the pre-Malthusian age, 'often the criterion by which the value of any social and political proposal or institution was gauged' (1988: 8). Hume here assesses the population (and the political, economical and social systems) of the modern world *relative* to the ancient, retaining his underlying assumption of the universality of human nature. Consequently, Hume's advocacy for the benefits of modern civilisation does not contradict his fundamental view of history as a pendulum movement.

A related school of thought, basing its argument for the decline of the modern world upon admiration for ancient times, was also criticised by Hume. He observed in the essay 'Of Refinement' that '[t]o declaim against present times, and magnify the virtue of remote ancestors, is a propensity almost inherent in human nature' (E 278).[17] Applying this principle to historical analysis in the *History*, Hume rejected the argument for an idealised ancient English constitution as based upon nostalgia for the past (H II, 525), and again observed that '[t]he English constitution, like all others, has been in a state of continual fluctuation' (IV, 355 footnote [l]).

As some scholars have pointed out (Hont 2005: 288; see also Forbes 1975a: 194, 308; 1975b: 204–5, 308), Hume differs still more from those who posited a trade-off between wealth and virtue, in the sense that the more wealth a society amasses, the more corrupt it becomes (for example, Ferguson [1767] 1995: 241; Jack 1989: chap. 4, although Ferguson is far from deterministic on this point). In this vision – what István Hont calls 'the luxury-corruption model' (2005: 288) – the accumulation of wealth could be considered to be conditionally positive at best, or a silver lining to the cloud. Hume clearly states his concept of what it means to be 'civiliz'd' in the following passage from his correspondence: 'My Notion is, that the uncultivated Nations are not only inferior to civiliz'd in Government, civil, military, and eclesiastical [sic]; but also in Morals' (NL 198). In another letter to Horace Walpole, a Whig politician and man of letters, Hume begs him 'to consider the great difference in point of morals between uncultivated and civilized ages'. He summarises his point as follows:

> if you had been born a barbarian [...], you had certainly been an obliging, good-natured, friendly man; but at the same time, that reading, conversation, and travel have detracted nothing from those virtues, and have made a considerable addition of other valuable and agreeable qualities to them. (L II, 111)

A similar idea is repeated in the *Political Discourses*: 'We cannot reasonably expect, that a piece of woollen cloth will be wrought to perfection in a nation, which is ignorant of astronomy, or where ethics are neglected' (E 'Refinement' 270–1). Hume argued for the realisation of the interdependence of 'industry, knowledge, and humanity' rather than for their mutual exclusivity.

This chapter has illustrated the significance of Hume's cyclical view of civilisation in his political, economic and even metaphysical writings. The argument presented here is supported by three points. Firstly, Hume's cyclical view did not focus exclusively on the fine arts and literature, but ranged over a wider field, including that of what we now regard as economic. Secondly, despite his imprecision in articulating whether his cyclical view should be applied to particular cases or generalities, the emphasis should be rather upon his conviction that human societies are in a continual state of flux, from which Hume derives his observation of the universality and constancy of human nature. Thirdly, despite the wide circulation of the cyclical view among his contemporaries, such a belief seems to separate Hume from some other contemporary thinkers who were convinced of the attainability of indefinite progress in human civilisation and human nature on the one hand, and from those who foresaw the continual fall and decay of human nature and society on the other. Hume also differs from those who believed in a trade-off between the moral nature of a simple society and the progress of commerce and political liberty. For him, the blessings of civilisation cover economic, political and moral aspects. At the same time, this does not automatically mean that Hume's support of modern civilisation is unconditional. His narratives in the *History* are framed within his model of the pendulum movement of civilisations at the macro level (H II, 519), and by the changeability and unpredictability of opinion at the micro level (Chapter 3). In a similar way to his nuanced defence of luxury (Chapter 4), he is rather keenly aware of how contingent those merits are and how liable they are to excess and disorder.

To view Hume's historical vision within a naïve dichotomy constructed between the champions of modernity and its discontents is, therefore, to neglect the subtleties of his thought. If we take Hume's cyclical view of civilisation into consideration along with his persistent obsession with the instability of the British government, the characteristics of the Humean way of defending the refinement of luxury, the rule of law and the secularisation of morals will become clear. So far, Hume scholars have emphasised one of these two aspects to justify their images of Hume as either an Enlightenment thinker – in the conventional sense – or a philosopher of the Counter-Enlightenment. Both positions necessarily disregard the other aspect. Hume himself sees neither contradiction nor incompatibility between his cyclical (and *seemingly* pessimistic) view of civilisation and his adamant support for these modern values. Certainly, he flatly denies as groundless the supposition that liberty, once established, would never perish (L II, 216) or that human societies will continue to rise (or fall).[18] For Hume, to claim something more than that with confidence should be judged to transcend the boundary of 'the narrow capacity of human understanding' (EHU 12.25; 161). Notwithstanding, Hume implies, humankind can be improved; this can never occur through any transformation of its nature, but only through the continuous betterment of the ways in which we associate, socialise and converse with each other in this common life. This attitude can be discerned throughout his writings. An example occurs in the very last paragraph in the second volume of the medieval series within the *History*, which was originally the last published volume, before the work was reissued and compiled in the present form. Hume concludes his long narrative with the remark that the historical knowledge of various vicissitudes through which our government was formed 'is chiefly *useful* by instructing [the readers] to cherish their present constitution' and 'also *curious*' 'by instructing them in the great mixture of accident, which commonly concurs with a small ingredient of wisdom and foresight, in erecting the complicated fabric of the most perfect government' (H II, 525). In this context he refers to the British constitution, but a much wider applicability is implied. Hume's adamant support of modern civilisation coexists with – and exists only within – his acute awareness of the instability of human institutions, as well as his observations on the universality of human nature. It is rather reasonable to consider that he recommends both his contemporaries and us to foster these modern values, not in spite of, but because of their fragility and vulnerability.

Notes

1. Here I aim to amplify the remark made by Pocock: 'From Hume to Rousseau, the conservative and radical Enlightenments were at one in sharing a complex understanding of the movement from ancient to modern, a duality of acceptance and revulsion which made them see history with a double vision; in this sense it may be said that their thinking was increasingly historicist' (2008: 98–9).
2. According to Muthu, for instance, Diderot's cyclical vision is based upon his assumption that 'undercuts much of the imperial ideology that aims to "civilize" non-Europeans', by reminding his

contemporary European imperialists that any seemingly stable and refined societies would one day decline' (2003: 84; see also 194).

3. The Scottish historian William Robertson expressed a similar view ([1769] 1972: 21).
4. Potkay also points out that Velleius' *Historiæ Romanæ* is found in Hume's library (Potkay 2000: 153; Norton and Norton 1996: entry 951).
5. The similar view can also be found in Dubos (Jones 1982: 102).
6. Hume generally held Fontenelle in as high esteem as Temple: 'What wou'd his Friend, Fontenelle, have done in this Situation? I am as great a Lover of Peace as he, and have kept myself as free from all literary Quarrels' (L II, 81). His library contained Fontenelle's *Œuvres* (1742) (Norton and Norton 1996: entry 476) and he extensively mentions Fontenelle's works throughout his writings.
7. The analogy was used in varying ways by contemporary philosophers. According to Adam Smith, the French Physiocrats, using a metaphor between the natural body and the body politic, claimed that the political body 'would thrive and prosper only under a certain precise regimen, the exact regimen of perfect liberty and perfect justice' ([1776] 1982: 674 [IV.ix.28]).
8. In his unpublished manuscript 'Historical Essay on Chivalry and Modern Honour' Hume seems to have a different idea about the relationship between political organisation and the fine arts: 'But as without some such Revolution in public Affairs, 'tis impossible for a polite Nation, by slow Degree, & by an ill constituted Government alone to become altogether barbarous, their Change, however great, cou'd never extend to the entire banishment of all Arts, but in common Life at least, there must remain near the same Perfection in Handicraft Arts, & in Conversation a Tincture of their former Civility' (Hume 2012: 204 [1]; on this manuscript, see also note 20 in Chapter 4). However, despite the phrase 'near the same Perfection', Hume is not claiming here that political disorders never affect the condition of these arts, but only admits these arts would never be *entirely* banished. The same thing can be said on Hume's somewhat ambiguous statement on the durability of the law: 'when [the law] has once taken root, is a hardy plant, which will scarcely ever perish through the ill culture of men, or the rigour of the seasons' (E 'Rise and Progress' 124).
9. Bruce Truitt Elmslie stated that 'Hume's position was substantially altered' from his belief in endogenous retrogression at the stage of the *Essays, Moral and Political* to the theory of 'convergence' that

he advanced after the exchange of letters with Tucker in the mid-1750s (1995: 211), and he contrasts this position with Tucker's 'divergence' theory. In their earlier studies, J. M. Low (1952) and Bernard Semmel (1965) basically agreed that Hume and Tucker had held opposing opinions.

10. In a reply to James Oswald criticising the same point as Tucker does, written in 1750, he has already argued that '[t]he growth of every thing, both in arts and nature, at last checks itself' (L I: 143; on Oswald's letter to Hume, see Rotwein 1955: 190–6, esp. 194). In the so-called 'Early Memoranda' Hume also mentions 'a natural Course of Things, which brings on the Destruction of great Empires' (Hume 1948: 517, entry 259). 'Hume's pendulum-of-growth argument', Hont correctly argues, 'was used to precisely counter such intellectually complacent extrapolations into an indefinite future from the apparently widening gap between rich and poor countries in his own day' (2005: 288).
11. This had been a common view in the mercantilist writings (Mun [1664] 1967: 7; Barbon [1690] 1905: 9–10; Harris [1757–8] 1970: 14, for example).
12. Dugald Stewart considers Hume's 'Natural History of Religion' to be one of the origins of conjectural history as developmental history, not evidence of his pendulum view of history ([1792] 1982: 292). Such a tendency to narrow Hume's historical view into a one-sided account of progress from barbarism to civility seems especially prominent in studies of Hume's economic thought (Rotwein 1955: xxxii). Emerson acutely pointed out that while Hume's argument concerning flux and reflux within the human mind 'was a statement about the learned and the vulgar in all polite societies, it was also a statement about the societies in which men live and about the quality of life within them' (1984: 84).
13. 'Nothing comparable to [Dugald] Stewart's perfectibilist speculations can be found in Hume and Smith' (Collini et al. 1983: 39).
14. This word is coined by Rousseau, whose usage is slightly, but significantly, different from that of Turgot (Wokler 2012: 25–7).
15. On a related point, despite the influence of his theory among the early nineteenth-century philosophical radicals, David Hartley's alleged belief in the possibility of progress and amelioration of the human condition was extremely conditional. His Christian faith in Divine Providence and conviction of the depravity of human nature would not lead him to a naïve progressivism, but rather to mysticism and pessimism, although he nonetheless believed in the possibility of

'the progress of the individual mind from carnality to a spirituality' (Leslie 1972: 631; see also Popkin 1976: 86, 89).

16. Nevertheless, Tracy does not expect that many people will have the time, willingness or capability to learn the system of moral science through educational programmes; he considers that such education should be given only to an elite cadre of promising students, in order to train them to be superior legislators or governors ([1798] 2011: 138–9).
17. Hume here seems to paraphrase Machiavelli's statement in the preface of Book II of the *Discorsi* (*Discourses on Livy*), that '[m]en always praise ancient times and condemn the present, but not always with good reason' ([1531] 1997: 149).
18. Heilbroner's statement about Adam Smith holds true for Hume: 'the conception of history as a cyclical process, or a vast drama ending in tragedy, would by no means have struck him, as an eighteenth-century thinker, with the same unpleasant force as it does ourselves, who still tend to conceive of history in the linear terms of the late nineteenth century' (1973: 256).

8

'The Prince of Sceptics' and 'The Prince of Historians': Hume's Influence and Image in Early Nineteenth-Century Britain

As has emerged from the arguments in previous chapters, Hume's contemporaries' evaluations of his works were far from unified. This last chapter deals in more detail with the reception of Hume in the late eighteenth- and early nineteenth-century British context. Some explanation seems necessary as to why such receptions should occupy the final chapter of this book. Firstly, as we saw in Chapter 1, despite recent analysis of the relationship between Hume's philosophy and history (Norton 1965; Wertz 2000; Schmidt 2004; Holthoon 2013 and others), John Stuart Mill's evaluation of the relationship between Hume's sceptical philosophy and his political conservatism continues to exert influence. The image of Hume as conservative has also been reinforced by Hume's contemporaries' evaluation of him as a Tory historian. Certainly, there are some significant differences between Toryism and political conservatism as technical terms. Livingston, for example, considers Hume not a Tory, but 'the first conservative philosopher', though he does not expatiate how different these two terms are (1998: 181, 286; see also Livingston 1984: 310; Livingston 1995). However, we do not need to dwell on this point now.[1] When his contemporary and nineteenth-century readers casually labelled Hume as a Tory historian, they emphasised his alleged prejudicial support of monarchy, the established Church and the house of Stuart. It seems to have been easy to associate or sometimes confuse these factors with Hume's supposed endorsement of the *status quo* and his abhorrence of hasty reforms among later generations. Furthermore, Isaiah Berlin (1979; 2000) and Laurence Bongie ([1965] 2000) emphasise the wide acceptance in Germany and France respectively of Hume among those they class as Counter-Enlightenment or Counter-Revolutionary thinkers, although both admit that such acceptance does not imply any inclination of Hume's own thought towards the Counter-Enlightenment (see also Redmond 1987). These various strands have combined, intentionally or otherwise, to consolidate the view of Hume as a conservative thinker. To settle the issue of 'liberal/conservative' readings of Hume is not the theme of this book, but how Hume's contemporaries and later generations attempt to integrate or adjust his images as philosopher and as historian seems to matter for our understanding of the 'historical' Hume. In addition to this, it will be found that his contemporaries and immediately succeeding generation paid attention to some important topics and arguments in Hume's writings that now tend to go unheeded. Some of them are also illuminating with regard to the discussions of the previous chapters.

Although the subject of the contemporary and later receptions of Hume's writings in a British context has already been addressed by James Fieser's series of *Early Responses to Hume*, this elaborate compilation of receptions deals with Hume's various aspects *separately*, and the problematic issue of the relationship between Hume as a philosopher and historian is insufficiently addressed in his series. The same thing can be said with Phillips and Smith (2005), which is still an excellent survey of the popularity and evaluations of Hume as the author of the *History* in late eighteenth- and early nineteenth-century Britain. A series of works by Donald Winch (1978, 1996, Collini et al. 1983) are significant contributions to our historical understanding of the assessment of Hume and Adam Smith in the late eighteenth and the early nineteenth centuries. However, his focus is rather placed on the latter, and the former is mentioned mainly in relation to Smith as an ally of the Sceptical Whig (Collini et al. 1983: 43; Winch 1978: chap. 2).

With the help of these studies, this chapter will discuss the perceived relationship, often thought to be mainly exhibited in the *History*, between Hume's philosophy and his political ideology. For this purpose, the evaluations of Hume as a political philosopher should also be taken into account. As recent historiographical research demonstrates, a wide range of his contemporaries cited and utilised Hume's political writings (Winch 1978; 1996; Spencer 2005). They did so not only in accordance with their evaluations of Hume as philosopher and historian; the latter has also been significantly affected in turn by evaluations of Hume as a political philosopher. In this reassessment, I do not wish to commit the error of going from one extreme to another: there is little doubt that Hume's Toryism as allegedly exhibited in the *History* was widely (though not universally) accepted. A fact that has received less attention is that some of Hume's arguments in his political essays and even his *History* were used by some radicals and reform-minded political writers. On the one hand, for their oppositional purposes Hume's alleged 'Country' aspects were useful. On the other hand, among those loosely called the 'Romantics', while his historical writings stimulated their imagination, the subversive nature of his scepticism overshadowed his reputation as historian. It is worthwhile exploring (or rather re-exploring) more diversified or even divided images of Hume that existed in the early nineteenth century, which will serve to demonstrate the complexity and difficulties encountered by his contemporaries and later generations in representing the 'historical' Hume.

My investigation ranges up to roughly the 1830s, except for some of Mill's comments on Hume, which take us up to the 1870s. This periodisation is justified on two grounds. Firstly, Mill's assessment of Hume (quoted in Chapter 1 and below) appeared in 1838, which has been one of the starting points for our reconsideration of the 'historical' Hume. It seems sufficient for our present purposes to investigate similarities and differences between the images of Hume both as philosopher and as historian among his contemporaries and the following generations up to Mill. Secondly, the first volume of T. B. Macaulay's *History of England* was published in 1849, which is claimed to have displaced Hume's *History* as the standard national history. This seems to justify our focus on the first part of the nineteenth century. Moreover, beyond the preference for Macaulay, much wider and more gradual changes were taking place in the world of academia. As Fieser's *Early Responses to Hume* series attest, Hume's various works were continually cited by the generations before and after this period. However, such references become increasingly compartmentalised throughout the nineteenth century into those that treat Hume as a historian, and those that regard him as a philosopher. The fact that many key testimonies in the following concentrate around the 1800s might be a part of the proof of such segmentalisation.

1 The Evaluations of Hume by J. S. Mill and Other Radicals

John Stuart Mill's evaluation of Hume is perhaps the most appropriate starting point for a reassessment of Hume's influence, not because of the correctness of the evaluation itself, but because of its wide influence on later generations (Miller 1981: 13; Whelan 1985: 312; Stewart 1992: 3–4. All quote the following remarks of Mill, though not necessarily positively). In one of the footnotes to 'Bentham', to quote it again, Mill strongly condemned Hume's 'negative' philosophy as follows:

> Hume, the prince of *dilettanti*, from whose writings one will hardly learn that there is such a thing as truth, far less that it is attainable [...]. This absolute scepticism in speculation very naturally brought him round to Toryism in practice; for if no faith can be had in the operations of human intellect, and one side of every question is about as likely as other to be true, a man will commonly be inclined to prefer that order of things which, being no more wrong than every other, he has hitherto found compatible with his private comforts. ([1838] 1963–91: 80n.q–q 38; see also Mill [1865] 1963–91: 499n.)

One of the points to note here is that Mill's evaluation in this note should not be considered completely neutral, because he here tries to highlight the positive contributions of Bentham to moral and political philosophy compared with the 'negative' and 'destructive' philosophies of Hume and other eighteenth-century philosophers. While Mill was not a straightforward Benthamite by the time he wrote this article, it is natural to consider that the Philosophic Radical would have no intention of praising the sceptical philosopher/Tory historian.

Mill also had reason to despise Hume the historian, with whom he was familiar since his childhood ([1873] 1963–91: 10–11). This is closely related to the young Mill's support of the principle of the greatest happiness of the greatest number. In his review of the *History of the British Empire* written by George Brodie, an ardent Whig historian, which appeared in *The Westminster Review* in 1824, the young Mill predictably agrees with Brodie's minutely detailed criticism of Hume's errors in the *History*. After emphasising once again Hume's scepticism and thus his inability to attain the truth, as well as his 'taste for literature', Mill undervalues

Hume as an authentic historian, and equates Hume's *History* with romances such as '*Old Mortality* or *Ivanhoe*' by Walter Scott. According to Mill, the main problem with Hume's *History* lies in its tendency to sympathise with the fate of the noble few in episodes such as the Civil War.[2] As a result, Mill argues that the nameless throngs must be ignored in Hume's *History*:

> Who is there that would not admit, that it is better one should suffer than a million? Yet among those who can feel and cannot reason, nothing is so rare as to sympathize with the million. The one, with them, is every thing, the million, nothing; merely because the one is higher in rank, and perhaps suffers rather more, than any one assignable individual among the million. [...] This propensity is so thoroughly incompatible with the pursuit of the only true end of morality, the greatest happiness of the greatest number [...]. (Mill [1824b] 1963–91: 4)

Mill's criticism is directed at 'the man, who had presumed to shed a generous tear for the fate of Charles I. and the Earl of Strafford' (E 'My Own Life' xxxvii). As Nicholas Phillipson (2000: chap. 1) argues, Hume's *History* is a landmark in terms of refocusing attention on the importance of the changing manners of nameless multitudes. Yet, Mill's anger here is not only directed at the alleged political bias of this Scottish historian, but also at his (allegedly) classical way of narrating English history, in which attention is focused on élites. In either case, Mill had sufficient reason to underrate Hume both as a philosopher and as a historian.

Then, to what extent was Mill's evaluation of Hume shared by other Philosophic Radicals? It is widely known that Book 3 of the *Treatise* provided Jeremy Bentham with one of the first inspirations for his utilitarianism. In addition, Bentham praises Hume's criticism of the theory of social contract ([1776] 1962: 268). What is not so well known is that Bentham also praises Hume's *History* in his 'Plea for the Constitution'. Interestingly, this founder of utilitarianism praises the Scottish historian as one sensitive to the rule of law and the breach of liberty in the same volumes of the *History*, those focusing on the Stuarts, which J. S. Mill was to criticise over twenty years later.

> If prejudices of any kind be deemed imputable to that prince of historians [Hume], they will hardly be of that cast, which would dispose

> a man to exaggerate the mischief resulting from a transgression of the limits prescribed by the constitution to the power of the crown. Whether to that dispassionate, acute, and comprehensive mind, the wounds given to the constitution on the ground of the penal colony would have presented themselves as matters of indifference [...] is a question, the answer to which may be read, I should suppose, without much difficulty, in the following passage [...].

In the rest of the work, Bentham continues to intersperse long quotations from Hume's *History* with favourable comments on the legal developments of political rights and liberty in English history ([1803] 1962: 283, n.ll; Fieser 2003).[3] Bentham was in no doubt that Hume would have been a supporter of these developments.[4]

Even among radicals of other persuasions,[5] the evaluation of Hume as a historian was not unified. James Mackintosh – though he was to alter his political position later in his life – acutely ascertained the difference between Hume and Burke. In the *Vindiciae Gallicae*, he vividly contrasts 'the specious and temperate Toryism of Mr. Hume' to 'the repulsive and fanatical invectives of Mr. Burke'. Although he admitted that both 'would be adverse to the Revolution', he claimed that it would not be difficult to distinguish 'between the undisguised fury of an eloquent advocate and the well dissembled partiality of a philosophical Judge':

> Such would probably be the difference between Mr. Hume and Mr. Burke, were they to treat on the French Revolution. The passions of the latter would only feel the excesses which had dishonoured it; but the philosophy of the former would instruct him, that the human feelings, raised by such events above the level of ordinary situations, become the source of a guilt and a heroism unknown to the ordinary affairs of nations [...]. (Mackintosh [1791] 2006: 90)[6]

One of the examples illustrative of this difference, according to Mackintosh, is their divergence on the issue of the established church after the Revolution. He elaborated the difference as follows: Burke is critical of 'the degraded pensionary establishment' and 'the elective constitution of the new clergy of France' after the Revolution, because these changes would make religion less respectable and more contemptible among the people. Elsewhere, Mackintosh features Hume's argument on the ecclesiastical establishment as a contrast to Burke's:

> Mr. Hume vindicates the policy of an opulent establishment, as a bribe which purchases the useful inactivity of the priesthood. [...] Had that philosopher been now alive, he must on the same principle have remarked, that an elective clergy and a scantily endowed Church, had a far greater tendency to produce fanaticism than irreligion. [...] But he would have been consoled by the reflection, that the dissolution of the Church as a corporation had broken the strength of the priesthood; that religious liberty without limit would disarm the animosity of sects; and that the diffusion of knowledge would restrain the extravagances of fanaticism. ([1791] 2006: 63–4; Winch 1996: 185–91)[7]

Mackintosh was not alone on this point. John Thelwall, a radical reformer and lecturer, also frequently mentioned Hume's *History* (sometimes his *Essays*) as a historical source throughout his periodical, *The Tribune*. He admitted Hume's conservative aspects in 'the very partial and pleader-like history he wrote', in which, he argues, Hume 'was always favourable enough to the Court party' (1795–6: I, 18–19, 23). Despite his judgement of the *History*, Thelwall also emphasises Hume's hostility to the clergy in quoting the passage that '[t]he clergy have much lost their credit' from his essay 'Whether the British Government inclines more to Absolute Monarchy, or to a Republic' (E 51):

> Hume himself [...] is obliged to acknowledge, in his essay on the British Government, that mankind are now no longer held in chains, by a superstitious veneration to mere forms and trappings; and he observes, that even those things, which, in former times, claimed the utmost veneration of mankind, seemed to sink into oblivion, from the persevering reason and enquiry that mankind have directed towards them'. (Thelwall 1795–6: II, 260)

While these aspects of Hume as an infidel philosopher might not be unconditionally accepted among some Radicals, especially Millenarian or Unitarian, others seem to ascertain the potentiality of Hume's subversive arguments to criticise the established religion.

Hume's credentials as a historian among the radicals in general, has been much underestimated among scholars, possibly as a result of Catharine Macaulay's republican attack on Hume's 'Tory' *History* (see also Hume's letter to Macaulay in NL 80–2). Such evaluations were fairly common at the end of the eighteenth and the early nineteenth century. However, there were some prominent radicals who favourably cited and mentioned Hume's *History*. This is because these radicals had to refute the Burkean complacent understanding of English history. For this purpose, Hume's claim that the establishment of liberty was not based on the ancient constitution, but just a modern invention was convenient. Daniel I. O'Neill indicates that '[i]n her first *Vindication* Wollstonecraft deployed Hume's *History of England* as a historical counter to Burke, as part of her attack on Burke's celebration of the supposed wisdom of our forefathers' (O'Neill 2007: 106–7).[8] Hume's descriptions of the uncivilised, barbarous and factious state of the past England were also utilised by Wollstonecraft's husband William Godwin. In his *Considerations on Lord Grenville's and Mr. Pitt's bills*, Godwin compares Grenville's attempts to introduce oppressive legislation (the Treasonable Practices Bill) to Elizabeth's arbitrary maxims of government. He does this by citing at length (the description occupying six pages of the eighty-six page pamphlet) Hume's depiction in the *History* of Elizabeth's repressive responses to a move made by a puritan, Robert Bell, against an exclusive patent granted to a company of merchants ([1795] 1993: 61–7).

In spite of Thelwall's claim that Hume 'was always favourable enough to the Court party', some of his political arguments were a part of his supposedly 'Country' aspects. Above all, his warnings against public credit attracted some radicals. Discussions of financial policy were an area in which an important ideological divide opened up between the establishmentarians and the dissidents. It is also concerned with the historical context of somewhat complex markers of ideological identity in British politics. In the middle of the eighteenth century, Hume's pessimism on the issue of public credit naturally associated him with the 'Country-Tory' side and has been interpreted to 'support a "Tory" interpretation of his political sympathies' (Winch 1978: 126; Kramnick 1992: 43).[9] In the latter half of the eighteenth century, however, Hume's anxiety concerning the possible consequences of public credit increasingly attracted the attention of some Opposition or extra-parliamentary radicals. James Burgh, a Scottish-born Whig politician, an educational reformer, criticises his contemporaries' negligence on the issue of public credit: 'If you go to altering any thing, they cry, it will produce disturbance, and then public credit may suffer. But will public credit be safe, if you do not alter any thing?' Then he named '[s]uch men as *Price*, and *Hume*, and *Grenville*' as patriotically-minded men who entertain apprehension about 'the highest probability of a national bankruptcy' (Burgh 1774–5: III, 328). Richard Price in fact quotes Hume's famous phrase '[e]ither the nation must destroy public credit, or public credit will destroy the nation' (E 360–1) both in a footnote of his *Observations on Reversionary Payments* (1773: 162) and in his *Additional Observations on the Nature and Value of Civil Liberty* (1777: 153). He also recommended his readers to refer to Hume's essay 'Of Public Credit' in a footnote of *An Appeal to the Public, on the Subject of the National Debt* (1772: 51). On this point – what Jack Fruchtman terms 'Apocalyptic politics' (1983: 76–7) or what Kramnick considers the influence of 'Tory radicalism' (1994: 170–1) – Hume could even be associated with another radical – Thomas Paine, who was also concerned about the consequences of the English public credit. Although the latter did not name Hume in the pamphlet *The Decline and Fall of the English System of Finance* (1796) (Claeys 1989: 86), it is possible that Hume's influence had contributed to rendering his general attitude toward the issue of national debt less sanguine since *Common Sense* (1776).

Hume's somewhat enigmatic treatment of the '*pressing of seamen*' in the essay 'Of Some Remarkable Customs' also received some attention among his contemporaries and later generations. He concludes this essay by claiming that '[t]he wild state of nature is renewed, in one of the most civilized societies of mankind' (E 376). What is less known among commentators is the fact that Hume mentions the same topic in the *History* a few times. As we saw in Chapter 3, Hume's support of established practices does not necessarily negate his advocacy of the establishment of 'the regular plan of liberty': 'The power of pressing, both for sea and land service', Hume argues in the *History*, 'was another prerogative totally incompatible with freedom' (H IV, 360). Hume's primary concern seems to lie not in convincing his readers to acquiesce to the *status quo*, but in confronting a contradiction with his readers and causing among them much astonishment and bewilderment of how such a gross neglect of liberty does happen in 'a civilized nation, like the English, who have happily established the most perfect and most accurate system of liberty that was ever found compatible with government' (II, 525). Most of the opponents of the extra-legal practice of impressing sailors for the navy in England considered Hume their strong ally. For example, an anonymous author of *The Manual of Liberty* (1795), which is a compilation from writings of Helvétius, Godwin and Rousseau, quotes some sentences from Hume's essay with the clear intention of demonstrating the absurdity of the custom and its contradiction of English liberty (Anon. 1795: 366). Another anonymous author, of *A Discourse on the Impressing of Mariners*, a pamphlet criticising the compulsory draft, also favourably quotes Hume's comments in its postscript (Anon. c.1778: 119). Michael J. Franklin argues that the author of this pamphlet was plausibly William 'Oriental' Jones, the English philologist and radical Whig (Franklin 2011: 143–4; see also 128–9). Opposition to the press gangs was common among radicals such as Wollstonecraft (1995: 14). Oddly enough, however, Charles Butler, a defender of this prerogative, in *An Essay on the Legality of Impressing Seamen* (1777), to which the former pamphlet was addressed, spent a few pages quoting Hume's essay in question when concluding his own essay. He even expressed admiration of Hume's essay 'which bears the strongest marks of that penetration and depth of thought for which he has been so highly celebrated'. Unless Butler here quoted Hume with sarcasm (which seems unlikely), it has to be admitted that Hume's comment on the 'press-gang' is sufficiently ambiguous to produce such opposing evaluations. His expressions employed for depicting this practice are so ironic and cryptic as to produce extremely divided interpretations of his attitude on this issue even among our contemporary commentators.[10]

In fields other than history and politics, Hume enjoyed a less ambiguous reception among the nineteenth-century radicals. One of the most important contributions of Hume to their philosophical ideology is his theory of the association of ideas: his contribution on this point was far from exclusive. His name frequently appears alongside those of Locke, Hartley and Condillac in this context. In some cases, Hume's authority was much overshadowed by these other 'associationists'. This is partly because Reid's Common Sense philosophy, which aimed to rebut Hume's scepticism, was itself identified with Scottish philosophy throughout the nineteenth century (Craig 2006: 267–8). In this sense Hume's contribution to this newly born science seems to be indirectly inherited by the Philosophic Radicals mainly via the French intellectuals such as Condillac and Tracy, and partly through Dugald Stewart (see Chap. 2 in this book and Stephen 1900: II, chap. 7, esp. 268–87, 309–11; Halévy 1955: 435–7). Élie Halévy is right in arguing that 'Hume was a far deeper thinker than Hartley. In spite of this, or perhaps even because of it, there is in his philosophy a fundamental ambiguity which will always cause adherents of the doctrine of association to hesitate to accept him as their master' (1955: 9). This 'ambiguity' is most exemplified in James Mill, a pupil of Dugald Stewart. He gave a higher, though conditioned, evaluation of Hume in his essay 'Education' and summarises the latter's contributions to the development of the theory of associationism. Here, Mill focuses on Hume's account of contiguity in time and place that he expanded from Hobbes's 'succession of ideas', and his attempt to account for complex ideas by the same principle of contiguity. The elder Mill asserts that the second point 'was a great discovery; but it must at the same time be owned, that it was very imperfectly developed by Mr. Hume. [...] He was misled by the pursuit of a few surprising and paradoxical results, and when he had arrived at them he stopped' (Mill [c.1828] 1992: 150). Despite such qualifications and Halévy's allegation that 'he never seems to have had a high opinion of Hume's works' (1955: 435), James Mill finally described Hume's *Treatise* as 'a work which, according to its author, had fallen dead-born from the press, was philosophical and sagacious in the highest degree' (Mill [c.1828] 1992: 151). This seems to suggest that, as James McCosh acutely points out, J. S. Mill 'is scarcely aware of the extent of the resemblance between his doctrines and those of the Scottish sceptic' because 'he seems to have wrought out his conclusion from data supplied to him by his own father, Mr James Mill, who, however, has evidently drawn much from Hume' (1875: 133; cited in Craig 2006: 268).[11] If this evaluation is correct, then Halévy's general conclusion would still stand solid: 'the influence of Hume and the perhaps stronger influence of Hartley were exercised on the leaders of the Utilitarian movement' (1955: 487). However, the influence of Hume's associationism was not confined to the radicals. As we will see later, recent literary studies of the nineteenth century have revealed that his theory of association was widely and actively discussed and critiqued among the Romantics.

2 The Evaluations of Hume in *The Edinburgh Review* and their Inconsistencies

In order to decipher John Stuart Mill's relatively negative assessment of Hume, it is helpful to turn to the treatment of Hume in *The Edinburgh Review*, which was the periodical that Mill strongly criticised. Although most of the mentions of Hume in review articles of literary journals and periodicals might be suspected to be cursory and passing, these media were becoming no less essential in influencing and propagating his various images in contemporary readers' minds than more highbrow discussions and criticisms of his writings in scarcely available and expensive books (St. Clair 2004: 100, 186–7). On this point, James Fieser correctly argues that '[a]n analysis of Hume's reception in *The Edinburgh* and the *Quarterly* is a study in itself' (1996: 653). Additionally, the authority of Hume to *The Edinburgh Review* was obviously important, partly because of this magazine's indigenousness to Scottish intellectual culture. For example, John Allen wrote in an article in *The Edinburgh Review* in 1814:

> We subscribe unreservedly to the doctrine of Mr. Hume, that every people, not absolutely subdued by foreign force, must be governed by opinion; or, if the admirers of Mr. Paine object to that word, by prejudice. Government is founded – not on divine right – not on a social contract, but on the general consent and tacit agreement of the people, as at the moment subsisting. (Allen 1814: 380, cited in Mill [1824a] 1963–91: 293–4)[12]

Eight years later, in one of his articles in *The Westminster Review*, J. S. Mill was to pick up on the above quotation in order to lambast this 'Whig' journal for its opportunism. Mill's criticism is simple: 'This passage is a specimen of the vague language, so convenient for the purpose of compromise, which the Opposition party makes use of when it takes the popular side of any question': *The Edinburgh Review* 'has never proposed any plan of reform which would, to any practical purpose, diminish the power of the aristocracy, or add to the people's securities for good government'. Mill continues to pinpoint 'the spirit of compromise', the 'aristocratic bigotry' and the 'see-saw' in *The Edinburgh Review* (Mill [1824a] 1963–91: 294, 296, 302, 305 and 303).

Mill's criticism has some justification. The several mentions of Hume in *The Edinburgh Review* did not converge to present any coherent image of Hume. This is understandable not only since many contributors committed themselves to this long-established journal, but also because of the difficult position of the 'Whig' principles between revolutionary and conservative forces after the French Revolution reflected in this journal. Events across the Channel seriously affected the party's political identity in this period as well as the editorial policy of *The Edinburgh Review* as the most influential Whig journal (Fontana 1985: 15; see also Claeys 1989: 131; Duncan 2007: 49).

More importantly, throughout the early history of *The Edinburgh Review*, the evaluation of Hume as one of their most important intellectual forefathers was closely related to the issue of how to reconcile Hume as a philosopher and as a historian, although he remained one of the most important theorists and defenders of modern commercial society (Fontana 1985: 9, 13–14). One possible way to solve this difficulty seems to have been to depict Hume's alleged Toryism as a purely personal issue or the result of happenstance. For example, James Mackintosh in 1821 partly echoed Mill's claim that 'there was a tendency in infidelity to produce Toryism. In England alone, we might appeal to the examples of Hobbes, Bolingbroke, Hume, and Gibbon', but he finally attributed Hume's alleged Toryism to his cultural background of the time: 'In [Hume's] youth, the Presbyterians, to whose enmity his opinions exposed him, were the zealous and only friends of civil liberty in Scotland; and the close connexion of liberty with Calvinism, made both more odious to him' (1821: 257, 260; Copinger 1895: 33). He repeated the same point in 1812: he admitted that Hume along with Montaigne and Bayle were 'advocates of absolute power', but he wondered if his alleged absolutism could be attributed rather to the result of 'the fanaticism of the Scottish Presbyterians' (1835: II, 244; see also Halévy 1955: 141).

Francis Jeffrey, one of the founders of *The Edinburgh Review*, attributed to Hume contemporary political apathy and the exclusive pursuit of personal happiness in a review of 1808: 'Mr Hume, we are afraid, is chiefly responsible for the prevalence of this Epicurean and ignoble strain of sentiment in this country, – an author from whose dispositions and understanding, a very different doctrine might have been anticipated'. Again, the issue of concern is the relationship between his infidel and sceptical philosophy, and his political creed as supposedly exhibited in the *History*. Jeffrey noticed the inconsistency between Hume's personal 'disposition' and the effect produced by his philosophy. The reviewer added a footnote to the sentence just quoted, and repeated the difficulty of accounting for this inconsistency:

> Mr Fox seems to have been struck with the same surprise at this strange trait in the character of our philosopher. In a letter to Mr Laing, he says, 'He was an excellent man, and of great powers of mind; but his partiality to kings and princes is intolerable. Nay, it is, in my opinion, quite ridiculous; and is more like the foolish admiration which women and children sometimes have for kings, than the opinion, right or wrong, of a philosopher'. (Jeffrey 1808: 277; Copinger 1895: 16; see also Fontana 1985: 89–90)[13]

In another review, published in 1824, Jeffrey tries to explain Hume's Toryism by his abhorrence of the Calvinism to which he had been exposed in Scotland in his childhood, echoing the view Mackintosh had expressed in 1821 (see also Jeffrey's review of M'Crie's *Life of Knox* (1812) cited in Phillips and Smith 2005: 304). In doing so, the same reviewer underestimates the talent of Hume as a historian. His strategy for depicting the competing opinions of different parties is 'deservedly admired for the singular clearness, brevity, and plausibility with which they are composed'; 'But,' Jeffrey continues, 'in reality, they belong rather to *conjectural* than to *authentic* History' (1824: 94, 97n.; Copinger 1895: 36).[14] Interestingly, Mackintosh and Jeffrey took up the same issue as Mill, and Jeffrey and Mill undervalued Hume's *History* as a romance or '*conjectural*' history, while they gave a slightly different answer to the account of Hume's Toryism. Mill emphasizes the (alleged) logical consequence from Hume's scepticism to his political Toryism, while admitting the latter was Hume's 'private' comfort. On the other hand, Mackintosh and Jeffrey attempt to excuse it as the result of his cultural background. The latter evaluation reminds us of Johnson's claim that 'the fellow [Hume] is a Tory by chance' (Fieser (ed.) 2003: I, 288).[15]

To the embarrassment of contemporaries, the same journal provided another interpretation. This is to emphasise Hume's rather progressive attitudes by contrasting him to a more conservative historian. Some reviewers of *The Edinburgh Review* could mention Hume as a possible supporter of liberty in the same journal.[16] In 1811, for example, an anonymous reviewer (but probably James Mill) of *Mémoires de Candide, sur la liberté de la presse* quoted Hume's essay 'Of the Liberty of the Press' to demonstrate the positive effects of decreasing the influence of the crown, although the reviewer (consciously or not) quoted the fourth edition of the essay ([Mill] 1811: 122), which neither reflects Hume's omission of the last few (but long) paragraphs, nor contains his more cautious assessment of the effect of the liberty of the press, which appears only in his newly added concluding paragraph to the 1772 edition: 'It must however be allowed, that the unbounded liberty of the press [...] is one of the evils, attending those mixt forms of government' (E 13).[17] The rather atypical tone of this review is no wonder, considering that around this time James Mill became acquainted with Bentham and started to secede from *The Edinburgh Review* group.[18]

In 1825, John Allen anonymously reviewed in *The Edinburgh Review* the *History of England* written by John Lingard, a Catholic historian. In order to devalue Lingard's *History*, Allen praises Hume as a historian, and even claims that 'it has always appeared to us that Mr Hume was in reality an admirer of popular government in preference to monarchy', however paradoxical it may sound (Forbes 1975b: 182n.1). Allen's evaluation remains ambivalent: he asserts that Hume was 'in his speculative tenets a republican' on the one hand, but he also admits that 'the general tenor of his History of England is unfavourable to the popular party in our Constitution' on the other. The reviewer finally declares what he believes to be the historian's political principle, despite his occasional aberrations, as follows:

> But, though too much disposed, in his History of England, to take part with the Crown against the people, no historian had a stronger sense than Mr Hume of the benefits of civil liberty; no one has pleaded with more success, or defended with more steadiness, the cause of humanity and toleration; and, on great occasions, no one has expressed a deeper interest in the struggles for liberty and limited government. (Allen [1825] 2002: II, 297)

Although he admitted Hume's inclination to the Stuart side and ascribes it to a 'strong tincture of Jacobitism' that he received 'from education' as Jeffrey did (Allen [1825] 2002: II, 298; Phillips and Smith 2005: 306), the above evaluation seems rather closer to Bentham's in his 'Plea for the Constitution', which we saw above.

Considering such divergent evaluations of Hume in the same journal, it is no wonder that it attracted the criticism of John Stuart Mill and others. In 1827, *The London Magazine* pointed out that 'this jealousy of Hume is, above all things, absurd and inconsistent in the Edinburgh Review, who have so lately lent all their aid to the exposure of his errors' in Jeffrey's review of Brodie's *History of the British Empire* in 1824. This anonymous reviewer not only delivers the verdict that Hume is unqualified as a historian, but also advances a prototype of the obsolete opinion that Hume became more conservative in his later years:

> To these indictments and recorded sentences of Hume, which have now justly outlawed him as *historian,* we can state, that we have collated the early editions of the Political Essays with the last, as *corrected* by the author, and have marked with astonishment the change of *sentiments* – a change which may nevertheless there, as well as in his historical work, be traced in its progress, by the following useful graduated scale of political or sinister influence. It is the fashion to consider Mr. Hume a *philosopher* in his personal character, a gentleman who neither valued nor sought the good things of this world. The following is something more than 'a hypothetical integration' of places in which, at different periods of his life, he was pleasantly seated. (Anon. 1827: 424)

The reviewer went to the effort of listing Hume's career as successive service as Secretaries to the British Embassy in Paris, as librarian at the Edinburgh Advocate's Library and as a pensionary, with the intention of undermining Hume as an independent philosopher. In relation to this devaluation, the reviewer execrates Hume's *History* because 'his "Philosophy of History" is a romance, we despise, as a degrading part of his literary labours. And lament it, as a drawback upon his intellectual influence'. The reviewer of *The London Magazine* is thus, accidently, in accordance with J. S. Mill and Francis Jeffrey in underrating Hume as a historian (424–5).

3 The Evaluations of Hume among the Romantics

As we have seen in the previous two sections, proponents of the differing evaluations of Hume in early nineteenth-century Britain were variously concerned about the relationship between Hume's scepticism in his philosophical writings and his allegedly conservative creed in his *History*. While John Stuart Mill judged Hume's Toryism to be an inevitable result of his scepticism, the reviewers of *The Edinburgh Review* rather tended to minimise Hume's alleged favour towards the house of Stuart and monarchy more generally, which they typically treat as a peripheral point. Alternatively, Hume could be deemed a champion of liberty, in accordance with the evaluation of Bentham and of Mackintosh before 1792. These considerations suggest that the difficulty of unifying the images of Hume both as a philosopher and as a historian continued to embarrass nineteenth-century commentators. However, it is safe to say that given Hume's dual role as philosopher and historian, he was better attuned to contemporary political realities than these explanations suggest. This also seems to have been realised by those commentators with a more politically conservative orientation. As Phillips and Smith correctly argue, some Tory critics, such as Isaac D'Israeli, the father of Benjamin Disraeli, championed Hume's *History* from Brodie's indictment (2005: 309). For other critics, however, Hume's alleged conservatism looks more dubious, and his scepticism more serious.

Although Edmund Burke's mentions of Hume are few, Burke himself seems *not* to consider Hume as a comrade in his support for the established system; rather he became 'an outspoken critic' of Hume's philosophical and religious principles (Mossner 1980: 394). As O'Neill demonstrates, Burkean evaluations of Hume can be fathomed through *The Annual Register*, which Burke founded and wrote most articles for until the 1760s (2007: 66–70). After then he kept his editorial influence over it. A reviewer in the 1771 issue of *The Annual Register* highly praises James Beattie's work, *An Essay on the Nature and Immutability of Truth in Opposition to Sophistry and Scepticism*. This reviewer animadverted on Hume's scepticism at great length:

> If an inhabitant of another planet were to read *The Treatise of Human Nature*, what notions of human nature could he gather from it? [...] That the perfection of human knowledge is to doubt [...] – That we ought to doubt of every thing, yea of our doubts themselves; and therefore the utmost that philosophy can do, is to give a doubtful solution of doubtful doubts [...]. (Anon. [1771] 1803: 257)

Here, the reviewer emphasises the essential connection between 'our sceptics in philosophy' and 'infidels in religion' both of which are contrasted with 'men of taste', that is, men 'of sensibility and imagination' (259). According to O'Neill, the reviewer was plausibly Burke himself, though the authorship of this review has not yet been fully established. Burke and Beattie, who personally admired each other, formed a united front against Humean scepticism. 'In fact,' O'Neill argues, 'there is abundant evidence in the pages of the *Annual Register* that Burke saw Humean skepticism as a mirror image of the descent into moral, political, and social anarchy that necessarily followed from Bolingbroke's rationalism' (2007: 66–7).[19] This interpretation can be confirmed by one of the earliest biographers of Burke. In his *Life of Edmund Burke*, Robert Bisset notes that Burke 'seems to have been as partial *for* Beattie as *against* Hume' (1800: I, 262). He also (not surprisingly) observes that '[p]erhaps the religious sentiments of Hume might have been one cause of Mr. Burke's disapprobation [...]' (II, 428).

On the other hand, O'Neill assumes that 'Burke held a high opinion of Hume's abilities as a historian, if not as a moral philosopher', based on his review of Hume's *History* in the *Register* in 1761 (2007: 79), despite his disagreements with Hume on the Irish Massacre and Marian controversy (Mossner 1980: 394; Sato 2014: 691). On this point, however, Bisset reveals an understanding different from O'Neill's: 'Burke was prejudiced against Hume. – That Hume was friendly to despotism', which, according to Bisset, 'is an opinion more consistent with a cursory reading of his works than an accurate perusal'. Bisset defends the fact that Hume 'appears rather to palliate than justify' the conduct of Stuart monarchs (1800: I, 440; see also I, 439). He attempts to demonstrate that Hume offers a more balanced view of English history than Burke. Hume ridiculed not only puritans' 'theological absurdities' but also 'the high church bigotry'. Bisset, calling Hume 'this philosophical observer and surveyor of the progress of men', finally concludes that '[i]f Burke had not been incensed against Hume, it is probable that he would have considered the general scope, rather than particular passages of his writings' (I, 442).

Burke's critical attitude towards Hume can be confirmed by Burke's own words – as Bisset argued, his criticism is probably directed not at Hume's overall style or narrative, but at the particular exposure of his alleged political principles. In *Three Memorials on French Affairs*, Burke is anxious about the advent of 'a system of French conspiracy' or the atheistic republicanism advocated by Condorcet and Priestley:

> A predominant inclination towards it [a system of French conspiracy] appears in all those who have no religion, when otherwise their disposition leads them to be advocates even for despotism. Hence Hume,

> though I cannot say that he does not throw out some expressions of disapprobation on the proceedings of the levellers in the reign of Richard the Second, yet affirms that the doctrines of *John Ball* were 'conformable to the ideas of primitive equality, *which are engraven in the hearts of all men*'. (Burke 1797: 53; Hume, H II, 289–90. Burke's Italics; see also Bisset 1800: II, 349n.)

What is important in this context is that Hume's alleged Toryism and favour to the Stuart monarchs and the Church looked, at least to Burke, like red herrings. Similar points were made by another reviewer in *The Annual Register*:

> Under the pretext of exposing the delusions of fanaticism, the weakness of bigotry, and the arts of selfish and designing ecclesiastics, [Hume] indirectly endeavours to sap the fabric of religion itself, and undermine the dearest interests of society. His political principles are averse to the claims of freedom. (Anon. [1798] 1806: 432)

This reviewer's notion of the 'claims of freedom' seems to be a Burkean one, supported by religion and order. Hence, a kind of 'conspiratorial' interpretation of Hume's influence was introduced and became popular. In the 'Explanation of New Terms' in the *Register* of 1792, the author mentions the pernicious effects of 'The New or Modern Philosophy': 'The doctrine of Rousseau, Voltaire, Hume, Diderot, and others' who 'have devoted, or continue to devote their lives to the seduction of mankind, into a mockery of the Christian religion, and the adoption of a system of atheism and licentiousness'. After they outdid their predecessors, the reviewer continues, 'so they themselves were, in their turn, outdone by Condorcet, Brissot, Sieyes, Mr. Paine, and a whole herd of other philosophers, who actually attempted to carry the dreams of metaphysicians, on political subjects, into practice' (Anon. [1792] 1799: xi–xii). In 1800, a reporter of French affaires (mentioning the French new constitution) left a short comment in a footnote that Hume 'was very popular, and almost adored by the French. And certainly, though he is partial to absolute monarchy, and a sworn enemy to democracy, his writing had a great share in bringing about the revolution' (Anon. [1800] 1801: 61n.).

Similarly, *The Anti-Jacobin Review and Magazine* depicted Hume and Gibbon as 'one of them much superior to the Socinian teachers, and the other equal to most in the nation, whose writings, though friendly to kingly government, and indeed intended to be so to ecclesiastical establishments, as political institutions, yet co-operated with the enemies of religion' (Anon. 1798: 715). Although mentions of and quotations from Hume were much less common in the *Quarterly Review* than in either *The Edinburgh Review* or *The Westminster Review*, such a 'conspiracy' theory rather abounds in the Anti-Jacobin journals and some Romantic writings after the French Revolution and Burke.[20]

As Schilling (1943) argues, Voltaire became deemed to be the chief villain of the Revolution after 1800 in Britain. Rousseau and other French philosophes can be added to this list. What matters is that some Romantics counted Hume among their confederates. Despite his early enthusiasm for the French Revolution, Coleridge deemed Hume as his *bête noir* as early as 1799. In the 'Advice to the Friends of Freedom', which appeared in the *Morning Post*, Coleridge depicted 'Humists in opinion, debauchees in conduct' as one of the three types of the pretended apologists of freedom:

> they have lost all power of sympathysing with whatever exists in society, and mistake for philosophy, and a love of freedom, that restlessness of mind and body which results from lewd habits and embarrassed circumstances. These men find, from each successive explosion in France, a stimulus so necessary and so pleasurable, that each in its turn is first palliated and finally justified. Their mode of justifications are, indeed, laughably inconsistent with each other; but this formed no objection with men who love fashions in philosophy, and would deem it a proof of intellectual poverty to appear thrice together in the same habiliments. (Coleridge [1799] 1978–2001: I, 38 footnote 4)

As the editor of this text suggests, the Humist (or Humean) here is the same as what Charles Lamb termed in a letter 'the Damned philosophical Humeian [sic] indifference, so cold, and unnatural, and unhuman!' (Lamb 1968: I, 177). Although this does not mention Hume himself but suggests the people who were affected by Hume's (alleged) sceptical philosophy, the allusions to Hume in this context always accompany and invoke the drastic changes in our morals after the Revolution. In the writings of Coleridge, the name of Hume often appears as part of the triad of 'Hume, Paley and Condillac' as the 'parents or foster-fathers of modern ethics' ([1809] 1978–2001: II, 82), or 'Hume, Hartley, and Condillac [who] have exploded all *Ideas*, but those of sensation' ([1816]

1978–2001: 102).[21] Sometimes the list of the dramatis personae changes, but Hume and Condillac are commonly used examples. According to this poet, even the abolishment of the Catholic Church in France after the Revolution could be considered one of Hume's ideas that were later adopted by philosophes:

> The French, as is usual with them, evidently stole the original idea [of abolishing the National Church] from our ingenious countryman, and then with some trifling additions, passed it off on the world as a brilliant thought of their own. I am glad of this opportunity of restoring the honour of the invention to its original author. (Coleridge [1812] 1978–2001: II, 342)[22]

The editor of this text added in the footnote to the above sentence that 'the "ingenious" British atheist is probably Hume'.

Hume's anti-religious attitude is, for Coleridge, one of the principal causes of the ethical devastation that he believed was evident in society after the Revolution: Hume was above all the philosopher 'who devoted his life to the undermining of the Christian religion' ([1816] 1978–2001: 22). Despite Coleridge's strong commitment to Hartley's associationism in his youth (Roe 1988: 113) (he even named his first child 'David Hartley' (Craig 2007: 42)), Hume's version was and has been insufficient for him, because it ultimately fails to explicate the positive and creative powers of imagination, 'whose function it is to control, determine, and modify the phantasmal chaos of association' (Coleridge [1817] 1978–2001: I, 116), which means, Coleridge believes, that we are deprived of access to the Eternal truth. Cairns Craig is right to argue that 'Hume is Coleridge's ultimate adversary because Hume's version of the imagination offers no such consolation: it is purely social, entirely contingent; generating associations without end, it is always detached from any ground and never capable of reaching an ultimate conclusion' (Craig 2007: 58). Compared with Hume, Hartley remained a favourite for Coleridge who in the *Biographia Literaria* of 1817 still called him 'that great master of Christian philosophy' regardless of his assumed materialistic orientation (Coleridge [1817] 1978–2001: I, 121; Leslie 1972). These general evaluations of Hume were the same as in Thomas Carlyle: 'the Anti-church of Hume and Paine', 'the Paine and Hume Atheistic theory of "things well let alone", with Liberty, Equality and the like [...]' ([1843] 2005: 168). William Hazlitt also called David Hume 'a languid, Epicurean philosopher, of a reasonable corpulency, who was hurried away by no violent passions, or intense desire, but looked on most things with the same eye of lifelessness and indifference' ([1813] 1930–4: 260–1).[23]

Compared with these critical comments on Hume as a philosopher, nevertheless, it is rather difficult to find flattering comments on Hume's historical works as literary creations among these Romantics, probably because his historical narratives appeared too calm and detached, or his insistence on the uniformity of human nature sounded too 'unhistorical'.[24] Coleridge's evaluation of Hume as a historian is rather ambivalent: he finds some merits in Hume's historical works along with Robertson's and Gibbon's, because of their emphasis on large-scale social changes, while criticising them for their lack of interest in the role of heroic individual wills affecting such historical trends (Coleridge 1956: VI, 583 [a letter to John Hookham Frere, 6 June 1826]; Edwards 2004: 156–7). Interestingly enough, Coleridge's evaluation is the opposite of Mill's attack noted above on Hume's historical writings because of their overemphasis on the role of great figures. As Edwards and Morrow emphasise, Coleridge also draws some influence from Hume (along with Adam Smith and James Steuart) in his 'sceptical' defence of commercialisation through the works of John Crawfurd (Edwards 2004: 3, 193–4, 212; see also Morrow 1990).[25]

Julius Charles Hare, a disciple of Coleridge, dismissively contended that 'few men have been more poorly endowed with the historical spirit, or less capable of understanding or sympathizing with any unseen form of human nature' than Hume (quoted in Forbes 1952: 191n.203). Behind such evaluations obviously lies the burgeoning interest in imagination and sensibility in Romantic historiography (Stronberg 1951; Phillips and Smith 2005: 310–11). There is a parallel between these uncomplimentary evaluations of Hume the historian and the generally negative assessment of his contribution of the associationist theory to the literary genre among the Romantics. Unsurprisingly, his allegedly mechanical treatment of the human mind and its atomistic implication has been a target of criticism among the Romantics in a way different from the Philosophic Radicals, although, as Cairns Craig points out, there is much more intellectual indebtedness of British Romanticism to Hume than has been considered (Craig 2007: chap. 1; see also Duncan 2007: chap. 5).

Another feature of the depiction of Hume as an infidel writer is the claim that Hume recommended 'adultery'. In some passages of his novel *The Vagabond* (1799), which has been described as an 'Anti-Revolutionary novel' (Harvey 1977: 290–300), George Walker mentioned 'the *fashionable* Hume' (1799: I, 42), whom he describes as a sceptical philosopher who reduces all ideas to mere impressions. For example, Walker mocked Hume's scepticism as follows: '"I am fearful," said the Doctor Alogos, "that even Mr. Hume must allow this storm to be something more than idea"' (II, 115).[26] According to Harvey, Walker seems to regard Hume's ideas as 'the most characteristic example of the essential topsy-turviness of reform ideology' in this novel (1977: 298). In chapter 8 of the *Vagabond* with the title 'Mr. Hume's Arguments for Adultery, with practical Consequences – the new Method of Benevolence', the fictional narrator says that he 'read over the Essays of the fashionable Hume, where I found that adultery was one of the moral virtues, and perfectly agreeable to political justice'. To support his image of Hume, Walker went as far as forging his text and citation: 'In volume 2, page 409, of his Essays, edition 1767':

> 'Adultery,' says [Hume], 'must be practised, if men would obtain all the advantages of life, if generally practised, it would soon cease to be scandalous; and if practised secretly and frequently, it would, by degrees, come to be thought no crime at all'. (Walker 1799: I, 174)

It seems almost unnecessary to point out that there is no counterpart anywhere in Hume's writings to the statement that is attributed to him here. This is actually a quotation from what James Beattie claimed to represent a summary of Hume's moral philosophy in his *Essay on the Nature and Immutability of Truth* (1771) – Walker's reference to the page and edition is exactly the same as Beattie's ([1771] 1783: 140). Following the dictate of 'Immortal Hume', 'I' started to address a lady who 'was in company with an ill-humoured, jealous-looking, illiberal man'. That lady was found to hate her own slavery and 'wanted to exert the inborn freedom of her sex'. Suggestively, the character who Walker is obviously mocking is taken from 'Mrs. Wollstonecraft' (1799: I, 174, 175). Due to her husband's sudden death, this widow – whom the narrator calls 'Mary' – openly met him in public. Before long, the fact that other gentlemen gave her 'some handsome presents' caused the calumny that 'I kept my wife as a prostitute' in their neighbourhood. In the event, this fictional widow soon got bored with the narrator, transferring her affections to the protagonist's friend, Williams (I, 181–3). The rest of the story proceeds to the Godwinian issue of political justice of private property and need not be discussed in detail here. What is important is that for this anti-Revolutionary writer, Hume was not only religiously an infidel, but also a generally immoral author complicit in the Revolutionary cause along with Wollstonecraft and Godwin. On this point, even James Mackintosh in his later years laments that Hume 'treats vice with too much indulgence', and claimed that '[h]ad he lived fourteen years longer [...] he would have seen, that the virtues which guard the natural seminaries of the affections are their only true and lasting friends' (Mackintosh [1830] 1846: I, 142–3). While neither Walker nor Mackintosh clearly indicated any specific writings of Hume when they accused him of recommending 'adultery', it clearly derives from Hume's claim in 'A Dialogue' of the second *Enquiry* (EPM, 'A Dialogue' 47; 339) and his essay 'Of Refinement in the Arts' (E 271).[27]

Among the writers closely involved with the *Quarterly Review*, John Gibson Lockhart can be considered to give one of the most comprehensive evaluations of Hume among the Romantics. He was one of the founders of the *Blackwood Magazine*, the editor of the *Quarterly Review* since 1825, and the husband of Walter Scott's daughter, and is now best known as a biographer of Scott. Lockhart published a novel, *Peter's Letters to his Kinsfolk* (1819), on the model of his future father-in-law's epistolary novel, *Paul's Letters to his Kinsfolk* (1816). Although this work has been 'neglected outside the field of Scottish literary studies', Ian Duncan argues, '*Peter's Letters* offers the first programmatic account of the ideological formation of a romantic cultural nationalism in Great Britain' (2007: 47; see also 58–9). In this novel, the sender of letters depicted the scenery, historical monuments and various episodes of people in Scotland, mainly Edinburgh and Glasgow. Unsurprisingly, Hume's alleged 'ardent feeling' on 'the ideas of ancient loyalty and attachment to the blood of his native princes' was again an issue of concern. Despite the oft-expressed claim for the influence of his early education, he writes:

> I am rather inclined to be of opinion, that David had really persuaded himself, by the exercise of his speculative understanding, that the

> greatest danger, to which his country was likely to be exposed, would be nothing else than a too great dereliction of those ideas, on which the national character and constitution had been formed, and determined, in his capacity of philosopher, to make use of his powers as a historian to controvert, and, if possible, counterbalance this perilous tendency of his times. (Lockhart 1819: 82; see also Duncan 2007: 60)

In spite of his seemingly balanced account of the causes of Hume's alleged conservative bias, Lockhart's final judgement was harsh, because he considers that Hume's personal and sporadic zeal for the Stuart monarchs was undermined and overwhelmed by his own relentless assault on the religious establishment. According to the sender of letters in this novel, therefore, Hume's 'consolation, if such there might be, was a very deceitful thing' because his worries were due to his own deeds of 'convulsing the whole soil, wherein feelings both religious and national had taken root':

> and others saw well enough, although he himself might not, the absurdity of his undertaking to preserve, in the midst of the ruin occasioned by his own exertions, any particular item of that produce, for the sum total of which he had manifested so little reverence.

Such an evaluation is closely related to the confrontation between Hume as a philosopher and as a historian. Lockhart summarises the point succinctly: 'the Prince of Sceptics has himself been found the most potent instrument for diminishing, almost for neutralizing, the true and grave influence of the Prince of Historians' (Lockhart 1819: 83–4).[28]

The source of anxiety for Lockhart and other Romantics does not only lie in Hume's supposed influence among their contemporaries. Rather, their concern also centres on their belief in the perpetuity and the contagious nature of Hume's philosophy and its potential influence on the future world: 'Whatever may be his future fate, this much is quite certain, that the general principles of his philosophy still continue to exert a mighty influence over by far the greatest part of the literary men of his country [...]'.[29] Lockhart clearly detects the discordance between Hume's philosophy and history. He went on to argue that:

> almost the only subject on which these his pious disciples dare to apply his principles in a different way from what he himself exemplified – is

> that of politics. Among them, as indeed I have hinted already, David's Toryism is always talked of, as one little foible which should not be too hardly thought of in the character of so great a man. (1819: 86–7)

Those whom he called 'his pious disciples' appear to refer to the same group that Coleridge called 'Humists in opinion'. His reference to politics seems to suggest that he would have regarded the frivolous social habits and loose morals of people after the French Revolution much as Coleridge did. Lockhart did not consider that these allegedly harmful effects were Hume's own intention, because he believed that Hume's 'object, in most cases, was to see what the mere power of ratiocination would lead to, and wherever he met with an illogical sequence of propositions, he broke it down without mercy' (91). In spite of Hume's (alleged) naïveté, however, Lockhart would have been hard put to deny that Hume the philosopher should not be judged innocent of the results. The evaluation of Hume the philosopher by Lockhart basically accords with J. S. Mill's evaluation of Hume as a 'negative philosopher', or 'a man, the peculiarities of whose mind qualified him to detect failure of proof, and want of logical consistency' (Mill [1838] 1963–91: 80 note q–q 38), despite the difference in their interpretations of the relationship between the two Humes. On the other hand, Lockhart and Francis Jeffrey concur in regarding Hume's Toryism as supposedly exhibited in the *History* as less significant than his philosophical influence, because both take more seriously the impact of his allegedly irreligious, sceptical and hedonistic philosophy.[30] In addition, Lockhart and Jeffrey saw serious discrepancies between Hume's personal disposition and the outcome of his philosophy: both Scots might have had access to personal memories of 'le bon David'.[31]

These diverse evaluations of Hume in the early nineteenth century never converge to produce a simple profile. Nor were they free from each political standpoint. Nevertheless, this evidence sufficiently demonstrates that Mill's familiar interpretation that Hume's scepticism logically led to his Toryism was not universally shared by his contemporaries and later generations. Even Hume's *History* was sometimes mentioned favourably among the Radicals. Above all, James Mackintosh in the 1790s did not overlook the significant difference between Hume and Burke. For the reviewers of *The Edinburgh Review*, Hume was one of the most famous and important intellectual figures of local origin;

his evaluations among them, however, were no less divided than the political position taken by this journal, as John Stuart Mill critically noted. The conflicting images of Hume appearing even in the same journal might be considered to be partly a reflection of the ambivalence in the 'Philosophic Whiggism' (Fontana 1985: 183–4). When Coleridge and Burke mentioned Hume, even in passing, one of their intentions was to implicate him in the moral deterioration they perceived as having occurred in society after the French Revolution. For them, Hume's Toryism was nothing but a blatant excuse.

Surprisingly or not, he has been listed in the British Library catalogue as 'David Hume, historian' and many modern commentators believe that Hume's reputation as a historian dominated that of Hume the philosopher through the nineteenth century. However, even in the early nineteenth century, the influence of 'the Prince of Sceptics' was far from overshadowed by his fame as 'the Prince of Historians'. Rather, the former has continued to shake, disturb and plague the latter. As Lockhart correctly predicted, the name of David Hume continues to be revered even in the twenty-first century, especially among philosophers. The issue of the relationship between the two Humes was not only being earnestly discussed as early as the end of the eighteenth century, but also continues and will continue to be so. This situation had already appeared in his lifetime. George Keith, the Earl Marischal of Scotland, reportedly remarked to Hume that '[t]o the highflyers you are therefore a sad Whig, to the Whigs an hidden Jacobite, and to reasonable men, *le bon David*, a Lover of truth' (quoted in Mossner 1980: 318). The consequence is what Hume himself seemed to intend: 'Whether am I Whig or Tory? Protestant or Papist? Scotch or English? I hope you do not all agree on this head; & that there [are] disputes among you about my principles' (L I, 195).

Notes

1. On the distinction between the old/new Tory and Whig definitions of conservatism, see Mossner 1941b: 227–8; Pocock 1985b: chap. 11.
2. Mill also despises Hume's lack of historical imagination and sympathy in contrast with Carlyle's *French Revolution*: 'If there be a person who, in reading the histories of Hume, Robertson, and Gibbon [...] has never felt that this, after all, is not history [...], such

a person [...] feels no need of a book like Mr. Carlyle's; the want, which it is peculiarly fitted to supply, does not yet consciously exist in his mind' (Mill [1837] 1963–91: 134; see also 135–6; Phillips and Smith 2005: 311–12).

3. Bentham cited Hume's *History* V, 247, 246, 329–30, 281, 249–50, 248 and 293. See also Forbes's quotation from Bentham's mention of Hume in his *Theory of Legislation* (Forbes 1975b: 292n.1).
4. Élie Halévy also argues that '[a]t this time [when he published his *Fragment on Government*] Bentham clearly held himself to be Hume's ally in irreligion', referring to Bentham's manuscripts and letters (1955: 141n.1).
5. As for the opposition between the Philosophic Radicals and Philosophic Whigs, see Collini et al. 1983: chap. 3.
6. The same point is discussed by a reviewer in the *Monthly Review*: Thomas Pearne, a classical scholar, argues that Hume 'defended religious establishments on the ground of their being excellent and necessary soporifics to check the intemperate zeal of the clergy, and to prevent them from being too eager and assiduous in the discharge of their duty' (1790: 443). As for the attribution of this review to Pearne, see Nagle 1955: 52–3, 97. Nagle described Pearne's political and religious principles as 'extremely liberal' (53). As for the 'Humean influence on Mackintosh', see Haakonssen 1996: 268–70.
7. On this point, John Stuart Mill fundamentally disagrees with Mackintosh, because the former judged that Hume should be considered not 'a good witness against the church', but 'a man who sold his conscience for them, a writer who violated every law of historical veracity in order to screen the church [...]' ([1828] 1963–91: 423).
8. O'Neill also points out that Wollstonecraft criticises Hume's notion of gallantry in her *Vindication of the Rights of Woman* (2007: 106–7).
9. This is also evinced by the fact that Bolingbroke's 'Some Reflections on the Present State of the Nation' is appended to a French translation of Hume's *Political Discourses* (Hume 1754: 331–429; see also Hont 2005: 337). On other British contemporary responses to Hume's argument on public credit, see Sonenscher 2007: esp. 52–67, 300–1.
10. For the 'conservative' interpretations on this issue, see Livingston 1990: 126; 1998: 194; Miller 1981: 180; Israel 2011: 230. And for the 'liberal' reading, see Baier 2011: 79–80. Outside the discipline of Hume study, it seems more common to interpret Hume as an

opponent of impressing seamen (Radzinowicz 1986: 86; Franklin 2011: 128).

11. 'I do not think that [J. S.] Mill was very familiar with Hume's writings. A note to the concluding chapter of the *Examination of Hamilton* seems to imply that he was not acquainted with the *Treatise*; nor does he appear from his posthumous Essays to have studied Hume's writings upon theology' (Stephen 1900: III, 86n.1).
12. As for John Allen, see Jacyna 1994: chap. 2.
13. On the ideological positions of *The Edinburgh Review* and the *Quarterly Review*, see Shattock 1989.
14. The reviewer points out that '[s]uch a hypothetical integration of the opinions likely to prevail in any particular circumstances' can be found in his four essays on happiness. On Jeffrey's general view of Hume's *History* in his review of George Brodie's *History of the British Empire*, see Phillips and Smith 2005: 308.
15. When Boswell mentioned this character sketch to William Burke, the latter quipped: 'Yes, as he was an Epicurean, it must be by chance' (Boswell 1993: 79). The humour is, of course, based on the Epicurean natural philosophy that all things are made by the contingent connections of atoms and that there is no such thing as Providence. Thomas Carlyle wrote in his 'Characteristics' published in *The Edinburgh Review* (1831) that '[a]s Johnson became the father of all succeeding Tories; so was Hume the father of all succeeding Whigs, for his own Jacobitism was but an accident, as worthy to be named Prejudice as any of Johnson's' (Fieser (ed.) 2003: II, 177).
16. Thomas Erskine also favourably cited Hume's opinion on the liberty of the press for the defence of Paine in his trial. Erskine admitted that Hume held 'the highest monarchical principles of Government', but claimed that he 'considers, that this Liberty of the Press extends not only to abstract speculation, but to keep the public on their guard against all the acts of their Government' (Gurney 1793: 162; E 12–13). Erskine again cited a passage from Hume's essay 'Of the Liberty of the Press' (Gurney 1793: 175), but this was actually 'That Politics may reduced to a Science' and that passage was deleted from the *Essays* after 1777 editions (E 605).
17. Eugene F. Miller's 'Variant Readings' (E 602), which are based on Green and Grose's identification of the editions of Hume's *Essays and Treatises* (Hume 1992 [1886]: III, 86), mistakenly attribute this addition to the 1777 edition because both do not reflect the 1772 edition.

18. For the attribution of this review to James Mill, see Houghton (ed.) 1966–89: I, 448 (entry 559). I thank Yuichiro Kawana for this and the bibliographical information on James Mill.
19. However, attitudes towards Beattie and Hume among *The Annual Register* reviewers were not consistent. Another reviewer in the same journal is more critical of Beattie, who, 'more than thirty years after the publication of that sceptical system, has been so successfully as to obtain a pension by his *Essay on the Immutability of Truth*; in which he discovers all the violence of a sectary, and all the illiberality of a pedant, and rather abuses than confutes Mr. Hume' (Anon. [1776] 1788: 28). This reviewer made rather flattering remarks about Hume's ingenuity (29). The title of this review is 'An Account of the Life and Writings of the late David Hume, Esq. as given to the World in one of the periodical publications' but it is not specified on which 'periodical publication' the original version appears. On this short biography, see Fieser (ed.) 1995.
20. The similar 'conspiracy' theory was also found in a dissenter's journal. An anonymous reviewer of *The Annual Review and History of Literature* argued that Hume 'hinted to the continental writers the expediency of puffing the quakers' because he considers them 'the most innocent enthusiasts that have yet been known', while completely free from the priestly bondage in the essay 'Of Superstition and Enthusiasm' (E 75). 'The French philosophists', the reviewer argues, used this information to demonstrate the 'inutility both of chistianity and its clergy' (Anon. 1805: 713).
21. Coleridge in other places laments that 'Bacon, Harrington, Machiavel, and Spinoza, are not read, because Hume, Condilliac, and Voltaire are' ([1817] 1978–2001: I, 54). A similar argument is also found in a German critic, Friedrich Schlegel, who attributes a modern anomie to the philosophies of Hume, Rousseau and Voltaire (Duncan 2007: 57).
22. Coleridge was the very person who doubted the originality of Hume's associationist theory, and he believed that the Scottish philosopher plagiarised it from Aristotle. This suspicion was rejected by James Mackintosh ([1830] 1846: notes T–U, 1: 302–4; Rep. in Fieser (ed.) 2000: II, 147–8).
23. Hume's first *Enquiry* was also mentioned together with Bayle's *Dictionnaire* as an example of 'a sceptical dispassionate, Epicurean work' that 'gives the finishing blow to what little remains of dogmatical faith in established systems' (Hazlitt [1821] 1930–4: 'Guy Faux', 102).

24. Yet, a reviewer of the *Quarterly Review* could use Hume to counteract the Whiggish history of Henry Hallam (Anon. 1828).
25. I thank Daisuke Odagawa for information on these points.
26. Walker also satirised another 'fashionable' Hume's theory of identity by saying through the mouth of Doctor Alogos that 'Mr. Hume, who finished the essays, was not the Mr. Hume who wrote the Treatise on Human Nature' (II, 224). Harvey infers that the model for Dr. Alogos would be Joseph Priestley (1977: 295).
27. This point was also ridiculed by Anon. (c.1755) and Bonar ([1755] 2003: I, 41–2). See also Fieser (ed.) 2003: II, 120.
28. Lockhart continues to affirm that Hume's utilitarianism along with the co-operation with Adam Smith 'was undoubtedly the most dangerous present ever conferred by men of high and powerful intellects upon the herd of the species'.
29. The interpretation of Hume as an infidel and pernicious writer was not limited among the Romantics, but was found even among political reformists. 'Major' John Cartwright was amazed at 'how universally, especially among that polite and lettered world, his [Hume's] pernicious tenets had spread themselves' together with the writings of Voltaire and Rousseau. At the same time, Cartwright admitted that, 'however they may hurt the present generation, posterity will benefit by these friends of infidelity, for truth will always benefit by discussion' ([1826] 1969: 49–50). He confessed that he himself was much influenced by Hume when he was young (51).
30. At the same time, as Biancamaria Fontana argues, *The Edinburgh Review* not only 'defend[ed] Hume from the current charges of atheism, materialism and impiety; but, like [Dugald] Stewart, the reviewers were ready to recognise that Hume's opinion about the limits of human knowledge had not in fact prevented him from making a substantial contribution to moral science' (Fontana 1985: 90).
31. James Beattie also admitted that Hume's 'manners in private life are said to be so agreeable to many of his acquaintance', although complaning that he 'should yet, in the public capacity of an author, have given so much cause of just offence to all the friends of virtue and mankind, is to me matter of astonishment and sorrow, as well as of indignation' ([1770] 1778, 10–11).

Conclusion

This book has delineated the nature of Hume's own visions of the Enlightenment as an on-going movement in his contemporary Europe, and the ways in which he committed to several central issues of the Enlightenment while keeping his spirit of scepticism alive throughout his political, social and historical analyses. In order *not* to exaggerate the idiosyncrasy of Hume by presupposing a naïve and caricatured notion of 'the Enlightenment', I provide a more enlarged definition of this intellectual movement. The provisional definition of Enlightenment that I have proposed aims, not to exclude, but rather to encourage investigations undertaken on an individual basis, without missing the larger picture. As demonstrated in this book, not a few of Hume's particular arguments were indebted to his predecessors and shared with his contemporaries. Because every philosopher is unique in one way or another, the point is to elucidate as much as possible on what point, in what way, and to what degree we can differentiate Hume's arguments and others', while recognising the concepts, discourses, mind-sets, sensitivities, prejudices and values they shared with one another. As is the case with almost every thinker, Hume's commitment to some key issues in the Enlightenment discourses should be seen as a matter of degree, but as such it is most revealing. This leads us to investigate the 'historical' Hume. What Duncan Forbes observes in his *Hume's Philosophical Politics* seems still worth listening to: 'The history of ideas would be easier to write about, more dramatic, if what looked like chiaroscuro did not nearly always on closer inspection cease to be so. The colours always run, and the picture becomes complex and messy' (Forbes 1975b: 308).

If Hume's 'spirit of scepticism' plays a central role in his social, political and historical writings, his singularity as an Enlightenment thinker can be best described, I believe, by delineating the ways in which he remains faithful in his mitigated scepticism throughout the various topics he addresses. I have termed this the 'Sceptical Enlightenment' and tried to understand the 'historical' Hume through this concept, while endeavouring to avoid the error of explaining this concept by exploiting his ideas. Admittedly, the intellectual weapon of scepticism lies at the very heart of the Enlightenment: there were no philosophes (in the broadest sense of the term) who did not employ this powerful armament to attack and devastate many established paradigms and existing (religious, moral or social) institutions. Nevertheless, Hume is the philosopher who most consciously aimed scepticism at himself in his own enquiry. Thus, one of the biggest intellectual challenges for Hume is how to avoid all types of dogmatism, including the philosophical variety, while recognising the overall social benefits of civilisation. This is why his endorsement of modern values is often conditional to the extent that its seriousness appears dubious. For example, he was well aware that learning, generally regarded as the source of development in politics, law and culture, could be a double-edged sword. In his depiction of the Civil War, he remarked that '[l]earning itself, which tends so much to enlarge the mind, and humanize the temper, rather served on this occasion to exalt that epidemical frenzy which prevailed' (H V, 348; see also IV, 312). As he shows in his psychological analysis of '*artificial* lives' in the second *Enquiry*, extreme theory or philosophical chimera is far from a cure. Hume's critique of (vulgar) philosophy has often been claimed to be one of the most important characteristics of Hume as a (proto-)conservative thinker. This book has claimed instead that this aspect of his thought should be comprehended as a part of his ubiquitous 'spirit of scepticism'.

Based upon his philosophical arguments regarding the workings of human imagination and opinions, Hume emphasises the essential instability of civilisation, while retaining a positive assessment of modern values such as liberty, politeness and refinement. He also underlines the possible improvement of politics as a science by augmenting the regularity of our political behaviours, while cautiously suspending his theoretically perfect plan at the hypothetical and speculative level. As a corollary to this 'spirit of scepticism', Hume cannot be so naïve in his view of civilisation as to claim the perpetual progress and improvement of human societies. Hume's seemingly paradoxical stance is buttressed by his indeterminate argumentation, and further intensified by his ironical style. Considering these, there is no wonder that what Forbes calls 'terrible campaign country' has continued to produce the divided, one-sided and fragmentary images of Hume both as philosopher and historian that have endured since the late eighteenth century. As we saw in the last chapter, the diverse images of Hume among later generations are nothing but a reflection of this complexity.

In this conclusion, some further discussions concerning the nature of Hume's Sceptical Enlightenment will be advanced. A few more comparisons between Hume and Voltaire will be useful, since their specific similarities and differences can tell a great deal about the peculiarity of Hume's thought. An examination of Beattie's diatribe against Hume might also be illuminating.

Despite the similarities in their intellectual strategies for secularising the world (Chapter 4), Hume, the 'Scottish Voltaire', is more cautious than Voltaire in acknowledging the salutary effects of (false) religions (Chapter 5). They also differ in evaluation of their intellectual hero – Isaac Newton. Voltaire was one of the most adamant and official admirers of this intellectual giant. In *Éléments de la philosophie de Newton* (*The Elements of Sir Isaac Newton's Philosophy*) he declares that Newton 'has discovered Truths; but he has searched for, and placed them in an Abyss, into which it is necessary to descend, in order to bring them out, and to place them in full Light' (Voltaire [1738] 1967, 4; 1968–: XV, 549. This 'avant-propos' appeared only in the two 1738 French editions). To take another example, 'after three thousand years of fruitless research', he praises in *Le Siècle de Louis XIV* (*The Age of Louis XIV*), 'Newton was the first to find and demonstrate the great natural law by which all elements of matter are mutually attracted, the law by which all the stars are held in their courses. He was indeed the first to see the light; before him it was unknown'. To emphasise his monumental achievement, Halley's eulogy of Newton was also cited: 'it is not permitted to any mortal to approach nearer to divinity' (Voltaire [1751] 1961: 378). Obviously, behind Voltaire's praise of Newton lies his deistic interest in the orderliness and harmony of this universe.

On the other hand, Hume evaluates Newton, not for his discovery of the eternal truth of this world, but rather for maintaining his modest and sceptical attitude even in his odyssey: 'While Newton seemed to draw off the veil from some of the mysteries of nature, he shewed at the same time *the imperfections* of the mechanical philosophy; and thereby restored *her ultimate secrets to that obscurity, in which they ever did and ever will remain*' (H VI, 542. Italics added). In the first *Enquiry* Hume asserts that Newton 'was so cautious and modest as to allow, that it was a mere hypothesis, not to be insisted on, without more experiments' (EHU footnote 16 to 7.25; 73n.1). Here Hume seems to ignore Newton's religious aspects, expressed in his *Chronology of Ancient Kingdoms* and *Observations upon the Prophecies of Daniel, and the Apocalypse of St. John* (Popkin 1976: 88). Voltaire shares some important aspects of scepticism with Hume and both admire the same intellectual giant (although the Scottish Voltaire is not quite as enthusiastic as his French counterpart). Nevertheless, there is a significant difference in the underlying causes of their respect for Newton, which seems to parallel the differences in their religious views.

Such differences can be considered to permeate their styles and behaviours. Voltaire was consciously a philosophe-militant, polemist and activist. Hume can hardly be considered in these terms. Despite the controversy many of his writings provoked among his contemporaries, Hume resolved 'never to reply to any body' (E 'My Own Life' xxxvi) and tried, in vain, to avoid any quarrels ('Controversy, however civilly conducted, has unavoidably something harsh in its Nature, & what I would willingly avoid' (Hume 2014: 31)). This difference did not escape their contemporaries' attention. Gustave Phillipe, comte de Creutz, poet and Swedish Ambassador at Madrid and Paris, sent a letter to Hume on 4 February 1765. In this rarely cited letter, the Swedish correspondent recorded Voltaire's optimism in a succinct way: Voltaire 'see within 50 years from now on that universal reason will spread its empire over the world. Asia will have no more slaves; nor will Europe have any more prejudice. All the nations would be free and all the people philosophers' (Greig 1932: 853–4).* On the other hand, a similar optimism can rarely be found in Hume. Even when he occasionally expresses his ideals, he puts up a front of cool control: 'though it is much to be hoped, that the progress of reason will, by degrees, abate the acrimony of opposite religions all over EUROPE; *yet the spirit of moderation has, as yet, made too slow advances to be entirely trusted*' (E 'Protestant Succession' 510.

* 'Il [Voltaire] vois dans 50 ans d'ici la raison universelle etendre son empire sur l'univers. L'Asie n'aura plus d'esclaves; l'Europe plus de préjugés. Toutes les nations seront libres et tous les hommes philosophiques'.

Italics added). This reflects Hume's uncertainty over the prospect of the future of party political opposition in Britain (L I, 336–7; I, 385–6; II, 251–2; H VI, 381). More importantly, comte de Creutz goes on to contrast Voltaire and Hume in this letter, while mentioning the former's favourable opinion of the latter: 'Monsieur Voltaire is preoccupied with you, my dear philosopher. He calls you his "St. David." I told him that you could draw a better part of the life than he could, and that *you could live with the amicable ignorant as if you had never been destined to enlighten the humankind*' (Greig 1932: 854. Italics added).*

Despite this contrast by the Swedish ambassador, we should not unduly exaggerate it, or relapse into the anachronistic – extremely optimistic and reformist – image of Enlightenment thinkers exemplified by the quotation from Engels given in Chapter 1 (p. 11). Voltaire can say in a letter (written in 1759) without any embarrassment that 'the enlightened times will only enlighten a small number of right-thinking people; The common people will always be fanatics' (Voltaire 2013: D7118; cited in and translated by Blanning 1998: 22).† In 'Letter XIII' of the *Lettres philosophiques* he more directly affirms this point: 'Never will philosophers set up a religious sect. Why? Because they do not write for the people' ([1733] 2003: 58). He was not exceptional on this point. Not only the French, but most Enlightenment thinkers (with a few exceptions) did not so naïvely believe in the possibility of enlightening the common people, much less did they attempt to eliminate the distinction between the elite and the vulgar. The same attitude can be found about Hume, who repeatedly directs his appeals not to the vulgar, but rather to those of 'a philosophical mind' (H V, 459; VI, 142). In the *Treatise* he asserts that 'I pretend not to make philosophers [of 'many honest gentlemen' in England], nor do I expect them either to be associates in these researches, or auditors of these discoveries' (T 1.4.7.14; 272) – the 'common people' seem to be still further beyond his scope. More clearly, the essay 'The Sceptic' declares that '[t]he empire of philosophy extends over a few; and with regard to these too, her authority is

* 'Monsieur de Voltaire est pleine de Vous, mon cher philosophe. Il vous appelle son St David. Je luy ai dit que vous savés tirer meilleur parti de la vie que luy et que vous saviés vivre avec les ignorens aimables comme si vous n'aviés jamais eté déstiné a eclairer les homme'.

† 'Les temps éclaires n'éclaireront qu'un petit nombre d'honnêtes gens. Le vulgaire sera toujours fanatique'.

very weak and limited' (E 169). This shared indifference towards their social, cultural or intellectual inferiors should not necessarily be regarded as a blemish. As Muthu (2003) argues, it enabled these eighteenth-century thinkers to escape the paternalistic and imperialistic arguments for interventionism that arose among their nineteenth-century counterparts (here I will not dwell on Hume's negative views on the Africans in a footnote of the essay 'Of National Characters' because this topic is beyond the scope of this book. On this point, see Sebastiani 2013: chaps. 1 and 4). If so, the above-mentioned difference in both philosophers' characters should be construed within the bounds of their shared lack of interest in those they considered ignorant and vulgar.

Considering such a common prejudice among Enlightenment thinkers, it seems far more doubtful that Hume could believe or expect that society would become composed entirely of such mitigated sceptics as himself; probably he did not. It is unlikely that the man in the street could be expected to perfectly master this way of thinking (Herdt 1997: 15). Although his appeal to the changeability of opinion is one of his strongest methods for maintaining a balanced approach to politically and historically polemical issues (Chapter 3), Hume emphasises the difficulty in detaching ourselves from current prejudices in the essay 'Of the Standard of Taste':

> There needs but a certain turn of thought or imagination to make us enter into all the opinions, which then prevailed, and relish the sentiments or conclusions derived from them. But *a very violent effort is requisite* to change our judgment of manners, and excite sentiments of approbation or blame, love or hatred, different from those to which the mind from long custom has been familiarized. (E 247. Italics added)

If Hume's Sceptical Enlightenment relies on such sophisticated intellectual manipulation of historical and philosophical arguments, then the possible disadvantage might lie in its very nature.

Seen in this light, Hume's worst enemies among his contemporaries were not those whose ideas differed from his own, but those who attempt to subvert his self-professed appeal to soberness and moderation through scepticism. In the postscript of his *Essay on the Nature and Immutability of Truth*, James Beattie makes a dexterous attempt to overturn Humean strategic scepticism. After a pretended concession that scepticism tends to humble 'our pride of understanding' and aids '[t]he prevention of bigotry' ([1770] 1778: 452–3; see also Beattie [1767] 1948/2003), he delivers the defiant rejoinder that scepticism 'prevents all bigotry, and all strong attachment on the side of truth and common sense; but in behalf of its own paradoxes, it establishes bigotry the most implicit and the most obstinate' ([1770] 1778: 456). In this way, he turns the allegation of bigotry towards his adversary by taking the side of common sense. Beattie is even willing to admit to the charge of bigotry as it is framed by his opponent: 'Is it bigotry to believe these sublime truths with full assurance of faith? I glory in such bigotry' (458). There is no more provocative and effective way to undermine Hume's appeal to soberness through scepticism. Beattie's rebuttal does not finish here. Hume is not only a bigot, avers Beattie, but also 'affected and hypocritical', if he will 'keep up the appearance of as much coolness, as if he were disputing about an indifferent matter' (461). Thus, Beattie criticises the sceptic with his affected indifference as a 'dogmatist', while he justifies his own ardent advocacy of truth as a legitimate form of bigotry (469). Beattie's *coup de grâce* seems to have been no less influential than the contents of his critique of Hume's philosophy. J. S. Mill, Coleridge and Hazlitt similarly criticised Hume's or Humean indifference (Chapter 8). This attack on Hume's supposed bigotry must have been particularly painful and provocative for him, given that it accused him of the sin he was most proud of avoiding: he avowed to a correspondent that 'I was resolved not to be an enthusiast in philosophy, while I was blaming other enthusiasms' (L I, 24). Although Hume continued to admire Thomas Reid, the founder of the Common Sense School, as a philosopher despite the severe attacks the latter made upon his work, he was less able to contain his anger with 'that bigotted silly Fellow Beattie' (L II, 301). According to Mossner, Hume is reported to have said: 'Truth! There is no truth in [Beattie's *Essay*]; it is a horrible large lie in octavo' (Mossner 1980: 581). Despite his fury, Hume continued to demonstrate the importance of maintaining a moderate, sober and indifferent outlook in the face of any philosophical, political or religious polemics. Was this his innate character? 'Hume seems to me', Roger Emerson presumes from Hume's biographical information, 'someone who struggled to be calm and adopted a jocular manner that concealed as much as [his pessimism] showed. Dissembling was probably second nature to'

Hume (2007: 92). He resolutely maintained this stance even in the face of his own death (Guimarães 2008).

Beattie's revulsion against Hume's scepticism and the latter's fury at the former seem to reveal a significant difference between what has been called Hume's 'philosophy of common life' and the Common Sense School. This difference is missed in Israel's dichotomy between the Moderate and Radical Enlightenments: he tends to lump, not only Hume and other Scottish Enlightenment thinkers (Spencer 2010), but also the Common Sense School philosophers into the former category. The Common Sense Realism (especially in the naïve version of Beattie) is quite different from Hume's recurrent incorporation of common life into his philosophy through the dialectics of scepticism. As Joseph Priestley comments negatively (1785: xx–xxi; Norton 1976; Popkin 1977), the Common Sense School philosophers set the point of reference as a common sense, by which we can judge – or rather *sense* – the right or wrong in moral issues. Such a pre-fixed starting point is more different from Humean meta-analytic orientation to common practice or 'what is established' through mitigated scepticism than might first be surmised. Hume's contemporaries never failed to discern this subverting tendency in his writings – his scepticism (even in his non-epistemological writings) was far from moderate, but rather continued to be a public nuisance. As recent archival research demonstrates, quite a few Scottish contemporary readers abhorred Hume's scepticism and irreligion revealed not only in his *Essays and Treatises*, but also in the *History*. Many of them turned to the Common Sense School philosophers in order to counteract his allegedly dangerous religious and philosophical tenets (Towsey 2010a: chap. 8; 2010b). Hume was too sceptical to acquiesce to a 'common-sense' approach or view.

Despite his own recognition that he could not fundamentally change his contemporaries' ways of thinking, nevertheless, Hume seems to illustrate the way in which we (only if we are already intelligent, educated and decent to a certain degree) can ameliorate our judgement in his political and historical writings as well as in his aesthetic writings. Certainly Hume admits in some essays on aesthetics that real connoisseurs are and must be limited to 'the company of a few select companions' (E 'Delicacy of Taste' 7), which appears to be consistent with Hume's aloof attitude about the possibility of cultivating the judgement of the common people. However, a close and a little reconstructive reading of these essays can provide us with a hint of the Humean method. This is not a paternalistic approach that aims high-handedly to illuminate the ignorant, but one that hopes to facilitate our improvement of ourselves, while operating within the limits of our capacities. He is far from completely indifferent to the way of improving our own taste and judgement. In these essays he consistently emphasises the importance of 'practice' and 'comparison' (Jones 1976a; 1976b). In the essay 'Of the Delicacy', for example, he opines that '[i]n order to judge aright of a composition of genius, there are so many views to be taken in, so many circumstances to be compared, and such a knowledge of human nature requisite' (E 6). In 'Of the Standard of Taste' he concludes his defence of the universality of the standard of taste as follows: 'Strong sense, united to delicate sentiment, *improved by practice, perfected by comparison*, and cleared of all prejudice, can alone entitle critics to [such] valuable character' as 'a true judge in the finer arts' (241. Italics added). Certainly he mentions here not the speculative sciences or political principles, but what can be called the 'fine arts' such as poetry, music or painting. He sees greater differences in opinion in the 'moral principles, as with speculative opinions of any kind' than in fine arts (246). In the essay 'Of the Rise and Progress', however, the distinction between the arts and sciences becomes more blurred. As we saw in Chapter 7, he asserts here that '[a] noble emulation is the source of every excellence' (135). Mentioning the situation of the ancient Greek republics, he depicts how the 'contention and debates [by various artists and philosophers] sharpened the wits of men' (121). This repeated emphasis on 'practice' and 'comparison' in his aesthetic essays should not be considered to be exclusively for professional critics. Hume also suggests the plausible – although not inevitable – betterment of our taste and judgement through the enjoyment of luxury and conversation in our everyday life: 'The more these refined arts advance, the more sociable men become' (E 'Refinement' 271). Hume also endorses the same vision in the second *Enquiry*, which is written around the same time as the above essay in the *Political Discourses*: 'the more we converse with mankind, and the greater social intercourse we maintain, the more shall we be familiarized to these general preferences and distinctions without which our conversation and discourse could scarcely be rendered intelligible to each other' (EMP 5.42; 228).

Such an interpretive linkage between Hume's aesthetic writings and his social and political ones might evoke Hannah Arendt's reading of Kant's aesthetics; she ingeniously discovers his (or her own) political philosophy in his theory of aesthetic judgement (Arendt 1982). Here I will dwell neither on the validity of Arendt's interpretations, nor on the comparison between the Scottish and German philosophers (on this point, for example, see Guyer 2008). Still, we can consider Hume's aesthetic writings to be as embedded in his overall social philosophy as his other writings. It might be added: despite the wide-ranging differences between Hume and Kant, it is no wonder (and no coincidence) that the latter also acknowledges the significance of sociability (*Geselligkeit*) and humanity (*Humanität*) in his arguments on taste (Kant [1790] 1952: § 41, 60); considering the latter's indebtedness to the former's various essays, as well as to other Scots' aesthetical arguments (see, for example, Kant's mention in *The Contest of Faculties* of a passage of Hume's *Political Discourses* (Kant [1798] 1970: 189–90)).

Obviously Hume's emphasis on practice and comparison does not necessarily neglect the role of philosophy; like other philosophes, he acknowledges its positive role in cultivating our judgement. In the posthumously published essay 'Of Suicide' he emphasises anew the role of 'sound philosophy' as the antidote to superstition and false religions, while seemingly discarding the effectiveness of 'all other remedies':

> Plain good sense and the practice of the world, which alone serve most purposes of life, are here found ineffectual: History, as well as daily experience furnish instances of men endowed with the strongest capacity for business and affairs, who have all their lives crouched under slavery to the grossest superstition. Even gaiety and sweetness of temper, which infuse a balm into every other wound, afford no remedy to so virulent a poison [...] (E 577–8)

It is needless to say that Hume does not attest to the ineffectiveness of the practice of the world, good sense and conversation, but rather verifies that none of them would work by themselves. The same can be said of philosophy (Lemmens 205: 60–1). As he affirms in one of his earliest but later deleted essays, 'Of Essay Writing', one could gain a lot through the mutual active communication between the conversable world and the learned (534–5). His famous phrase, after all, encapsulates this point – 'Be a philosopher; but, amidst all your philosophy, be still a man'. He also rephrases this as follows: 'man is a sociable, no less than a reasonable being' (EHU 1.6; 9). This passage provides further evidence of his characteristic way of thinking, including his reluctance to appeal to any single principle.

Almost no one can claim to have an exhaustive understanding of such a multifaceted and equivocal thinker as David Hume. James Beattie's allegations provide an illustration of how Hume and his philosophy were considered to be riven with contradiction: 'But why is this author's character so replete with inconsistency! why should his principles and his talents extort at once our esteem and detestation, our applause and contempt!' ([1770] 1778, 10–11). By emphasising particular (if not one-sided) aspects of his thought, he could be interpreted as a Moderate, Radical or even Counter-Enlightenment thinker, or as one of the contemporary classifications such as conservative, liberal or utilitarian. At the same time, however, he could be rejected from any of them. Rather than thrusting Hume into any one particular category, it seems more fruitful to comprehend why his social philosophy has been so variously exploited among his contemporaries and later generations, or even by some post-modernists. Hume continues to confound almost all classifications of thought, whether those of his time, those which emerged later to define the period, or even our own present categories of philosophical inquiry. Not despite, but because of this, he seems to represent possibly one of the best starting points from which to open up a dialogue between the extremely divided intellectual camps of today, with their split evaluations of the nature of modernity.

Bibliography

Hume's Manuscripts, Writings, Translations and Unpublished Letters

Hume, David [1745] (1967), *A Letter from a Gentleman to his Friend in Edinburgh*, ed. Ernest C. Mossner and John V. Price, Edinburgh: Edinburgh University Press.

—— [1751] (1997), *The Petition of the Grave and Venerable Bellmen (or Sextons) of the Church of Scotland, to the Hon. House of Commons*, [Ninewells, Berwickshire?], transcribed by M. A. Stewart, 'Hume's 'Bellmen's Petition': The Original Text', *Hume Studies*, 23: 1 (1997), pp. 3–8.

—— [1754] (1970), *The History of Great Britain, Vol. I, Containing the Reigns of James I. and Charles I.*, Edinburgh: Printed by Hamilton, Balfour and Neill, ed. Duncan Forbes, Harmondsworth: Penguin.

—— (1755), *Discours politiques de Monsieur Hume, traduits de l'anglois par Monsieur l'abbé Le Blanc, A Dresde*, 2 vols, Amsterdam; et se vend à Paris: M. Lambert.

—— (1756), *The History of Great Britain, Vol. II, Containing the Commonwealth, and the Reign of Charles II and James II*, London: Printed for A. Millar.

—— (1757), *Four Dissertations* [...], London: Printed for A. Millar.

—— (1760), *Essais de morale, ou Recherches sur les principes de la morale* [trans. by J. B. R. Robinet], Amsterdam: Chez J. H. Schneider.

—— (1764), *Œuvres philosophiques de M. D. Hume. Traduits de l'anglois, Nouvelle édition*, Londres: Chez David Wilson.

—— [1886] (1992), *David Hume: The Philosophical Works*, ed. Thomas Hill Green and Thomas Hodge Grose, 4 vols, New ed., London: Longmans, Green and Co.; Rep. Darmstadt: Scientia Verlag Aalen.

—— (1948) 'Hume's Early Memoranda, 1729–1740: The Complete

Text', ed. Ernest Campbell Mossner, *Journal of the History of Ideas*, 9: 4 (1948), pp. 492–518.
—— (1962), 'New Letters to Lord Elibank, 1748–1776', ed. Ernest Campbell Mossner, *Texas Studies in Literature and Language*, 4 (1962), pp. 431–60.
—— (1970), 'Lettre et Corrections Inédites de David Hume', ed. Jérôme Vercruysse, *Dix-huitième Siècle*, 2 (1970), pp. 33–7.
—— (1991), '"And Time Does Justice to All the World": Ein unveröffentlichter Brief von David Hume an William Strahan', ed. Heiner Klemme, *Journal of the History of Philosophy*, 29: 4 (1991), pp. 657–64.
—— (2012) 'An Historical Essay on Chivalry and Modern Honour', transcribed by E. C. Mossner, *Modern Philology*, 45 (1947), pp. 54–60; transcribed by John P. Wright, Appendix 'Transcription of Hume's "Essay on Chivalry"', to his article 'Hume on the Origin of "Modern Honour": A Study in Hume's Philosophical Development', in Savage (ed.) 2012: 204–9. The page number of the new transcription is given with paragraph numbers of the original text inserted parenthetically.
—— (2014), *Further Letters of David Hume*, ed. Felix Waldmann, Edinburgh: Edinburgh Bibliographical Society.

Primary (Pre-1900) Sources

Addison, Joseph and Richard Steele [1711–12] (1965), *The Spectator*, ed. Donald Frederic Bond, 5 vols, Oxford: Clarendon Press.
Allen, John (1814), Review of *Teoria de las Cortes* [...], *Edinburgh Review*, 23: 46 (Sept. 1814), pp. 347–84.
—— [1825] (2002), Review of *A History of England* by John Lingard, *Edinburgh Review*, 42: 85 (April 1825), pp. 1–31, Rep. in Fieser (ed.) 2002: II, 295–300.
Anon. (1741 or 42), 'Remarks on Essays, Moral and Political', transcribed by James Fieser, in Fieser (ed.) 1999: II, 1–8.
Anon. (1752), Review of *Political Discourses* by David Hume Esq. [...], in Matthieu Maty and M. de Mauves (eds), *Journal Britannique*, 7 (March 1752), pp. 243–67.
Anon. (c.1752), *The Quintessence of Modern Philosophy Extracted from Ten Late Essays, and Intended to Show* [...], [Edinburgh]: n. p.
Anon. [1755] (2002), Review of *The History of Great Britain*, vol. 1, in *Göttingische Anzeigen von gelehrten Sachen* (8 Dec. 1755), pp. 1350–4, Rep. in Fieser (ed.) 2002: I, 22–5.

Anon. [1771] (1803), *A Review of an Essay on the Nature and Immutability of Truth* [...], *The Annual Register*, 6th edn, London: Printed (by assignment of the executors of the late Mr. James Dodsley) for W. Otridge and Son, pp. 252–60.

Anon. [1776] (1788), 'An Account of the Life and Writings of the Late David Hume, Esq., as given to the World in one of the periodical publications', *The Annual Register*, London: Printed for J. Dodsley, pp. 27–33, reproduced in Fieser 1995.

Anon. (c.1778), *A Discourse on the Impressing of Mariners* [...], London: Printed for T. Cadell.

Anon. [1792] (1799), 'Explanation of New Terms', *The Annual Register*, 34 (1792), London: Printed for W. Otridge & Son [...], pp. xi–xvi.

Anon. (1795), *The Manual of Liberty, or Testimonies in Behalf of the Rights of Mankind* [...], London: Printed for H. D. Symonds.

Anon. (1798), 'The Rise, Progress, Effects of Jacobinism', *The Anti-Jacobin Review and Magazine, or, Monthly Politique and Literary Censor*, 1 (1798), pp. 712–18.

Anon. [1798] (1806), 'Criticism of the Historians of England: from Coote's *History of England*', *The Annual Register*, 40 (1798) 2nd edn, London: Printed by R. Wilks, pp. 432–3.

Anon. [1800] (1801), 'History of Europe', *The Annual Register*, 42 (1800), London: Printed by T. Burton, pp. 41–65.

Anon. (1805), Review of *The Society of Friends Examined* [...], *The Annual Review and History of Literature*, 4 (Jan. 1805), pp. 713–17.

Anon. [1816] (2002), 'Coincidences. Hume and Dryden', *The Port Folio*, vol. 2 [series 5] (1816), p. 126, Rep. in Spencer (ed.) 2002: II, 79.

Anon. [1822] (2000), *Quarterly Review*, 26 (1822), pp. 512–13; Rep. in Fieser (ed.) 2000: II, 161.

Anon. (1827), 'Dr. Lingard and the Edinburgh Review', *The London Magazine*, 7: 27 (Mar. 1827), pp. 421–9.

Anon. (1828), Review of *The Constitutional History of England* [...], by Henry Hallam, *Quarterly Review*, 37: 73 (Jan. 1828), pp. 194–260.

B-de, Monsieur (1790), *Reflections on the Causes and Probable Consequences of the Late Revolution in France* [...] *by Mons. B–De*, Dublin: Printed for William Porter.

Balfour, James (1753), *A Delineation of the Nature and Obligation of Morality* [...], Edinburgh: Printed for Hamilton and Balfour.

Barbon, Nicholas [1690] (1905), *A Discourse of Trade*, Rep. Baltimore: Johns Hopkins University Press.

Bayle, Pierre [1682] (2000), *Various Thoughts on the Occasion of a Comet*, trans. with notes and an interpretive essay by Robert C. Bartlett, Albany: State University of New York Press.

—— [1697] (1965), *Historical and Critical Dictionary: Selections*, ed. and trans. Richard H. Popkin, Indianapolis: Bobbs-Merrill.

Beattie, James [1770] (1778), *Essay on the Nature and Immutability of Truth* [...], 6th edn, corrected, London: Printed for Edward and Charles Dilly.

—— (1783), *Dissertations Moral and Critical*, 2 vols, Dublin: Printed for Mess. Exshaw, Walker, Beatty, White, Byrne, Cash and M'Kenzie.

—— (1948/2003), 'Beattie's "The Castle of Scepticism": An Unpublished Allegory against Hume, Voltaire, and Hobbes', ed. Ernest Campbell Mossner, *Studies in English*, 27 (1948), pp. 108–45; newly transcribed in Fieser (ed.) 2003: I, 178–97.

Bentham, Jeremy [1776] (1962), *Fragment on Government* [...], in *The Works of Jeremy Bentham*, ed. John Bowring, 11 vols, New York: Russell & Russell, vol. 1, pp. 221–95.

—— [1803] (1962), 'A Plea for the Constitution shewing the Enormities committed, to the Oppression of British subjects, innocent as well as guilty [...]', in J. Bentham, *Works*, vol. 4, pp. 249–84.

Berkeley, George [1732] (1993), *Alciphron, or the Minute Philosopher*, in *Alciphron, or the Minute Philosopher: in Focus*, ed. David Berman, London: Routledge.

Bisset, Robert (1800), *The Life of Edmund Burk* [...], 2 vols, London: Printed by George Cawthorn.

Bonar, John [1755] (2003), *An Analysis of the Moral and Religious Sentiments contained in the Writings of Sopho, and David Hume, Esq.* [...], Edinburgh: n. p., Rep. in James Fieser (ed.) 2003: I, 41–2.

Boswell, James (1993), *Laird of Auchinleck, 1778–1782*, ed. Joseph W. Reed and Frederick Albert Pottle, Edinburgh: Edinburgh University Press.

Brougham, Henry Peter (1816), Review of *Reflections on the Progressive Decline of the British Empire* [...], by H. Schultes, and *Liberty, Civil and Religious*, by a Friend to Both, *The Edinburgh Review*, 27: 53 (Sept. 1816), pp. 245–63.

Brown, John (1757–8), *An Estimate of the Manners and Principles of the Times*, 6th edn, 2 vols, London: Printed for L. Davis and C. Reymers.

—— (1765), *Thoughts on Civil Liberty, on Licentiousness, and Faction* [...], 2nd ed., London: Printed for L. Davis and C. Reymers.

Burgh, James (1766–7), *Crito or Essays on Various Subjects*, 2 vols, London: Printed for Dodsley, Becket and De Hondt, White, Payne and Cooke.

—— (1774–5), *Political Disquisitions or, an Enquiry into Public Errors, Defects, and Abuses* [...], 3 vols, Philadelphia: Printed and sold by Robert Bell.

[Burke, Edmund] [1761] (1800), Review of *The History of England, from the Invasion of Jurius Caesar to the Accession of Henry VII* [...], *The Annual Register*, London: Printed for J. D. Dewick, pp. 301–4.

Burke, Edmund [1790] (2014), 'Reflections on the Revolution in France', in *Revolutionary Writings: Reflections on the Revolution in France and the First Letter on a Regicide Peace*, ed. Iain Hampsher-Monk, Cambridge: Cambridge University Press, pp. 1–250.

—— [1791] (1992), 'An Appeal from the New to the Old Whigs', in *Further Reflections on the Revolution in France*, ed. Daniel L. Ritchie, Indianapolis: Liberty Fund, pp. 73–201.

—— (1797), *Three Memorials on French Affairs. Written in the Years 1791, 1792 and 1793*, London: Printed for F. and C. Rivingston.

Burton, John Hill (ed.) (1849), *Letters of Eminent Persons Addressed to David Hume*, Edinburgh; London: William Blackwood and Sons.

Burton, Robert [1621] (2001), *The Anatomy of Melancholy*, ed. and with an introduction by Holbrook Jackson, and with a new introduction by William H. Gass, New York: New York Review Books.

Carlyle, Alexander [1860/1910] (1990), *The Autobiography of Dr. Alexander Carlyle of Inveresk 1722–1805*, ed. John Hill Burton, Rep. with a new introduction by Richard B. Sher, Bristol: Thoemmes Continuum.

Carlyle, Thomas [1843] (2005), *Past and Present*, in T. Carlyle, *Norman and Charlotte Strouse Edition of the Writings of Thomas Carlyle*, introduction and notes by Chris R. Vanden Bossche; text established by Chris R. Vanden Bossche, Joel J. Brattin and D. J. Trela, 4 vols, Berkeley: University of California Press, vol. 4.

—— [1881] (2012), *Reminiscences*, ed. James Anthony Froude, 2 vols, Cambridge: Cambridge University Press.

Cartwright, F. D. (ed.) [1826] (1969), *The Life and Correspondence of Major Cartwright*, Rep. 2 vols, New York: M. Kelly.

Chalmers, James (1776), *Plain Truth: Addressed to the Inhabitants of America* [...], 2nd edn, Philadelphia; Dublin: Rep. by M. Mills.

Chandler, Samuel (1735–38), *The Old Whig: or, The Consistent Protestant*, No. 1–160, London: Sold by J[ames]. Roberts.

Cicero (1991), *On Duties*, ed. E. M. Atkins and M. T. Griffin, and trans. by M. T. Griffin, Cambridge: Cambridge University Press.

Coleridge, Samuel Taylor [1799] (1978–2001), 'Advice to the Friends of Freedom' in *The Morning Post*, 12 Dec. 1799, *Essays on his Times*

in *The Morning Post and The Courier*, ed. David V. Erdman, 3 vols, in S. T. Coleridge, *Collected Works*, 16 vols, Princeton: Princeton University Press, vol. 3 (vol. 1 in 3 vols), pp. 37–40.
—— [1809] (1978–2001), 'Letters on the Spaniards: Letter VII' in *The Courier*, 22 Dec. 1809, *Essays on his Times*, in *Collected Works*, vol. 3 (vol. 2 in 3 vols), pp. 79–85.
—— [1812] (1978–2001), 'A Modest Proposal for Abolishing the Church of England' in *The Courier*, 1 April 1812, *Essays on his Times*, in *Collected Works*, vol. 3 (vol. 2 in 3 vols), pp. 341–7.
—— [1816] (1978–2001), 'The Statesman's Manual', *Lay Sermons*, ed. R. J. White, in *Collected Works*, vol. 6, pp. 3–114.
—— [1817] (1978–2001), *Biographia Literaria or Biographical Sketches of My Literary Life and Opinions*, ed. James Engell and W. Jackson Bate, 2 vols, in *Collected Works*, vol. 7 (2 vols).
—— (1956), *Collected Letters of Samuel Taylor Coleridge*, ed. Earl Leslie Griggs, 6 vols, Oxford: Clarendon Press.
Comber, Thomas (1758), *Vindication of the Great Revolution in England*, London: Printed for J. Robinson.
—— (1978–2001), *Table Talk*, recorded by Henry Nelson Coleridge (and John Taylor Coleridge), ed. Carl Woodring, 2 vols, in *Collected Works*, vol. 14.
Condillac, Étienne Bonnot de [1746] (1756), *An Essay on the Origin of Human Knowledge* [...], London: Printed for J. Nourse.
—— [1755] (1766), *Traité des animaux* [...], Amsterdam: Chez Ch. Ant. Jombert.
Condorcet, Marie-Jean-Antoine-Nicolas de Caritat, marquis de [1795] (2012), 'The Sketch', in *Condorcet: Political Writings*, ed. Steven Lukes and Nadia Urbinati, Cambridge: Cambridge University Press.
Copinger, W. A. (1895), *On the Authorship of the First Hundred Numbers of the "Edinburgh Review"*, Manchester: Privately Printed.
Dennis, John (1711), *An Essay upon Publick Spirit* [...], London: Printed for Bernard Lintott.
Descartes, René [1641] (2008), *Meditations on First Philosophy: With Selections from the Objections and Replies*, trans. by Michael Moriarty, Oxford: Oxford University Press.
—— [1649] (1989), *The Passions of the Soul*, trans. by Stephen H. Voss, Indianapolis: Hackett Publishing Co.
Dickinson, John (1768), *Letters, from a Farmer in Pennsylvania, to the Inhabitants of the British Colonies* [...], Dublin: Printed for J. Sheppard.
Dubos, Jean-Baptiste, abbé [1719] (1748), *Critical Reflections on Poetry*

and Painting, trans. by Thomas Nugent, 2 vols, London: Printed for John Nourse.

Engels, Friedrich [1880] (1920), *Socialism, Utopian and Scientific*, trans. by Edward Aveling, 5th edn, London: George Allen & Unwin.

Epicurus (1994), *The Epicurus Reader: Selected Writings and Testimonia*, trans. and ed. Brad Inwood and L. P. Gerson, with introduction by D. S. Hutchinson, Indianapolis: Hackett Publishing Co.

Ferguson, Adam [1767] (1995), *An Essay on the History of Civil Society*, ed. Fania Oz-Salzberger, Cambridge: Cambridge University Press.

—— (1776), *Remarks on a Pamphlet Lately Published by Dr. Price* [...], London: Printed for T. Cadell.

—— (1783), *The History of the Progress and Termination of the Roman Republic*, 3 vols, London: Printed for W. Strahan; T. Cadell; W. Creech.

—— (1792), *Principles of Moral and Political Science* [...], 2 vols, Edinburgh: W. Creech.

Filmer, Robert [1680] (1949), *Political Discourses, viz. Patriarcha, or the Natural Power of Kings*, in *Patriarcha and Other Political Writings of Sir Robert Filmer*, ed. Peter Laslett, Oxford: Basil Blackwell.

Fletcher, Andrew (1997), *Political Works*, ed. John Robertson, Cambridge: Cambridge University Press.

Fontenelle, Bernard Le Bovier de [1688] (1742), 'Digression sur les Anciens et les Modernes', in *Œuvres de Monsieur de Fontenelle: Nouvelle édition augmentée*, 6 vols, Paris: Chez M. Brunet, vol. 4, pp. 170–200.

Garden, Francis [1791] (2002), *Miscellanies in Prose and Verse*, Edinburgh: Printed by J. Robertson, Rep. in Fieser (ed.) 2002: II, 193–200.

Gerard, Alexander [1760] (1762), *The Influence of the Pastoral Office on the Character Examined* [...], 2nd edn, London: Printed for A. Millar.

Gibbon, Edward (1961), *The Autobiography of Edward Gibbon*, with an introduction by Dero A. Saunders, New York: Meridian Books.

Godwin, William [1793] (1993), *An Enquiry concerning Political Justice*, ed. Mark Philp; researcher, Austin Gee, in *Political and Philosophical Writings of William Godwin*, general editor, Mark Philp, 7 vols, London: Pickering and Chatto, vol. 3.

—— [1795] (1993), *Considerations on Lord Grenville's and Mr. Pitt's bills,* [...], in *Political and Philosophical Writings*, vol. 2 (vol. 1 in 2 vols), pp. 125–62.

—— [1801] (1993), 'Thoughts occasioned by the Perusal of Dr. Parr's

Spital Sermon [...]', in *Political and Philosophical Writings*, vol. 2 (vol. 1 in 2 vols), pp. 165–208.
—— (1993), *An Enquiry concerning Political Justice Variants*, ed. Mark Philp, in the *Political and Philosophical Writings*, vol. 4.
Goldsmith, Oliver [1771] (2002), *History of England, from the Earliest Times to the Death of George II*, 4 vols, London: printed for T. Davies, Rep. in Fieser (ed.) 2002: I, 343–4.
Gurney, Joseph (1793), *The Whole Proceedings on the Trial of an Information exhibited* ex Officio *by the King's Attorney-General against Thomas Paine* [...], *taken in short-hand by Joseph Gurney*, 2nd edn, London: Sold by Martha Gurney.
Hardy, Francis (1812), *Memoirs of the Political and Private Life of James Chaufield, Earle of Charlemont*, 2nd edn, 2 vols, London: Printed for T. Cadell and W. Davies.
Harrington, James [1656] (1992), *The Commonwealth of Oceana and a System of Politics*, ed. J. G. A. Pocock, Cambridge: Cambridge University Press.
Harris, Joseph [1757–8] (1970), *An Essay upon Money and Coins*, Part 1, Rep. New York: Johnson Reprint Corp.
Hartley, David (1749), *Observations on Man, his Frame, his Duty, and his Expectations*, 2 vols, London: Printed by S. Richardson.
Hazlitt, William [1813] (1930–4), *Lectures on English Philosophy*, in *The Complete Works of William Hazlitt*, ed. P. P. Howe, after the edition of A. R. Waller and Arnold Glover, 21 vols, London: Dent, vol. 2, pp. 121–284.
—— [1821] (1930–4), 'Guy Faux', *Miscellaneous Writings*, in *Complete Works*, vol. 20, pp. 96–112.
Hegel, Georg Wilhelm Friedrich [1837] (1980), *Lectures on the Philosophy of World History*, with introduction by Duncan Forbes, trans. by Hugh Barr Nisbet, Cambridge: Cambridge University Press.
Helvétius, Claude-Adrien (1777), *A Treatise on Man, his Intellectual Faculties and his Education. A Posthumous work of M. Helvétius* [...], trans. by W. Hooper, 2 vols, London: Printed for B. Law and G. Robinson.
—— (1781), *Œuvres complètes de M. Helvétius. Nouvelle édition* [...], 2 vols, Londres: n. p.
Hobbes, Thomas [1640] (1969), *The Elements of Law, Natural and Politic*, ed. Ferdinand Tönnies, 2nd edn, with introduction by M. M. Goldsmith, New York: Barnes & Noble.
—— [1642] (1997), *On the Citizen* (*De Cive*), ed. Richard Tuck and

trans. by Michael Silverthorne, Cambridge: Cambridge University Press.

—— [1651] (1996), *Leviathan*, ed. Richard Tuck, Cambridge: Cambridge University Press.

Holbach, Paul-Henri Thiry, baron d' (1766), *Le Christianisme dévoilé, ou examen des principes et des effets de la religion chrétienne* [...], A Londres [i.e. Nancy]: n. p.

—— (1768), *La Contagion sacrée, ou histoire naturelle de la superstition* [...], 2 vols, Londres [Amsterdam?]: n. p.

—— (1795), *Christianity Unveiled; being, an Examination of the Principles and Effects of the Christian Religion*, New York: Printed at the Columbian Press.

Home, John (1757), *Douglas a Tragedy*, Belfast: Printed by and for James Magee.

—— (1976), *A Sketch of the Character of Mr. Hume and Diary of a Journey from Morpeth to Bath 23 April–May 1776*, ed. David Fate Norton, Edinburgh: The Tragara Press.

Hooker, Richard [1593, 1597, 1662] (1989), *Of the Laws of Ecclesiastical Polity*, ed. Arthur Stephen McGrade, Cambridge: Cambridge University Press.

Horne, George (1786), *Letters on Infidelity. The 2nd ed. To which is prefixed a letter to Dr. Adam Smith*, Oxford: Clarendon Press.

Hurd, Richard [1759] (2002), *Moral and Political Dialogues*, Rep. in Fieser (ed.) 2002: I, 175–80.

Hutcheson, Francis [1725] (1990), *An Inquiry into the Original of Our Ideas of Beauty and Virtue* [...], Rep. in *Collected Works of Francis Hutcheson*, 7 vols, Hildesheim: Georg Olms, vol. 1.

—— [1726] (1997), *Letters to the Dublin Journal*, 4 February 1726, Rep. in Stafford (ed.) 1997: 383–407.

—— [1728] (1990), *An Essay on the Nature and Conduct of the Passions and Affectations*, Rep. in *Collected Works*, vol. 2.

—— [1755] (1990), *A System of Moral Philosophy*, 2 vols, in *Collected Works*, vols 5 and 6.

Jeffrey, Francis (1808), Review of *A History of the Early Part of the Reign of James the Second*, *Edinburgh Review*, 12: 24 (Jul. 1808), pp. 276–7.

—— (1824), Review of *A History of the British Empire, from the Accession of Charles I. to the Restoration*, *Edinburgh Review*, 40: 79 (Mar. 1824), pp. 92–146.

Kames, Lord (Henry Home) (1747), *Essays upon Several Subjects concerning British Antiquities*, Edinburgh: Printed for A. Kincaid.

King, William (1731), *An Essay on the Origin of Evil* [...] *translated from the Latin*, London: Printed for W. Thurlbourn.

Lamb, Charles (1968), *The Letters of Charles Lamb to which are added those of his Sister Mary Lamb*, ed. E. V. Lucas, 3 vols, New York: AMS Press.

Law, Edmund (ed.) (1777), *The Works of John Locke*, 8th edn, 4 vols, London: Printed for W. Strahan.

Locke, John [1689/90] (1975), *An Essay concerning Human Understanding*, ed. with an introduction by Peter H. Nidditch, Oxford: Clarendon Press.

—— [1690] (1988), *Two Treatises of Government* [...], ed. Peter Laslett, Cambridge: Cambridge University Press.

—— [1693] (1996), *Some Thoughts Concerning Education*, in *Some Thoughts Concerning Education; and, Of the Conduct of the Understanding*, ed. with introduction by Ruth W. Grant and Nathan Tarcov, Indianapolis: Hackett Publishing Co., pp. 1–161.

—— [1697] (1996), 'Of the Conduct of the Understanding', in *Some Thoughts Concerning Education; and, Of the Conduct of the Understanding*, 163–227.

—— (1967), *Two Tracts on Government*, ed. with an introduction, notes and trans. by Philip Abrams, Cambridge: Cambridge University Press.

Lockhart, John Gibson (1819), *Peter's Letters to his Kinsfolk*, 2nd edn, 2 vols, Edinburgh: Printed for William Blackwood.

Lucretius (1997), *On the Nature of the Universe*, trans. by Sir Ronald Melville, with introduction and explanatory notes by Don and Peter Fowler, Oxford: Clarendon Press.

McCosh, James (1875), *Biographical, Expository, Critical from Hutcheson to Hamilton*, New York: Robert Carter and Brothers.

Machiavelli, Niccolò [1531] (1997), *Discourses on Livy*, trans. by Julia Conaway Bondanella and Peter Bondanella, Oxford: Oxford University Press.

Mackintosh, James [1791] (2006), *Vindiciae Gallicae* [...], in *Vindiciae Gallicae and Other Writings on the French Revolution*, ed. Donald Winch, Indianapolis: Liberty Fund, pp. 1–165.

—— (1818), Review of *Plan of Parliamentary Reform, in the Form of a Catechism*, *Edinburgh Review*, 31: 61 (Dec. 1818), pp. 165–203.

—— (1821), 'A General View of the Progress of Metaphysical, Ethical, and Political Science', *Edinburgh Review*, 36: 71 (Oct. 1821), pp. 220–67.

—— [1830] (1846), 'Dissertation on the Progress of Ethical Philosophy', *The Miscellaneous Works of the Right Honourable Sir James*

Mackintosh, 3 vols, London: Longman, Brown, Green and Longmans, vol. 1, pp. 1–314.

—— (1835), *Memoirs of the Life of the Right Honourable Sir James Mackintosh*, ed. by Robert James Mackintosh, 2 vols, London: Edward Moxon.

MacQueen, Daniel [1756] (2002), *Letters on Mr. Hume's History of Great Britain*, Edinburgh: Printed by Sands, Donaldson, Murray and Cochran. For A. Kincaid and A. Donaldson, Rep. in Fieser (ed.) 2002: I, 34–145.

Malebranche, Nicolas [1674–5] (1997), *The Search after Truth*, trans. and ed. Thomas M. Lennon and Paul J. Olscamp, Cambridge: Cambridge University Press.

Mandeville, Bernard [1714/1729, 1732] (1988), *The Fable of the Bees or Private Vices, Publick Benefits*, with a commentary by F. B. Kaye, 2 vols, Indianapolis: Liberty Fund.

—— [1720] (1729), *Free Thoughts on Religion, the Church, and National Happiness*, 2nd edn, London: Printed for John Brotherton.

May, Sir Thomas Erskine [1871] (1912), *The Constitutional History of England Since the Accession of George the Third: 1760-1860*, New ed., 3 vols, London: Longmans Green and Co.

Melon, Jean-François (1734), *Essai politique sur le commerce*, [Amsterdam], n. p.

—— (1738), *A Political Essay upon Commerce* [...], trans. by David Bindon, Dublin: Printed for Philip Crampton.

[Mill, James] (1811), Review of *Memoires de Candide, sur la liberté de la presse* [...], *Edinburgh Review*, 18: 35 (May 1811), pp. 98–123.

Mill, James [c. 1828] (1992), 'Education', rep. in *Jame Mill: Political Writings*, ed. by Terence Ball, Cambridge: Cambridge University Press, pp. 137–94.

Mill, John Stuart [1824a] (1963–91), 'Periodical Literature: Edinburgh Review' [originally published in *The Westminster Review*, 1 (April, 1824), pp. 504–41], *Autobiography and Literary Essays*, ed. John M. Robson and Jack Stillinger, with introduction by Lord Robbins, in *Collected Works of John Stuart Mill*, 33 vols, vol. 1, pp. 291–325.

—— [1824b] (1963–91), 'Brodie's History of the British Empire' [originally published in *The Westminster Review*, 2 (Oct. 1824), pp. 346–402], *Essays on England, Ireland, and the Empire*, ed. John M. Robson, Introduction by Joseph Hamburger, in *Collected Works*, vol. 6, pp. 1–58.

—— [1828] (1963–91), '25. Church' (15 February, 1828), *Journals and*

Debating Speeches Part I, ed. John M. Robson, in *Collected Works*, vol. 26, pp. 418–27.

—— [1837] (1963–91), 'Carlyle's French Revolution' [originally published in *The London and Westminster Review*, 5 & 27 (July 1837), pp. 17–53], *Essays on French History and Historians*, ed. John M. Robson, with introduction by John C. Cairns, in *Collected Works*, vol. 20, pp. 131–66.

—— [1838] (1963–91), 'Bentham', *Essays on Ethics, Religion and Society*, ed. John M. Robson, with introduction by F. E. L. Priestley, in J. S. Mill, *Collected Works*, 33 vols, Toronto: University of Toronto Press, vol. 10, pp. 75–85.

—— [1865] (1963–91), *An Examination of Sir William Hamilton's Philosophy and of the Principal Philosophical Questions discussed in his Writings*, ed. John M. Robson, with introduction by Alan Ryan, in *Collected Works*, vol. 9.

—— [1873] (1963–91), *Autobiography*, in *Collected Works*, vol. 1, pp. 1–290.

Millar, John (1771), *Observations concerning the Distinction of Ranks in Society*, London: Printed by W. and J. Richardson.

Milton, John [1660] (1993), 'The Readie & Easie Way to Establish a Free Commonwealth', in *The Works of John Milton*, 18 vols, New York: Columbia University Press, Rep. Tokyo, Hon-no-Tomosha, vol. 6, pp. 111–49.

Mirabeau, Victor de Riqueti, marquis de (1756–60), *L'Ami des hommes*, 4 vols, Avignon: n. p.

Monboddo, Lord (James Burnett) (1773–92), *Antient Metaphysics or, the Science of Universals*, 6 vols, London: Printed for T. Cadell.

Montesquieu, Charles-Louis de Secondat, baron de [1721] (1730), *Persian letters*, trans. by Mr. Ozell, 2 vols, London: Printed for J. Tonson.

—— [1734] (1949–51), *Considérations sur les causes de la grandeur des Romains et de leur décadence*, in *Œuvres complètes de Montesquieu*, ed. Roger Caillois, Nouv. éd., 2 vols, Paris: Gallimard, Bibliothèque de la Pléiade, vol. 2, pp. 69–209.

—— [1734] (1999), *Considerations on the Causes of the Greatness of the Romans and Their Decline*, trans. with introduction and notes, by David Lowenthal, Indianapolis: Hackett Publishing Co.

—— [1748] (1989), *The Spirit of the Laws*, trans. and ed. A. M. Cohler, Basia C. Miller and Harold S. Stone, Cambridge: Cambridge University Press.

—— [1750] (1777), *A Defence of the Spirit of Laws, To which are*

added, some explanations, in *Complete Works of Montesquieu*, 4 vols, London: Printed for T. Evans, vol. 4, pp. 219–81.
—— (1949–51), *Mes pensées*, in *Œuvres complètes*, vol. 1, pp. 973–1574.
—— (2012), *My Thoughts (Mes Pensées)*, trans., ed., and with an Introduction by Henry C. Clark, Indianapolis: Liberty Fund.
Moyle, Walter [1723] (1969), *An Essay upon the Constitution of the Roman Government*, Rep. in *Two English Republican Tracts*, ed. Caroline Robbins, Cambridge: Cambridge University Press.
Mun, Thomas [1664] (1967), *England's Treasure by Forraign Trade*, Rep. Oxford: Blackwell.
Paine, Thomas (1776), *Common Sense; with the Whole Appendix the Address to the Quakers also, the Large Additions* [...], Philadelphia: Printed by R. Bell.
—— (1796), *The Decline and Fall of the English System of Finance*, Paris: Printed by Hartley, Adlard and Son.
[Pearne, Thomas] (1790), Review of *Mr. Burke's Reflections on the Revolution in France*, *Monthly Review*, 3 (Dec. 1790), pp. 438–65.
Philips, Ambrose (ed.) (1740), *The Free-thinker or, Essays of Wit and Humour* [...], 3rd edn, 3 vols, London: Printed for J. Hinton.
Price, Richard (1772), *An Appeal to the Public, on the Subject of the National Debt*, 2nd edn, London: Printed for T. Cadell.
—— (1773), *Observations on Reversionary Payments on Schemes for Providing Annuities for Widows* [...], London: Printed for T. Cadell.
—— (1777), *Additional Observations on the Nature and Value of Civil Liberty* [...], London: Printed for T. Cadell.
Priestley, Joseph (1771), 'An Essay on the Analogy there is between the Methods by which the Perfection and Happiness of Men are promoted, according to the Dispensations of Natural and Revealed Religion', *The Theological Repository; consisting of Original Essays, Hints, Queries, &c. calculated to promote Religious Knowledge*, 3 (1771), pp. 4–31.
—— (1775), *Hartley's Theory of the Human Mind on the Principle of the Association of Ideas* [...], London: Printed for J. Johnson.
—— (1785), *An Examination of Dr. Reid's Inquiry into the Human Mind on the Principles of Common Sense* [...], 2nd edn, London: Printed for J. Johnson.
Rapin-Thoyras, Paul de (1711), *Dissertation sur les Whigs & les Torys, or an Historical Dissertation upon Whig and Tory*, trans. by Mr. Ozell, London: Printed for E. Curll.
Raynal, Guillaume-Thomas-François, abbé [and Denis Diderot] (1780), *Histoire philosophique et politique des établissements et du commerce des Euoropéens dans les deux Indes*, 10 vols, Genève: Chez Berry.

Reid, Thomas [1965] (1997), 'Unpublished Letters of Thomas Reid to Lord Kames, 1762–82', ed. Ian S. Ross, *Texas Studies in Literature and Language*, 7: 1 (1965), pp. 17–65, Rep. in Reeder (ed.), *On Moral Sentiments: Contemporary Responses to Adam Smith*, Bristol: Thoemmes Press, pp. 65–8.

—— [1984] (1997), 'A Sketch of Dr Smith's Theory of Morals', transcribed in J. C. Stewart-Robertson and David Fate Norton, 'Thomas Reid on Adam Smith's Theory of Morals', *Journal of the History of Ideas*, 45: 2 (1984), pp. 310–21, Rep. in John Reeder (ed.), *On Moral Sentiments*, pp. 69–88.

Rich, Henry (1826), Review of *Charte Constitutionelle de Portugal*, *Edinburgh Review*, 54: 89 (Dec. 1826), pp. 199–247.

Ritchie, Thomas Edward (1807), *An Account of the Life and Writings of David Hume*, London: Printed for T. Cadell and W. Davies.

Robertson, William [1769] (1972), *The Progress of Society in Europe: a Historical Outline from the Subversion of the Roman Empire to the Beginning of the Sixteenth Century* (The first section of the author's *History of the Reign of the Emperor Charles V*), ed. Felix Gilbert, Chicago: University of Chicago Press.

Rousseau, Jean-Jacques [1755] (1997), *Discourse on the Origin and Foundations of Inequality Among Men* or *Second Discourse*, in *Rousseau: The Discourses and Other Early Political Writings*, ed. Victor Gourevitch, Cambridge: Cambridge University Press.

—— [1762] (1990–2010), *Emile or On Education: Includes Emile and Sophie, or the Solitaires*, trans. and ed. Christopher Kelly and Allan Bloom, in J. J. Rousseau, *Collected Writings of Rousseau*, 12 vols, Hanover, NH: Published for Dartmouth College by University Press of New England, vol. 13.

—— [1762] (1997), *The Social Contract*, in *The Social Contract and Other Later Political Writings*, ed. Victor Gourevitch, Cambridge: Cambridge University Press.

—— [1782] (1990–2010), *The Confessions*, ed. Roger D. Masters and Christopher Kelly, in *Collected Writings*, vol. 5.

—— [1782] (1997), *Considerations on the Government of Poland*, in *The Social Contract and Other Later Political Writings*, pp. 177–260.

Saint-Évremond, Charles de Marguetel de Saint-Denis, seigneur de (1714), *The Works of Monsieur de St. Evremond* [sic], *made English from the French original. With the author's life, by Mr. des Maizeaux* [...], 3 vols, London: Printed for J. Churchill, J. Darby, J. Round, E. Curll, R. Gosling and T. Baker.

Saint-Lambert, Jean François, marquis de [1764] (1965), 'Luxury', Diderot, D'Alembert (et al.), *Encyclopedia: Selections*, trans. by Nelly S. Hoyt and Thomas Cassirer, Indianapolis: Bobbs-Merrill, pp. 203–32.

—— (1797–1801), *Analyse de l'homme et de la femme* [...], in *Œuvres philosophiques de Saint-Lambert*, 6 vols, Paris: Chez H. Agasse, vol. 1.

Sextus Empiricus (1994), *The Outlines of Scepticism*, trans. by Julia Annas and Jonathan Barnes, Cambridge: Cambridge University Press.

Shaftesbury, the third earl of (Anthony Ashley Cooper) [1711] (1999), *Characteristics of Men, Manners, Opinions, Times*, ed. Lawrence E. Klein, Cambridge: Cambridge University Press.

—— (1900), *The Life, Unpublished Letters, and Philosophical Regimen of Anthony, Earl of Shaftesbury*, ed. Benjamin Rand, London: S. Sonnenschein & Co, Rep. New York: Macmillan.

Smith, Adam [1756] (1982), 'A Letter to the Authors of the *Edinburgh Review*', in *Essays on Philosophical Subjects*, ed. W. P. D. Wightman and J. C. Bryce, in *The Glasgow Edition of the Works and Correspondence of Adam Smith*, 7 vols, Indianapolis: Liberty Fund, vol. 3.

—— [1759] (1982), *The Theory of Moral Sentiments*, ed. A. L. Macfie and D. D. Raphael, in *Works and Correspondence*, vol. 1.

—— [1776] (1982), *An Inquiry into the Nature and Causes of the Wealth of Nations*, ed. Roy Hutcheson Campbell and Andrew S. Skinner; textual editor William B. Todd, 2 vols, in *Works and Correspondence*, vol. 2.

—— (1777), 'Letter from Adam Smith, LL.D. to William Strahan, Esq.' appended to *The Life of David Hume, Esq. Written by himself*, London: Printed for W. Strahan, pp. 37–62.

—— (1982a), *Lectures on Jurisprudence*, ed. R. L. Meek, D. D. Raphael and P. G. Stein, in *Works and Correspondence*, vol. 5.

—— (1982b), *The Correspondence of Adam Smith*, ed. Ernest Campbell Mossner and Ian Simpson Ross, in *Works and Correspondence*, vol. 6.

[Smith, Adam, Thomas Sherlock and Alexander Gordon] [1755–6] (1818), *The Edinburgh Review for the Year 1755*, 2nd edn with a preface and explanatory notes, Edinburgh: Printed by Richard and Arthur Taylor.

Smith, Charles (1758), *A Short Essay on the Corn Trade and Corn Laws* [. . .], Edinburgh: n. p.

Spinoza, Benedict de [1670] (2007), *Theological-Political Treatise*, ed. Jonathan Israel, trans. by Michael Silverthorne and Jonathan Israel, Cambridge: Cambridge University Press.

—— [1677a] (1955), *The Ethics*, in *On the Improvement of the Understanding, The Ethics, Correspondence*, trans. from the Latin with an Introduction by R. H. M. Elwes, New York: Dover Publication, pp. 43–271.

—— [1677b] (1955), *On the Improvement of the Understanding*, in *On the Improvement of the Understanding, The Ethics, Correspondence*, pp. 1–41.

Stephen, Leslie (1876), *History of English Thought in the Eighteenth Century*, 2 vols, London: Smith, Elder & Co.

—— (1900), *The English Utilitarians*, 3 vols, London: Duckworth and Co.

Stewart, Dugald [1792–1827] (1854–60, 1994), *Elements of the Philosophy of the Human Mind*, 3 vols, in D. Stewart, *Collected Works*, ed. Sir W. Hamilton, Edinburgh, Rep., Bristol: Thoemmes Press, vol. 2.

—— [1821] (2000), *Dissertation on the Progress of Philosophy*, Part 2, supplemental volumes to the 1821 edition of the *Encyclopædia Britannica*, Rep. in Fieser (ed.) 2000: II, 162–81.

Swift, Jonathan [1726] (2012), *Gulliver's Travels*, ed. David Womersley, in *The Cambridge Edition of the Works of Jonathan Swift*, 18 vols, Cambridge: Cambridge University Press, vol. 16.

—— [1730] (1778), 'Of Publick Absurdities in England', in *The Works of Jonathan Swift* [...], 18 vols, Edinburgh: Printed for W. Johnston, vol. 11.

Temple, William (1692), *Memoirs of What Past in Christendom, from the War Begun 1672 to the Peace Concluded 1679* (*Memoirs, Part II*), 2nd edn, London: Printed by R. R. for Richard Chiswell.

—— (1754), *The Works of William Temple*, 4 vols, Edinburgh: Printed for G. Hamilton and J. Balfour, A. Kincaid and A. Donaldson, L. Hunter, W. Gordon, J. Yair and C. Wright; and for A. Stalker at Glasgow.

Thelwall, John (1795–6), *The Tribune, a Periodical Publication* [...], 3 vols, London: Printed for the author.

Tracy, Destutt de [1797] (1992), *Mémoire sur la faculté de penser, De la métaphysique de Kant et autres textes*, Rep. Paris: Fayard.

—— [1798] (2011), 'Quels sont les moyens de fonder la morale chez un peuple', in *Œuvres complètes I, Premiers écrits, Sur l'éducation et l'instruction publique*, Introduction, édition et notes par Claude Jolly, Paris: Vrin.

—— [1811] (1969), *Commentary and Review of Montesquieu's Spirit of Laws*, Rep. New York: Burt Franklin.

Trenchard, John (1709), *The Natural History of Superstition*, London: Sold by A. Baldwin.

Trenchard, John and Thomas Gordon [1720–1] (1994), *The Independent Whig*, Rep. in *The English Libertarian Heritage*, ed. David L. Jacobson, foreword by Ronald Hamowy, San Francisco: Fox & Wilkes.

—— [1720–3] (1995), *Cato's Letters: or Essays on Liberty, Civil and Religious, and other Important Subjects*, ed. and annotated by Ronald Hamowy, 2 vols, Indianapolis: Liberty Fund.

Tucker, Josiah [1749] (1753), *A Brief Essay on the Advantages and Disadvantages which respectively attend France and Great Britain, with regard to trade*, 2nd edn, London: Printed for T. Trye.

—— [1774] (1993), *Four Tracts, together with Two Sermons on Political and Commercial Subjects*, in *Collected Works of Josiah Tucker*, with a new introduction by Jeffrey Stern, London: Routledge/Thoemmes, vol. 2.

Turgot, Anne-Robert-Jacques (1973), *On Progress, Sociology and Economics*, ed. and trans. by Ronald L. Meek, Cambridge: Cambridge University Press.

Turnbull, George (1740), *The Principles of Moral Philosophy: An Enquiry into the Wise and Good Government of the Moral World*, 2 vols, London: Printed for John Noon.

Velleius Paterculus (1924, 1955), *Compendium of Roman History; Res Gestae Divi Augusti*, trans. by Frederick W. Shipley, Cambridge, MA: Harvard University Press.

Voltaire (François-Marie Arouet) [1733] (2003), *Philosophical Letters (Letters concerning the English Nation)*, trans. with an introduction by Ernest Dilworth, Mineola, NY: Dover Publications.

—— [1738] (1967), *The Elements of Sir Isaac Newton's Philosophy*, trans. by John Hanna, London: Printed for S. Austen, Rep. London: Frank Cass & Co. Ltd.

—— [1751] (1961), *The Age of Louis XIV*, trans. by M. P. Pollack, London: Everyman's Library.

—— [1763] (2000), *Voltaire: Treatise on Tolerance*, trans. by Simon Harvey and Brian Masters, Cambridge: Cambridge University Press.

—— [1764] (2004), *Philosophical Dictionary*, ed. and trans. by Theodore Besterman, London: Penguin.

—— [1764] (2010), *Philosophical Dictionary*, trans. by H. I. Woolf, New York: Knopf.

—— [1769] (2010), *God & Human Beings*, trans. by Michael Shreve, intro. by S. T. Joshi, Amherst: Prometheus Books.

—— (1877–85), *Œuvres complètes de Voltaire*, éd. Louis Moland, 52 vols, Paris: Garnier.

—— (1968–), *Œuvres complètes de Voltaire* (*The Complete Works of Voltaire*), Oxford: Voltaire Foundation.

—— (1994), *Voltaire: Political Writings*, ed. David Williams, Cambridge: Cambridge University Press.

—— (2012), *Digital Correspondence of Voltaire*, ed. Theodore Besterman, online supplement by Nicholas Cronk et al., including the 2nd tranche, Oxford: Voltaire Foundation, based on Besterman's *Correspondence and Related Documents*, 2nd edn, 51 vols, *Les Œuvres complètes de Voltaire*, Geneva, Banbury & Oxford: Institut et Musée Voltaire & Voltaire Foundation, 1968–1977 (http://www.e-enlightenment.com/coffeehouse/project/voltaire2011/ [accessed 25 Nov. 2014]).

Walker, George (1799), *The Vagabond*, 2 vols, London: Printed for G. Walker.

Wallace, Robert [1761] (1969), *Various Prospects of Mankind, Nature, and Providence*, Rep. New York: A. M. Kelley.

Warburton, William [1737–41] (1742), *The Divine Legation of Moses Demonstrated, on the Principles of a Religious Deist*, 3rd edn, 2 vols, London: Printed for the executor of the late Mr Fletcher Gyles.

—— (1748), *The Alliance Between Church and State* [...], 3rd edn, London: Printed for J. and P. Knapton.

Whiter, Walter (1794), *A Specimen of a Commentary on Shakspeare* [sic], London: Printed for T. Cadell.

Wollstonecraft, Mary [1790] (1995), *A Vindication of the Rights of Men*, in Wollstonecraft, *A Vindication of the Rights of Men and A Vindication of the Rights of Woman*, ed. Sylvana Tomaselli, Cambridge: Cambridge University Press.

Secondary Sources

Adair, Douglas (1965), '"That Politics May Be Reduced to a Science": David Hume, James Madison, and the Tenth Federalist', *Huntington Library Quarterly*, 20: 4 (1965), pp. 343–60.

Ahnert, Thomas and Susan Manning (eds), *Characters, Self, and Sociability in the Scottish Enlightenment*, New York: Palgrave Macmillan.

Allan, David (2013), 'Reading Hume's *History of England*: Audience and Authority in Georgian England', in Spencer (ed.) 2013: 103–20.

Archer, John (1983), 'The Beginnings of Association in British Architectural Esthetics', *Eighteenth-Century Studies*, 16: 3 (1983), pp. 241–64.

Arendt, Hannah [1963] (1990), *On Revolution*, New York, Rep. Harmondsworth: Penguin.

—— (1982), *Lectures on Kant's Political Philosophy*, ed. and with an interpretive essay by Ronald Beiner, Chicago: The University of Chicago Press.

Arkin, Marc M. (1995), 'The Intractable Principle: David Hume, James Madison, Religion, and the Tenth Federalist', *American Journal of Legal History*, 39: 2 (1995), pp. 148–76.

Armitage, David (2000), *The Ideological Origins of the British Empire*, Cambridge: Cambridge University Press.

Baier, Annette C. (1989), 'Hume on Women's Complexion', in Peter Jones (ed.), *The 'Science of Man' in the Scottish Enlightenment: Hume, Reid and their Contemporaries*, Edinburgh: Edinburgh University Press, pp. 33–53.

—— (1991), *A Progress of Sentiments: Reflections on Hume's Treatise*, Cambridge, MA: Harvard University Press.

—— (2008), *Death and Character: Further Reflections on Hume*, Cambridge, MA: Harvard University Press.

—— (2010), *The Cautious Jealous Virtue: Hume on Justice*, Cambridge, MA: Harvard University Press.

—— (2011), *The Pursuit of Philosophy*, Cambridge, MA: Harvard University Press.

Baker, Eric (2007), 'Lucretius in the European Enlightenment', in Stuart Gillespie and Philip Hardie (eds), *The Cambridge Companion to Lucretius*, Cambridge: Cambridge University Press, pp. 274–88.

Baker, Keith Michael (1990), *Inventing the French Revolution*, Cambridge: Cambridge University Press.

Baumstark, Moritz (2008), *David Hume: The Making of a Philosophical Historian A Reconsideration*, PhD thesis, Edinburgh: University of Edinburgh.

—— (2012), 'The End of Empire and the Death of Religion: A Reconsideration of Hume's Later Political Thought', in Savage (ed.) 2012: 231–57.

Beauchamp, Tom L. (2007), 'The Intellectual Background: A Concise Account, with Bibliography' in *David Hume: A Dissertation on the Passions; The Natural History of Religion*, Oxford: Clarendon Press, pp. 205–28.

Berdell, John F. (1996), 'Innovation and Trade: David Hume and the Case for Freer Trade', *History of Political Economy*, 28: 1 (1996), pp. 107–27.

Berlin, Isaiah (1979), 'Hume and the Sources of German Anti-Rationalism', in *Against the Current: Essays in the History of Ideas*, ed. Henry Hardy, with an introduction by Roger Hausheer, Princeton: Princeton University Press, pp. 162–87.

—— (2000), 'The Magus of the North', in *Three Critics of the Enlightenment: Vico, Hamann, Herder*, ed. Henry Hardy, Princeton: Princeton University Press, pp. 243–361.

Berry, Christopher J. (1982), *Hume, Hegel and Human Nature*, The Hague: Martinus Nijhoff.

—— (1994), *The Idea of Luxury: A Conceptual and Historical Investigation*, Cambridge: Cambridge University Press.

—— (1997), *Social Theory of the Scottish Enlightenment*, Edinburgh: Edinburgh University Press.

—— (2003), 'Lusty Women and Loose Imagination: Hume's Philosophical Anthropology of Chastity', *History of Political Thought*, 24: 3 (2003), pp. 416–33.

—— (2006), 'Hume and the Customary Causes of Industry, Knowledge and Humanity', *History of Political Economy*, 38: 2 (2006), pp. 291–317.

—— (2008), 'Hume and Superfluous Value (or the Problem with Epictetus' Slippers)', in Wennerlind and Schabas (eds) 2008: 49–64.

—— (2009), *David Hume*, New York: Continuum.

—— (2013), *The Idea of Commercial Society in the Scottish Enlightenment*, Edinburgh: Edinburgh University Press.

Besterman, Theodore (1976), *Voltaire*, Chicago: University of Chicago Press.

Betts, C. J. (1984), *Early Deism in France: From the So-called 'déistes' of Lyon (1564) to Voltaire's 'Lettres Philosophiques' (1734)*, The Hague: Martinus Nijhoff.

Blanning, T. C. W. (1998), *The French Revolution: Class War or Culture Clash?* 2nd edn, Hampshire: Palgrave Macmillan.

Bongie, Laurence L. (1958), 'David Hume and the Official Censorship of the Ancien Régime', *French Studies*, 12: 3 (1958), pp. 234–46.

—— (1961), 'Hume, "Philosophe" and Philosopher in Eighteenth-Century France', *French Studies*, 15: 3 (1961), pp. 213–27.

—— [1965] (2000), *David Hume: Prophet of the Counter-Revolution*, 2nd edn with a foreword by Donald W. Livingston, Indianapolis: Liberty Fund.

Box, M. A. (1990), *The Suasive Art of David Hume*, Princeton: Princeton University Press.

——, David Harvey and Michael Silverthorne (2003), 'A Diplomatic Transaction of Hume's "Volunteer Pamphlet" for Archibald Stewart: Political Whigs, Religious Whigs, and Jacobites', *Hume Studies*, 29: 2 (2003), pp. 223–66.

—— and Michael Silverthorne (2013), 'The "Most Curious & Important of All Questions of Erudition": Hume's Assessment of the Populousness of Ancient Nations' in Spencer (ed.) 2013: 225–54.

Boyd, Richard (2000), 'Reappraising the Scottish Moralists and Civil Society', *Polity*, 33: 1 (2000), pp. 101–25.

Brahami, Frédéric (2009), 'Criticism and Science in Hume', in José R. Maria Neto, Gianni Paganini and John Christian Laursen (eds), *Skepticism in the Modern Age*, Leiden; Boston: Brill, pp. 365–80.

Brewer, Daniel (2008), *The Enlightenment Past*, Cambridge: Cambridge University Press.

Brewer, John (1989), *The Sinews of Power: War, Money and the English State, 1688-1783*, London: Unwin Hyman.

Broadie, Alexander (2009), *A History of Scottish Philosophy*, Edinburgh: Edinburgh University Press.

—— (2012), *Agreeable Connexions: Scottish Enlightenment Links with France*, Edinburgh: Birlinn.

Brooke, Christopher (2012), *Philosophic Pride: Stoicism and Political Thought from Lipsius to Rousseau*, Princeton: Princeton University Press.

Brumfitt, J. H. (1972), *The French Enlightenment*, London: Macmillan.

Buckle, Stephen (2007), 'Hume's Sceptical Materialism', *Philosophy*, 82: 4 (2007), pp. 553–78.

—— (2011), 'Hume and the Enlightenment', in Craig Taylor and Stephen Buckle (eds), *Hume and The Enlightenment*, London: Pickering and Chatto Publishers, pp. 13–37.

—— and Dario Castiglione (1991), 'Hume's Critique of the Contract Theory', *History of Political Thought*, 12: 3 (1991), pp. 457–80.

Burson, Jeffrey D. and Ulrich L. Lehner (eds) (2014), *Enlightenment and Catholicism in Europe: A Transnational History*, Notre Dame: University of Notre Dame Press.

Carey, Daniel (2006), *Locke, Shaftesbury and Hutcheson: Contesting Diversity in the Enlightenment and Beyond*, Cambridge: Cambridge University Press.

Castiglione, Dario (1994), 'History, Reason and Experience: Hume's Arguments against Contract Theory', in David Boucher and Paul Kelly (eds), *The Social Contract from Hobbes to Rawls*, London; New York: Routledge, pp. 95–114.

—— (2006), 'Hume's Two Views of Modern Scepticism', *History of European Ideas*, 32: 1 (2006), pp. 1–27.

Chamley, P. E. (1975), 'The Conflict between Montesquieu and Hume', in A. S. Skinner and T. Wilson (eds), *Essays on Adam Smith*, Oxford: Oxford University Press, pp. 274–305.

Champion, J. A. I. (1992), *The Pillars of Priestcraft Shaken: The Church of England and its Enemies, 1660–1730*, Cambridge: Cambridge University Press.

Charles, Loïc (2008), 'French "New Politics" and the Dissemination of David Hume's *Political Discourses* on the Continent, 1750–70', in Wennerlind and Schabas (eds) 2008: 181–202.

Charles, Sébastien (2012), 'Entre pyrrhonisme, académisme et dogmatisme: le "scepticism" de Voltaire', *Cahiers Voltaire*, 11 (2012), pp. 125–48.

—— (2013), 'Introduction', in Charles and Smith (eds) 2013: 1–15.

—— and Plíno J. Smith (eds) (2013), *Scepticism in the Eighteenth Century: Enlightenment, Lumières, Aufklärung*, Dordrecht; New York: Springer.

Cherel, Albert (1926), *Un Aventurier religieux au XVIIIe siècle, André Michel Ramsay*, Paris: Librairie académique Perrin et Cie.

Chisick, Harvey (1989), 'David Hume and the Common People', in Jones (ed.) 1989: 5–32.

—— (2002), 'Public Opinion and Political Culture in France during the Second Half of the Eighteenth Century', *The English Historical Review*, 117: 470 (2002), pp. 48–77.

Christensen, Jerome (1987), *Practicing Enlightenment: Hume and the Formation of a Literary Career*, Wisconsin, MA: The University of Wisconsin Press.

Claeys, George (1989), *Thomas Paine: Social and Political Thought*, London; New York: Routledge.

—— (1994), 'The Origins of the Rights of Labour', *Journal of Modern History*, 66: 2 (1994), pp. 249–90.

—— (2007), *The French Revolution Debate in Britain: The Origins of Modern Politics*, New York: Palgrave.

Clark, John P. (1977), *The Philosophical Anarchism of William Godwin*, Princeton: Princeton University Press.

Colley, Linda (1981), 'Eighteenth-Century English Radicalism Before Wilkes', *Transactions of the Royal Historical Society*, 5th Series, 31 (1981), pp. 1–19.

Collini, Stefan, Donald Winch and John Burrow (eds) (1983), *That Noble Science of Politics: A Study in Nineteenth-Century Intellectual History*, Cambridge: Cambridge University Press.

Conniff, James (1955), *The Useful Cobbler: Edmund Burke and the Politics of Progress*, Albany, NY: State University of New York.

—— (1976), 'Hume's Political Methodology: A Reconsideration of "That Politics may be Reduced to a Science"', *The Review of Politics*, 38: 1 (1976), pp. 88–108.

—— (1980), 'The Enlightenment and American Political Thought: A Study of the Origins of Madison's *Federalist Number 10*', *Political Theory*, 8: 3 (1980), pp. 381–402.

Costelloe, Timothy M. (2013), 'Fact and Fiction: Memory and Imagination in Hume's Approach to History and Literature', in Spencer (ed.) 2013: 181–200.

Coyle, Sean (2009), 'The Reality of the Enlightenment', *British Journal for the History of Philosophy*, 17: 4 (2009), pp. 849–58.

Craig, Cairns (2006), 'Nineteenth-Century Scottish Thought', in Ian Brown, Thomas Clancy, Susan Manning and Murray Pittock (eds), *Edinburgh History of Scottish Literature*, 3 vols, Edinburgh: Edinburgh University Press, vol. 2, pp. 267–76.

—— (2007), *Associationism and the Literary Imagination: From the Phantasmal Chaos*, Edinburgh: Edinburgh University Press.

Cunningham, Andrew S. (2005), 'David Hume's Account of Luxury', *Journal of the History of Economic Thought*, 27: 3 (2005), pp. 231–50.

Davie, George (1994), 'Hume, Reid, and the Passion for Ideas', in *A Passion for Ideas: Essays on the Scottish Enlightenment, Vol. II*, ed. Murdo Macdonald, Edinburgh: Polygon, pp. 1–19.

Davies, J. D. (2004), 'Temple, Sir William, baronet (1628–1699)', *Oxford Dictionary of National Biography*, ed. H. C. G. Matthew and Brian Harrison, 60 vols, Oxford: Oxford University Press, vol. 54, pp. 84–9.

Davis, Michael T. (ed.) (2002), *London Corresponding Society, 1792–1799*, 6 vols, London: Pickering & Chatto.

De Dijn, Herman (2003), 'Hume's Nonreductionist Philosophical Anthropology', *The Review of Metaphysics*, 56: 3 (2003), pp. 587–603.

—— (2012), Spinoza and Hume on Religion as a Natural Phenomenon, *Hume Studies*, 38: 1 (2012), pp. 3–21.

Dees, Richard H. (1992), 'Hume and the Contexts of Politics', *Journal of the History of Philosophy*, 30: 2 (1992), pp. 226–7.

—— (2005), '"The Paradoxical Principle and Salutary Practice": Hume on Toleration', *Hume Studies*, 31: 1 (2005), pp. 145–64.

Delacampagne, Christian (2001), 'The Enlightenment Project: A Reply to Schmidt', *Political Theory*, 29: 1 (2001), pp. 80–5.

Deleule, Didier (1979), *Hume et la naissance du libéralisme économique*, Paris: Aubier Montaigne.

Deleuze, Gilles [1953] (1991), *Empiricism and Subjectivity: an Essay on Hume's Theory of Human Nature*, trans. and with an introduction by Constantin V. Boundas, New York: Columbia University Press.

Dickinson, H. T. (1977), *Liberty and Property: Political Ideology in Eighteenth-Century Britain*, London: Methuen.
—— (1995), *The Politics of the People in Eighteenth-Century Britain*, New York: Macmillan Press, St. Martin's Press.
Dinwiddy, John (1989), *Bentham*, Oxford: Oxford University Press.
Draper, Theodor (1982), 'Hume and Madison: The Secrets of Federalist Paper No. 10', *Encounter*, 58: 2 (1982), pp. 34–47.
Duncan, Ian (2007), *Scott's Shadow: The Novel in Romantic Edinburgh*, Princeton: Princeton University Press.
Edelstein, Dan (2010), *The Enlightenment: A Genealogy*, Chicago: University of Chicago Press.
Edwards, Pamela (2004), *The Statesman's Science: History, Nature, and Law in the Political Thought of Samuel Taylor Coleridge*, New York: Columbia University Press.
Ekelund Jr., R. B., R. F. Hébert and R. D. Tollison (2005), 'Adam Smith on Religion and Market Structure', *History of Political Economy*, 37: 4 (2005), pp. 647–60.
Elmslie, Bruce Truitt (1995), 'Retrospectives: The Convergence Debate between David Hume and Josiah Tucker', *Journal of Economic Perspectives*, 9: 4 (1995), pp. 207–16.
Emerson, Roger L. (1984), 'Conjectural History and Scottish Philosophers', *Historical Papers: Communications Historiques*, 19 (1984), pp. 63–90.
—— (1994), 'The "Affair" at Edinburgh and the "Project" at Glasgow: the Politics of Hume's Attempts to become a Professor', in Stewart and Wright (eds) 1994: 1–22.
—— (1997), 'Hume and the Bellman, Zerobabel MacGilchrist', *Hume Studies*, 23: 1 (1997), pp. 9–28.
—— (2007), 'Review of Roderick Graham, *The Great Infidel: A Life of David Hume*', *Eighteenth-Century Life*, 31: 1 (2007), pp. 88–96.
—— (2008), *Academic Patronage in the Scottish Enlightenment: Glasgow, Edinburgh and St Andrews University*, Edinburgh: Edinburgh University Press.
—— (2009), *Essays on David Hume, Medical Men and the Scottish Enlightenment: 'Industry, Knowledge and Humanity'*, Farnham: Ashgate.
—— (2013), 'Hume and Ecclesiastical History: Aims and Contexts', in Spencer (ed.) 2013: 13–36.
Evans III, Frank B. (1940), 'Shelley, Godwin, Hume and the Doctrine of Necessity', *Studies in Philosophy*, 37: 4 (1940), pp. 632–40.
Evnine, Simon (1993), 'Hume, Conjectural History, and the Uniformity

of Human Nature', *Journal of the History of Philosophy*, 31: 4 (1993), pp. 589–606.
Farr, James (1988), 'Political Science and the Enlightenment of Enthusiasm', *The American Political Science Review*, 82: 1 (1988), pp. 51–69.
Fieser, James (1996), 'The Eighteenth-Century British Reviews of Hume's Writings', *Journal of the History of Ideas*, 57: 4 (1996), pp. 645–57.
—— (1995), 'Hume's Concealed Attack on Religion and His Early Critics', *Journal of Philosophical Research*, 20 (1995), pp. 431–49.
—— (ed.) (1995), 'Early Biographies of David Hume' (http://www.skeptic tank.org/treasure/HUME/ACCOUNT.TXT [accessed 25 June 2014]).
—— (ed.) (1999), *Early Responses to Hume's Moral, Literary and Political Writings*, 2 vols, Bristol: Thoemmes Press.
—— (ed.) (2000), *Early Responses to Hume's Metaphysical and Epistemological Writings*, 2 vols, Bristol: Thoemmes Press.
—— (ed.) (2002), *Early Responses to Hume's* History of England, 2 vols, Bristol: Thoemmes Press.
—— (ed.) (2003), *Early Responses to Hume's Life and Reputation*, 2 vols, Bristol: Thoemmes Press.
—— (ed.) (2005), *Early Responses to Hume's Moral, Literary and Political Writings*, 2 vols, 2nd edn, Rev., Bristol: Thoemmes Press.
—— (2003), *A Bibliography of Hume's Writings and Early Responses* (http://www.rrbltd.co.uk/bibliographies/hume_web_bibiog_2e.pdf) [accessed 11 Oct. 2012]).
Finlay, Christopher J. (2007), *Hume's Social Philosophy: Human Nature and Commercial Sociability in* A Treatise of Human Nature, London: Continuum.
Fontana, Biancamaria (1985), *Rethinking the Politics of Commercial Society: The Edinburgh Review 1802–1832*, Cambridge: Cambridge University Press.
Forbes, Duncan (1952), *The Liberal Anglican Idea of History*, Cambridge: Cambridge University Press.
—— (1954), 'Scientific Whiggism: Adam Smith and John Millar', *Cambridge Journal*, 7: 2 (1954), pp. 643–70.
—— (1963), 'Politics and History in David Hume', *The Historical Journal*, 6: 2 (1963), pp. 280–323.
—— (1975a), 'Skeptical Whiggism, Commerce, and Liberty', in Andrew S. Skinner and Thomas Wilson (eds), *Essays on Adam Smith*, Oxford: Oxford University Press, pp. 179–201.
—— (1975b), *Hume's Philosophical Politics*, Cambridge: Cambridge University Press.

—— (1977), 'Hume's Science of Politics', in G. P. Morice (ed.) 1977: 39–50.

—— (1978), 'The European, or Cosmopolitan Dimension in Hume's Science of Politics', *The British Journal for Eighteenth-Century Studies*, 1: 1 (1978), pp. 57–60.

Force, Pierre (2007), *Self-Interest Before Adam Smith: A Genealogy of Economic Science*, Cambridge: Cambridge University Press.

Fosl, Peter S. (1994), 'Doubt and Divinity: Cicero's Influence on Hume's Religious Skepticism, *Hume Studies*, 20: 1 (1994), pp. 103–20.

Foucault, Michel [1984] (1991), 'What is Enlightenment? (*Qu'est-ce que les Lumières?*)', in *The Foucault Readers: An Introduction to Foucault's Thought*, ed. Paul Rabinow, New edn, London: Penguin, pp. 32–50.

Franklin, Michael J. (2011), *'Orientalist Jones': Sir William Jones, Poet, Lawyer, and Linguist, 1746–1794*, Oxford: Oxford University Press.

Frazer, Michael L. (2010), *The Enlightenment of Sympathy: Justice and the Moral Sentiments in the Eighteenth Century and Today*, Oxford: Oxford University Press.

Frey, R. G. (1995), 'Virtue, Commerce, and Self-Love', *Hume Studies*, 21: 2 (1995), pp. 275–87.

Fruchtman, Jr., Jack (1983), *The Apocalyptic Politics of Richard Price and Joseph Priestley*, Philadelphia: American Philosophical Society.

Garrett, Aaron (2006), 'Human Nature', in Haakonssen (ed.) 2006: 160–233.

Gaskin, J. C. A. (1988), *Hume's Philosophy of Religion*, 2nd edn, London: Macmillan.

—— (1994), Introduction to Thomas Hobbes, *The Elements of Law, Human Nature and De Corpore Politico*, Oxford: Oxford University Press.

Gautier, Claude (2005), *Hume et les savoirs de l'histoire*, Paris: Vrin.

—— (ed.) (2001), *Hume et le concept de société civile*, Paris: PUF.

Gay, Peter (1966–69), *The Enlightenment: An Interpretation*, 2 vols, London: Weidenfeld & Nicolson.

Gilbert, Felix (1944), 'The English Background of American Isolationism in the Eighteenth Century', *The William and Mary Quarterly*, 3rd Series, 1: 2 (1944), pp. 138–60.

Gill, Michael (2000), 'Hume's Progressive View of Human Nature', *Hume Studies*, 26: 1 (2000), pp. 87–108.

Goldie, Mark (1987), 'The Religion of James Harrington', in Anthony Pagden (ed.), *The Languages of Political Theory in Early-Modern Europe*, Cambridge: Cambridge University Press, pp. 197–222.

—— (1991), 'The Scottish Catholic Enlightenment', *Journal of British Studies*, 30: 1 (1991), pp. 20–62.

—— (1993), 'Priestcraft and the Birth of Whiggism', in Nicholas Phillipson and Quentin Skinner (eds), *Political Discourse in Early Modern Britain*, Cambridge: Cambridge University Press, pp. 209–31.

—— and Robert Walker (eds) (2006), *The Cambridge History of Eighteenth-Century Political Thought*, Cambridge: Cambridge University Press.

Goldsmith, M. M. (1988), 'Regulating Anew the Moral and Political Sentiments of Mankind: Bernard Mandeville and the Scottish Enlightenment', *Journal of the History of Ideas*, 49: 4 (1988), pp. 587–606.

—— (1994), 'Liberty, Virtue, and the Rule of Law, 1689–1770', in David Wootton (ed.), *Republicanism, Liberty and Commercial Society, 1649–1776*, Stanford: Stanford University Press, pp. 197–232.

Gray, John [1995] (2007), *Enlightenment's Wake: Politics and Culture at the Close of the Modern Age*, Rep. London: Routledge.

Greenblatt, Stephen (2011), *The Swerve: How the World became Modern*, New York: W. W. Norton & Co.

Greig, J. S. T. (1932), 'Some Unpublished Letters to David Hume', *Revue de littérature comparée*, 12 (1932), pp. 826–56.

Guimarães, Lívia (2008), 'Skeptical Tranquility and Hume's Manner of Death', *Journal of Scottish Philosophy*, 6: 2 (2008), pp. 115–34.

—— (2009), 'Skepticism and Religious Belief in *A Treatise of Human Nature*', in José R. Maria Neto et al. (eds), *Skepticism in the Modern Age*, pp. 345–64.

Gunn, J. A. W. (1983), *Beyond Liberty and Property: The Process of Self-Recognition in Eighteenth-Century Political Thought*, Kingston & Montreal: McGill Queen's University Press.

—— (1993), 'Opinion in Eighteenth-Century Thought: What did the Concept Purport to Explain?' *Utilitas*, 5: 1 (1993), pp. 17–33.

—— (1995), *Queen of the World: Opinion in the Public Life of France from the Renaissance to the Revolution*, Oxford: Voltaire Foundation.

Guyer, Paul (2008), *Knowledge, Reason, and Taste: Kant's Responses to Hume*, Princeton and Oxford: Princeton University Press.

Haakonssen, Knud (1981), *The Science of a Legislator: The Natural Jurisprudence of David Hume and Adam Smith*, Cambridge: Cambridge University Press.

—— (1996a), *Natural Law and Moral Philosophy: From Grotius to the Scottish Enlightenment*, Cambridge: Cambridge University Press.

—— (1996b), 'Enlightened Dissent: an Introduction', in Haakonssen (ed.) 1996: 1–11.

—— (2009), 'The Structure of Hume's Political Philosophy', in Norton and Taylor (eds) 2009: 341–80.

—— (ed.) (1996), *Enlightenment and Religion: Rational Dissent in Eighteenth-Century Britain*, Cambridge: Cambridge University Press.

—— (ed.) (2006), *The Cambridge History of Eighteenth-Century Philosophy*, 2 vols, Cambridge: Cambridge University Press.

Halévy, Élie (1901), *La Formation du radicalisme philosophique*, 3 vols, Paris: Ancienne Librairie Germer Baillière et Cie., Félix Alcan, Éditeur.

—— [1934] (1955), *The Growth of Philosophic Radicalism*, trans. by Mary Morris, with a preface by A. D. Lindsay, London: Faber & Faber Limited, Rep. Boston: The Beacon Press.

Hamowy, Ronald (2005), *The Political Sociology of Freedom: Adam Ferguson and F. A. Hayek*, foreword by Mario J. Rizzo, Cheltenham: Edward Elgar.

Hampsher-Monk, Iain (1992), *A History of Modern Political Thought: Major Political Thinkers from Hobbes to Marx*, Oxford: Blackwell.

—— (2002), 'From Virtue to Politeness' in Marin van Gelderen and Quentin Skinner (eds), *Republicanism: A Shared European Heritage, Vol. II, The Values of Republicanism in Early Modern Europe*, Cambridge: Cambridge University Press, pp. 85–105.

—— (2006), 'British Radicalism and the Anti-Jacobins', in Goldie and Wokler (eds) 2006: 660–87.

Hardin, Russell (2007), *David Hume: Moral & Political Theorist*, Oxford: Oxford University Press.

Harris, Ian (1993), Introduction to 'Substance of the Speech [...] In the Debate on the Army Estimates', in *Edmund Burke, Pre-Revolutionary Writings*, ed. Ian Harris, Cambridge: Cambridge University Press, pp. 298–305.

Harris, James A. (2003), 'Answering Bayle's Question: Religious Belief in the Moral Philosophy of the Scottish Enlightenment', in Daniel Garber and Steven Nadler (eds), *Oxford Studies in Early Modern Philosophy*, Oxford: Oxford University Press, pp. 229–54.

—— (2005a), *Of Liberty and Necessity: the Free Will Debate in Eighteenth-Century British Philosophy*, Oxford: Oxford University Press.

—— (2005b), 'The Reception of Hume in Nineteenth-Century British Philosophy', in Jones (ed.) 2005: 314–26.

—— (2009), 'The Epicurean in Hume', in Leddy and Lifschitz (eds) 2009: 161–81.

—— (2011), 'Reid and Hume on the Possibility of Character', in Ahnert and Manning (eds) 2011: 31–48.

—— (2012), 'The Early Reception of Hume's Theory of Justice', in Savage (ed.) 2012: 210–30.

Harvey, A. D. (1997), 'George Walker and the Anti-Revolutionary Novel', *Review of English Studies*, New Series, 28: 111 (1977), pp. 290–300.

Hayashi, Seiyu (2013), 'Hume doutokutetsugaku niokeru "Hitobito no Iken" ('"The Opinions of Men" in Hume's Moral Philosophy') (in Japanese), Rinrigaku Kenkyu (*Annals of Ethical Studies*), 43 (2013), pp. 56–67.

Hayek, Friedrich August von (1967), 'The Legal and Political Philosophy of David Hume', in *Studies in Philosophy, Politics and Economics*, London: Routledge and Kegan Paul, pp. 106–21.

Head, Brian William (1985), *Ideology and Social Science: Destutt de Tracy and French Liberalism*, Dordrecht: Martinus Nijhoff.

Heilbroner, Robert L. (1973), 'The Paradox and Progress: Decline and Decay in *The Wealth of Nations*', *Journal of the History of Ideas*, 34: 2 (1973) pp. 243–62.

Henderson, G. D. (1952), *Chevalier Ramsay*, London: T. Nelson.

Herdt, Jenifer A. (1997), *Religion and Faction in Hume's Moral Philosophy*, Cambridge: Cambridge University Press.

—— (2013), 'Artificial Lives, Providential History, and the Apparent Limits of Sympathetic Understanding', in Spencer (ed.) 2013: 37–59.

Holthoon, F. L. van (1997), 'Hume and the 1763 Edition of His History of England: His Frame of Mind as a Revisionist', *Hume Studies*, 23: 1 (1997), pp. 133–52.

—— (2013), 'Hume and the End of History', in Spencer (ed.) 2013: 143–62.

Hont, István (2005), *Jealousy of Trade: International Competition and the Nation-State in Historical Perspective*, Cambridge, MA: Harvard University Press.

—— (2006), 'The Early Enlightenment Debate on Commerce and Luxury', in Goldie and Walker (eds) 2006: 379–418.

—— (2008), '"The Rich Country-Poor Country" Debate Revisited: The Irish Origins and French Reception of the Hume Paradox', in Wennerlind and Schabas (eds) 2008: 243–323.

Houghton, Walter E. (ed.) (1966–89), *The Wellesley Index to Victorian Periodicals 1824–1900*, 5 vols, Toronto: Routledge, University of Toronto Press.

Hundert, E. J. (1974), 'The Achievement Motive in Hume's Political Economy', *Journal of the History of Ideas*, 35: 1 (1974), pp. 139–43.

—— (1992), 'Augustine and the Sources of the Divided Self', *Political Theory*, 20: 1 (1992), pp. 86–104.

—— (2005), *The Enlightenment's Fable: Bernard Mandeville and the Discovery of Society*, Cambridge: Cambridge University Press.

Immerwahr, John (1977), 'The Failure of Hume's *Treatise*', *Hume Studies*, 3: 3 (1977), pp. 57–71.

—— (1989), 'Hume's Essays on Happiness', *Hume Studies*, 15: 2 (1989), pp. 307–24.

—— (1991), 'The Anatomist and the Painter: The Continuity of Hume's Treatise and Essays', *Hume Studies*, 17: 1 (1991), pp. 1–14.

Inuzuka, Hajime (2004a), *David Hume no Seiji-Gaku* (*David Hume and the Traditions of Political Thought*) (in Japanese), Tokyo: University of Tokyo Press.

—— (2004b), 'David Hume's Politics: Inheritance and Renewal of the Traditional Political Thought', Discussion Paper Series, No. F–113, Institute of Social Science, University of Tokyo (http://jww.iss.u-tokyo.ac.jp/publishments/dp/dpf/pdf/f-113.pdf [accessed 12 Aug. 2014]).

Israel, Jonathan I. (2001), *Radical Enlightenment: Philosophy and the Making of Modernity, 1650–1750*, Oxford: Oxford University Press.

—— (2006), *Enlightenment Contested: Philosophy, Modernity, and the Emancipation of Man 1670–1752*, Oxford: Oxford University Press.

—— (2010), *A Revolution of the Mind: Radical Enlightenment and the Intellectual Origins of Modern Democracy*, Princeton: Princeton University Press.

—— (2011), *Democratic Enlightenment: Philosophy, Revolution, and Human Rights 1750–1790*, Oxford: Oxford University Press.

Jack, Malcolm (1989), *Corruption & Progress: The Eighteenth-Century Debate*, New York: AMS Press.

Jacob, Margaret C. (2006), *The Radical Enlightenment: Pantheists, Freemasons and Republicans*, 2nd Revised edn, Lafayette: Cornerstone.

Jacyna, Stephen (1994), *Philosophic Whigs: Medicine, Science and Citizenship in Edinburgh, 1789-1848*, London: Routledge.

Jaffro, Laurent (1998), *Éthique de la communication et art d'écrire: Shaftesbury et les Lumières anglaises*, Paris: PUF.

—— (2012), 'Toland and the Moral Teaching of the Gospel', in Savage (ed.): 77–89.

James, Susan (1997), *Passion and Action: The Emotions in Seventeenth-Century Philosophy*, Oxford: Oxford University Pres.

—— (2005), 'Sympathy and Comparison: Two Principles of Human Nature', in Marina Frasca-Spada and P. J. Kail (eds), *Impressions of Hume*, Oxford: Oxford University Press, pp. 107–24.

Johnson, E. A. J. (1960), *Predecessors of Adam Smith: the Growth of British Economic Thought*, New York: Prentice Hall.

Johnson, Peter (1998), 'Hume on Manners and the Civil Condition', *British Journal for the History of Philosophy*, 6: 2 (1998), pp. 209–22.

Johnson, W. R. (2000), *Lucretius and the Modern World*, London: Duckworth.

Jones, Howard (1989), *The Epicurean Tradition*, London; New York: Routledge.

Jones, Peter (1976a), 'Cause, Reason, and Objectivity in Hume's Aesthetics', in Donald W. Livingston and James T. King (eds), *Hume: A Re-evaluation*, New York: Fordham University Press, pp. 323–42.

—— (1976b), '"Art" and "Moderation" in Hume's Essays', in Norton et al. 1976: 161–80.

—— (1978), 'Hume on Art, Criticism and Language: Debts and Premises', *Philosophical Studies*, 33: 2 (1978), pp. 109–34.

—— (1982), *Hume's Sentiments: Their Ciceronian and French Context*, Edinburgh: Edinburgh University Press.

—— (ed.) (1989), *The 'Science of Man' in the Scottish Enlightenment: Hume, Reid and their Contemporaries*, Edinburgh: Edinburgh University Press.

—— (ed.) (2005), *The Reception of David Hume in Europe*, London; New York: Thoemmes Continuum.

Kail, Peter J. E. (2013), 'Shaftesbury, Hutcheson and Moral Scepticisms', in Charles and Smith (eds) 2013: 95–107.

Kallich, Martin (1970), *The Association of Ideas and Critical Theory in Eighteenth-Century England: A History of a Psychological Method in English Criticism*, The Hague: Mouton.

Kalyvas, Andreas and Ira Katznelson (2008), *Liberal Beginnings: Making a Republic for the Moderns*, Cambridge: Cambridge University Press.

Kapposy, Béla (2002), 'Neo Roman Republicanism and Commerical Society: The Example of Eighteenth-century Berne', in van Gelderen and Skinner (eds), *Republicanism, Vol. II*, pp. 227–47.

Kavanagh, Thomas M. (2010), *Enlightened Pleasures: Eighteenth-Century France and the New Epicureanism*, New Haven: Yale University Press.

Kemp Smith, Norman (1941), *The Philosophy of David Hume: A Critical Study of its Origins and Central Doctrines*, London: Macmillan.

Kennedy, Emmet (1978), *A* Philosophe *in the Age of Revolution: Destutt de Tracy and the Origins of "Ideology"*, Philadelphia: American Philosophical Society.

Klein, Lawrence E. (1994), *Shaftesbury and the Culture of Politeness*, Cambridge: Cambridge University Press.

Klever, Wim (1990), 'Hume Contra Spinoza?' *Hume Studies*, 16: 2 (1990), pp. 89–106.

Kors, Alan Christian (2013), 'An Uneasy Relationship: Atheism and Scepticism in the Late French Enlightenment', in Charles and Smith (2013): 221–30.

Kramnick, Isaac (1992), *Bolingbroke & His Circle: The Politics of Nostalgia in the Age of Walpole*, Ithaca, NY: Cornell University Press.

Laird, John (1932), *Hume's Philosophy of Human Nature*, London: Methuen.

Laursen, John Christian (1992), *The Politics of Skepticism in the Ancients, Montaigne, Hume and Kant*, Leiden; New York: Brill Academic Publishing.

LaVopa, Anthony J. (2009), 'A New Intellectual History? Jonathan Israel's Enlightenment', *The Historical Journal*, 52: 3 (2009), pp. 717–38.

Leathers, Charles G. and J. Patrick Raines (2008), 'Adam Smith on Religion and Market Structure: The Search for Consistency', *History of Political Economy*, 40: 2 (2008), pp. 345–63.

Leddy, Neven and Avi S. Lifschitz (2009), 'Epicurus in the Enlightenment: an introduction', in Leddy and Lifschitz (eds) 2009: 1–11.

—— (eds) (2009), *Epicurus in the Enlightenment*, Oxford: Voltaire Foundation.

Lee, Janice (1982), 'Political Antiquarianism unmasked: the Conservative Attack on the Myth of the Ancient Constitution', *Historical Research*, 55: 132 (1982), pp. 166–79.

Le Jallé, Éléonore (2001), 'Les Mœurs chez Hume: Des règles du Traité aux "secrètes révolutions" de l'Histoire d'Angleterre', *Les Cahiers philosophiques de Strasbourg*, 11 (2001), pp. 119–35.

Lemmens, Willem (2005), 'The Melancholy of the Philosopher: Hume and Spinoza on Emotions and Wisdom', *Journal of Scottish Philosophy*, 3: 1 (2005), pp. 47–65.

Lennon, Thomas M. (1977), *Introduction to Malebranche*, [1674–5] 1997: vii–xxiii.

Leslie, Margaret (1972), 'Mysticism Misunderstood: David Hartley and the Idea of Progress', *Journal of the History of Ideas*, 33: 4 (1972), pp. 625–32.

Letwin, Shirley Robin (1998), *The Pursuit of Certainty: David Hume, Jeremy Bentham, John Stuart Mill, and Beatrice Webb*, Indianapolis: Liberty Fund.

Levine, Joseph M. (1991), *The Battle of the Books: History and Literature in the Augustan Age*, Ithaca, NY: Cornell University Press.

Levin, Lawrence M. (1936), *The Political Doctrine of Montesquieu's Esprit des Lois: Its Classical Background*, New York: Columbia University Press.

Livingston, Donald W. (1984), *Hume's Philosophy of Common Life*, Chicago: University of Chicago Press.

—— (1990), 'Hume's Historical Conception of Liberty' in Nicholas Capaldi and Donald W. Livingston (eds), *Liberty in Hume's* History of England, Dordrecht: Kluwer, pp. 105–53.

—— (1995), 'On Hume's Conservatism', *Hume Studies*, 21: 2 (1995), pp. 151–64.

—— (1998), *Philosophical Melancholy and Delirium: Hume's Pathology of Philosophy*, Chicago: University of Chicago Press.

—— (2009), 'David Hume and the Conservative Tradition', *The Intercollegiate Review*, 44: 2 (2009), pp. 30–41.

Long, Douglas (2013), 'Hume's Historiographical Imagination', in Spencer (ed.) 2013: 201–24.

Long, Roderick T. (2008), 'No Matter, No Master: Godwin's Humean Anarchism', a paper read at the SEASECS (Southeastern American Society for Eighteenth-Century Studies) Conference (February 2008) (http://praxeology.net/RTL-nomatternomaster-final.doc [accessed 10 Oct. 2012]).

Lough, John (1985), 'Reflections on *Enlightenment* and *Lumières*', *British Journal for Eighteenth-Century Studies*, 8: 1 (1985), pp. 1–15.

Low, J. M. (1952), 'An Eighteenth Century Controversy in the Theory of Economic Progress', *The Manchester School of Economic and Social Studies*, 20: 3 (1952), pp. 311–30.

Luehrs, R. B. (1987), 'Population and Utopia in the Thought of Robert Wallace', *Eighteenth-Century Studies*, 20: 3 (1987), pp. 313–35.

McArthur, Neil (2007), *David Hume's Political Theory: Law, Commerce, and the Constitution of Government*, Toronto: University of Toronto Press.

McCormick, Miriam Schleifer (2013), 'Hume's Skeptical Politics', *Hume Studies*, 39: 1 (2013), pp. 77–102.

MacIntyre, Alasdair (1981), *After Virtue: A Study in Moral Theory*, Notre Dame: University of Notre Dame Press.

MacLean, Kenneth (1936), *John Locke and English Literature of the Eighteenth Century*, New Haven: Yale University Press.

McLynn, F. J. (1983), 'Jacobitism and David Hume: The Ideological Backlash Foiled', *Hume Studies*, 9: 2 (1983), pp. 171–99.

McMahon, Darrin M. (2001), *Enemies of the Enlightenment: The French Counter-Enlightenment and the Making of Modernity*, Oxford: Oxford University Press.

—— (2007), 'What are Enlightenments?' *Modern Intellectual History*, 4: 3 (2007), pp. 601–16.

Macpherson, C. B. (1943), 'Sir William Temple, Political Scientist?' *The Canadian Journal of Economics and Political Science*, 9: 1 (1943), pp. 39–54.

McShea, Robert J. (1978), 'Human Nature and Political Science', *American Journal of Political Science*, 22: 3 (1978), pp. 656–79.

Malherbe, Michel (2003), 'The Impact on Europe', in Alexander Broadie (ed.), *The Cambridge Companion to the Scottish Enlightenment*, Cambridge: Cambridge University Press, pp. 298–315.

—— (2005), 'Hume's Reception in France', in Jones (ed.) 2005: 43–9.

Mankin, Robert (2005), 'Can Jealousy be Reduced to a Science? Politics and Economics in Hume's *Essays*', *Journal of the History of Economic Thought*, 27: 1 (2005), pp. 59 –70.

Manning, Susan (1990), *The Puritan-Provincial Vision: Scottish and American Literature in the Nineteenth Century*, Cambridge: Cambridge University Press.

—— (2002), *Fragments of Union: Making Connections in Scottish and American Writing*, Basingstoke: Palgrave.

—— (2011a), 'Introduction: Character, Self, and Sociability in the Scottish Enlightenment', in Ahnert and Manning (eds) 2011: 1–30.

—— (2011b), 'Historical Characters: Biography, the Science of Man, and Romantic Fiction', in Ahnert and Manning (eds) 2011: 225–48.

Marburg, Clara (1932), *Sir William Temple: A Seventeenth Century "Libertin"*, New Haven: Yale University Press; London, H. Milford: Oxford University Press.

Marshall, Geoffrey (1954), 'David Hume and Political Scepticism', *The Philosophical Quarterly*, 4: 16 (1954), pp. 247–57.

Mason, H. T. (2003), Introduction to 'Le Mondain: Critical Edition', *Writing of 1737, Les Œuvres complètes de Voltaire*, vol. 16, Oxford: Voltaire Foundation, pp. 273–94.

Mason, Hayden (1996), 'Optimism, Progress, and Philosophical History', in Goldie and Wokler (eds) 2006: 195–217.

Mason, Sheila Mary (1975), *Montesquieu's Idea of Justice*, The Hague: Martinus Nijhoff.

Maurer, Christian (2012), 'Archibald Campbell's Views of Self-Cultivation and Self-Denial in Context', *The Journal of Scottish Philosophy*, 10: 1 (2012), pp. 13–27.

—— and Laurent Jaffro (2013), 'Reading Shaftesbury's Pathologia: An Illustration and Defence of the Stoic Account of the Emotions', *History of European Ideas*, 39: 2 (2013), pp. 207–20.

May, Henry F. (1976), *The Enlightenment in America*, New York: Oxford University Press.

Mayo, Thomas Franklin (1934), *Epicurus in England: 1650-1725*, Dallas: Southwest Press.

Mazza, Emilio (2005), 'Hume's "Meek" Philosophy among the Milanese', in Marina Frasca-Spada and P. J. E. Kail (eds), *Impression of Hume*, Oxford: Oxford University Press, pp. 213–44.

—— and Emanuele Ronchetti (eds) (2007), *New Essays on David Hume*, Milan: FrancoAngeli.

Merrill, Thomas W. (2005), 'The Rhetoric of Rebellion in Hume's Constitutional Thought', *The Review of Politics*, 67: 1 (2005), pp. 257–82.

Meyer, Paul H. (1951), 'Voltaire and Hume's Descent on the Coast of Brittany', *Modern Language Association*, 66: 7 (1951), pp. 429–35.

—— (1958), 'Voltaire and Hume as Historians: A Comparative Study of the *Essai sur les moeurs* and the *History of England*', *PMLA (Proceedings of Modern Language Association of America)*, 73: 1 (1958), pp. 51–68.

Miller, David (1981), *Philosophy and Ideology in Hume's Political Philosophy*, Oxford: Oxford University Press.

Mizuta, Hiroshi (2000), *Adam Smith's Library: A Catalogue*, Oxford: Oxford University Press.

Moore, James (1976a), 'Hume's Theory of Justice and Property', *Political Studies* 24: 2 (1976), pp. 103–19.

—— (1976b), 'The Social Background of Hume's Science of Human Nature', in Norton et al. (eds) 1976: 23–41.

—— (1977), 'Hume's Political Science and the Classical Republican Tradition', *Canadian Journal of Political Science*, 10: 4 (1977), pp. 809–39.

—— (1994), 'Hume and Hutcheson', in Wright and Stewart (eds) 1994: 23–57.

—— (2002), 'Utility and Humanity: The Quest for the Honestum in Cicero, Hutcheson, and Hume', *Utilitas*, 14: 3 (2002), pp. 365–86.

—— (2004), 'Burnet, Gilbert (1690–1726)', *ODNB*, vol. 8, pp. 923–4.

—— (2007), 'The Eclectic Stoic, The Mitigated Skeptic', in Mazza and Ronchetti (eds) 2007: 133–70.

—— (2009), 'Montesquieu and the Scottish Enlightenment' in Rebecca E. Kingston (ed.), *Montesquieu and His Legacy*, Albany: SUNY Press, pp. 179–95.

Morgan, Edmund S. (1986), 'Safety in Numbers: Madison, Hume, and the Tenth *Federalist*', *Huntington Library Quarterly*, 49: 2 (1986), pp. 95–112.

Mori, Naohito (2010), *Hume niokeru Seigi to Touchi: Bunmei-shakai no Ryougisei* (*Hume and his Ambivalent Idea of Civilized Society*) (in Japanese), Tokyo: Sobunsha.

Morize, André (1909), *L'Apologie du luxe au XVIIIe siècle et « Le Mondain » de Voltaire: Étude critique sur le Mondain et ses sources*, Paris: H. Didier.

Morrice, G. P. (ed.) (1977), *David Hume: Bicentenary Papers*, Austin: University of Texas Press.

Morrow, John (1990), *Coleridge's Political Thought*, New York: Palgrave Macmillan.

Mortimer, Sarah and John Robertson (2012), 'Nature, Revelation, History: Intellectual Consequences of Religious Heterodoxy C. 1600 –1750', in Mortimer and Robertson (eds) 2012: 1–46.

—— (eds) (2012), *The Intellectual Consequences of Religious Heterodoxy 1600–1750*, Leiden; Boston: Brill.

Mossner, Ernest Campbell (1941a), 'An Apology for David Hume, Historian', *PMLA*, 56: 3 (1941), pp. 657–90.

—— (1941b), 'Was Hume a Tory Historian? Facts and Reconsiderations', *Journal of the History of Ideas*, 2: 2 (1941), pp. 225–36.

—— (1949), 'Hume and the Ancient-Modern Controversy, 1725–1752: A Study in Creative Scepticism', *The University of Texas Studies in English*, 28 (1949), pp. 139–53.

—— (1950), 'Hume's "Four Dissertations": An Essay in Biography and Bibliography', *Modern Philology*, 48: 1 (1950), pp. 37–57.

—— (1962), 'New Hume Letters to Lord Elibank, 1748–1776', *Texas Studies in Literature and Language*, 4: 3 (1962), pp. 437–8.

—— (1980), *The Life of David Hume*, 2nd edn, Oxford: Clarendon Press.

Muthu, Sankar (2003), *Enlightenment against Empire*, Princeton: Princeton University Press.

Nakagami, Yumiko (2003), *Jissen toshiteno Seiji, Aato toshiteno Seiji: John Locke Seijishisou no Saikousei* (*Prudence and the Art of Politics*) (in Japanese), Tokyo: Sobunsha.

Nakhimovsky, Isaac (2003), 'The Enlightened Epicureanism of Jacques Abbadie: *L'Art de se connoître soi-même* and the Morality of Self-Interest', *History of European Ideas* 29: 1 (2003), pp. 1–14.

Nangle, Benjamin Christie (1955), *The 'Monthly Review' Second Series 1790-1815*, Oxford: Clarendon Press.

Nelson, Eric (2004), *The Greek Tradition in Republican Thought*, Cambridge: Cambridge University Press.

Neserius, Philip George (1926), 'Voltaire's Political Ideas', *American Political Science Review*, 20: 1 (1926), pp. 31–51.

Niblett, Matthew (2009), 'Man, Morals and Matter: Epicurus and Materialist Thought in England from John Toland to Joseph Priestley' in Leddy and Lifschitz (eds) 2009: 137–59.

Norton, David Fate (1965), 'History and Philosophy in Hume's Thought', in Norton and Popkin (eds) 1965: xxxii–l.

—— (1975), 'George Turnbull and the Furniture of the Mind', *Journal of the History of Ideas*, 36: 4 (1975), pp. 701–16.

—— (1976), 'Hume and his Scottish Critics', in Norton et al. (eds) 1976: 309–24.

—— (2005), 'Hume and Hutcheson: the Question of Influence', in Daniel Garber and Steven Nadler (eds), *Oxford Studies in Early Modern Philosophy*, Oxford: Clarendon Press, vol. 2, pp. 211–56.

—— (2007), 'Editorial Material including Historical Account of *A Treatise of Human Nature* from its Beginnings to the Time of Hume's Death', in *A Treatise of Human Nature: A Critical Edition*, 2 vols, Oxford: Oxford University Press, vol. 2.

—— and Richard H. Popkin (eds) (1965), *David Hume: Philosophical Historian*, Indianapolis: Bobbs-Merrill.

——, Nicholas Capaldi and Wade L. Robison (eds) (1976), *McGill Hume Studies*, San Diego: Austin Hill Press.

—— and Mary J. Norton (eds) (1996), *The David Hume Library*, Edinburgh: National Library of Scotland.

—— and Jacqueline Taylor (eds) (2009), *The Cambridge Companion to Hume*, 2nd edn, Cambridge: Cambridge University Press.

Oberg, Barbara Bowen (1976), 'David Hartley and the Association of Ideas', *Journal of the History of Ideas*, 37: 3 (1976), pp. 441–54.

O'Brien, Karen (1997a), 'Robertson and Eighteenth-Century Narrative History', in Stewart J. Brown (ed.), *William Robertson and the Expansion of Empire*, Cambridge: Cambridge University Press, pp. 74–91.

—— (1997b), *Narratives of Enlightenment: Cosmopolitan History from Voltaire to Gibbon*, Cambridge: Cambridge University Press.

O'Neill, Daniel I. (2007), *The Burke-Wollstonecraft Debate: Savagery, Civilization, and Democracy*, University Park: Pennsylvania State University Press.

Ozouf, Mona (1988), '"Public Opinion" at the End of the Old Regime', *The Journal of Modern History*, 60: Supplement (1988), pp. S1–S21.

Paganini, Gianni (1996), 'Hume et Bayle: conjonction locale et immatérialité de l'âme', in Michelle Magdelaine, Maria-Cristina Pitassi, Ruth Whelan and Antony McKenna (eds), *De l'humanisme aux Lumières, Bayle et le protestantisme*, Oxford: Voltaire Foundation, pp. 701–13.

—— (2013), 'Hume and Bayle on Localization and Perception: A New Source for Hume's Treatise 1.4.5', in Charles and Smith (eds) 2013: 109–24.

Parkin, Jon (2007), *Taming the Leviathan: The Reception of the Political and Religious Ideas of Thomas Hobbes in England 1640–1700*, Cambridge: Cambridge University Press.

Parusniková, Zuzana (1993), 'Against the Spirit of Foundations: Postmodernism and David Hume', *Hume Studies*, 19: 1 (1993), pp. 1–18.

Penelhum, Terence (2008), 'Hume's View on Religion: Intellectual and Cultural Influences', in Radcliffe (ed.) 2008: 323–37.

Perinetti, Dario (2006), 'Philosophical Reflection on History', in Haakonssen (ed.) 2006: 1107–40.

Petsoulas, Christina (2001), *Hayek's Liberalism and its Origin: His Idea of Spontaneous Order and the Scottish Enlightenment*, London and New York: Routledge.

Phillips, Mark Salber, *Society and Sentiment: Genres of Historical Writings in Britain, 1740–1820*, Princeton: Princeton University Press.

—— and Dale R. Smith (2005), 'Canonization and Critique: Hume's Reputation as a Historian', in Jones (ed.) 2005: 299–313.

Phillipson, Nicholas (1983), 'Politeness and Politics in the Reigns of Anne and the Early Hanoverians', in J. G. A. Pocock (ed.), *Varieties of British Political Thought 1500–1800*, Cambridge: Cambridge University Press, pp. 583–605.

—— (2010), *Adam Smith: An Enlightened Life*, New Haven: Yale University Press.

—— (2011), *David Hume: The Philosopher as Historian*, London: Penguin.

Philp, Mark (1986), *Godwin's Political Justice*, London: Duckworth.

—— (2014), *Reforming Ideas in Britain: Politics and Language in the Shadow of the French Revolution, 1879–1815*, Cambridge: Cambridge University Press.

Pittion, J. P. (1977), 'Hume's Reading of Bayle: An Inquiry into the

Source and Role of the Memoranda', *Journal of the History of Philosophy*, 15: 4 (1977), pp. 373–86.
Pocock, J. G. A. (1957), *The Ancient Constitution and the Feudal Law: A Study of English Historical Thought in the Seventeenth Century*, Cambridge: Cambridge University Press.
—— (1975), *The Machiavellian Moment: Florentine Political Thought and the Atlantic Republican*, Princeton: Princeton University Press.
—— (1982), 'Superstition and Enthusiasm in Gibbon's History of Religion', *Eighteenth-Century Life*, 8: 1 (1982), pp. 83–94.
—— (1985a), 'Clergy and Commerce: The Conservative Enlightenment in England', in R. Ajello (ed.), *L'Età dei Lumi: Studi storici sul settecento europeo in onore de Franco Venturi*, Naples: Jovene, pp. 524–62.
—— (1985b), *Virtue, Commerce, and History: Essays on Political Thought and History, Chiefly in the Eighteenth Century*, Cambridge; New York: Cambridge University Press.
—— (1989a), 'Conservative Enlightenment and Democratic Revolutions: The American and French Cases in British Perspective', *Government and Opposition*, 24: 1 (1989), pp. 81–105.
—— (1989b), *Politics, Language, and Time: Essays on Political Thought and History*, Chicago: University of Chicago Press.
—— (1990), *Barbarism and Religion, Vol. II, Narratives of Civil Government*, Cambridge: Cambridge University Press.
—— (1997), 'Enthusiasm: The Antiself of Enlightenment', *Huntington Library Quarterly*, 60: 1–2 (1997), pp. 7–28.
—— (2008), 'Historiography and Enlightenment: a View of their History', *Modern Intellectual History*, 5: 1 (2008), pp. 83–96.
Pomeau, René [1954] (1969), *La Religion de Voltaire*, Nouvelle éd., Paris: Chez Nizet.
Popkin, Richard H. (1965), 'Skepticism and the Study of History', in Norton and Popkin (eds) 1965: ix–xxxi.
—— (1976), 'Hume: Philosophical Historian Versus Prophetic Historian', in Kenneth R. Merrill and Robert W. Shahan (eds), *David Hume: Many-sided Genius*, Norman: University of Oklahoma Press, pp. 83–95.
—— (1977), 'Joseph Priestley's Criticisms of David Hume's Philosophy', *Journal of the History of Philosophy*, 15: 4 (1977), pp. 437–47.
—— (1979), 'Hume and Spinoza', *Hume Studies*, 5: 2 (1979), pp. 65–93.
—— [1963] (1997), 'Scepticism in the Enlightenment', Rep. in Popkin et al. (eds) 1997: 1–16.
—— [1976] (1997), 'Scepticism and Anti-Scepticism in the Latter Part of the Eighteenth-Century', Rep. in Popkin et al. (eds) 1997: 17–34.

—— [1992] (1997), 'New Views on the Role of Scepticism in the Enlightenment', Rep. in Popkin et al. (eds) 1997: 157–72.

—— (2003), *The History of Scepticism: From Savonarola to Bayle*, Rev. and expanded ed., Oxford: Oxford University Press.

——, Ezequiel de Olaso and Giorgio Tonelli (eds) (1997), *Scepticism in the Enlightenment*, Dordrecht: Kluwer.

Porter, Roy (2001), *The Enlightenment*, 2nd edn, New York: Palgrave Macmillan.

Postema, Gerald J. (1986), *Bentham and the Common Law Tradition*, Oxford: Clarendon Press, Oxford University Press.

Potkay, Adam (2000), *The Passion for Happiness: Samuel Johnson and David Hume*, Ithaca: Cornell University Press.

—— (2001), 'Hume's "Supplement to Gulliver": The Medieval Volumes of *The History of England*', *Eighteenth-Century Life*, 25: 2 (2001), pp. 32–46.

Price, John Valdimir (1964), 'Sceptics in Cicero and Hume', *Journal of the History of Ideas*, 25: 1 (1964), pp. 97–106.

—— [1965] (1992), *The Ironic Hume*, Rep. Bristol: Thoemmes Press.

—— (1990), Introduction to Daniel MacQueen, *Letters on Mr. Hume's History of Great Britain*, with a new introduction by John Valdimir Price, Bristol: Thoemmes, Kinokuniya.

Primer, Irwin (1975), 'Mandeville and Shaftesbury: Some Facts and Problems', in Irwin Primer (ed.), *Mandeville Studies: New Explorations in the Art and Thought of Dr. Bernard Mandeville (1670–1733)*, The Hague: Martinus Nijhoff, pp. 126–41.

Pujol, Stéphane (2012), 'Voltaire et la question du scepticisme', *Cahiers Voltaire*, 11 (2012), pp. 104–23.

—— (2013), 'Forms and Aims of Voltairean Scepticism', in Charles and Smith (eds) 2013: 189–204.

Radcliffe, Elizabeth S. (ed.) (2008), *A Companion to Hume*, Malden, MA: Blackwell.

Radzinowicz, Leon (1986), *Grappling for Control*, in *A History of English Criminal Law and its Administration from 1750*, 5 vols, London: Stevens and Sons, vol. 4.

Raphael, D. D. (1969), 'Adam Smith and "The Infection of David Hume's Society": New Light on an Old Controversy, Together with the Text of a Hitherto Unpublished Manuscript', *Journal of the History of Ideas*, 30: 2 (1969), pp. 225–48.

—— (1977), '"The True Old Humean Philosophy" and its Influence on Adam Smith', in G. P. Morice (ed.) 1977: 23–38.

Rasmussen, Dennis C. (2008), *The Problems and Promise of Commercial*

Society, Adam Smith's Response to Rousseau, Pennsylvania: Pennsylvania State University Press.
—— (2014), *The Pragmatic Enlightenment: Recovering the Liberalism of Hume, Smith, Montesquieu, and Voltaire*, Cambridge: Cambridge University Press.
Rawson, Elizabeth (1991), *The Spartan Traditions in European Thought*, Oxford: Clarendon Press.
Raynor, David (1982), 'Hume's Critique of Helvétius's *De l'esprit*', *Studies on Voltaire and the Eighteenth Century*, 215 (1982), pp. 223–9.
—— (1998), 'Who invented the invisible hand? Hume's Praise of Laissez-Faire in a newly discovered pamphlet', *Times Literary Supplement* (14 Aug. 1998).
—— (2009), 'Why did David Hume dislike Adam Ferguson's *An Essay on the History of Civil Society*?' in Eugene Heath and Vincenzo Merolle (eds), *Adam Ferguson: Philosophy, Politics and Society*, London: Pickering & Chatto, pp. 45–72 (n., pp. 179–88).
Real, Hermann J. and Ian Simpson Ross (2003), 'The "Extreme Difficulty Understanding the Meaning of the Word Opinion": Some Limits of Understanding Dean Swift', in Herman J. Read and Helgard Stöver Leidig (eds), *Reading Swift: Papers from the Fourth Münster Symposium on Jonathan Swift*, München: Wilhelm Fink, pp. 349–61.
Redmond, M. (1987), 'The Hamann-Hume Connection', *Religious Studies*, 23: 1 (1987), pp. 95–107.
Rivers, Isabel (2000), *Reason, Grace, and Sentiment: A Study of the Language of Religion and Ethics 1660–1780, Vol. II, Shaftesbury to Hume*, Cambridge: Cambridge University Press.
—— (2001), 'Responses to Hume on Religion by Anglicans and Dissenters', *The Journal of Ecclesiastical History*, 52: 4 (2001), pp. 675–95.
Robbins, Caroline (1959), *The Eighteenth-Century Commonwealthman: Studies in the Transmission, Development and Circumstance of English Liberal Thought from the Restoration of Charles II until the War with the Thirteen Colonies*, Cambridge, MA: Harvard University Press.
Robertson, John (1983), 'The Scottish Enlightenment at the Limits of the Civic Tradition', in István Hont and Michael Ignatieff (eds), *Wealth and Virtue: The Shaping of Political Economy in the Scottish Enlightenment*, Cambridge: Cambridge University Press, pp. 137–78.
—— (1985), *Scottish Enlightenment and the Militia Issue*, Edinburgh: J. Donald; Atlantic Highlands, NJ: Humanities Press.
—— (1993), 'Universal Monarchy and the Liberties of Europe: David Hume's Critique of an English Whig Doctrine', in Nicholas Phillipson

and Quentin Skinner (eds), *Political Discourse in Early Modern Britain*, Cambridge: Cambridge University Press, pp. 349–73.
—— (2000), 'The Scottish Contribution to the Enlightenment', in Paul Wood (ed.) 2000: 37–62.
—— (2005), *The Case for the Enlightenment: Scotland and Naples 1680–1760*, Cambridge: Cambridge University Press.
Roe, Nicholas (1988), *Wordsworth and Coleridge: The Radical Years*, Oxford: Clarendon Press.
Roe, Shirley A. (1985), 'Voltaire Versus Needham: Atheism, Materialism, and the Generation of Life', *Journal of the History of Ideas*, 46: 1 (1985), pp. 65–87.
Ronchetti, Emanuele (2007), 'Appropriating Hume: Joseph de Maistre, Benjamin Constant and the "History of England"', in Mazza and Ronchetti (eds) 2007: 365–88.
Rorty, Richard (1987), 'Thugs and Theorists: A Reply to Bernstein', *Political Theory*, 15: 4 (1987), pp. 564–80.
—— (1993), 'Human Rights, Rationality and Sentimentality', in Stephen Shute and Susan Hurley (eds), *On Human Rights: The Oxford Amnesty Lectures 1993*, New York: Basic Books, pp. 111–34.
—— (1998), *Truth and Progress*, Cambridge: Cambridge University Press.
Rosen, Frederick (2003), *Classical Utilitarianism from Hume to Mill*, London; New York: Routledge.
Ross, Ian Simpson (1972), *Lord Kames and the Scotland of His Day*, Oxford: Clarendon Press.
—— (1995), *The Life of Adam Smith*, Oxford: Clarendon Press.
Rothschild, Emma (2001), *Economic Sentiments: Adam Smith, Condorcet, and the Enlightenment*, Cambridge, MA: Harvard University Press.
—— (2008), 'David Hume and the Seagods of the Atlantic', in Susan Manning and Francis D. Cogliano (eds), *The Atlantic Enlightenment*, Hampshire: Ashgate, pp. 81–96.
Rotwein, Eugene (1970), Editor's Introduction to *David Hume: Writings on Economics*, Madison: University of Wisconsin Press.
Russell, Paul (2008), *The Riddle of Hume's* Treatise*: Skepticism, Naturalism, and Irreligion*, Oxford: Oxford University Press.
—— (2003/2013), 'Hume on Religion', in *The Stanford Encyclopedia of Philosophy* (http://plato.stanford.edu/entries/hume-religion/ [accessed 15 Oct. 2014]).
Ryan, Todd (2013), 'Hume's Reply to Baylean Scepticism', in Charles and Smith (eds) 2013: 125–38.
Sabl, Andrew (2009), 'The Last Artificial Virtue: Hume on Toleration and Its Lessons', *Political Theory*, 37: 4 (2009), pp. 511–38.

—— (2012), *Hume's Politics: Coordination and Crisis in the* History of England, Princeton: Princeton University Press.

Sagar, Paul (2013), 'Sociability, Luxury and Sympathy: The Case of Archibald Campbell', *History of European Ideas*, 39: 6 (2013), pp. 791–814.

Sakamoto, Tatsuya (1995), *Hume no Bunmei Shakai: Kinrou, Chishiki, Jiyuu* (*David Hume's Civilized Society: Industry, Knowledge, Liberty*) (in Japanese), Tokyo: Sobunsha.

—— (2003), 'Hume's Political Economy as a System of Manners', in Tatsuya Sakamoto and Hideo Tanaka (eds), *The Rise of Political Economy in the Scottish Enlightenment*, London; New York: Routledge, pp. 86–102.

—— (2006), 'Genesis of Hume's Political Economy of "Manners"', in George Stathakis and Gianni Vaggi (eds), *Economic Development and Social Change: Historical Roots and Modern Perspectives*, London; New York: Routledge, pp. 190–9.

—— (2011a), *Hume: Kibou no Kaigishugi: Aru Shakai-kagaku no Tanjou* (*Hume's Sceptical Optimism: the Birth of a Social Science*) (in Japanese), Tokyo: Keio University Press.

—— (2011b), 'Hume's "Early Memoranda" and the Making of His Political Economy', *Hume Studies*, 37: 2 (2011), pp. 131–64.

—— (forthcoming), 'The Philosophical Nature and Origin of Hume's Science of Economics', in Paul Russell (ed.), *The Oxford Handbook of Hume*, Oxford: Oxford University Press.

Sato, Sora (2014), 'Edmund Burke's Ideas on Historical Change', *History of European Ideas*, 40: 5 (2014), pp. 675–92.

Savage, Ruth (ed.) (2012), *Philosophy & Religion in Enlightenment Britain*, Oxford: Oxford University Press.

Schilling, Bernard N. (1943), 'The English Case against Voltaire: 1789-1800', *Journal of the History of Ideas*, 4: 2 (1943), pp. 193–216.

Schliesser, Eric (2003), 'The Obituary of a Vain Philosopher: Adam Smith's Reflections on Hume's Life', *Hume Studies*, 29: 2 (2003), pp. 327–63.

Schmidt, Claudia M. (2004), *David Hume: Reason in History*, University Park: Penn State University Press.

—— (2013), 'David Hume as a Philosopher of History', in Spencer (ed.) 2013: 163–80.

Schmidt, James (1996), 'Introduction: What is Enlightenment? A Question, Its Context, and Some Consequences', in *What is Enlightenment? Eighteenth-Century Answers and Twentieth-Century Questions*, ed. Schmidt, Berkley: University of California Press, pp. 1–44.

—— (2001), 'Projects and Projections: A Response to Christian Delacampagne', *Political Theory*, 29: 1 (2001), pp. 86–90.

Schofield, Robert E. (1997), *The Enlightenment of Joseph Priestley: A Study of his Life and Works from 1733 to 1773*, University Park: Pennsylvania State University Press.

Schuurman, Paul (2001), 'Locke's way of ideas as context for his theory of education in *Of the Conduct of the Understanding*', *History of European Ideas*, 27 (2001), pp. 45–59.

Scott, Jonathan (2002), 'Classical Republicanism in Seventeenth-century England and the Netherlands', in Martin van Gelderen and Quentin Skinner (eds), *Republicanism: A Shared European Heritage, Vol. I, Republicanism and Constitutionalism in Early Modern Europe*, Cambridge: Cambridge University Press, pp. 61–81.

—— (2004), *Commonwealth Principles: Republican Writings of the English Revolution*, Cambridge: Cambridge University Press.

Sebastiani, Silvia (2011), 'National Characters and Race: A Scottish Enlightenment Debate', in Ahnert and Manning (eds) 2011: 187–205.

—— (2013), *The Scottish Enlightenment: Race, Gender and the Limits of Progress*, New York: Palgrave-Macmillan.

Sekora, John (1977), *Luxury: The Concept in Western Thought, Eden to Smollett*, Baltimore: Johns Hopkins University Press.

Semmel, Bernard (1965), 'The Hume-Tucker Debate and Pitt's Trade Proposals', *The Economic Journal*, 75: 300 (1965), pp. 759–70.

Serjeantson, Richard (2012), 'David Hume's *Natural History of Religion* (1757) and the End of Modern Eusebianism', in Mortimer and Robertson (eds) 2012: 267–95.

Sessions, William Lad (1991), 'A Dialogic Interpretation of Hume's Dialogues', *Hume Studies* 17: 1 (1991), pp. 15–40.

Shattock, Joanne (1989), *Politics and Reviewers: The* Edinburgh *and the* Quarterly *in the Early Victorian Age*, London; New York: Leicester University Press.

Sheehan, Colleen A. (2002), 'Madison and the French Enlightenment: The Authority of Public Opinion', *The William and Mary Quarterly*, 3rd Series, 59: 4 (2002), pp. 925–56.

—— (2005), 'Public Opinion and the Formation of Civic Character in Madison's Republican Theory', *The Review of Politics*, 67: 1 (2005), pp. 37–48.

Sheldon, R. D. (2004), 'Smith, Charles (1713–1777)', *Oxford Dictionary of National Biography*, vol. 51, p. 60.

Sher, Richard B. (1985), *Church and University in the Scottish*

Enlightenment: The Moderate Literati of Edinburgh, Princeton: Princeton University Press.
—— (1990), 'Professor of Virtue: The Social History of the Edinburgh Moral Philosophy Chair in the Eighteenth Century', in M. A. Stewart (ed.), *Studies in the Philosophy of the Scottish Enlightenment*, Oxford: Oxford University Press, pp. 87–126.
Shklar, Judith N. (1959), 'Ideology Hunting: The Case of James Harrington', *The American Political Science Review*, 52: 3 (1959), pp. 662–92.
—— (1969), *Men and Citizens: A Study of Rousseau's Social Theory*, Cambridge: Cambridge University Press.
Shovlin, John (2006), *The Political Economy of Virtue: Luxury, Patriotism, and the Origins of the French Revolution*, Ithaca: Cornell University Press.
—— (2008), 'Hume's *Political Discourses* and the French Luxury Debate', in Wennerlind and Schabas (eds) 2008: 203–22.
Siebert, Donald T. (1990), *The Moral Animus of David Hume*, Newark: University of Delaware Press.
Skinner, Andrew S. (1979), *A System of Social Science: Papers Relating to Adam Smith*, Oxford: Clarendon Press.
Sonenscher, Michael (2007), *Before the Deluge: Public Debt, Inequality, and the Intellectual Origins of the French Revolution*, Princeton: Princeton University Press.
—— (2008), *Sans-Culottes: An Eighteenth-Century Emblem in the French Revolution*, Princeton: Princeton University Press.
Spadafora, David (1990), *The Idea of Progress in Eighteenth-Century Britain*, New Heaven; London: Yale University Press.
Spencer, Mark G. (2002), 'Hume and Madison on Faction', *The William and Mary Quarterly* 3rd Series, 59 (2002), pp. 869–96.
—— (2005), *David Hume and Eighteenth-Century America*, Rochester: University of Rochester Press.
—— (2010), Review of Jonathan Israel, *A Revolution of the Mind: Radical Enlightenment and the Intellectual Origins of Modern Democracy*, *History of Intellectual Culture*, 9: 1 (2010) (http://www.ucalgary.ca/hic/files/hic/Spencer%20on%20Israel.pdf [accessed 25 Oct. 2014]).
—— (2013), 'Introduction: Hume as Historian', in Spencer (ed.) 2013: 1–12.
—— (ed.) (2002), *Hume's Reception in Early America*, 2 vols, Bristol: Thoemmes.
—— (ed.) (2013), *David Hume: Historical Writer, Historical Thinker*, Pennsylvania State University Press.

St. Clair, William (2004), *The Reading Nation in the Romantic Period*, Cambridge: Cambridge University Press.

Stafford, J. Martin (ed.) (1997), *Private Vices, Publick Benefits? The Contemporary Reception of Bernard Mandeville*, Solihull: Ismeron.

Starobinski, Jean [1957] (1988), *Jean-Jacques Rousseau: Transparency and Obstruction*, trans. by Arthur Goldhammer, Chicago: University of Chicago Press.

Steenbakkers, Piet (2004), 'Spinoza on Imagination', in L. Nauta and D. Pätzold (eds), *The Scope of Imagination: Between Medieval and Modern Times*, Leuven: Peeters, pp. 175–94.

Steensma, Robert C. (1970), *Sir William Temple*, New York: Twayne Publishers.

Steintrager, James A. (2012), 'Oscillate and Reflect: La Mettrie, Materialist Physiology, and the Revival of the Epicurean Canonic', in Brooke Holmes and W. H. Shearin (eds), *Reading: Studies in the Reception of Epicureanism*, Oxford: Oxford University Press, pp. 162–98.

Stewart, John B. (1963), *The Moral and Political Philosophy of David Hume*, New York; London: Colombia University Press.

—— (1992), *Opinion and Reform in Hume's Political Philosophy*, Princeton: Princeton University Press.

Stewart, M. A. (1991), 'The Stoic Legacy in the Early Scottish Enlightenment', in M. J. Osler (ed.), *Atoms, 'Pneuma' and Tranquillity*, Cambridge: Cambridge University Press, pp. 273–96.

—— (1994), 'An Early Fragment on Evil', in Stewart and Wright (eds) 1994: 160–70.

—— (1995), *The Kirk and the Infidel* (an Inaugural Lecture delivered at Lancaster University on 9 November 1994), Lancaster: Lancaster University Publication Office.

—— (2000), 'The Dating of Hume's Manuscripts', in Wood (ed.) 2000: 267–314.

—— (2002), 'Two Species of Philosophy: the Historical Significance of the First *Enquiry*', in Peter Millican (ed.), *Reading Hume on Human Understanding*, Oxford: Oxford University Press, pp. 67–95.

—— (2003), 'Religion and Rational Theology', in Alexander Broadie (ed.), *The Cambridge Companion to the Scottish Enlightenment*, Cambridge: Cambridge University Press, pp. 31–59.

—— (2005), 'Hume's Intellectual Development, 1711–1752', in Marina Frasca-Spada and P. J. E. Kail (eds), *Impressions of Hume*, Oxford: Oxford University Press, pp. 11–58.

—— and John P. Wright (eds), *Hume and Hume's Connexions*, Edinburgh: Edinburgh University Press.

Stockton, Constant Noble (1971), 'Hume – Historian of the English Constitution', *Eighteenth-Century Studies*, 4: 3 (1971), pp. 277–93.

—— (1976), 'Economics and the Mechanism of Historical Progress in Hume's *History*', in Livingston and King (eds) 1976: 296–320.

Striker, Gisela (2010), 'Adacemics versus Pyrrhonists, reconsidered', in Richard Bett (ed.), *The Cambridge Companion to Ancient Scepticism*, Cambridge: Cambridge University Press, pp. 195–207.

Stromberg, R. N. (1951), 'History in the Eighteenth Century', *Journal of the History of Ideas*, 12: 2 (1951), pp. 295–304.

Susato, Ryu (2007), 'The Idea of Chivalry in the Scottish Enlightenment: The Case of David Hume', *Hume Studies*, 33: 1 (2007), pp. 155–78.

—— (2009), Review of Neil McArthur, *David Hume's Political Theory: Law, Commerce, and the Constitution of Government*, *Journal of the History of Philosophy*, 47: 1 (2009), pp. 146–7.

—— (2010), Review of Christopher J. Berry, *David Hume*, *Hume Studies*, 36: 2 (2010), pp. 242–4.

—— (forthcoming), 'Hume as an "ami de la liberté": the Reception of his "Idea of a Perfect Commonwealth"', *Modern Intellectual History*, forthcoming.

Tapper, Alan (1996), 'Priestley on Politics, Progress and Moral Theology', in Haakonssen (ed.) 1996: 272–86.

Taylor, Charles (1989), *Sources of the Self: The Making of the Modern Identity*, Cambridge, MA: Harvard University Press.

Thomson, Ann (2008), *Bodies of Thought: Science, Religion and the Soul in the Early Enlightenment*, Oxford: Oxford University Press.

Tolonen, Mikko (2013), *Mandeville and Hume: Anatomists of Civil Society*, Oxford: Voltaire Foundation.

Tomaselli, Sylvana (1988), 'Moral Philosophy and Population Questions in Eighteenth Century-Europe', *Population and Development Review*, 14 (Supplement: Population and Resources in Western Intellectual Tradition) (1988), pp. 7–29.

Tonelli, Giorgio (1997), 'The "Weakness" of Reason in the Age of Enlightenment', in Popkin et al. (eds) 1997: 35–50.

Towsey, Mark R. M. (2010a), *Reading the Scottish Enlightenment: Books and their Readers in Provincial Scotland, 1750–1820*, Leiden: Brill.

—— (2010b), '"Philosophically Playing with the Devil": Recovering Readers' Responses to David Hume and the Scottish Enlightenment', *Historical Research*, 83: 220 (2010), pp. 301–20.

—— (2013), '"The Book Seemed to Sink into Oblivion": Reading Hume's *History* in Eighteenth-Century Scotland', in Spencer (ed.) 2013: 81–102.

Traiger, Saul (2008), 'Hume on Memory and Imagination', in Radcliffe (ed.) 2008: 58–71.

Trevor-Roper, Hugh (2010), *History and the Enlightenment*, New Haven; London: Yale University Press.

Tuck, Richard (1992), 'The Civil Religion of Thomas Hobbes', in Nicholas Phillipson and Quentin Skinner (eds), *Political Discourse in Early Modern Britain*, Cambridge: Cambridge University Press, pp. 120–38.

—— (1997), Introduction to Hobbes [1642] 1997, viii–xxxiii.

—— (1999), *The Rights of War and Peace: Political Thought and the International Order from Grotius to Kant*, Oxford: Oxford University Press.

Turco, Luigi (2007), 'Hutcheson and Hume in a Recent Polemic', in Mazza and Ronchetti (eds) 2007: 171–98.

Velk, Tom and A. R. Riggs (1985), 'David Hume's Practical Economics', *Hume Studies*, 11: 2 (1985), pp. 154–65.

Venturi, Franco (1971), *Utopia and Reform in the Enlightenment*, Cambridge: Cambridge University Press.

Voparil, Christopher J. (2006), *Richard Rorty: Politics and Vision*, Lanham, MD: Rowman & Littlefield Publishers.

Vyverberg, Henry (1958), *Historical Pessimism in the French Enlightenment*, Cambridge, MA: Harvard University Press.

—— (1989), *Human Nature, Cultural Diversity, and the French Enlightenment*, New York; Oxford: Oxford University Press.

Yolton, John W. (1965), *John Locke and the Way of Ideas*, Oxford: Oxford University Press.

—— (1984), *Thinking Matter: Materialism in Eighteenth-Century Britain*, Oxford: Basil Blackwell.

—— (1991), *Locke and French Materialism*, Oxford: Clarendon Press.

Young, B. W. (1998), '"Scepticism in Excess": Gibbon and Eighteenth-Century Christianity', *The Historical Journal*, 41: 1 (1998), pp. 179–99.

—— (1998), *Religion and Enlightenment in Eighteenth-Century England: Theological Debate from Locke to Burke*, Oxford: Clarendon Press.

Wade, Ira O. [1947] (1967), *Studies on Voltaire: With Some Unpublished Papers of Mme. du Châtelet*, Rep. Princeton: Princeton University Press.

—— (1970), *The Intellectual Development of Voltaire*, Princeton: Princeton University Press.

Wennerlind, Carl (2008), 'David Hume's Political Philosophy: A Theory of Commercial Modernization', *Hume Studies*, 28: 2 (2008), pp. 247–70.

—— and Margaret Schabas (eds) (2008), *David Hume's Political Economy*, London and New York: Routledge.

Werner, John M. (1972), 'David Hume and America', *Journal of the History of Ideas*, 33: 3 (1972), pp. 439–56.

Wertz, Spencer K. (2000), *Between Hume's Philosophy and History: Historical Theory and Practice*, Oxford: University Press of America.

Whelan, Frederick G. (1985), *Order and Artifice in Hume's Political Thought*, Princeton: Princeton University Press.

Williams, Michael (2003), 'Rorty on Knowledge and Truth', in Charles Guignon and David R. Hiley (eds), *Richard Rorty*, Cambridge: Cambridge University Press, pp. 61–80.

Wilson, Catherine (2008), *Epicureanism at the Origins of Modernity*, Oxford: Oxford University Press.

—— (2009), 'Epicureanism in Early Modern Philosophy', in James Warren (ed.), *The Cambridge Companion to Epicureanism*, Cambridge: Cambridge University Press, pp. 266–86.

Wilson, Margaret D. (1996), 'Spinoza's Theory of Knowledge', in Don Garrett (ed.), *The Cambridge Companion to Spinoza*, Cambridge: Cambridge University Press, pp. 89–141.

Winch, Donald (1978), *Adam Smith's Politics: An Essay in Historiographic Revision*, Cambridge: Cambridge University Press.

—— (1996), *Riches and Poverty: An Intellectual History of Political Economy in Britain, 1750–1834*, Cambridge: Cambridge University Press.

Wokler, Robert (2012), *Rousseau, the Age of Enlightenment, and Their Legacies*, ed. Bryan Garsten, with an introduction by Christopher Brooke, Princeton: Princeton University Press.

Wolfe, Charles T. (2009), 'A Happiness fit for Organic Bodies: La Mettrie's Medical Epicureanism', in Leddy and Lifschitz (eds) 2009: 69–84.

Wolin, Sheldon (1954), 'Hume and Conservatism', *American Political Science Review*, 48: 4 (1954), pp. 999–1016.

Wood, Neal (1992), 'Tabula Rasa, Social Environmentalism, and the "English Paradigm"', *Journal of the History of Ideas*, 53: 4 (1992), pp. 647–88.

Wood, Paul (ed.) (2000), *The Scottish Enlightenment: Essays in Reinterpretation*, Rochester, NY: Rochester University Press.

Wood, P. B. (1994), 'Hume, Reid and the Science of the Mind', in Stewart and Wright (eds) 1994: 119–39.

Woodbridge, Homer E. (1940), *Sir William Temple: The Man and his Work*, New York: Modern Language Association of America.

Wootton, David (2009), 'David Hume, "the Historian"', in Norton and Taylor (eds) 2009: 447–79.
Wright, Johnson Kent (1997), *A Classical Republican in Eighteenth-Century France: The Political Thought of Mably*, Stanford: Stanford University Press.
Wright, John P. (1983), *The Sceptical Realism of David Hume*, Minneapolis: University of Minnesota Press.
—— (2002), 'Materialism and the Life Soul in Eighteenth-Century Scottish Physiology', in Paul Wood (ed.) 2000: 177–96.
—— (2003), 'Dr. George Cheyne, Chevalier Ramsay, and Hume's Letter to a Physician', *Hume Studies*, 29: 1 (2003), pp. 125–41.
—— (2006), 'The *Treatise*: Composition, Reception, and Response', in Saul Traiger (ed.), *The Blackwell Guide to Hume's* Treatise, Oxford: Blackwell, pp. 5–25.
—— (2009), *Hume's* 'A Treatise of Human Nature'*: An Introduction*, Cambridge: Cambridge University Press.
—— (2012), 'Hume on the Origin of "Modern Honour": A Study in Hume's Philosophical Development', in Savage (ed.) 2012: 187–209.

Index